Saints and Feast Days

Lives of the Saints: with a Calendar and Ways to Celebrate

Sisters of Notre Dame of Chardon, Ohio

Loyola Press

Chicago

Adapted from the *Christ our Life* series

 Loyola Press

3441 North Ashland Avenue
Chicago, Illinois 60657
1-800-621-1008

Cover art: Sister George Ellen Holmgren, C.S.J.

98 99 00 01 02 / 10 9 8 7 6 5 4

Dedication

**To Saint Julie Billiart
founder of the Sisters of Notre Dame
in gratitude for her inspiration and example**

A Calendar of Feasts to Celebrate

Sketches and suggested activities are provided in this book for the following saints and feast days. Entries for saints whose names are italicized are in the Supplement, which is at the back of this book.

22	Cecilia
23	Clement I
	Columban
	Bl. Miguel Agustín Pro
24	*Andrew Dung-Lac and His Companions*
30	Andrew
	Christ the King (Last Sunday of Ordinary Time)

DECEMBER

3	Francis Xavier
4	John Damascene
6	Nicholas
7	Ambrose
8	Immaculate Conception
9	*Bl. Juan Diego*
11	Damasus I
12	Our Lady of Guadalupe
13	Lucy
14	John of the Cross
21	Peter Canisius
23	John of Kanty
25	Christmas
26	Stephen
27	John the Evangelist
28	Holy Innocents
29	Thomas Becket
31	Sylvester I
	Holy Family (Sunday within Octave of Christmas)

JANUARY

1	Solemnity of Mary, Mother of God
2	Basil the Great and Gregory Nazianzen
4	Elizabeth Ann Seton
5	John Neumann
	Epiphany (Sunday between January 2 and January 8)
6	*Bl. André Bessette*
	Baptism of the Lord (Sunday after January 6)
7	Raymond of Peñafort
13	Hilary
17	Anthony
20	Fabian
	Sebastian
21	Agnes
22	Vincent
24	Francis de Sales
25	Conversion of Paul
26	Timothy and Titus
27	Angela Merici
28	Thomas Aquinas
31	John Bosco

FEBRUARY

2	Presentation of the Lord
3	Blase
	Ansgar
5	Agatha
6	Paul Miki and His Companions
8	Jerome Emiliani
10	Scholastica
11	Our Lady of Lourdes
14	Cyril and Methodius
17	Seven Founders of the Order of Servites
21	Peter Damian
22	Chair of Peter
23	Polycarp

MARCH

3	*Bl. Katharine Drexel*
4	Casimir
7	Perpetua and Felicity
8	John of God
9	Frances of Rome
17	Patrick
18	Cyril of Jerusalem
19	Joseph, Husband of Mary
23	Turibius de Mogrovejo
25	Annunciation of the Lord

APRIL

2	Francis of Paola
4	Isidore of Seville
5	Vincent Ferrer
7	John Baptist de la Salle
8	Julie Billiart
11	Stanislaus
13	Martin I
21	Anselm
23	George
24	Fidelis of Sigmaringen
25	Mark
28	Peter Chanel
29	Catherine of Siena
30	Pius V

MAY

1 Joseph the Worker
2 Athanasius
3 Philip and James
10 *Bl. Damien*
12 Nereus and Achilleus
   Pancras
14 Matthias
15 Isidore the Farmer
18 John I
20 Bernardine of Siena
25 Bede the Venerable
   Gregory VII
   Mary Magdalene de Pazzi
26 Philip Neri
27 Augustine of Canterbury
30 Joan of Arc
31 Visitation
   Immaculate Heart of Mary

JUNE

1 Justin
2 Marcellinus and Peter
3 Charles Lwanga and His Companions
5 Boniface
6 Norbert
9 Ephrem
11 Barnabas
13 Anthony of Padua
19 Romuald
21 Aloysius Gonzaga
22 Paulinus of Nola
   John Fisher and Thomas More
24 Birth of John the Baptist
27 Cyril of Alexandria
28 Irenaeus
29 Peter and Paul
30 First Martyrs of Rome

JULY

1 *Bl. Junípero Serra*
3 Thomas
4 Elizabeth of Portugal

5 Anthony Zaccaria
6 Maria Goretti
11 Benedict
13 Henry
14 *Bl. Kateri Tekakwitha*
   Camillus of Lellis
15 Bonaventure
16 Our Lady of Mount Carmel
21 Lawrence of Brindisi
22 Mary Magdalene
23 Bridget of Sweden
25 James
26 Joachim and Ann
29 Martha
30 Peter Chrysologus
31 Ignatius of Loyola

AUGUST

1 Alphonsus Liguori
2 Eusebius of Vercelli
4 John Vianney
5 Dedication of St. Mary Major
6 Transfiguration
7 Sixtus II and His Companions
   Cajetan
8 Dominic
10 Lawrence
11 Clare
13 Pontian and Hippolytus
14 *Maximilian Mary Kolbe*
15 Assumption
16 Stephen of Hungary
18 Jane Frances de Chantal
19 John Eudes
20 Bernard of Clairvaux
21 Pius X
22 Queenship of Mary
23 Rose of Lima
24 Bartholomew
25 Louis of France
   Joseph of Calasanz
27 Monica
28 Augustine
29 Martyrdom of John the Baptist

Saints and Feast Days

INTRODUCTION

The Church calendar in the West (Roman calendar) revolves around the one great feast of the year, the Lord's resurrection, or Easter. The Church gives special emphasis to the Paschal Mystery and the life and teachings of Jesus. Therefore, the year is divided into Easter and the Easter cycle of feasts, Christmas and the Christmas cycle, and ordinary time.

Traditionally, the Church has celebrated the way certain men and women have lived the Paschal Mystery and honored them as saints. These human beings responded to God through Jesus, and overcame their weaknesses and sins through the power of grace. Their lives praise Christ, give hope to His followers, and offer an example for people to imitate. *Saints and Feast Days* provides sketches of many saints and feast days listed in the Roman calendar. Suggested activities help the students to realize that in their own lives rich opportunities are given them to become saints, too.

SUGGESTED ACTIVITIES

1. At the beginning of class, read — or have a student read — the sketch provided in the supplement.

2. In the case of summer saints, have the students named after these saints present the sketches on their birthdays, baptismal anniversaries, or at another suitable time.

3. Make copies of the supplement pages and distribute them to the students for use at home.

4. Encourage the students to do additional research on the saints, especially their patrons, and share their findings with the class. These could eventually be assembled into a class booklet. Assigning research of patrons is a significant activity for students.

5. Have the students find out the meaning, or etymology, of their own names or the names of the saints.

6. On the feast days, use the opening prayer of the Mass for the class prayer.

7. Post a calendar that contains the name days of the students as well as their birthdays and baptismal anniversaries.

8. After presentations of the lives of the saints, relate their lives to the present day. Stress that a lived faith is a powerful witness to the world.

9. Encourage the students and their families to celebrate the feast days of patron saints in some way:
   - Prepare for the celebrations by observing vigils the night before, during which they should read about their patrons, read from Scripture, pray the Rosary, or use their own form of prayer.
   - Attend Mass on the feast day of their patron.
   - Prepare a special dessert for the day.
   - Light a baptismal candle or Christ candle in honor of the saint.

10. Have the students write their own prayers to the saints, or have them compose their own personal litanies. A general starting point would be a prayer to God the Father, Christ, the Holy Spirit, Mary, Joseph, and then any saints whom they wish to include.

11. Keep a saint mural in progress. As each saint is studied, he or she may be added to the mural. The students themselves might be included in the mural — at least approaching the land of the saints!

12. Have the students imagine that they are the saints presented. What would they have done? Felt?

5

The calendar of saints represents men and women from every walk of life, every period of history, and every part of the world. They became saints because they loved. They remind us that it is possible for us to change and grow in the love of God and of others. Through the power of Jesus working in us all, we can become holy and can help the world come to know and love God. Praying to the saints encourages us to live up to our full potential so that we may join them in eternal life.

The Second Vatican Council made it very clear that all men and women are called to holiness. "All Christ's followers, therefore, are invited and bound to pursue holiness and the perfect fulfillment of their proper state" (Dogmatic Constitution on the Church #2). All of us are called to be close to God, to listen and to pray, to respond to His teachings, whatever the cost, as did the saints. The saints are our companions, and we thank God for the example of their lives that makes Christ more present to us, and we ask their intercession. By suffering and dying, the saints bore witness to the faith, and their witness encouraged others to remain strong.

Sometimes when we read the lives of the saints of earlier centuries, we are amazed and even shocked by the things they did. It is true that the world we live in is very different from theirs. When we read about the extraordinary events of their lives, we wonder if these stories are really true. We must remember that, since books were scarce, people of earlier times passed on the lives of the saints by telling stories. In the retelling, some of the stories were naturally embellished; yet the substance of these stories is to be considered true. Some stories of the saints are called legends. This does not mean that they are fictional. It literally means they were "to be read" in the Divine Office, and are to be understood in the spirit in which they were written. When reading the lives of the saints, we must remember that their lives and their deaths give purpose and meaning to ours. When we see how God is glorified in them, we are encouraged to strive ever more eagerly to win the crown of everlasting life.

SEPTEMBER 3: ST. GREGORY THE GREAT

It is often during difficult times that the strongest, most faith-filled leaders emerge. These are the people who meet the challenges of the times, who struggle with the problems before them and, at the same time, plan for the future. Such a man was Gregory the Great. Gregory was born sometime around the year 540 in Rome. He was the son of Gordianus, a wealthy Roman senator. Like most of the nobility of his time, he was well-educated. But unlike many, he was generous and concerned about the poor.

Little is known about Gregory's childhood, but we do know he lived during a period of wars, invasions by hostile tribes, famine and destruction. When he was in his early thirties, Gregory was made the chief prefect, or governor, of Rome. He had long been attracted to the religious life, however, and so left his position before very long. He converted the family estate in Rome into the Abbey of St. Andrew, became a monk there, and founded six Benedictine monasteries on his estates in Sicily. His life of quiet and prayer did not last long, for around 578 he was ordained one of the seven deacons of Rome and sent as the papal ambassador to Constantinople, where he served until 585. When he arrived back in Rome, he was made the abbot of St. Andrew's.

In 590, Pope Pelagius II died and Gregory was acclaimed pope by the clergy and the people of Rome. Unwillingly, Gregory accepted the role, calling himself the "servant of the servants of God." Because of his political skill, learning, talents, and deep devotion to God, Gregory was able to make peace with the invading Lombards, save the city from famine by reorganizing the property and granaries of the Church, and restore order within the Church itself. Even though there were tremendous problems in Rome, Gregory was able to look beyond his land to the needs of people in foreign lands. In 596 he sent Augustine (of Canterbury), who was the prior at St. Andrew Monastery, and forty other monks to England to teach the Angles the faith. So great was Gregory's interest in them that he has come to be called the "Apostle of England," even though he himself was unable to travel there to preach.

Gregory died on March 12, 604. Although his achievements were many and had a widespread effect on those times, Gregory became a saint because of his love for God, which was reflected in all that he did.

SUGGESTIONS

1. "The times make the man." Discuss with the students how Gregory I responded to the needs of his era. Ask them what qualities a person would need today to be considered a great saint.

2. Although Gregory's full influence on the music of his day is debatable, he is sometimes accredited with the Church's liturgical chant form, "Gregorian chant." Play some samples of Gregorian chant for the students and teach them one of the Latin responses. Gregory was known for liturgical

reform as well, and for encouraging the praying of the Stations of the Cross and participation in daily Mass during Lent.

3. Along with Augustine, Ambrose, and Jerome, Gregory the Great is considered one of the four key Fathers of the Western Church. Have the students research any of these Fathers of the Church. Encourage them to discover what is necessary in order to be called a "Father" of the Church.

4. Gregory supported mission work. During his life he sent groups of monks to evangelize Britain. At that time the practice of sending monks as missionaries was not usual. Have a missionary present a program on the work being done in the missions. Or have students do research on the many active missionary congregations in the Church, especially those in your diocese. Invite a Benedictine, if possible, since Gregory was a Benedictine.

5. Gregory is known as a patron of teachers, scholars, and singers. Discuss with the students why these areas are especially related to Gregory. Have them make Gregory the Great medals or certificates for outstanding teachers, students, and singers.

6. Gregory the Great is known for his numerous writings on theology, scripture, and morality. His book *Pastoral Care* contains a powerful description of the qualities and duties of a bishop. Invite the students to find out more about the pope as bishop of Rome, the duties of the local bishops, various organizations of bishops (particularly the Synod of Bishops), and other areas related to bishops. After the students have found out more about bishops, encourage them to write supportive letters to their bishop and to follow the statements and activities of the bishops by reading the Catholic paper in the diocese.

SEPTEMBER 8: BIRTH OF MARY

God chose Mary to be the Mother of Jesus. So open was she to God's action in her life that she was chosen to bring Christ to the waiting world. The Gospels are silent about her actual birth, but from the part she was to play in Christ's life, we know how special it was — even though the world did not know it at the time.

We cannot be certain about what the future holds for any newborn infant, but we do know that each life has meaning and purpose. We know that we are gifted and loved by God, and that He has given us a part to play in life that cannot be duplicated by any other person. We honor Christ by celebrating His mother's birth. So, too, let us honor Him by showing respect and concern for one another — for God loves us and has called us each to something very special in life.

SUGGESTIONS

1. Encourage the students to pray to Mary during the day, or pray the Memorare; Hail, Holy Queen; Litany of Loreto; or Hail Mary with them. Close the day with a hymn honoring Mary.

2. The date of the feast of the Birth of Mary was used to fix the date of the feast of the Immaculate Conception. This situation occurs a couple of times during the Church year. (The Annuniation/the Nativity.) But all the Marian feasts are closely related to the mysteries in Christs's life. Have the students explain how these feasts point to Christ as the center of Mary's life.

3. Traditionally this feast is believed to have originated in Jerusalem and was celebrated in the Eastern Church before it came to be observed in the Western (sometime around the eighth century). Use this opportunity to have the students research the Eastern Church or devotions celebrated in the Eastern Catholic communities, e.g., Akathistos (NCD #143). Or have the students present nationality customs honoring Mary. Such presentations could include displays, samples of music and food characteristic of these celebrations, etc.

SEPTEMBER 9: ST. PETER CLAVER

Peter Claver was a man with a mission. Born in Spain in 1581, Peter studied under and was trained by the Jesuits. In 1602, he entered the Jesuit novitiate at Tarragona. As a young man, he met Alphonsus Rodriguez, the porter of the college. Alphonsus greatly influenced Peter, urging him to follow the call to be a missionary. And so in 1610 Peter was sent as a missionary to Cartagena (in what is now Colombia), South America. There he continued his studies, ministered to the people, and was ordained (1616).

Cartagena was a busy city, but its economic success came from dealings in human misery, for Cartagena was the principal market for the slave trade in the New World. Hundreds of thousands of blacks were brought there, herded into warehouses, and auctioned off to the highest bidder. These slaves had been captured in Africa, chained together in groups of six, crowded into the lower holds of the ships, and mistreated continually during the long journey to Colombia. Ships meant to hold 100-200 were carrying 600-800 human beings. So terrible and inhuman were the conditions that an estimated one-third of the slaves died during the journey. These were the people that came to mean so very much to Peter Claver. Whenever a boat arrived in port, Peter would hurry down to it with medicine, fruits, vegetables, bread, and clothing. He would greet the slaves by giving them water to drink. His first concern was to tend to their human needs — to somehow restore their sense of dignity after they had suffered so much. He nursed many back to health and, while they were in warehouses awaiting their sale, would teach them and administer the sacraments to them.

At the time there was little that Peter Claver could do to change the social structure. The hearts and the consciences of the people had been so hardened that they refused to see this evil of slavery in their midst. Peter and Father Alphonsus Sandoval tried to be visible signs to the people, showing them that these slaves were indeed human beings, children of God. By bringing Christianity to these slaves, these men were laying the foundations of justice and charity for the future. During his forty years in Colombia, Peter Claver baptized nearly 300,000 blacks.

A man of deep prayer, unbounded energy, and steady devotion, Peter Claver realized that it was his relationship with Christ that nourished his spirit and gave him the courage to go on when so many problems surrounded his work. In 1650, worn out from his work, Peter became bedridden. For four years he was unable to actively serve the people, and on September 8, 1654, he died. The city that had opposed so many of his efforts honored him greatly after his death. In 1888 he was canonized by Pope Leo XIII.

It takes a rare kind of courage and love to continue to reach out to others when evil seems so strong in a society. But Peter Claver had the kind of courage and love necessary to bring peace to the hearts of those who suffered. He saw the suffering Jesus in the slaves he served. And he heard in their cry: "What you do unto others, you do unto Me."

SUGGESTIONS

1. Peter Claver's life was a vivid demonstration of the works of mercy in action. Review with the students the spiritual and corporal works of mercy. Have them draw pictures of Peter's ministry, showing how he was involved in these various works.

2. Have the students find Spain and Colombia on maps. Refer to history books for the various slave trade routes of the era.

3. Alphonsus Rodriguez (1598-1628) figured in Peter Claver's life story. Have the students discover more about this saint.

4. Peter Claver was canonized by Pope Leo XIII, who also championed the rights of workers. This pope encouraged missionary activity and the abolition of slavery. Have the students find out more about this pope and his writings, and about other saints canonized by him.

5. Invite a representative from the lay missions, the Jesuits, or any other group that is involved in evangelization to speak on missionary spirit and activities.

6. On his solemn profession, Peter Claver signed himself "slave of the black forever." Discuss the problems of racial tensions, prejudice, and equality. Refer to the bishops' pastoral, *Racism in Our Days for Church Teaching.*

7. Have the students compose a prayer to Peter Claver asking for his intercession for peace. Ask how they can be modern Peter Clavers.

8. Peter Claver bought eighteen blacks to help and act as interpreters and catechists for his work. Encourage the students to do research on black history and the contributions of blacks to various cultures. Also discuss with the class the need for the various groups in any social structure to help one another.

9. Have the students research Scripture texts to discover what the apostles and disciples needed and did on their earliest missionary journeys: Matthew 10:1-42, Luke 9:1-6, Luke 9:57-62, Luke 10:1-20.

SEPTEMBER 13: ST. JOHN CHRYSOSTOM

People who are willing to stand up for what is right and condemn what is evil leave their mark on the world. But they also may find themselves with a lot of enemies! John Chrysostom, an eloquent bishop-preacher of the fourth century, certainly understood this.

John was born around the year 347 in Antioch (where the believers in Jesus were first called Christians). His father died when he was a child, and so his mother guided his education. A gifted student, John studied under Libanius, a famous orator of his time. Recalling his years as an adolescent, John considered himself too involved in the evils of the world. At eighteen, he experienced some type of religious conversion and began to study the Bible. Three years later, after the death of his mother, John went to join a group of monks living in the mountains. After four years, he left them to live the life of a hermit in a cave. But so strenuous was this life that his health suffered, and he returned to the city of Antioch.

Here others quickly noticed his gifts: a monk, a biblical scholar, an eloquent speaker. Soon he was ordained to the diaconate, and when he was thirty-nine he was ordained a priest. One role of a priest or bishop is to teach, and teach he did! John was quick to see how greed and lust infected society and he was not hesitant about condemning it. Of particular concern to him was the widespread indifference to the poor.

In 397 John was made the bishop-patriarch of Constantinople — a position of extraordinary influence. He himself lived a very simple life, giving his wealth over for the building of hospitals, and he set about reforming the clergy and the city. He deposed bishops for buying their way into office. He sold much of the expensive furniture in the bishop's residence and gave the money to serve the poor. He urged other bishops to spend more time in their own areas rather than in the palaces of city officials. He attacked the wealthy for misuse of their riches. He sought to reform the lax clergy, to straighten out the badly managed budget, to rid the land of violence. The list was endless. Such a champion of charity and justice was he that it was not long before he stirred up the anger of the empress, Eudoxia, and the jealousy of Theophilus, the patriarch of Alexandria. With such enemies mounting an attack against him, John was impeached and exiled. Even though he had the support of Pope Innocent I, the love of the poor, and the devotion of so many others, John was exiled even further and died en route in 407.

It is said that the role of a true prophet is to comfort the disturbed and to disturb the comfortable. In that case John Chrysostom was a powerful prophet of his day, for he was not afraid to speak out against wrong, no matter who was involved. Who are the prophets of today? Who are the prophets in your classroom? Your family? Your group of friends? Is it you or will the world have to wait for someone else?

SUGGESTIONS

1. John was given the title *Chrysostom*, meaning 'Golden Mouth', because of his eloquence in speaking. Hold a John Chrysostom Day for which the students prepare speeches dealing with any moral theme relevant to their school, home, or society. Awards may be given to students for clarity of thought and powerful expression.

2. Since John was a Scripture scholar, he devoted extra time during the day to reading and meditation on the Bible. Encourage the students to read the Bible daily for about five minutes.

3. Invite the pastor or associate pastor in to speak on the diaconate program of his time and the present program. Also, have the students find the Scriptural passages related to the role of the deacon in the early Church. Acts 6:8-15 describes the first deacon, Stephen.

4. In 387, John Chrysostom helped ease tensions in Antioch after a tax riot broke out. The emperor had levied a heavy tax to increase his defense budget, and the people revolted in protest. It was John's first year as a priest and he interceded, calling for restraint and peace. Such situations still occur. Have the students relate contemporary issues and the directives from the Church regarding such issues. These can often be found in newspaper and magazine reports on the activities and speeches of the pope and the local bishops.

SEPTEMBER 14: TRIUMPH OF THE CROSS

The one symbol most often identified with Jesus and His Church is the cross. Today we celebrate the feast of the Triumph of the Cross. This feast traces its beginning to Jerusalem and the dedication of the church built on the site of Mount Calvary in 335. But the meaning of the cross is deeper than any city, any celebration, any building. The cross is a sign of suffering, a sign of human cruelty at its worst. But by Christ's love shown in the Paschal Mystery, it has become the sign of triumph and victory, the sign of God Who is love itself.

Believers have always looked to the cross in times of suffering. People in concentration camps, in prisons, in hospitals, in any place of suffering and loneliness, have been known to draw, trace, or form crosses and focus their eyes and hearts on them. The cross does not explain pain and misery. It does not give us any easy answers. But it does help us to see our lives united with Christ's.

We often make the Sign of the Cross over ourselves. We make it before prayer to help fix our minds and hearts on God. We make it after prayer, hoping to stay close to God. In trials and temptations, the cross is a sign of strength and protection. The cross is the sign of the fullness of life that is ours. At Baptism, too, the Sign of the Cross is used; the priest, parents, and godparents make the sign on the forehead of the child. A sign made on the forehead is a sign of belonging. By the Sign of the Cross in Baptism, Jesus takes us as His own in a unique way. Today, let us look to the cross often. Let us make the Sign of the Cross and realize we bring our whole selves to God — our minds, souls, bodies, wills, thoughts, hearts — everything we are and will become.

O cross, you are the glorious sign of our victory. Through your power may we share in the triumph of Christ Jesus.

(Prayer of Christians)

9

SUGGESTIONS

1. Teach the students the Prayer to Christ Crucified or run off copies of it for the students to pray together.

A PRAYER TO CHRIST CRUCIFIED

Behold, O kind and most sweet Jesus, I cast myself upon my knees in Your sight, and with the most fervent desire of my soul I pray and beseech You that You would impress upon my heart lively sentiments of faith, hope, and charity, with true repentance for my sins, and a firm desire of amendment, while with deep affection and grief of soul I ponder within myself and mentally contemplate Your five most precious wounds, having before my eyes that which David the prophet put in Your own mouth concerning you, O good Jesus: "They have pierced my hands and feet: they have numbered all my bones."

2. Encourage the students to do research on St. Helena and the true cross. Or have them research Constantine, the emperor at the time of the dedication. You may wish to suggest that they read *Builders and Destroyers* (Book Four of *God's Hand in History A.D. 300-700*) by Mary Wilson (Our Sunday Visitor, Inc., Huntington, Indiana 46750; 1977) for the background it provides.

3. Have the students construct crosses of their own using wood, cardboard, foil, stones (pebbles), clay, or any other material available. Or have them make a matchstick cross:

BURNT MATCH CROSS

Materials needed:

- 275 or so burnt wooden matches (Strike them and blow them out at once so only the tips are black.)
- a piece of cardboard or wood cut in the shape of a cross
- all purpose glue
- varnish or wood stain

Steps:

- Cut the cardboard as shown:

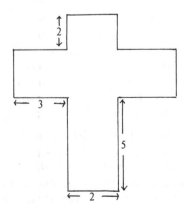

- Lay four matches on the cardboard with the black tips cut off as shown in the diagram ①②③④. They form a cross in the center of the cardboard. Glue them down.

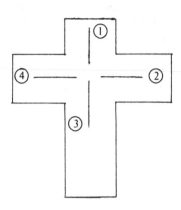

- Lay five more matches down, ⑤ - ⑨ as shown. Do not cut off the black tips. All but ⑨ should extend over the cardboard edge.

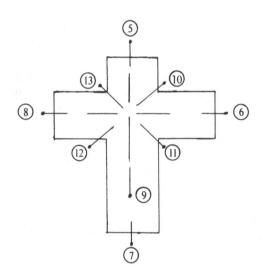

- Lay four more matches diagonal to the center. See ⑩ - ⑬ in the diagram. Continue to glue matches diagonally as shown for each section. Paint over or varnish the matches. Let dry one hour.

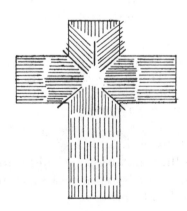

4. Take the students to the church or prayer room, if one is available, for a short prayer or meditation on the cross/crucifix. Often churches have specially designed crosses/crucifixes. If this is the case, invite someone familiar with the design or church architecture to explain the symbolism of the one there.

Provide Scripture references for meditation (e.g., John 19; Mark 15-16; 2 Timothy 2:10-12) or appropriate music (e.g., "Behold the Wood," "With What Great Love," etc.).

5. Pray the Way of the Cross with the students or have them compose their own meditations and drawings for the stations.

SEPTEMBER 15: OUR LADY OF SORROWS

When you love people very much, you share in all their joys and all their sorrows. When your parents, brothers and sisters, or friends are happy, it is easier for you to be happy, too. But when they are sick or suffering, you carry the pain in your own heart. That's how it was for Mary, the Mother of Jesus. When people accepted Jesus and found their lives changed, Mary was filled with joy. But when she saw her Son rejected and hurt, she experienced that pain very deeply. Today we remember Our Lady's share in the sufferings of her Son and we call upon her as Our Lady of Sorrows. Because Mary loved Jesus so much, she suffered along with Him. Neither complaining nor feeling sorry for herself, she carried these sufferings in silence — knowing that God understood and cared.

Mary is our mother, too. That means she rejoices when we draw closer to God. It means she understands our daily pains and sufferings. We may not always understand the mystery of the cross in our lives, but we do know we need never carry it by ourselves. For we are brothers and sisters of Jesus Who gave His life for us on the cross, and we are children of Mary, Our Lady of Sorrows. Today, let us turn to Mary with our complaints and our sufferings, with the times we are misunderstood and lonely. She is near to us and will help us by praying for us. Mary, Our Lady of Sorrows, pray for us.

SUGGESTIONS

1. Traditionally, the major sorrows of Mary are listed as seven. Direct the students to research these incidents in Scripture. Have them illustrate the events or design banners for each.
   1) The prophecy of Simeon (Jesus is presented in the temple): Luke 2:33-35
   2) The flight into Egypt: Matthew 2:13-18
   3) The loss of Jesus in the temple in Jerusalem: Luke 2:41-50
   4) Meeting Jesus on the way to Calvary (Jesus is crowned with thorns): Matthew 27:27-31; Mark 15:16-20
   5) Mary at the foot of the cross (The crucifixion and death of Jesus): Matthew 27:45-56; John 19:25-27
   6) Jesus is taken down from the cross (The placing of Jesus in the arms of His mother): Luke 23:47-55
   7) The burial of Jesus: Matthew 27:57-61; John 19:38-42

You will note that several of the last references are not explicit in the Scriptures, but rather come from the traditional understanding of Mary's role in the passion and death of her Son.

2. Teach or review with the students several Marian prayers or devotions: the Stabat Mater; Marian ejaculations; the Memorare; Hail, Holy Queen; the Litany of Loreto; or the Sorrowful Mysteries of the Rosary.

3. Show the students either a picture or replica of Michelangelo's *Pieta*. Display it in the room during the day as a reminder of Mary's love for Jesus and her love for us.

SEPTEMBER 16: STS. CORNELIUS AND CYPRIAN

Beginnings can be very difficult. The beginning years of the Church are an example of this, as the lives of Cornelius and Cyprian clearly show. These two martyr-saints lived in the third century and found themselves confronting heresies, persecutions, and divisions of every kind.

The emperor at the time was a man named Decius. He was a severe ruler who believed that Rome could be great only by staying faithful to the worship of pagan idols. He made a law stating that all who would not give up their Christian faith should be killed. The pope (Fabian, at that time) was martyred along with many others. But there were Christians who did give up their faith, out of fear, weakness, or lack of real commitment. The Emperor Decius thought that without a pope the Church would simply fade away, and so he prevented any election of another bishop of Rome. But the Church did not fade. Instead, a council of priests secretly carried on the work. After a year, the emperor was forced to leave the area to lead his soldiers against the invading Goths. During his absence, Church elections were held and Cornelius was made pope.

Cornelius found himself in the midst of problems from the moment he became pope. One source of difficulties was Novatian. Novatian had hoped to become pope, and so immediately he challenged Cornelius. Novatian also believed that those who had

11

given up their faith during the persecutions could not be accepted back into the Church — even if they had sincerely repented. Cornelius called a council of bishops together to settle these disputes. The council reaffirmed Cornelius' position as pope and condemned Novatian's view. After two years as pope, Cornelius was arrested under the emperor's rule and sentenced to banishment. He died in the year 253 while he was in exile.

A close friend and courageous supporter of Cornelius during this time was a man named Cyprian, the bishop of Carthage (near what is now called Tunis) in North Africa. Cyprian was born in Carthage around 210 and was the son of pagan parents. He was extremely intelligent and was a powerful speaker. He converted to Christianity as an adult. After that he lived a very virtuous, penitential life. His reputation for holiness grew and he was made a priest, and eventually bishop.

Cyprian was bishop of Carthage for nearly ten years. During that time, he had only one year of peace. After that, the persecutions under Decius began, as well as disagreements over what to do with those who gave up their faith during these persecutions. Just as Pope Cornelius had to deal with Novatian, Bishop Cyprian had to deal with a priest named Novatus. Novatus believed that all the people who had denied their faith should be accepted back without any restrictions. Eventually the Church took a middle course on the whole issue. New persecutions broke out under Valerian. Cyprian was arrested and put on trial for being a Christian. When he was read his death sentence, he exclaimed, "Blessed be God!" He was martyred in front of a large crowd on September 14, 258.

Both Cornelius and Cyprian knew what it was like to remain faithful to Jesus and to the Church in the midst of difficulties. Although separated by many miles, they were good friends and supported one another in seeking the truth. In their lives, we see not only the overwhelming power of God but also the power of good friendship. They encouraged one another to lead good, virtuous, self-sacrificing, and loving lives for God. There is no greater gift that one friend can offer to another.

Today let us think of ways to help our friends grow closer to God.

SUGGESTIONS

1. We often take the Sacrament of Penance for granted. The lives of Cornelius and Cyprian show us how the Church has always struggled for a deeper, clearer understanding of this sacrament. The Church continually tries to discern the mind and spirit of Christ. Have the students discuss the importance of this sacrament in their lives and the need to ask forgiveness from those they have offended. Prepare a short penance celebration or have the students exchange some sign of peace.

2. Cyprian was converted largely through the influence of a priest. Have the students interview priests, religious, teachers, or new converts in the parish on the people and things that have influenced their lives and their major decisions. If your parish is involved in a catechumenate program, invite the leaders of this group to come in and explain the importance of community support.

3. The students may wish to do further research in one of the following areas:

   The catacombs (Cornelius eventually was buried in a crypt near the catacomb of Callistus)

   Apostates (Those who reject the faith they once professed.)

   Anti-pope (Novatian was one of the first anti-popes.)

   Decius, Valerian, and other persecutors and persecutions of the early Church

4. A document from Cornelius describes the mid-third century Church at Rome as having 46 priests, 7 deacons, 7 sub-deacons, and an estimated 50,000 Christians. Have the students find similar statistics on their own diocese.

SEPTEMBER 17: ST. ROBERT BELLARMINE

It is said that Robert Bellarmine was so short he used to stand on a stool in order to be seen in some of the high pulpits of Europe. But he was a giant in many other ways.

Robert Bellarmine was born in Italy in 1542. He was the third of ten children in a family where prayer and serving others were priorities. In 1560 he entered the Society of Jesus, the Jesuits. While he attended the Roman College, he was considered a brilliant student. He eventually taught at Louvain. As a matter of fact, he was the first Jesuit to become a professor there. His sermons and his defense of the faith were so powerful that people were attracted to him from all over, and many were eventually converted. Bellarmine was ordained a priest in 1570. He became rector at the Roman College in 1592 and provincial of Naples in 1594. By 1598 he was named a cardinal and in 1602 he became archbishop of Capua. He was called to Rome in 1605 to work in defense of the Church against the heresies of the day. All in all, Robert Bellarmine was advisor to five different popes. He was involved in all sorts of controversies. One of the most famous of these involved the teachings of Galileo, the scientist, who was also a friend of Bellarmine.

As we have seen in so many other cases, great leaders seem to surface during difficult times in the Church. Many of the men Bellarmine knew and aided also became leaders in the Church and some, such as Aloysius Gonzaga and Francis de Sales, became saints. This is all part of the mystery of the Paschal Mystery of Christ. For those who love and depend on God, there is no challenge too great, no sacrifice too difficult. In our own lives, too, we may find the strength to hold to all that Jesus has taught as we grow in love of Him. Today, like Robert Bellarmine, let us use all our gifts for God. May we study hard, pray much, and serve others, so that the world will see how great is our God.

SUGGESTIONS

1. Robert Bellarmine wrote and taught during the Protestant Reformation (1517-1648). You may wish to have the students research some aspect of the Reformation and Robert Bellarmine's role during it.

2. Many of Bellarmine's students went on to become missionaries in England and Germany. Encourage the students to support current missionary activity in the Church.

3. Bellarmine was known as an outstanding student. Have the students discuss the importance of studying their faith in order to witness more effectively to others. Let them design posters illustrating some of the main beliefs of the Catholic faith. Recommend that they refer to the Apostles' Creed or the Nicene Creed as a basis.

4. Have the students do research on the Society of Jesus. What activities are the Jesuits involved in currently? Why would people expect the saints of this community to be not only loving and virtuous but also highly educated?

5. Bellarmine wrote a great deal in defense of the faith, and in 1931 was declared a Doctor of the Church. Have the students find out what it means to be a "Doctor of the Church." Then ask them to write essays on some truth of the faith that has come to mean more to them in the past year.

SEPTEMBER 19: ST. JANUARIUS

Little is actually known about Januarius except that he was a bishop of Benevento (near Naples, Italy) and was probably martyred during the persecutions under Diocletian around 305. But there are a number of legends connected with this saint. According to these stories, Januarius went to visit some Christians who had been imprisoned. He himself was then arrested and condemned to death for being a Christian. Januarius and his companions were thrown to wild beasts in the amphitheater of Pozzuoli, but the animals refused to harm them. They were beheaded

instead and the blood and body of Januarius were brought back to Naples. Januarius is regarded as the patron saint of Naples, and his protection is sought when there is the danger of volcanic eruption.

SUGGESTIONS

1. When Diocletian became emperor of the Roman Empire in 284, he knew he would need to divide the land in order to rule better. At first he did not demand much in the realm of homage, but as the number of Christians increased, he feared rebellion and began a series of persecutions. Those who refused to burn incense before a statue of the emperor as proof of their loyalty were executed. Perhaps Januarius was among those who refused to show such worship. Have the students reflect on the need to live their faith even during difficult times. Call their attention to various occasions throughout the day when they have an opportunity to live their faith.

2. The relics of Januarius have gained more fame than the saint himself. These relics, including a four-inch flask of his blood, have been attracting people since the fifteenth century. Each year the substance in the flask liquefies eighteen times (usually in May, September 19-26, and December). Refer the students to the *New Catholic Encyclopedia* (McGraw-Hill) for additional reading on liquefactions. You may wish to discuss the purpose of miracles and miraculous events, but also the role of faith without such signs. "The Church also honors the other saints who are already with the Lord in heaven. We who come after them draw inspiration from their heroic example, look for fellowship in their communion, and in prayer seek their intercession with God on our behalf." (NCD #107).

See Supplement for September 20.

SEPTEMBER 21: ST. MATTHEW

Matthew, the apostle, is the patron of bankers — and for a good reason. Matthew, also known as Levi, was a tax collector in Capernaum. Most tax collectors were hated by the Jews because they worked for the Romans, who had conquered the land. A tax collector could use his position honestly or dishonestly. But the temptation of riches was often too great.

Yet Matthew was one of those special people chosen by Christ to follow Him, to learn from Him, and to go out and spread the Good News to others. So powerful was the call from Jesus that Matthew left his work as tax collector. He even invited Jesus to a special dinner where other tax collectors (publicans) and sinners were gathered. The Pharisees were upset when they saw this and they said to the disciples, "Why does your master eat with tax collectors and sinners?" Jesus heard them and replied, "It is not the healthy who need the doctor, but the sick. Go and learn the meaning of the words: What I want is mercy, not sacrifice. And indeed I did not come to call the virtuous, but sinners" (see Matthew 9:9-13). We know nothing other than that about Matthew from the Scriptures, but we do know that Matthew preached the Good News of Christ and that at least part of the Gospel attributed to him was first written for the Jewish converts in Palestine. Our copy of the Gospel of Matthew has come to us in Greek. It has been translated into Latin and into English.

There is some uncertainty about where Matthew preached and where and how he died. Some say Matthew labored in Persia; some say Syria and Greece, while others say Ethiopia. His shrine is in Salerno, Italy.

There is much that we can learn from Matthew. He was a man who knew quite well the power of money. He knew the comfort it could ensure, the recreation it could buy, the luxury it could provide. But he was wise enough to know what it could not do. Money could never give him that sense of peace deep inside. It could never befriend him when he was lonely or give him the strength and courage to go on when all else seemed lost. Money could never buy him forgiveness or love. But the love of Christ could do all this and more. Let us pray today that through the intercession of St. Matthew we may not be fooled into thinking money can provide us with the most important things in life. Let us also recall that Christ will provide us with all we need to grow in what really matters. St. Matthew, pray for us.

SUGGESTIONS

1. Encourage the students to pray for those who work with money as their occupation that they may remain honest and keep a sense of priorities in their lives.

2. Have the students share with the poor: collect money for the missions, sponsor a canned goods drive for the hungry, seek donations of clothes and toys for the local thrift shop or other group serving the poor.

3. Have the students locate Capernaum on a map.

4. It is believed that the Gospel of Matthew was written between 80-90 AD. He wrote to show that Jesus was the Messiah, the Savior-King foretold by the prophets. In the Gospel of Matthew there are almost more Old Testament references than in all the other Gospels combined. If there is a Scripture study group in the parish, invite the members in to share what they have learned about the Gospel of Matthew. Enthrone the Bible, open to the Gospel of Matthew, and read from it. Have the students look through the Gospel for its Old Testament references.

5. There are several symbols for Matthew. Explain them to the students. Then have the students use one or more to design a lectern for their church, a statue, a window, a banner, a shrine, or some other object.

Symbols for Matthew:

a man: represents the Gospel of Matthew, since the Gospel begins with the genealogy of Christ, His human family line

sitting at a desk: represents Matthew as an author of the Gospel

holding a money box and/or glasses: represents his life as tax collector and reader of account books

SEPTEMBER 26: STS. COSMAS AND DAMIAN

There are some saints of whom we know very little. People from all over the world may honor them. Shrines and churches may be built in their names. But the facts and details of their lives have faded from our memories or they may never have been recorded.

Cosmas and Damian are saints like these. Little is known about them except that they suffered martyrdom for their faith in Syria sometime during the persecutions of Diocletian (around 303). We may never know exactly what happened, but we do know that their witness to the faith was so strong that people automatically turned to them for prayerful help.

Legends about these two saints abound. According to these stories, Cosmas and Damian were twin brothers, born in Arabia, who went to Syria to study and practice medicine. But they were concerned about more than healing bodies. They brought their belief in Christ to those to whom they ministered. Not only that, but they also served people without charging any fees. Lysias, the governor of Celicia, heard about these two brothers and he summoned them before him. When Cosmas and Damian proclaimed they were Christians, Lysias had them tortured and finally beheaded. Their bodies were taken to the city of Cyr (Cyrrhus) in southern Syria. There great devotion to these two doctors grew and many cures were said to have been worked through their intercession. Later a church in their honor was constructed over the site of their burial. When the Emperor Justinian was sick, he prayed to Saints Cosmas and Damian for a cure. Out of gratitude for receiving this favor, he enlarged the city of Cyr and the church there. Numerous other churches were erected for them at Constantinople and Rome. Their names are also included in the First Eucharistic Prayer (the Roman Canon).

If so little about these saints is actually known, why do we honor them? Part of the answer can be found in tradition. When so many believers continue to honor the memory of martyrs, year after year and all over the world, there is good reason to believe that their lives were true witnesses to the Gospel. People who live and die according to their convictions and faith give hope to the world long after their deaths. Their lives can inspire us and encourage us to be faithful during our little trials and sorrows. Let us pray today.

> Lord, we honor the memory of Saints Cosmas and Damian. Accept our grateful praise for raising them to eternal glory and for giving us your fatherly care. We ask this through our Lord Jesus Christ, your Son, who lives and reigns with you and the Holy Spirit, one God for ever and ever.

SUGGESTIONS

1. Along with St. Luke, Saints Cosmas and Damian are the patrons of doctors, surgeons, and druggists. Lead the students in prayer for all those in the medical profession and those who minister to others in time of sickness.

2. The stories about Cosmas and Damian have inspired many artists through the centuries. Check local art museums and libraries for possible reprints of these pictures, e.g., one painted by Fra Angelico.

3. Cosmas and Damian have been given the name "the moneyless ones" because they did not charge any fee to their patients. Have the students think of some word or phrase by which they would like others to remember them. Have them write this title and why they chose it in their journals. Encourage them to live up to their ideals.

4. Ask the students to read the First Eucharistic Prayer and note the saints listed there. Have them do research on the martyrologies.

5. Some legends indicate that three of their brothers were also martyred with Cosmas and Damian. Discuss with the students how family support can help them live their faith.

6. Review the corporal works of mercy. Also review the correct form for the abbreviation of the plural of *saints: Sts.* Cosmas and Damian.

SEPTEMBER 27: ST. VINCENT DE PAUL

Remarkable! What better word is there to describe a man who organized charitable groups to provide food and clothing for the poor, founded a congregation of priests, helped found another congregation for women, began hospitals and homes for orphans and for the aged, established training programs and retreats for seminarians, raised money for the victims of war, and sent missionaries to countries — just to name a few of his projects! This remarkable man was Vincent de Paul.

Vincent de Paul was born in Gascony (France) in 1580. He was the son of peasant farmers. As a young boy, he was educated by the Franciscans at Dax, and then went on to study at the University of Toulouse. When he was nearly twenty, Vincent was ordained a priest. Being ordained at such an early age is somewhat unusual, but was not so at that time. Vincent had not planned on a life of extraordinary service and self-sacrifice, but rather on one of security and ease. It would take a few more years and many influences before he would respond more fully to God's love and the needs of those around him.

For a couple of years after his ordination, there was little known about him. There are stories that explain that during this time, while on board a ship, Vincent was seized by pirates and sold into slavery in Tunis, North Africa. Eventually he escaped and made his way back to Rome. From Rome he went to France, and there he was appointed court chaplain to Queen Margaret of Valois. He seemed well on the way to the life of wealth and comfort. But at the same time he came to know Pierre de Berulle, who later became a cardinal. Berulle helped Vincent understand more deeply what it meant to be a true Christian. Vincent came face-to-face with himself and his empty goals.

As he became more aware of God's love and his call to serve, Vincent changed the whole thrust of his life. He worked for a year in a small parish in a peasant area and saw how destitute the people were. So he organized charitable confraternities — groups of people who would provide food and clothing for the poor on a regular basis. But Vincent saw another kind of poverty, a spiritual poverty. Many of the people had no real understanding of their faith. So Vincent organized priests who would go out to the poorer sections and preach to the people. Eventually this group of priests became the Congregation of the Mission, also known as the Vincentian fathers.

As Vincent saw the needs of others, he reached out to them. At night he would search the city for abandoned babies and he founded homes for them. He cared for the prisoners who had been made slaves on the galleys. He remained good friends with many of the rich and influential people and involved them in his work with the poor and needy. So much had he done for so many that after his death in 1660 he was canonized a saint (by Pope Clement XII in 1737) and eventually was named the patron of all charitable societies by Pope Leo XIII.

Sometimes we need the help of others to see the needs of those around us. Vincent de Paul was challenged to forget about himself and serve others. From that time on, he did not limit his love. Orphans, the poor, the sick, the aged, the mentally ill, prisoners, slaves — all these people found a friend in Vincent de Paul.

How large is our world? Do we limit our love to only a few? Or are we like Vincent de Paul — reaching out to all people? Will people be able to look upon what we have done for others out of our love for God and say, "Remarkable!"? Let us make today a giving day.

SUGGESTIONS

1. It is said that Vincent de Paul wrote over 3,000 letters. Discuss with the students how much good can be done through letter writing (to relatives, to the sick or lonely, to policy makers in defense of the poor and in support of programs for the needy, etc.) Have the students write letters to those who need encouragement and care.

2. Vincent de Paul founded two congregations: the Congregation of the Missions (Vincentians) and the Sisters of Charity. Have the students research the history of these communities and their present apostolate. Or better yet, invite members of these communities in for a firsthand presentation of their ministry. Also have the students research the Saint Vincent de Paul Society, founded in 1833 by Frederic Ozanam. Some students may wish to organize their efforts in support of this group. Other people associated with Vincent de Paul that the students may wish to research or read about include:

- St. Louise de Marillac (With whom Vincent founded the Congregation of the Daughters of Charity)
- Frederic Ozanam (Founder of the St. Vincent de Paul Society)
- Pope Clement XII (Canonized Vincent de Paul a saint)
- Pope Leo XIII (Named Vincent patron of all charitable societies)
- Pierre Cardinal de Berulle (Influenced Vincent)
- Francis de Sales (Friend of Vincent de Paul)

3. Visit the Vincent de Paul Society of your city. Have someone explain the purpose of the organization and where and how they distribute their goods to the poor.

4. Vincent loved the aged. He never wanted them to be lonely. Have a "Grandparents Day." Let each person in the class invite an elderly friend or relative to school. Have games and activities you could share together.

5. Vincent was a great supporter of life. Find out the organizations in your diocese that support life. Invite someone in to speak to you about these. Ask how you can get involved.

6. It is said that Vincent's life was the Gospel alive! For each charitable work that Vincent did, find a quote from the Scripture that matches. Make banners of these quotes and hang them in the school hallway.

SEPTEMBER 28: ST. WENCESLAUS

A king, a jealous brother, and a plotting mother make the life of St. Wenceslaus read like a murder mystery. Wenceslaus was born in Bohemia in 907. His father was killed in battle when Wenceslaus was young. This left the kingdom of Bohemia in the hands of his pagan mother, who favored the anti-Christian factions. Ludmilla, Wenceslaus' grandmother, took over the education of her grandson. Ludmilla was determined Wenceslaus would do two things: be a Christian and rule his country rather than his mother. But the grandmother was never to see one part of her dream come true on earth. Nobles of pagan heritage killed Ludmilla by the time Wenceslaus was ready to assume the throne. Yet Ludmilla had done her work well and Wenceslaus became the ruler, a well-educated Christian one.

In a country that was only partially Christian, Wenceslaus was undaunted. He first made peace with his mother so that he could govern. He worked in close cooperation with the Church, ended the persecution of the Christians, brought back exiled priests and built churches. Wenceslaus was severe to the barbarous, pagan nobles. Even though he was king, he set an example all could follow. People called him the "Good King" of Bohemia. He gave alms, was just to rich and poor, visited prisoners and, at the advice of the clergy, promoted the religious and educational improvement of his people. To do this Wenceslaus had to make peace with the king of the German empire at the expense of Bohemian nationalism. This caused opposition. Nobles grew restless and angry because they were ruled by a Christian king.

Boleslaus, the brother of Wenceslaus, was jealous that he was king. Taking advantage of the feelings of vengeful nobles, Boleslaus invited Wenceslaus to celebrate with him at a banquet on the feast of Cosmas and Damian. The next morning as Wenceslaus was on his way to Mass, Boleslaus hit him. As they struggled, the friends of Boleslaus ran up and killed Wenceslaus at the chapel door. Before he died, Wenceslaus asked God's mercy for his brother. Wenceslaus was immediately recognized as a martyr. He was proclaimed patron of Bohemia, now modern-day Czech Republic. His picture was engraved on coins, and the crown of Wenceslaus was regarded as a symbol of Czech nationalism and independence. His life shines as a brilliant example of love of one's country and one's neighbor.

SUGGESTIONS

1. Ludmilla, Wenceslaus' grandmother, was responsible for his faith. She passed on an outstanding example of Christian life. Suggest that each student write a letter to his/her grandmother (or other elderly person to whom they are close) to cheer her and tell her how much she is appreciated.

2. Have the students listen to the song "Good King Wenceslaus." Ask how the words fit his political and Christian life. Why is St. Wenceslaus associated with Christmas?

3. Let the students research Bohemian Christian customs and explain these to the class. Have them share nationality customs that their families celebrate.

4. Wenceslaus was a man of peace. Suggest that the students write petitions for peace for their nation, their families, the class and for inner peace.

5. Wenceslaus wanted to heal the bitter disputes of his people. Have the students reflect on the sign of peace that is given in the Eucharistic liturgy. Ask what it means to them. Ask if they are uncomfortable doing this with someone who has hurt them. Give them a moment to offer forgiveness to someone who has injured them.

See Supplement for September 28.

SEPTEMBER 29: FEAST OF STS. MICHAEL, GABRIEL AND RAPHAEL (Archangels)

God has numerous ways to show His loving concern for us. One of these is through the angels. God has sent angels to intervene in people's lives when they need protection on their way to heaven. The Archangels, Michael, Gabriel and Raphael, are three such messengers.

In art, St. Michael is usually pictured as youthful, strong, clothed in armor and wearing sandals. Biblical accounts of Michael present him as a mighty leader bringing justice and strength. The Book of Daniel describes him as a heavenly prince who stands guard over God's people, helping the Israelites return from their Persian captivity. Michael, whose name means "Who is like God?" is the principal fighter in the battle against Lucifer, or Satan, as related in the Book of Revelation. The early Christians of the second century took courage from these accounts. They believed that Michael's intercession was powerful in rescuing souls from Hell. In the fourth century Emperor Constantine built a church to honor Michael.

Art depicting Gabriel most often shows him as communicating God's message. Biblically he is portrayed in three events as a messenger. The first is to explain to Daniel a vision he had concerning the Messiah. Another time he comes to Zachary, who is burning incense in the temple, and tells him that John the Baptist will be born. But most people associate Gabriel with the Annunciation and his message to Mary of the birth of Jesus. Gabriel's name means "Strength of God."

When you see the archangel Raphael in any picture, you see him pictured as a companion to Tobit with a fish. Raphael appears in the Book of Tobit. The blind Tobit wants to send his son Tobias on a journey to collect a debt. He finds Raphael and invites him to be a companion and guide. After an adventure-filled journey, Tobias collects the debt, finds a bride and restores Tobit's sight with the fish's gall.

Tobit's family accredits the success of the journey and the healing to the presence of Raphael. When they offer Raphael a reward, he announces who he is: "I am Raphael, one of the seven angels who stand ever ready to enter the presence of the glory of the Lord" (Tobit 12:15). Since it was through Raphael that Tobit was cured of his blindness, the angel's name means "God's healing" or "God has healed."

Because of their closeness to God, the Church urges people to pray to the archangels to help them in their needs. In times of temptation, people pray to Michael; in trying to do God's will, people look to Gabriel; and in sickness people turn to Raphael. In a mysterious and powerful way the angels protect the Church and her people. They assure the faithful that God cares and is with His people.

SUGGESTIONS

1. There is a special prayer to St. Michael (formerly recited after Mass) because he is the leader of God's power against Satan. Have the students learn the prayer to St. Michael. Pray it at the end of the school day. It is a good prayer to know in times of temptation.

PRAYER TO ST. MICHAEL

St. Michael the Archangel, defend us in battle;
be our defense against the wickedness and snares of the devil.
May God rebuke him, we humbly pray;
and do you, O prince of the heavenly host, by the power of God,
thrust into hell Satan and the other evil spirits who prowl
about the world for the ruin of souls. Amen.

2. Discuss why Gabriel is called the "Messenger of Redemption."

3. Gabriel is the patron of post offices and telephone and telegraph workers because he is God's messenger. Have the students read the accounts in Scripture that record Gabriel's messages and write a statement telling what they were.

Daniel 8:15; 9:21   Luke 1:11-20   Luke 1:26-38

Point out that even though an angel may not appear to us, there are other ways in which God reveals His messages. Ask the students to write down three of these ways.

4. Raphael brought healing to Tobit's blindness. Explain to the students that we have the ability to see physically and we have the inner ability to see called "insight." Our faith is a kind of "insight." Through faith in Christ, we can find real meaning in our lives. Suggest that they write in their journals things they did today, because of their faith, to help people feel happier.

5. Draw the crossword puzzle on the angels on the board — without the answers — and give the students the clues. Let them complete the puzzle.

DOWN

1) Who was the archangel sent to communicate God's message to Daniel, Zachary, and Mary?

2) Who is the archangel whose name means "Who is like God?"

4) What job was Raphael hired to do for Tobias on the journey? To be a _____ .

6) To whom did Gabriel announce the Incarnation?

ACROSS

3) What type of angel has God given to each person to protect him/her on the way to heaven?

5) Who is the archangel who was a companion to Tobias?

7) What kind of angel carries out important and special missions for God?

8) Against whom did Michael wage war?

6. Each archangel has a name that fits the mission God gave to him. Ask the students if meanings of their names fit their missions in life. Have them look up their names and relate the meanings given to their lives. Let them tell the others whether they feel their names express their goals and why.

Two books that may help the students discover the Christian meanings of their names are *A Saint for Your Name: Saints for Girls* and *A Saint for Your Name: Saints for Boys* by Albert J. Nevins (Our Sunday Visitor, Inc., 200 Noll Plaza, Huntington, Indiana 46750).

SEPTEMBER 30: ST. JEROME

Jerome was a man of extremes. His real name was extremely long: Eusebius Hieronymus Sophronius. He lived to an extreme old age, 91, even though he undertook extreme penances. Jerome had an extremely fierce temper, but an equally intense love of Christ. He went to extremes in criticism of what he considered heresy, but those who really knew him considered him extremely tender.

This brilliant, ambitious saint was born in present day Yugoslavia around 345. His Christian family was able to send him to Rome at age twelve for a good education. He studied there until he was twenty. When he wasn't studying, he enjoyed the spectacles, games, and amusements of Rome. Later, these would be a source of temptation for him. But what kept Jerome close to his faith were the frequent visits he made to the catacombs. In his heart was born the desire to imitate the spirit of the holy martyrs. He took his religion seriously and was baptized at age nineteen. This late date of Baptism was not uncommon at that time.

When Jerome's studies were over, he followed his desire to live a penitential life. He and his friends lived in a little monastery for three years. But this ended when the group dissolved over a real or supposed scandal. Jerome then set out for Palestine, but when he reached Antioch he fell seriously ill. He dreamt one night that he was taken before the judgment seat of God and condemned for being a heretic rather than a Christian. This dream made a deep impression on him.

Jerome was ordained a priest, a privilege he never asked for. Jerome never wished to minister as a priest within the local churches, but rather desired to study. Again he tried the life of a monk in the desert. But impure temptations of earlier days plagued him. To fight off temptation he studied Hebrew, wrote letters to his friends counseling them in the spiritual life, and copied books by hand. Finally Jerome left the desert life and moved to Constantinople. He continued his pursuit of education by studying Scripture under the Greek theologian and preacher, Gregory Nazianzen. Jerome liked the sophisticated city and the work. Pope Damasus saw Jerome's talents and summoned him to Rome to be a papal secretary. The pope also knew Jerome's love of Scripture, so he commissioned him to translate the Bible from Hebrew and Greek into Latin. This was a long, exhausting work. His translation was called the "Vulgate" and became the official text of the Catholic Church. Jerome was just the man to do this because he had great self-discipline and knowledge.

Jerome's cross was his temperament. He was strong-willed and quick-tempered. His writings were sometimes explosive. His temperament helped him do impossibly difficult tasks, but it also made him enemies wherever he went. His acid pen condemned the rich and reprimanded the lax clergy. He sometimes made biting comments about marriage. To conquer his faults, Jerome prayed and did much penance. He grew in love for Christ and His Church.

Jerome championed three causes that were to help the Church greatly and make him known as a Doctor of the Church. The first was his translation of the Bible. Jerome tried to get an accurate text by using the original languages. The second was his writings on monastic life. Jerome felt monks should make a prayerful study of the Scriptures and the Fathers of the Church. Men of God should know and love the Gospels, Paul, and Our Lady. Thirdly, in the controversy on theological opinions, Jerome believed the See of Rome was where these matters should be settled.

Jerome also guided a group of Christian widows: Paula, Marcella, Eustochium and others, who were practicing a semi-monastic life. He gave them lectures on the Scriptures and advised them in their spiritual life. Some people considered it scandalous that he spent so much time with women. This gossip led Jerome to move these women to Bethlehem. Here Jerome trained Paula and Eustochium to become Scripture scholars and they assisted him in his research. He continued to write commentaries on the Scriptures.

Jerome's tool was his pen. He did the Church a great service by translating the Bible so more people could read it. To do work like this takes not only scholarship but deep spirituality and love of the Church. May all pray to love the Church as Jerome did!

SUGGESTIONS

1. Point out to the students that it took Jerome thirty years to translate the Bible; he did it all by hand. Encourage them to do their homework this week with the enthusiasm of St. Jerome.

2. Jerome reverenced the Word of God. Enthrone the Bible in your classroom. Place candles by it. Take time to prayerfully read the Bible daily.

3. Tell the students that it is obvious Jerome thought highly of the talents of women because he trained them to study Scripture. Some people in the Middle Ages felt very strongly that women could not be competent in education. Have the stu-

dents discover what ministries women may perform in the Church now.

4. St. Jerome wanted the Bible to be read by everyone. Have the students memorize a Scripture quote a day. Some are listed below.
   Luke 9:46-48   Luke 9:21-27
   Luke 10:38-42   Luke 11:9-13

5. Jerome was a spiritual director for a convent of women. Ask the students to find out what a spiritual director is. Why do people have them? How can a spiritual director help a person lead a holy life?

6. Today the "Vulgate" is not the only translation of the Bible. Have the students find out what translation they use in school and what other translations are available. Ask if only one person translates the Bible, as Jerome did?

7. Have the students compare the personalities of the four original Western Doctors of the Church: Ambrose, Augustine, Jerome, and Gregory the Great. They should tell what was outstanding about each man.

8. Tell the students about Pope Damasus, who engaged St. Jerome. This pope had the combined talents of theologian and administrator. He sent missionaries to foreign lands, had churches restored, encouraged Scripture to be studied, and diplomatically avoided schisms. Ask the students to research the tasks of our present day pope. They should be able to describe his duties and the work he does for the Church.

9. Tell the students that St. Jerome wrote, "Whatever is proper to holy Scripture, whatever can be expressed in human language and understood by the human mind, is contained in the Book of Isaiah" (commentary on Isaiah by St. Jerome). Have them find out where Isaiah prophesies the birth of the Messiah and where he predicts Christ's death, burial, and resurrection.

10. Reading Scripture aloud is also important. Find a passage of the Gospels you like. Practice reading it clearly and distinctly. Proclaim it to your class!

OCTOBER 1: ST. THERESA OF THE CHILD JESUS

Twenty-eight years after St. Theresa's death, her autobiography, THE STORY OF A SOUL, was translated into thirty-five languages. Thirty-five years after her death, 800,000 copies of the book were sold and two and a half million of the abridged version. St. Theresa never went to a foreign land, never was awarded a medal of honor, never built a hospital, never argued with kings or started an organization. So why all of this popularity? Theresa proved we can become saints by doing the ordinary things extraordinarily well. She explained it in her autobiography: "I want to seek a way to heaven, a new way, very short, very straight — the way of trust and self-surrender . . . . I am a very little soul, who can offer only little things to Our Lord."

St. Theresa set an example everyone could follow because there was nothing dramatically unusual about her life. She was born into a middle-class family in France in 1873. Her father was a watchmaker, and her mother died when Theresa was five. There were nine children in the family, but only five lived. These five girls all entered religious life. Theresa was raised by her elder sisters and aunt, and she attended a school taught by the Benedictine sisters. Her family was loving and devout. Since Theresa was the youngest, her father had a special place for her in his heart. He called her "my little queen." When she was little, he would take her with him when he went fishing. She would sit on a hill, and the quiet and beauty of the sky and the meadow would give her inspiration and she would pray. She started to think seriously about God and prayed to love Him deeply.

Even at an early age, Theresa was fascinated by the idea of becoming a sister. When her two older sisters entered the Carmelite convent in Lisieux, she found out about contemplative sisters. Theresa had determination. She wanted to be a sister, and she did not want to wait until she was older. But common sense, Theresa's family, and the bishop told her she was too young at fourteen to make a commitment for the rest of her life. Theresa's single-minded wish to serve God as a sister remained with her as she and her family made a pilgrimage to Rome. For Theresa the most important part of the trip was not the sightseeing but the meeting with Pope Leo XIII. When Theresa's family entered the room to meet the Holy Father, they were given instructions not to talk, but just to kiss the pope's ring and to receive a blessing and a medal. When Theresa's turn came, she did what was expected, then blurted out, "Holy, Father, in honor of your jubilee let me enter Carmel at age fifteen." The Vicar General next to Pope Leo XIII cautioned him that the superiors must decide and the pope agreed. Spontaneously Theresa said, "If you say yes, everyone would be willing." The pope assured her, "You will, if it is God's will." Naturally Theresa was disappointed. She checked the mail every day when she got home to see if the bishop would send his approval. He finally did, and she entered Carmel at age fifteen.

Theresa prayed much and did the most ordinary tasks when she was a sister. Her jobs were scrubbing floors, washing dishes, setting the tables, sewing, dusting, and cooking. Later she helped the novice mistress, a sister who is in charge of the younger sisters' formation. A flu epidemic spread through the convent, killing three sisters. Theresa's health was strained in caring for the sick. She contracted tuberculosis and died at age twenty-four, only nine years a sister.

It was through Theresa's journal, THE STORY OF A SOUL, that people came to learn about her path to becoming a saint. Here Theresa's personality comes out, her struggles and her tremendous love of God. Theresa's greatest gifts were her intense concentration, which helped her grow in prayer, and her determination, which helped build her character. Her crosses were her shyness, sensitiveness, and stubbornness. Theresa set out to be a saint by what she called the "Little Way." She decided to do every act, even that of picking up a pin, for love of God. It is not easy, as everyone knows, not to complain, not to criticize, to smile when blamed, and to offer up the dullness of routine. But Theresa tried to do these things to show her love for Jesus. Hers was a simple way of saying yes to God by doing little duties of daily life well.

Her love was evident in her life and writings. The sisters she lived with were not perfect, but she loved them as she loved Christ. This took much faith and sacrifice. Theresa loved the Church. Because of her health, she could not go to the missions as she desired, but she offered up her sufferings for those who worked in the missions. She has been named Patroness of the Missions because she offered her life in a quiet way for the salvation of souls. Her life was so full of God that her last words were, "My God I love you."

SUGGESTIONS

1. St. Theresa is Patroness of the Missions, but she never left the town in which she grew up. Ask the students to think of ways they can make secret sacrifices for the missions today.

2. Theresa had a great interest in praying for priests. Encourage the students to make a special visit to the Blessed Sacrament to pray for their parish priests, and to make a point of talking with them after Sunday Mass.

3. The family of St. Theresa had a big effect on her vocation. This was because its members spent time together. The students might suggest to the members of their families an activity they can do together some weekend in order to strengthen family unity.

4. St. Theresa believed that charity which begins at home could have long-range effects. From this point of view, discuss with the students the question: "Can the power of love change the world?"

5. The book, *The Story of a Soul*, is really the story of St. Theresa's spiritual journey. Have the students write in their journals what they want to do for Christ right now to show their love for Him.

6. Direct the students to find prayers to St. Theresa and pictures of her. Display these in the classroom.

OCTOBER 2: GUARDIAN ANGELS

The ancient peoples were aware of invisible spirits. In our modern world we often forget about the real, invisible things. We need to be reminded of the guardian angels God gave us. St. Jerome wrote that the human soul is so valuable in heaven that every human person has a guardian angel from the moment the person comes into being. These pure spirits, which we can neither see nor feel, play an important role in our lives.

Angels are messengers from God. In Greek, "angel" meant messenger. In a real but unseen way, these powerful spirits point out to us the ways of God. Guardian angels assist us in work or study. In times of temptation, these spiritual beings direct us to do good.

Perhaps the guardian angels are best known for protecting us from physical danger, but their main role is to care for the salvation of our souls. It is wonderful to know that God has promised to love, protect, and be with us always. One way He does this is through the care of the angels. Whether we meet with danger or discouragement, our guardian angels are our personal, heavenly bodyguards. The angels also offer prayers to God for us. St. Thomas Aquinas has told us that the angel is the most excellent of creatures because he has the greatest intelligence next to God. Because angels always see and hear God, they can intercede for us. We should love our guardian angels, respect them, and pray to them.

In early Christianity there was no feast for the guardian angels, just for the archangels. But in the fifteenth and sixteenth centuries, the feast of the Guardian Angels was unofficially celebrated in Austria, Spain, and Portugal. In 1608, Pope Paul V made it a universal feast. In doing so, he helped to make us aware of the guardian angels, not just one day in October, but every day of our lives.

SUGGESTIONS

1. There are many prayers written to our guardian angels. One is traditional:

> Angel of God
> my guardian dear,
> to whom God's love
> commits me here,
> Ever this day
> be at my side,
> to light and guard,
> to rule and guide.
> Amen.

Another prayer is:

> Angel sent by God to guide me,
> be my light,
> and walk beside me;
> be my guardian and protect me;
> on the path of life direct me.

Have the students compose their own prayers or poems to the guardian angels. Display these in the classroom. Select one to pray on the feast of the Guardian Angels.

2. It is believed the guardian angels have a way of bringing people together in order to do God's work. Mary is "Queen of Angels." She also brings people together who need each other to work for God. Let the students share times in their lives when they have met someone who has done something that has influenced them greatly to serve God.

3. In art, angels have been pictured as chubby cherubs, stately winged guardians, or curly-haired beings playing harps, but these pictures are merely symbols of beings who are in actuality pure spirits. Allow the students to design symbols that represent angels and display these. They may wish to write scriptural passages under their symbols, or use Scripture to find ideas for their symbols. Suggested references are: Psalm 103:20; Psalm 138:1; Matthew 4:11; Matthew 18:10; Luke 9:26; Luke 15:10; Hebrews 13:2.

4. Theologians have studied angels. It is said there are nine choirs of angels. Have the students do research on the roles each choir of angels plays.

5. Great artists, especially of the Renaissance, have painted angels in their works. Urge the students to find art masterpieces of the angels. Let them explain why the artist represented the angels as he did.

6. Recommend that the students ask their parents to tell them about a time when God took special care of their families. Have each student write out his/her story. Make a scrapbook of these. When the students read one another's stories, they will see how carefully God cares for each person.

OCTOBER 4: ST. FRANCIS OF ASSISI

People who watched Francis of Assisi would have noticed his enthusiasm, his energy, his cheerfulness, his way of joking with bystanders and laughing at his own expense, his tendency to give playful pats to any wandering animals, and his grateful acceptance of anything that was offered to him. His warmth and gentleness and his love for people and nature might have given the impression that Francis was a stranger to discipline, misunderstanding, and suffering. But this would be a false impression. Let's look at his life to see who this man really was.

The son of a wealthy cloth merchant and a devout, loving mother, Francis learned to enjoy life. His fun-loving way and sunny personality made him very popular. Francis dreamed of becoming a noble knight who would accomplish fantastic deeds with raw courage. Finally, when Assisi and Perugia were at war, Francis had his chance to be a soldier, a defender of right. But the vicious hatred, fierce fighting, and humiliation of being held hostage in prison for a year were not what he had expected. After his imprisonment and a serious illness, he began to look for more purpose in life.

One day while he was praying in an old church, Francis heard a voice say, "Francis, go repair my house which, as you see, is falling into ruin." Impulsively, Francis rushed home, grabbed bales of cloth, sold them and took the money to the priest of the church. But the priest refused the money, and Francis's father was very angry about his actions. Francis returned the money, gave up his fancy clothes, and decided that he would rely on his heavenly Father for all that he needed.

For the next few years, Francis could be seen in his patched, mud-colored robe tied with a piece of rope, barefoot, rebuilding the church by hand. He worked cheerfully until one day at Mass he heard a reading from Matthew's Gospel 10:7-13. From this he realized that his life must be based on the Gospel and that he was called to do three things: to be one with his heavenly Father, to work for the Church, and to become as much like Jesus as possible. Because he believed that God was his Father, Francis felt a relationship to all people and to all created things, to animals, to fish, to summer and winter, to storms and stars. All were his brothers and sisters, and he was extremely courteous and welcoming even to tiny creatures like earthworms. He composed a prayer called "The Canticle of the Sun," acknowledging the good that creation accomplishes and calling all created things to praise God and thank Him for His care.

That passage from Matthew also helped Francis to realize that the Church is not just a building. The Church is made up of "living stones," that is, of the people of God. Francis saw clearly that he was to rebuild not churches, but the Church. All alone he started traveling from place to place, sleeping on the ground, begging for food, preaching about the Father's loving care and the need everyone has to repent and to turn back to Him. He tried to convince the rich to live a simpler life style and to create better conditions for the poor. He offered a sense of dignity and respect to the poor themselves. Francis was not a forceful speaker like John the Baptist, but he gently persuaded people to rely on God and to care about one another. Francis's joy, gentleness, sensitivity, and good humor were contagious. Many men joined him, living in poverty and traveling with him, preaching the Good News. So many came that Francis had to write guidelines for all his men based on the Gospels.

Although Francis influenced many to follow the poor Christ, some people were afraid that his followers, being so poor, would eventually begin to criticize the rich in the Church and attack Church authorities. To avoid misunderstanding, Francis met with Pope Innocent III to assure him that all of his men would respect and obey Church authorities in all matters. He also received papal approval for his group.

Francis wanted more than anything else to become like Jesus because he loved Jesus so much. He tried to be as poor as Jesus was, as humble as he was, and as compassionate toward those who suffered. Francis knew that Jesus had been mocked, ignored, and called names. Francis had a way of laughing at himself, of not taking these negative reactions too seriously, and his good sense of humor often won over even nasty critics.

At the end of his life, when he was dying, Francis asked to be laid on the ground so that he might keep the closest possible touch with creation, because through it he had always encountered his Creator.

SUGGESTIONS

1. Because Francis recognized God as Creator of all, he called all of creation — the bugs, the animals, the birds, the rain and the snow — to praise and thank Him for His care. The following is the poem called "The Canticle of the Sun" written by Francis.

THE CANTICLE OF THE SUN

O most high, almighty, good Lord God,
O most high, almighty, good Lord God,
to thee belong praise, glory, honor,
and all blessing!
Praised be my Lord God
through all his creatures;
and especially our brother the sun,
who brings us the day,
and who brings us the light;
fair is he, and shining
with a very great splendor:
O Lord, to us he signifies thee!
Praised be my Lord for our sister the moon,
and for the stars, which he has set
clear and lovely in heaven.
Praised be my Lord for our brother the wind,
and for air and cloud, calms and all weather,
by which thou upholdest in life all creatures.
Praised be my Lord for our sister water,
who is very serviceable unto us, and humble,
and precious, and clean.
Praised be my Lord for our brother fire,
through whom thou givest us light
in the darkness;
and he is bright, and pleasant,
and very mighty, and strong.
Praised be my Lord for our mother the earth,
which doth sustain us and keep us,
and bringeth forth divers fruits,
and flowers of many colors, and grass.
Praised be my Lord for all those who pardon
one another for his love's sake
and who endure weakness and tribulation;
blessed are they
who peaceably shall endure,
for thou, O most Highest,
shall give them a crown!
Praised be my Lord for our sister,
the death of the body, from whom
no man escapeth.
Woe to him who dieth in mortal sin!
Blessed are they who are found walking
by thy most holy will,
for the second death shall have no power
to do them harm.
Praise ye, and bless ye the Lord,
and give thanks unto him,
and serve him with great humility.

- Make copies of "The Canticle of the Sun" for your class. Divide the students into two groups and have one group read the opening address for each sentence and the other group read the rest of each sentence.

- Ask the students to write an original canticle of nature based on the form that Francis used, e.g., Praised be You, Lord, for (*Name creature*) who (*Name job that creature does*).

- Let the students write or print a section of the canticle of Francis neatly on paper and illustrate it. Post these in the room or hallway.

2. Francis often spent enjoyable hours contemplating the natural beauty of the woods. Take the students on a nature walk to view the rocks, the trees, the bugs, etc. as Francis viewed them — with reverence and courtesy. Direct them to carefully record the sights, sounds, smells, and textures that they encounter and to make a resolution to respect all life.

3. Francis once pleaded with King Ferdinand II of Germany to protect certain birds.
   - Have the students find information about individuals or groups who are working to protect wildlife and share their findings with the class.
   - Have them discuss the relationship between Francis's understanding of God and nature and his desire to protect wildlife.

4. To help the poor understand the great love that Jesus has for them, Francis decided to make a life-size scene of the Christmas crib, using real people and real animals. Let the students do research to find the answers to these questions:
   a) What is the story connected with Francis's starting the Christmas crib?
   b) How did the people respond to his new idea? How do people respond to the creche, or Christmas crib scene, in our present day?
   c) How have different countries in the world adapted Francis's idea during the Christmas season?

5. Francis, at first, felt that God wanted him to rebuild church buildings. Then he came to realize that God had chosen him to renew the Church, which is the people of God. Direct the students to make a list of ways they can help the parish community. They may want to begin their list with the idea of praying for the parish.

6. When he first started to follow Christ as a poor man, Francis was alone. Others seeing his freedom and joy joined him, and eventually there were so many men that the group became known as the Friars Minor or the Franciscans. Francis also founded the Poor Clares, an order for religious women and the Third Order secular for lay men and women. Since his time, many Franciscan orders have developed. The students may use the *New Catholic Encyclopedia* and other resources to research one order and write a one-page report on its history, its present work, its customs, and how it follows the spirit of St. Francis. A member of one of the local Franciscan groups might be asked to speak to the class on the spirit of St. Francis.

7. The spirit of St. Francis was a spirit of thanksgiving. In this spirit we should thank God for what Francis has done. Have the class make a list on the board of the contributions which St. Francis has made to the Church and the world. Then ask the students to consider the fact that gratitude and criticism do not go well together. Have them ask themselves: Has my attitude been one of gratitude for what others have done? Have I said the words "Thank you" often today? What attitude do my daily words convey?

8. When someone asked for his prayers, Francis would pray immediately so that he would not forget about it. Ask the students to think of someone that they promised to pray for or that they should pray for and take time to pray for these people.

9. Show the filmstrip "St. Francis of Assisi" (Ikonographics). Discuss with the students:

   • How could Francis be so joyful when he was so poor?

   • How can we imitate Francis in our daily lives?

10. "Let the brothers take care . . . that they show themselves glad in the Lord, cheerful and worthy of love and agreeable" (*Saints for Now*). Let this quote be the criteria for a St. Francis of Assisi award. Ask the students the following questions: Are there people in your class or in your school community who would qualify? Are there other people in your life who might qualify? The students may want to make the awards and present them to qualifying individuals.

11. St. Francis of Assisi is renowned in many countries by many Christians. Have the students find art work, books, poetry, and legends related to him. They might make a display or share their findings with the class.

OCTOBER 6: ST. BRUNO

Bruno was a master teacher. He not only became a great spiritual leader himself, but he inspired his students to do so. St. Hugh of Grenoble and Pope Urban II were two of his pupils. All through his life, he showed a talent for friendship. His deep appreciation for people and his loving personality made him an unforgettable man. Little is known of Bruno's childhood, but his education must have been carefully supervised because he was one of the most learned men of his day. He was a well-known teacher in theology for more than eighteen years and he headed schools. He wrote scholarly essays on the psalms and St. Paul's letters.

Truth and honesty meant more to Bruno than honors. He risked his reputation by opposing Manasses, the archbishop of Rheims. Manasses had acquired this position unfairly by buying it. This is called "simony." In doing this Manasses had given scandalous ex-

ample. When he was removed from his role as archbishop, he retaliated by confiscating Bruno's property. To escape further harm, Bruno hid in an associate's house where he was joined by two friends.

One day when Bruno and his friends were walking in the garden and talking about contemplative prayer, they decided to go to a hermitage where they could live a life of prayer. As time went on, however, Bruno was the only one of the three who remained enthused about this undertaking. He left his post as a teacher with six other companions. On the way, Bruno stopped to see an old friend, Hugh of Grenoble. Hugh greeted him with some amazement. The night before Hugh had dreamed of seven stars settling on the Chartreuse Alps, which he interpreted to mean Bruno with six companions. So Hugh took Bruno and his companions to the mountains, where they decided to build a chapel. They rejoiced at how fitting this site was for a life of prayer.

Bruno was not able to live the life of prayer and penance he loved for long. Six years later he was summoned to Rome by Pope Urban II. Although this was a big sacrifice for Bruno, he would not disobey the highest authority in the Church. In Rome Bruno was able to influence the pope greatly on Church matters. Vatican life gave Bruno very little time for the prayer and silence he desired. The pope offered to make him a bishop, but Bruno declined. He agreed to found another hermitage in Italy, where he died in 1101.

Though Bruno wrote no rule and never intended to start an order, he is considered the founder of the Carthusian monks. There is little change today in this strict observance of monastic life. Like their founder, each Carthusian monk still lives in a three-roomed cell. Their life style is one of poverty, silence, prayer, and penance. These monks come together for morning and evening prayer and the Eucharist. They only eat together on big feasts. Regularly they pray, work, and study in their own rooms.

Bruno is a saint, but he was never formally canonized. In 1623 his feast was put in the Roman liturgical calendar. Though Bruno's manner of living may seem unusual, Vatican II affirmed the contemplative life as always having a distinguished part to play in the Church.

SUGGESTIONS

1. At the death of St. Bruno, people praised him as an excellent teacher. He was able to influence his students to an active, enthusiastic love of the Church. The students might wish to write a letter of appreciation to the teacher who influenced them most.

2. Pope Urban II, who called St. Bruno to Rome so Bruno could advise him, was a man of conquest for the Church. One of his aims was to liberate the

24

shrine of the Holy Sepulchre. In a dramatic speech to the clergy and laity of France, he pleaded for this cause. In response, the First Crusade started. Have the students investigate the history of the crusades. After their research, have them compose the front page of a newspaper devoted to the crusades. It should have accounts of battles, stories of adventures encountered enroute to Jerusalem, an article on the spirit of the times, interviews with famous characters, a presentation of the ideals of the Church, comments on chivalry, a report on meeting the Turks, and descriptions of the Holy Land.

3. The Carthusian life is rarely heard of; vocations to it are few. Tell the students about Carthusian life. Explain that it is penitential and solitary. The monk lives in a hermitage consisting of a workroom and private garden on the ground floor and a living room above. Here he prays, works, studies, eats, and sleeps. The monk rises at midnight, goes to church, and prays the Divine Office. Then he returns to his room for a second period of sleep of about three hours. He rises at dawn for Mass, and in the evening he prays Vespers. The day is given to prayer, study, silence, and manual labor. In winter, one meal is taken at noon and bread and beverage are taken in the evening. In the summer, there are two meals. No meat is eaten. The students will find this life style foreign to them. Discuss with them why a person might want to join this group and might be happy living this kind of life. How do monks like these help us who are in the world? Why do we need people who will give their lives in penance and prayer for the world? Write on the board the Carthusian motto, "While the world changes, the cross stands firm."

4. Silence and prayer were ideals for St. Bruno, who put all his trust in Jesus Christ. Ask the students to spend a few minutes in silent prayer. A passage in Scripture they may wish to use is Luke 12:22-31.

5. St. Bruno believed all people need penance. He did not see penance as a negative thing, but rather as something that frees the spirit to be close to God. Suggest that the students fast from snacks between meals for one day.

See Supplement for October 6.

OCTOBER 7: OUR LADY OF THE ROSARY

In praying to Mary, we are praying to Christ. To the question, "Why honor Mary?" Pope Paul VI told us that Mary was to be honored and imitated because in her own life she fully accepted the will of God and did it. Mary placed her whole self at the service of God. Her yes to God was a perfect act of faith. We pray to her because of this yes. Her yes was an acceptance of the will of God. She will help us pray that God's will be done and that we can accept His will for us. Among the feasts of Mary, some celebrate her power of intercession.

The story of the feast of Our Lady of the Rosary is an interesting one. Pope Pius V was having trouble with the Ottoman Turks, who were a real danger to Christianity. After months of disagreements and bickering, he was able to unite Spain, Venice, and the States of the Church in a naval expedition to fight them. The day of the battle at Lepanto, 1571, the Rosary Confraternity of Rome was meeting at the Dominican headquarters. They knew the Christians needed a victory badly. The group recited the rosary for the special intention of the Christians at battle. The Turks were defeated. People believed it was the intercessory power of the Blessed Virgin that won the victory. Pope Pius V dedicated the day as one of thanksgiving to Our Lady of Victory! It was Pope Gregory XIII who changed the name to the feast of Our Lady of the Rosary.

The story of the feast of Our Lady of the Rosary is one of many that show how conscious Christian people are of the power of Mary's intercessory role. The story should renew our love of Mary. When a person is in pain, discouraged, or having trouble accepting God's will, he or she should go to Mary. She will pray to her Son for anyone who calls on her. Anyone who prays to her no longer feels alone. She loved Christ. She will help others love Him, too.

SUGGESTIONS

1. Review the Joyful, Sorrowful, and Glorious Mysteries of the Rosary. Divide the students into pairs and have each pair draw a picture of one of the mysteries of the rosary. Hang these up around the room and have the students explain the mysteries they have drawn.

2. Encourage the students to pray the rosary to honor Mary on her feast.

3. Ask the students to find five people and interview them on why they pray to Mary.

4. Rosaries can be obtained from most religious goods stores and at a minimal cost from the Blue Army — or free if a person cannot meet the cost. Try to make sure each student has a rosary. The address of the national office is: Blue Army Headquarters, Ave Maria Institute, Washington, New Jersey 07882.

5. Join together with other classes to form a living rosary. Each student represents a bead of the rosary and leads the class in the prayer.

6. Mary is the faithful disciple of the Lord. Give the students each a piece of paper. Have them list ways they can be disciples and give service to others. Put the papers in a box. Pass the box around the room. Have the students each draw a slip of paper. Encourage them to practice what is written on the slips they have drawn.

7. Write the word *rosary* on the board vertically. Let each letter become a word that describes a quality of Mary.

> seRvice
> Obedient
> Simple
> fAithful
> chaRitable
> holY

OCTOBER 9: ST. JOHN LEONARDI

"I can't do much." "I'm only one person" "Why should I even try to make a difference? I'll only make a mess of it." Have you ever had a big problem and felt that you were helpless to change the situation? John Leonardi was just one person, but he was able to make a real difference in the Church. Born in Italy in 1541, John grew up there and studied pharmacy. He used his knowledge while working in hospitals and prisons. But when he realized that God was calling him to serve His people, he became a priest.

The situation in the Church at the time was very confusing. In 1517 Martin Luther had denied some of the teachings of the Catholic Church. In the years following, many Catholics joined him and eventually pulled away from the Roman Catholic Church. Many others were very insecure about what to believe and what not to believe. John Leonardi grew up in these times, and soon after his ordination he began to train lay leaders and lay catechists who would teach the people the doctrine of the Catholic Church. In 1579 he founded the Confraternity of Christian Doctrine which is the Church's official association for those engaged in the work of Catholic religious education. He also published a summary of Christian doctrine. In 1573 he founded a religious order of men called the Clerks Regular of the Mother of God who would strengthen the faith of the people through religious education and other pastoral works. John had to pay a price for teaching the truth. His new order drew opposition, and eventually he was forced to leave his hometown in exile. His friend and spiritual guide, St. Philip Neri, found him a place to stay.

John's other works included helping to establish a seminary for the Propagation for the Faith, to re-form several religious orders, and to start several new orders. Even though he was very involved in the work of spreading the faith, he still kept an interest in helping the sick. In fact, it was while taking care of plague victims that he died in Rome in 1609. You are only one person. So was John Leonardi, but he proved by his life that God and one person can make a majority.

SUGGESTIONS

1. Have the students research the history and the present status of the Confraternity of Christian Doctrine and the Society of the Propagation of the Faith. Then have them find out how their parish or school is involved with these two groups.

2. Philip Neri was a friend and spiritual guide for John Leonardi. Friends can have a very strong influence for good in our lives. Direct the students to think of times when a friend of theirs really helped them to choose good or to want to change for the better. Let them share their ideas with the class.

3. John was struggling with the effects of the Lutheran Reformation on the Catholic Church. The students might do research to find out what these effects were. They should each make a list and bring it to class.

4. John published a summary of Catholic doctrine. Have the students find out about some of the Catholic catechisms. Let them look through a copy of the latest catechism for the entire Church: *Catechism of the Catholic Church.*

OCTOBER 9: ST. DENIS

Have you ever been mistaken for someone else? Perhaps you were standing by your locker, walking down the street, or waiting in line to see a movie. Suddenly a stranger came toward you, smiling and waving. When the two of you got closer, the other person realized the mistake, apologized, and left. Saint Denis was in a similar predicament. Research indicates that the title "St. Denis" has been given to two people — one named Dionysius and the other named Denis, (or Denys or Dennis). Each man has his own story, but in the course of history the identities of these two persons have become intertwined and confused, even though they did not live at the same time.

Little is known about the life of the saint named Denis except the story which Gregory of Tours told. According to Gregory, the Italian-born bishop, Denis, was sent with other bishops to preach the Good News of Jesus to the people of Gaul. Denis preached in a place that today is called Paris. He also organized the Church there. During a persecution, he was beheaded. After his death as a martyr, he became a very popular saint and the people of France took him as their patron. An abbey was built over his burial place and French kings were later buried there. Many legends evolved about the miracles which took place through him.

Little is known about the life of St. Dionysius also, but the story of his conversion can be found in the Acts of the Apostles 17:13-34. He was a very courageous Greek. One day at a large meeting where many of the most intelligent and logical Greek thinkers met, St. Paul, the apostle, was given permission to preach about the "unknown god" which was the true God. During his preaching, Paul was rudely interrupted, rejected, and ridiculed for saying that God had sent His Son to be crucified for people's sins. Having failed miserably, Paul sadly walked out of the meeting. A few courageous Greeks, who had been willing to listen and to whom God had given the gift of faith, followed him. Dionysius walked out with Paul amid the mocking of the others. In the 9th century the story of Dionysius became identified with that of St. Denis and caused a revival of interest in and devotion to this saint. Modern scholars now favor the interpretation that the Denis of Paris is the saint for this feast day and could not have had any connection with Dionysius. In any case, the witness of publicly declaring loyalty to Christ in the face of ridicule, rejection, and death is very clear in both men's lives.

SUGGESTIONS

1. Have the students make a chart, comparing and contrasting the lives of these two saints.

2. Read the Acts of the Apostles 17:13-34 to the students. Ask them to write a paragraph outlining the main points of Paul's argument. Then explain how Paul's example might have convinced Dionysius. The students might want to compose a letter from Dionysius, explaining his thoughts during Paul's preaching.

3. Let the students research legends which have evolved around Denis and Dionysius, and share their findings with the class.

4. Denis was declared patron of France. Direct the students to find out how the French people express their faith through particular traditions, art, literature, architecture, and devotions to certain saints. Have them share their findings with the class.

OCTOBER 14: ST. CALLISTUS I

What would you think of a man who had been born a slave and sentenced as a convict becoming a pope? This did happen to Pope St. Callistus.

Callistus was born as a slave to a Christian master. As he grew to maturity, his master noticed that Callistus had skill in finance and put him in charge of a bank. Some enemies of Callistus falsely accused him of embezzlement. Terrified because he knew he was innocent, Callistus tried to escape from Rome. He was caught and condemned to the mines of Sardinia. After partially serving his sentence, he was released so he could get some of the money back. In an effort to recover some of the debts, Callistus went to the Jewish moneylenders to plead for his money. He was arrested for fighting and sent back to the mines. Fortunately for him and for the other Christians, Marcia, the emperor's mistress, won their release.

Pope Zephyrinus recognized the talents of Callistus and gave him a fresh start. The pope made him manager of the burial grounds. Even today the land is named the cemetery of St. Callistus. Callistus proved himself responsible and was ordained a deacon. Pope Zephyrinus continued to rely on Callistus in whom he found extraordinary talents for leadership. It is not surprising then that in 217 Callistus was elected as the next pontiff. But Hippolytus and his followers were shocked that Callistus had been chosen. In rebellion this group elected Hippolytus as pope and he became the first anti-pope. Now there were two claimants to the papacy.

A schism or split in the Church went on for eighteen years. Callistus I knew this could be confusing for the people in the Church, but he also knew what real charity was. He gently tried to encourage Hippolytus to understand the error he had made. At the same time Pope Callistus I tried to make wise and understanding rules for the Church. He worried over rich Christian women who could not find husbands of their religion. He taught that marriages between a free woman and a slave were valid. Callistus also knew the struggle of people whose faith was challenged during times of persecution. He understood why some gave up the faith for fear of being killed. Callistus I felt there should be mercy for those who had fallen away but repented. The Church has the authority to forgive all sins said Callistus I. This angered Hippolytus, who felt Callistus was too easy on people. Hippolytus wrote bitterly about the pope. But the pope bore the insults calmly and humbly. Callistus I remained steady in his desire to bring peace to the Church. This great man of the Church was martyred in a riot. Callistus lived and died for Christ and His Church.

SUGGESTIONS

1. It is said that Hippolytus did not believe that the election of Pope Callistus I was valid. Recommend that the students study the method of electing a pope. Some questions to answer might be:

Who can elect a pope?

Who can be elected pope?

How is the election carried out?

Do cardinals actually cast the ballots? Explain.

How many votes does a pope need?

How secret is the balloting?

How will the public learn the identity of the new pope?

Are the cardinals who are voting allowed to leave the Vatican? Explain.

When did cardinals first start electing the pope?

Why have most popes been Italians?

Can any man be a pope?

2. Pope Callistus I was very forgiving. He encouraged the people who had committed serious sin to receive the Sacrament of Reconciliation. Plan a reconciliation service so the students may again participate in the powerful grace of the sacrament.

3. Pope Callistus I knew that loyalty to the Church is important to the believer. Have the students construct replicas of their own parish church out of boxes. To do this, first cover a box with paper. On the front of the box, draw the entrance to the church. Using construction paper, add to the top any addition such as spire, tower, cross, or dome. On the sides of the box, cut out pictures from a magazine that show facets of the parish community. Display the finished creations.

4. St. Callistus I proved that no matter how a person starts out in life he/she can live a life of holiness and win heaven. Callistus I was interested in sinners and merciful to the repentent. Have the students investigate the topic of evangelization in the Church. Find out what parishes can do to bring fallen away Catholics back to the faith.

5. St. Callistus knew what it was like to suffer and experience trouble. Start a petitions board. Post a sheet of paper on the bulletin board so the students can write petitions for suffering people for whom they would like the class to pray. It is good to remind others to pray for those who are suffering.

OCTOBER 15: ST. TERESA OF AVILA

"Forever!" was the favorite word of Teresa. She declared that if she made up her mind to love someone, it would be "forever!" Jesus Christ won her heart. Her love for Him was intense. The things she did and the books she wrote out of love for Him made an impact on the world.

Teresa was born into a wealthy Spanish family of ten children in 1515. She was endowed with a vivid imagination, as well as the qualities of determination and courage. After reading books on the saints, she desired nothing more than to be a martyr. At age seven she and her brother, Rodrigo, made a pact to run away from home to fight the Moors and to be beheaded for Christ. But their uncle found them before they had gone very far and brought them back. By age twelve Teresa was caught up, like any young girl, in fashion and romance. Instead of reading books on martyrs, she read of knights, love, and chivalry. Teresa was beautiful and charming. People liked her immediately, and her lively spirit and affectionate nature won her many friends.

Teresa's mother died when she was fifteen. Her father, at a loss as to how to raise girls, sent her to the Augustinian sisters to be educated. At the end of her schooling, her health failed and while she was recovering, she read the letters of St. Jerome. After that Teresa wanted more than anything else to be a sister. Out of the ten children, Teresa was "the most beloved of them all." It was not easy for her father to give his consent for her to enter the convent. At age twenty she left for the Convent of the Incarnation, a Carmelite monastery.

The Convent of the Incarnation looked like a convent from the outside, but it was really more like a hotel for upper-class women on the inside. It was overcrowded, with one hundred and forty nuns, and the rules were rarely observed. True, the sisters said their prayers, but the rest of the time was spent gossiping, entertaining visitors in the parlors, and going on vacations with friends. Teresa started out fervent and idealistic, but gradually she took on these ways, too. She had a generous nature and wanted the sisters to think well of her. The nuns loved her cheerful and personable ways. She was always doing favors for them and loved to be praised.

Even though it was in her nature to laugh, sing, dance, and have lively conversation, she had a secret doubt as to whether this was convent life. Another thing that bothered her was her prayer life. She was taught to imagine a scene in Christ's life and to reflect on it, but she did not make much progress in prayer doing this. She said, "Over a period of years I was much more occupied in wishing my hour of prayer over, and in listening whenever the clock struck than in thinking of things that were good." For eighteen years Teresa went on like this. Then one day, when she was trying to pray, Teresa noticed a new painting of Christ being scourged at the pillar. As she meditated on it, her heart was moved to love Christ more deeply. She knew that this was a special grace given her by Jesus. From this time on, Teresa had less trouble in prayer.

In these later years Teresa received much help from two deeply spiritual men, Francis Borgia and Peter Alcantara. They encouraged her and helped her to make much progress in prayer. Then Teresa began to receive special favors from God — visions and ecstasies. She promised she would live for God alone, but the convent in which she lived did not help. There was too much noise and too many distractions. At that time Teresa heard God calling her to reform the way the Carmelites were living. So with the help of friends, Teresa petitioned the pope to let her found a stricter order of Carmelites. The nuns of this reformed order would be called Discalced Carmelites because they would wear sandals instead of shoes.

Thirteen women joined the new convent, St. Joseph's, to live in strict poverty for love of Jesus. They slept on straw mats and ate no meat. These sisters did not have visitors and they earned their income by spinning and doing needlework. People were surprised when they saw the sisters' habit made of coarse brown wool. Some shook their heads and said women would never survive this type of life, but Teresa just laughed. She knew what could be done with God's help. With His help and her talent for leadership and organization, she was able to open sixteen more convents like this first one. Her common sense helped her to choose girls who had both a vocation and certain natural gifts. She would say, "God preserve me from stupid nuns." Although Teresa was the superior of the convent, she lived like the other sisters. She swept, spun and cooked meals as the others did.

When the provincial of the Carmelite friars saw what Teresa had done for the sisters, he asked her to help reform the monks, too. At this time Teresa met John of the Cross, a Carmelite friar, who became her spiritual director. John guided her when her life was full of crosses. One of these crosses was her assignment to return to the Convent of the Incarnation as prioress. The sisters at this convent did not want her because they liked living the easy way. The day she arrived one hundred and thirty sisters rose from their places and left weeping. But Teresa knew how to handle difficult situations. She placed the statue of Mary on the chair of the prioress with the keys to the convent and told the sisters that Our Lady was in charge. Before long Teresa won the respect, confidence, and love of all the sisters.

Teresa was a wholesome and intelligent person. She knew everything that was going on in her convents, even to the kind of material the sisters bought. Her spirit was joyful and contagious. At recreation she would play the flute. She travelled and met with kings and popes. In the midst of her work, she often had short talks with the Lord. Once when her carriage was caught in a mud hole, Teresa complained. The Lord answered her, "This is how I treat my friends." And Teresa replied, "Then it is no wonder you have so few of them."

Teresa's love for God was so great that once she said, "The desire to serve God came to me so intensely that I should like to shout it out and tell everyone how important is is not to just give a little." When Teresa died at sixty-eight years of age, people remembered her as a spontaneous and practical person, as well as a mystic who had gone to join her Lord FOREVER! In 1617 the Spanish government proclaimed her patroness of Spain and in 1622 the Vatican canonized her.

SUGGESTIONS

1. Teach the students this prayer of St. Teresa. They might write it on a card and design it.

> Let nothing disturb you,
> Let nothing frighten you.
> All things pass away:
> GOD is unchanging.
> Patience obtains everything.
> Whoever possesses GOD,
>   wants for nothing:
> GOD alone suffices.

2. Make a list of new vocabulary words the students may have learned from hearing and reading about St. Teresa. Have them look the words up and write down definitions for them.

prioress	mental prayer
convent	Discalced Carmelites
reform	spiritual director
vision	mystic
ecstasy	

3. St. Teresa and Catherine of Siena are the only two women Doctors of the Church. Direct the students to find out how the Church chooses a person to be a Doctor of the Church.

4. St. Teresa said she never liked gloomy saints. Recommend that the students try to be cheerful all day on her feast.

5. St. Teresa loved to meditate on the passion of Christ because it showed how much Jesus loved everyone. Suggest that the students read one of the Gospels on the passion to celebrate her feast.

6. In history there have always been men and women who have written, prayed, and worked together to help the Church. Have the students look up the histories of these "famous pairs" and write a sentence on the aspects of the Gospel which drew them together.

   John of the Cross and Teresa of Avila
   Vincent de Paul and Louise de Marillac
   Francis de Sales and Jane de Chantal
   Benedict and Scholastica

OCTOBER 16: ST. HEDWIG

"The power behind the throne is the queen" is an old saying. In the case of Hedwig it is a clear and refreshing truth. Born as the daughter of a count, Hedwig was educated in a monastery. At age twelve she married Henry I of Silesia. Henry was eighteen. In the 1200s this was the usual age for marriage. The couple had seven children.

Henry succeeded his father to the throne. Although it was rare for women in the feudal age to do anything but needlework and dancing, Henry depended on Hedwig to help him with the administration of the country. He recognized her qualities of fortitude, prudence, and remarkable insight. The most remembered incident of her great influence occurred when Henry was at war with Conrad of Masovia. Henry was captured by surprise at a church service. With rare courage, Hedwig persuaded Conrad to return her husband. Prince Henry adored Hedwig, not only because she was a beautiful woman, but because her virtue was outstanding.

The gentle queen was loved more for her kindness to the poor than for her political undertakings. She founded a hospital for lepers. The doors of her castle were open to travellers, the homeless, the sick and dying. It is said that Hedwig would go out herself to serve the poor. In the evenings she would visit their cottages. Late at night she would darn their clothes. Early in the morning, Hedwig would rise and pray for the kingdom. She did all this while taking very good care of her own family. Hedwig invited Franciscans, Dominicans, and the first convent of nuns, Cistercians, to build monasteries in the kingdom.

Hedwig experienced great suffering when two of her sons disagreed over land given them by Henry and went to war against one another. She bore this sorrow and the death of her son Henry with patience. The people of her kingdom loved her so much, they considered her a saint even when she was alive.

SUGGESTIONS

1. It is told that Hedwig would deny herself shoes in winter rather than see a poor person cold and barefoot. Review the spiritual and corporal works of mercy. Have each student make a banner depicting one of the works of mercy.

2. Hedwig lived during medieval times. Have the students do projects on medieval life. Understanding the flavor of Hedwig's historical setting will help understand the saint.

3. As a leader of her country, Hedwig set the example of how a queen could be concerned. Ask the students to read the newspaper and cut out articles that tell positive things people are doing in the world to help one another.

4. Hedwig is one of many who made the Polish country strong in faith. Find out how Poland kept the faith alive despite Communist rule.

OCTOBER 17: ST. IGNATIUS OF ANTIOCH

Every person's life affects that of others. No moment can be wasted. If St. Ignatius of Antioch were alive today, he would tell us that. Ignatius travelled as a prisoner from Antioch to Rome — a journey to martyrdom. He longed to die for Christ. And up to the moment of his death, Ignatius was influencing the lives of others for the better.

Ignatius was converted from paganism to Christianity in Syria. He became the second bishop of Antioch, a successor of St. Peter. In 107 the Emperor Trajan visited Antioch and tried to force the Christians to renounce their religion. At this time Ignatius gave the best witness a bishop can ever give his people. He allowed the company of soldiers to bind him in a rickety cart and lead him to Rome for martyrdom. So great was the witness of his faith and courage that, as his cart rolled into the different towns enroute to Rome, the local bishop and delegations of Christians would come to meet him and encourage him. St. Polycarp, the Bishop of Smyrna, received him with great honor, for he saw the holiness of Ignatius and cherished his friendship.

On the long tedious journey, Ignatius composed seven letters to the churches he left behind. The Church today is fortunate to have those letters, because they give valuable insight into the growth of theology in the early church. In his letters, Ignatius praises the brotherly love and support he experienced on his way to Rome. He insists that the people of the Church give obedience to their local bishop. "Wherever the bishop is, there let the people be, for there is the Catholic Church" (Smyrna 8.1-2).

He urged that nothing be done concerning the Church without the approval of the local bishop.

Ignatius loved the Eucharist and wrote that Christ was really present in the Blessed Sacrament. Of himself he said, "I am the wheat of Christ, may I be ground by the teeth of beasts to become the immaculate bread of Christ." He asked his people to gather around the Eucharist as a community and care for "the widow, the orphan, the oppressed, as well as those in prison, the hungry and the thirsty" (Smyrna 6.2). Ignatius renewed the people's courage by reminding them of the presence of Jesus in the Church and in each member. That is why Ignatius called himself "the bearer of God." Ignatius was martyred by being devoured by wild beasts in the arena.

SUGGESTIONS

1. St. Ignatius emphasized the important role of the local bishop in the Church. Direct the students to research the role the bishop plays in the Church. Have them write letters to their bishop expressing their appreciation for him and his work for the Church.

2. Luke 9:23-24 was a passage St. Ignatius took seriously. Have the class reflect on the Scripture passage today.

3. *Cathedra* means "chair." The church where the bishop presides is called this because of the presence of the bishop's chair. It is a sign of his leadership. But the cathedral belongs to everyone in the diocese. Plan a visit to the cathedral of your diocese and discover why it is an important part of the diocese.

4. Pretend that Ignatius is alive today. Have the students write a letter to him telling how they live their faith and how they encourage others to do likewise.

OCTOBER 16: ST. MARGARET MARY ALACOQUE

When we speak of heart, we often mean it to represent the whole person and all the love of which he or she is capable. Therefore, the heart seems a fitting symbol for the love God the Father has shown us through His Son Jesus. The symbol of the heart became a very important one for Margaret Mary Alacoque.

Born in 1647 into the refined, well-known Alacoque family, Margaret Mary had a rather unhappy childhood. Her father died when she was eight years old. After his death, her mother tried to collect money that people owed her husband but she did not succeed. Without this source of income, she was forced to share the farm with her husband's greedy relatives, who were delighted to have the Alacoques at their mercy. Margaret Mary had been sent to a boarding school after her father's death. But two years later she returned home because of illness. At the age of fourteen, she was cured after praying to Our Lady. However, she and her mother continued to be treated miserably. Margaret Mary once said that her greatest pain at this time was to see her mother suffer and not to be able to help the situation.

In 1671 Margaret Mary became a Visitation nun at the convent of Paray-le-Monial. When as a novice she was assigned to help the energetic practical nurse take care of the sick, she received much criticism for being slow, clumsy, and impractical. But she also was known to be humble, honest, patient, and kind. In these good qualities Jesus recognized something of Himself. Between 1673 and 1675 Margaret Mary received private revelations from Him. His message was, "See this Heart which has loved so much and received so little love in return. Tell everyone that I really love them and I want to be loved in return. If you love Me, pray and sacrifice for those who do not believe in My love or do not care about My love."

Margaret Mary worked hard to spread devotion to the Sacred Heart of Jesus, the heart which was a symbol of His overwhelming, always forgiving love. This was a difficult job because the false teaching of Jansenism was very popular. According to this teaching, Jesus did not die for all human beings, but only for those predestined to be saved. When Margaret Mary tried to explain how Jesus really died for everyone and cares for each individual, she met with opposition from all sides. Some theologians decided that she was imagining the whole thing and recommended that she eat more. Parents of students whom she taught called her an imposter. Even her own sisters at the convent became hostile and made life difficult for her. Finally she met Father Claude la Colombiere, who believed her and gave her encouragement and spiritual guidance. Gradually Margaret Mary, who returned kindness for criticism and patience for rejection, won the confidence of those around her. The devotion to the Sacred Heart was approved by the pope for liturgical observance in 1765, seventy-five years after Margaret Mary's death at the age of forty-three.

People did not believe that God would reveal His love so powerfully to someone so simple and plain as Margaret Mary. And yet in the Old Testament God revealed His merciful love to the sinful nation Israel. And in the New Testament Jesus revealed the forgiving love of God for all, including the poor, the fishermen, the prostitutes, and the tax collectors. Jesus Himself said, "Learn from Me, for I am gentle and humble of heart" (Mt. 11:29).

SUGGESTIONS

1. Enthrone the Sacred Heart in the classroom. Explain to the students that this practice shows that Jesus is really Lord, the One that all follow. It also shows that they believe in God's merciful, abundant love for them. Materials on the enthronement for schools and homes may be obtained by writing to The National Enthronement Center, 3 Adams Street, Fairhaven, Massachusetts 02719.

2. Send for information from the Apostleship of Prayer, 3 Stephen Avenue, New Hyde Park, NY 11040.

3. One of the devotions which evolved from Margaret Mary's work was the Holy Hour of Reparation. People agreed to meet and pray for an hour, to make up to Jesus for all the people who didn't care about His love and who ignored Him. Have the class plan a prayer service in which they pray for those who do not believe in His love for them. Possible readings are Ezekiel 34:11-16; Hosea 11:1-9; Isaiah 49; Romans 5:5-11; Ephesians 1:3-10, 3:14-19; Philippians 1:8-11; Luke 15:1-10, 11-32; John 15:1-8, 9-17, 19:31-34.

4. To identify with the Heart of Christ is to want what He wants. Followers of Jesus love the poor, especially poor sinners. Therefore, true devotion to the Sacred Heart will lead Christians to help those who are in spiritual or material need. Have the class write to the Catholic Relief Service for a list of projects in which they may become involved. The address is Catholic Relief Services, 1011 First Ave., New York, NY 10022.

5. Have the students research other devotions to the Sacred Heart: First Fridays; the feast of the Sacred Heart; consecrations to the Sacred Heart; the use of short prayers such as "Jesus meek and humble of heart, make my heart like Yours"; the votive Mass for the Sacred Heart and related songs and prayers.

OCTOBER 18: ST. LUKE

Luke was one of the evangelists. His gospel gives us a look at the compassionate, forgiving Christ. In the Acts of the Apostles, he gives us a detailed account of St. Paul's journeys. But we have little or no information on Luke himself. Luke's aim was to tell us who Jesus Christ was through His life, death, resurrection, and ascension. He did a masterful piece of work.

Since Luke's gospel is the best written in Greek, it is thought that Greek was his native tongue. Luke was a man who was careful in his sources. His writing is concrete and shows detail. His is a gospel of human interest and human sympathy. In this gospel we find that St. Luke puts stress on the gentleness of Christ as He heals the widow of Naim, speaks to the penitent woman at His feet, and comforts the weeping women on the way to the cross. It is Luke who includes the parables of mercy: the Good Samaritan and the Prodigal Son. The repentant thief is also his addition. His pagan origins probably gave him open-mindedness to all peoples. Samaritans, lepers, publicans, soldiers, public sinners, shepherds and the poor all find a special place in his gospel. Some people call his gospel the "Gospel of the Poor." Luke writes about Jesus as a master of prayer. Often Jesus is portrayed going alone to speak to His Father or helping his disciples to pray. Luke's gospel is a "Gospel of Joy" as well, and also a "Gospel of Total Abandonment." Luke presents the disciples as happy to give all, leave all, and suffer all joyfully.

Christian tradition recognizes Luke as the "beloved physician" (Col. 4:14), as Paul calls him. His account of the Acts of the Apostles gives valuable data for describing the post-resurrection Church.

We recognize Luke by the symbol of a man or a writer. Another symbol of Luke is the ox. The ox is chosen because Luke's writings make it clear that he was a man who placed all his faith and trust in Jesus.

SUGGESTIONS

1. Luke is the evangelist who wrote the most about Mary in Scripture. Have the students find the sources of the Joyful Mysteries of the Rosary in the first chapters of Luke. Let them make a list of these passages from Scripture.

2. Luke has six distinguishing themes. List them on the board. Ask the students to recall stories from Scripture that fit these themes. Let them draw an example for each theme and then make a mural of the drawings. The themes are:

   Gospel of the Poor
   Gospel of Joy
   Gospel of Universal Salvation
   Gospel of Mercy
   Gospel of Absolute Abandonment
   Gospel of Prayer

3. Have the students adapt a story from the Acts of the Apostles for a classroom theater. Props and costumes could be prepared.

4. Luke is considered the "Christmas Evangelist." Let the class make a set of Christmas cards by drawing or pasting appropriate pictures on construction paper and writing Lucan quotes beneath them.

OCTOBER 19: ST. PAUL OF THE CROSS

The feast of St. Paul has been changed to October 20.

"All the runners at the stadium are trying to win, but only one of them gets the prize. You must run in the same way, meaning to win" (1 Cor. 9:24). St. Paul the Apostle compares a Christian who is following Jesus to an athlete who is running a race. He admires the many sacrifices that an athlete willingly makes and suggests that a Christian should be willing to do even more. He uses himself as an example. These words of Paul apply very well to Paul Francis Danei, known as Paul of the Cross. A look at his life will prove this.

Born in Italy in 1694, Paul was the second of sixteen children. Because his father was often in financial difficulties, he had to leave boarding school to help support his family. Once he even had to pawn his possessions to raise money. At the age of fifteen Paul began to realize how much Jesus suffered for him out of love and that he should respond by praying and doing penance. So he took time to be alone and talk to God. He also did difficult things like sleeping on the floor instead of the bed and not eating the foods he liked in order to gain more control of himself and to follow Christ more closely. He wanted very much to share in the passion and death of Jesus.

At the age of twenty, he decided to join the Venetian army that was defending the faith. He thought he could give his life as a witness for Christ. But after a year, he went back to Italy, back to a life of prayer and penance while he waited to find out what God wanted him to do in life. During this time he noticed that many people felt guilty because they were caught in sin and didn't know how to gain control of themselves. He saw many hardened sinners who no longer felt guilty and were content in their evil ways. Then Paul realized that God was calling him to form a group of men who would be dedicated to preaching parish missions, which are similar to parish renewals. These men, called Passionists, would preach the mystery of Christ crucified — the mystery of God the Father's unlimited love manifested in the death of His Son. They hoped that Christians, hearing their preaching, would turn from their sins and rededicate their lives to a closer following of Christ. Paul developed a special method for giving missions that involved laypeople in street preaching, processions, vigils, prayer, penances, and sermons.

Paul's natural leadership ability showed itself both in his stubbornness and in his gentleness. Besides his natural gifts, Paul received gifts of prophecy and healing from the Holy Spirit. He was so powerful when he preached and so gentle with individuals in confession that he soon had an outstanding reputation for bringing sinners and lapsed Catholics back to the Lord. Paul also had a real concern for the British people, even though he had never been to England. He once said, "England is always before my eyes, and if ever again it becomes Catholic, the benefit to the Church will be immeasurable."

What Paul didn't know was that within sixty-five years a Passionist, Father Dominic Barberi, would go to England and help reconcile John Henry Newman and many others to the Catholic Church, thus aiding the revival of Catholicism in that country. When Paul died in 1775, people thought it was because he had performed such severe penances in his life. With St. Paul the Apostle, he could say, "I treat my body hard and make it obey me, for, having been an announcer myself, I should not want to be disqualified." (1 Cor. 9:27)

SUGGESTIONS

1. The Passionist habit, which has not changed since 1720, consists of a black tunic and mantle, a leather belt, and a rosary. The Passionists wear an emblem over their heart which looks like this:

   Have the students discuss the symbolism of this monogram and research various orders of Passionists, both men and women, in the United States.

2. Have the students make a banner using the emblem of the Passionists. Post it as a reminder of the life of Paul of the Cross.

3. Ask the students to research existing parish renewal programs or discover information on a renewal program in their own parish.

4. The reason for doing penance is to show our love for God and to gain self-control in order to overcome our sins and faults and become more faithful followers of Jesus. Have the class list possible penances which a student could perform this day (e.g. good posture, kind speech, cheerfulness). Ask the students to mentally choose one of the penances and do it to show their love for Jesus.

5. Have the students read 1 Corinthians 9:24-27 and Philippians 3:12-14 and write a short paragraph comparing the Christian life to running a race.

OCTOBER 19: STS. ISAAC JOGUES, JOHN DE BREBEUF, AND THEIR COMPANIONS

Among the most talented and intellectually gifted men of the 17th century were Isaac Jogues, John de Brebeuf, Gabriel Lalemant, Noel Chabanel, Charles Garnier, Anthony Daniel, Rene Goupil, and John de Lalande. The first six were Jesuits, the latter two laymen. It was inconceivable to most people that these personally dynamic men volunteered to be missionaries in the wilderness of North America, where the Indian tribes were their ministry. These great men would have been forgotten had not their revealing letters and journals survived them.

By 1632 the first Jesuits had established a mission center in Quebec ministering to the Huron Indians. The Huron nation was made up of twenty thousand people who lived in thirty villages. In this new land, there were dense forests and many rivers. Travel was extensive, and the missionaries suffered from cold and heat. They were not accustomed to the Indians' way of life. The Indians would sleep around a fire in smoke-filled rooms. Their culture and religion were filled with superstition, violence, and cannibalism. The life of the Huron Indians revolved around their hunting season and the attacks of their enemies, the fierce Iroquois.

The missionaries were not welcome in America. When they arrived, tramping over the hills in their "black robes," Indian children went running to their mothers afraid that the missionaries were sorcerers. A smallpox epidemic affected the tribe and the missionaries were blamed for it. In the midst of difficulties like these, they tried to bring the faith to the Indians. They tried to educate these people and teach them medical and agricultural skills.

Each missionary had his own talents. John de Brebeuf founded schools among the Hurons and wrote a catechism and dictionary in their native language. He was once condemned to death, but spoke so well and convincingly that the Indians spared his life. Noel Chabanel, a brilliant professor of languages in France, found he could barely stutter out Huron phrases. The food and life of the Indians repulsed him, but he made a vow he would stay there and try in humility to do the work of God. His silent suffering won graces for the missions. Rene Goupil and John de Lalande, lay missioners, gave their time without any pay. Charles Garnier would walk thirty and forty miles to baptize a single child.

All the efforts of these good men to love, forgive, heal, and suffer for the Indians seemed to be useless. The Indians were polite, but generally ignored them. It took years before the missionaries could win about two thousand converts. Then the Iroquois Indians, who resented the French, captured the missionaries and were merciless to them. They tortured the Jesuits by gnawing at their fingers and tearing out their nails. The missionaries were forced to run through a line of Indians who beat them with clubs. Their deaths were worse. Rene Goupil was tomahawked while trying to baptize a baby. Anthony Daniel was at Mass when a savage attack of the Iroquois came. He told his Indian friends to flee, saying, "I will stay here. We will meet in heaven." The attackers shot arrows at him and threw him into the fire. The Indians admired the bravery of John de Brebeuf so much that after his death they drank his blood and saved his heart for the chief to eat. They felt this way they could gain some of his courage.

Isaac Jogues, who had been a slave to the Iroquois, was able to escape back to France. His left hand was mutilated. But Pope Urban VIII allowed him to say Mass, saying, "It would be a shame that a martyr of Christ not drink the blood of Christ." Later Isaac Jogues bravely returned to America. This time, when on a peace mission to the Iroquois for the governor of New France, he was accused by the Indians of bringing a bad harvest. A box of religious goods he had with him was believed by the Indians to be a box containing a plague. They declared he should die. There is an account written of the death of Isaac Jogues and his companion, John de Lalande: "Before death both of their hearts were torn out. The barbarians feasted on these and while still alive on pieces of their thighs, calves, arms removed by butchers who roasted them over coals and ate them in their sight." Yet from the cruel sufferings of these missionaries came the seeds of the Church in America.

SUGGESTIONS

1. Even the barbaric Indians could not help but marvel at the courage of the martyrs. In imitation of these heroes of the faith, encourage the students to offer up their complaints silently today.

2. Show slides to accompany this native American prayer:

O Great Spirit
Whose voice I hear in the winds,
And whose breath gives life to all the world,
Hear me! I am small and weak,
I need your strength and wisdom.

Let me walk in beauty and make my eyes
ever behold the red and purple sunset!
Make my hands respect the things you have made
and my ears sharp to hear your voice.

Make me wise that I may understand
all things you have taught my people.
Let me learn the lessons
you have hidden in every leaf and rock.

I seek strength, not to be greater than my brother,
but to fight my greatest enemy, myself.
Make me always ready to come to you
with clean hands and straight eyes.

So when my life fades, as the fading sunset,
my spirit may come to you without shame.

Sioux Indian Prayer

3. The missionaries were able to teach the Indians about God by appealing to their love of and reverence for nature. Let each student make a poster using a picture of nature from a magazine

(or a collage of pictures) and a line of a psalm that praises God in His creation.

4. An Indian who has been beatified is Kateri Tekawitha. Read her story to find out how similiar her life was to the lives of the North American martyrs.

OCTOBER 23: ST. JOHN CAPISTRANO

It is hard to pin some people down to one place, one country, or one occupation. St. John Capistrano's one goal was to serve Jesus Christ. As a young man John was well educated, a successful lawyer and governor in fourteenth century Italy. He zealously rid the locality of political corruption. When John was sent as ambassador to another province at the age of twenty-six, his life underwent a major upset! He was imprisoned. During that long, unhappy stay in prison, John thought over his life. He realized that he could serve God more directly. A story is told that St. Francis appeared in a dream and asked him to become a Franciscan.

St. John Capistrano was a man of initiative. Once released from prison, he entered the Franciscan order. Here he did not show off his degrees, but worked as a humble novice. After his ordination, he studied under Bernardino of Siena. While Bernardino preached, John heard confessions. With the zeal that helped him drive out crime as a governor, John began to work for the salvation of souls. The world needed a man like him at this time. Schism had split the Church and several men were claiming to be pope. Thirty percent of the population had been killed by the plague, the "Black Death." Many people were losing faith. Cheerfully John travelled through Italy, Germany, Bohemia, Austria, Hungary, Poland, and Russia, preaching penance and prayer. He helped to reorganize and settle problems within the Franciscan order.

Pope Pius II recognized the strong convictions John had and solicited his help against a Turkish invasion of Hungary. With the preaching and enthusiasm of John and the skill of the Hungarian general John Hunyadi, seventy-thousand Christians stopped the Turkish attack. At seventy John was nothing but skin and bone, but he was still strong in spirit. He died of a disease caught in a battle. Eastern Europe was greatly influenced by John's preaching and penance. His determination, which earned him the title of defender of political law, later made him defender of God's law.

SUGGESTIONS

1. St. John Capistrano is the patron of jurists. His discerning mind developed because of his self-disciplined life. Have the students pray to St. John concerning any decisions they must make in life.

2. An organization in Brussels that takes its name from St. John Capistrano uses the motto "Initiative, Organization, Activity." Put those three words on the board for the week. Suggest that the students think up three words that describe their spirit in serving Christ and His Church.

3. St. John of Capistrano lived in changing times. People were less faithful to their Church. John wanted to build up more enthusiasm for the faith so the people could live a deeper Christian life. Have the students recommend a service project they could do in their school that would reflect how they are trying to build strong Christlike spirit.

4. St. John struggled to know what he was to become in life. Have the students write in their journals a prayer to know their own vocations.

OCTOBER 24: ST. ANTHONY CLARET

The well liked, farsighted Spanish priest, St. Anthony Claret, was born the fifth of eleven children. The family was poor, but hard working. Weaving was a family trade. Anthony's earliest remembrances of home were those of the family praying the rosary together and going to church. It was from this simple, pious environment that Anthony's deep love of Mary and devotion to Jesus grew.

By age twenty-one, Anthony had been educated and was in much demand for his skill as a weaver. At one time he suffered because of poor health, and during the days of recovery he imagined himself as a Carthusian monk. To get sound spiritual advice about this, Anthony went to the bishop. The bishop suggested that he go to the diocesan seminary and then, if he wished, leave and become a monk. Anthony did that and enjoyed seminary life. He was ordained to the priesthood two years earlier than usual due to the civil war being fought in Spain.

Anthony finally realized his health would prevent him from being a monk or a Jesuit missionary. Yet Anthony had a chance to discern the gifts God had given him. He was sent to a small mountain village where he studied medicine and helped many sick people. There he discovered his gifts. Anthony had the power to read hearts and possessed a wonderful ability for understanding people.

Anthony began an energetic schedule of preaching throughout Spain. His gentle conviction and undaunted courage in spreading devotion to the Immaculate Heart of Mary and to reviving devotion to the Eucharist made him a popular preacher. The effective work of preaching spurred his interest in other forms of communication. People could be reached through the printed word as well. Anthony began to publish. His book, THE CATECHISM

EXPLAINED, drew interest from a friend, the bishop of the Canary Islands. The bishop invited him to preach for a year on the islands. Anthony was delighted to go, for he had dreamed of becoming a missionary.

When Anthony returned to Spain, he secured permission to found a congregation called the Missionary Sons of the Immaculate Heart of Mary, or "Claretians." Here was where he wanted to concentrate his efforts, but surprisingly God had other plans. Anthony was assigned as archbishop of Cuba, a turbulent island that had not had an archbishop for fourteen years. If Anthony had ever desired missionary work, this was the fulfillment of his dream. But being bishop of Santiago, Cuba, did not provide ideal conditions for planting the cross of Christ. The island had relaxed its Christian standards. Most priests and politicians were happy without an archbishop, but Anthony set vigorously to work. He tried to renew the priests in their vocations. Anthony gave them an example by preaching in all of the churches and spending hours doing what he did best: hearing confessions, guiding souls to Christ.

He challenged the political system of Cuba by working for updated farm methods and credit unions. Anthony wanted the people to own their own farms and market their crops. He knew that stable material conditions would lead to good family life. He made political enemies by giving instructions to black slaves. On fifteen different occasions, people tried to assassinate him. Once he was stabbed by a knife-carrying individual. Yet when this man was given a death sentence for doing this, Anthony pleaded for him and obtained instead a prison sentence. His eight years of pastoral care as bishop in Cuba made a difference in the lives of those who lived there.

Just as Anthony got things in Cuba underway, he was brought back to Spain to be Queen Isabella II's confessor. Unhappily he obeyed, for Anthony had no interest in court functions. He and the queen agreed that he would not live at the palace and that he would come only to hear her confession and instruct the children. This freed much of his time for other things. Still interested in writing, he opened a religious publishing house and wrote over two-hundred books and pamphlets during this time. In 1886 a revolution took place, and all those associated with the court were being accused of treason. Anthony fled to Rome, where Vatican Council I was in session. Here he used his brilliant speaking abilities to defend the infallibility of the pope. Then he returned to a Cistercian monastery in Spain and stayed there in solitude until his death.

As a promoter of social justice, an archbishop, a publisher, a queen's confessor, a writer, a religious founder, a missionary and a weaver, Anthony was an outstanding and humble leader. He is remembered particularly as the spiritual father of Cuba.

SUGGESTIONS

1. Anthony's interest in the Catholic press should stimulate ours. With the class, set up a library in the back of the room for Catholic papers and magazines, as well as books on saints and the spiritual life. Discuss with the students ways of spreading Catholic literature.

2. Anthony Claret had the responsibility and the privilege of speaking at Vatican Council I. Help the students to study the importance of Vatican Council I. Some important points to cover are Pope Pius IX and the reason for the council, the membership and agenda, and the decisions of the council.

3. Anthony saw many difficulties in bringing Christ's healing to Cuba. He started in a small way. Recommend to the students that they make a small sacrifice, such as giving up their dessert and saving the money for the poor. Send this monetary donation to a mission.

4. The main issue of Vatican I was papal infallibility. Explain the definition of infallibility and discuss how the pope makes infallible statements.

5. Anthony was a pastoral bishop who cared about human dignity and the religious freedom of his people. Have the class give examples of how Pope John Paul II also has taken deliberate gospel action on this point.

OCTOBER 28: STS. SIMON AND JUDE

"This marketplace is probably the most crowded one in Jerusalem and the hottest," thought young Simon as he leaned against the wall of a hut. Then he noticed a bearded young man darting quickly through the mob of buyers and sellers. No one else seemed to notice him. Suddenly the man drew a knife from the folds of his robes, pointed it at a man carrying food, grabbed the bag of food from his hands and disappeared into the crowd. "He must be a Zealot!" Simon thought in stunned silence. "He's probably stealing food for his people." While this incident is imaginary, it demonstrates the type of people with whom Simon is identified in Luke's gospel.

The Zealots were a Jewish group who believed that the promise of the Messiah meant a free and independent Jewish nation where they would never have to pay taxes to the Romans again. Some Zealots were also very concerned that the spiritual ideals of their religion be kept. But others in the group acted more like modern day terrorists by raiding, killing and inciting riots.

After spending much time in prayer, Jesus decided to choose twelve men, twelve rather unlikely candidates, who would be His apostles and proclaim the kingdom of God to all people. Simon, the Zealot, was one who was called. At the same time, Jesus called Jude Thaddeus, brother of James, supposedly a fisherman by trade. Along with ten other men, these two followed Jesus, lived with Him, fled when He underwent His passion, and rejoiced when He rose from the dead. At Pentecost they were filled with the spirit and a burning desire to spread the Good News to all. Jude travelled to Mesopotamia to preach and Simon went to Egypt. Eventually they both ended up in Persia, where they worked together evangelizing the people until they were both martyred. These two unlikely candidates for apostleship finally witnessed to the risen Lord with their lives.

St. Paul understood that God chooses the very people that others look down upon. He taught this to the Corinthians, saying, "Take yourselves for instance, brothers, at the time when you were called; how many of you were wise in the ordinary sense of the word, how many were influential people, or came from noble families? No, it was to shame the wise that God chose what is foolish by human reckoning, and to shame what is strong that he chose what is weak by human reckoning; those whom the world thinks common and contemptible are the ones that God has chosen — those who are nothing at all to show up those who are everything" (1 Cor. 1:26-28).

SUGGESTIONS

1. Symbols have traditionally been associated with both apostles. Jude has been pictured with a club, which was the instrument of his death, and with a flame over his head to show the Spirit's influence upon him at Pentecost. Simon is pictured with a fish, symbol of the early Christians' identification with Christ (The Greek initials for "Jesus Christ, God's Son, Savior" spell "fish"). Both saints also have special shields. Jude's shield is red with a sailboat which has a cross on the mast. Simon has a red shield bearing two oars and a hatchet. Have the students design symbols for the two apostles and post them around the room.

2. Both Simon and Jude are mentioned in the first Eucharistic Prayer of the Mass. That prayer mentions twelve martyrs, five popes, one bishop, one deacon, one cleric, four laymen. Give the students copies of the prayer from the Missalette and let them share what they know about the saints named in this prayer.

3. St. Jude in modern days has come to be known as the "saint of hopeless cases." Have the students share any experiences they have had with people who are devoted to St. Jude. Then have them pray for someone who is suffering greatly. Let them pass around a prayer candle and take turns praying for some person. An example would be: "That the Lord will strengthen my Aunt Sarah through the intercession of St. Jude, we pray." The class responds, "Lord, hear our prayer."

4. Traditionally St. Jude, the apostle, is identified as the author of the Letter of Jude in the New Testament. Have the students read the Letter of Jude and follow these directions: find a passage that appeals to you; underline the key words; draw a picture which symbolizes the passage; write an explanation of the passage under the picture; memorize the passage.

NOVEMBER 1: ALL SAINTS

On the feast of All Saints, we honor those men and women who — whether they've been canonized or not — have led lives of heroic virtue that set an example for all Christians. They have truly witnessed to their faith. Although no two saints are alike (just as no two people are exactly alike), there are certain qualities that they all share.

Saints are BIG DREAMERS. They make the impossible seem possible. They do not let their weaknesses or those of others hold them back from doing good. They believe that with God on their side, no one and nothing can stop them.

Saints are GO-GETTERS. They believe what is written in the Gospel: give all, turn the other cheek, love God above all, feed the hungry, clothe the naked, sin no more, follow Me. They don't wait for someone else to do the good first. They jump right in.

Saints are LOVE-BRINGERS, in big and little ways. They try to see Christ in every person and in every situation.

The big dreamers, the go-getters, the love-bringers — we've read about them, we've heard about them, we've celebrated their feasts. But today we celebrate ALL the saints together — the ones we know and the ones we don't. These are the people who help us believe that love is the most important thing in the world. Their lives tell us that what matters most in life is not what we earn or own, not the job we have or the people we know. What really matters is how much we love God, others, and ourselves, and how well we show that love in all we do.

Perhaps there are big dreamers, go-getters, and love-bringers among your friends. Perhaps YOU are one of those special people who want to make this world a better place. Perhaps you are someone racing toward heaven with joy. Know that it begins with little things: a smile, a helping hand, a prayer. This is the road to sainthood. Leon Bloy wrote: "The only tragedy in life is not to be a saint." Remember, the whole world is waiting for St. You!

Let us pray today.

> Father, all-powerful and ever-living God,
>   today we rejoice in the holy men
>   and women of every time and place.
> May their prayers bring us your forgiveness
>   and love.
> We ask this through our Lord Jesus Christ,
>   your Son,
> who lives and reigns with you and the Holy
>   Spirit, one God, for ever and ever.
>   (Opening Prayer from All Saints)

SUGGESTIONS

1. Have the students research their patron saints and/or the patron saint of the parish. Or have them research their patron saints and prepare a fictitious front page of a newspaper as a report. Give the students the following directions:

   1) Read several books or articles on your saint. Take notes as you read, especially on events that might make good "front page items." Be sure to put page number references in your notes in case you need to check the information.

   2) After you have completed your research, choose one event from the saint's life for your headline story. Write your headlines and other events, clothing, etc., during the years your saint lived. Jot down ideas and use these in your smaller stories on the front page. Include the names of the reference books in your notes.

   3) Organize all your notes and articles and prepare a rough layout (arrangement) of your page. Articles should be written in columns. Pictures and/or drawings may be included, as in actual papers.

   4) Print your name in the lower right hand corner of the front page. May this activity help you make a new friend!

2. Let the students design banners representing their patron saints, including significant symbols where possible.

3. Encourage the students to find out and report on (a) how a person is nominated for canonization, (b) the process of becoming acclaimed as a saint, and (c) what it means to be proclaimed a saint by the Church.

4. As a school project, have each room select a saint as their patron. The students should then decorate the door to the classroom in honor of that saint. Or have the students draw their patron saints on cardboard, cut them out, and paste them on a long sheet of shelf paper suspended in the hall or on a large bulletin board, creating a mural of saints.

5. Have the students pretend to be their patron saints. Then ask them, as that saint, to write a letter to the pastor or any other designated parish leader on how people today can live the Gospel more completely.

6. Ask the students to explain the following quote:

   > Holiness consists not in doing uncommon things, but in doing all common things with an uncommon fervor.
   >   (Cardinal Manning, *The Eternal Priesthood*)

   Do the students agree or disagree with the quote? Have them explain their reactions.

NOVEMBER 2: ALL SOULS

Normally we remember the anniversaries of the death of people we knew and loved. We might bring flowers or plants to their graves as signs of our continuing love and prayers. We often save pictures and mementos of the loved ones. Somehow we know that death can separate us only for a while.

On this feast of All Souls and throughout the entire month of November, we recall our deceased relatives, friends, and all the faithful departed who may yet be waiting for the full joy of heaven. Christians have always prayed for those who have died. Anniversaries of death have been regarded as "birthdays" to a new life. In the eleventh century, St. Odilo, who was an abbot at Cluny, required that his monasteries pray for all the dead on the day after All Saints. Soon this custom spread.

Let us remember in our prayers today all who have died and say,

> Eternal rest give them, O Lord, and let perpetual light shine upon them. May they rest in peace. Amen.

SUGGESTIONS

1. Take the students to the church or the prayer center and allow them time to pray silently for the faithful departed.

2. Cut out of large construction paper a cross or a crown. Pass it around and have the students list any deceased relatives, friends, or others for whom they would like everyone to pray. Keep the cross/crown in the classroom prayer corner near the enthroned Bible for the entire month of November.

3. If there is a cemetery attached to the parish and easily accessible, take the students on a pilgrimage of prayer through it. Pray especially at the graves of those relatives or friends of students. Have the students make gravestone rubbings and note memorial verses on the markers. Some cemeteries have special sections for infants and you might wish to point this out to the students. If the

situation allows, you might involve the students in a cemetery beautifying project: pulling weeds, clearing away areas near markers, picking up debris, etc.

4. Encourage the students to write friendly letters to those parishioners or relatives who have lost members of their families throughout the past year. Also encourage visitation of the sick and care for the elderly; respect and kindness need never wait until after death to be shown.

5. Depending on the needs and sensitivities of the students with whom you are working, consider having a sharing session of different family customs concerning showing respect for the dead. There are some funeral directors who provide excellent programs and explanations concerning such rites of passage and mourning. Find out what is offered locally to determine if something appropriate for your class is available.

6. Find out the schedule of Masses for the day and provide a listing for the students and their families.

NOVEMBER 3: ST. MARTIN DE PORRES

Difficult times can make a person bitter or better. Martin de Porres certainly had his share of troubles, but he never let them turn him into a mean or selfish person. He was born in Lima, Peru in 1579. His father was a Spanish nobleman — a knight — and his mother was a black freed woman from Panama. Martin's father did not stay with them nor really support them except for a short time. So the three of them — Martin, his mother, and eventually his sister — made a living for themselves. But even in the midst of his own poverty, Martin cared for the needs of other poor people he saw. He often gave away his money or his goods.

When he was twelve years old, Martin became an apprentice to a barber/surgeon. He learned not only to care for hair but also to heal and mend ill and broken bodies. When he was fifteen, Martin entered the Dominicans, the Order of Preachers, as a lay brother. He did not enter as a religious or to become a priest because he did not feel worthy of it, even though nine years later the community asked that he make full religious profession. All his life, Martin chose to do only the lowest tasks. He was known to pray long hours, and when he was not praying, he was taking care of the needs of those around him.

Martin's care for others extended well outside the walls of his own residence. He cared for many sick throughout Peru. He handled the community's distribution to the poor. He founded an orphanage and a hospital, and he also ministered to the slaves who were brought from Africa. And in all of this he was known for his humility, kindness, and gentle manner.

Martin is sometimes pictured holding a basket and collecting mice from church drawers. The scene originated from the story that Martin found a mouse in a trap in the church. Mice had been nibbling away at the priests' vestments, so Martin told the mouse to tell his friends not to ruin the items in the church any more. He then released the mouse, and soon all the mice left the church. The closest they came to it was the garden where Martin would feed them daily. It is also said that Martin kept a hospital for dogs and cats at his sister's house. Other stories of Martin's way with animals abound!

Martin spent most of his days as the head of the infirmary at his residence. It was there that he died in 1639. He was canonized in 1962 by Pope John XXIII and was named the patron of interracial justice. At that time John XXIII said, "He excused the faults of others. He forgave the bitterest injuries, convinced that he deserved much severer punishments on account of his own sins. He tried with all his might to redeem the guilty; lovingly he comforted the sick; he provided food, clothing, and medicine for the poor; he helped, as best he could, farm laborers and Negroes, as well as mulattoes, who were looked upon at that time as akin to slaves. Thus he deserved to be called by the name the people gave him: Martin of Charity."

SUGGESTIONS

1. While Martin was working in Peru, Peter Claver was ministering in Colombia, and Vincent de Paul labored for the poor in France. At the same time, the Reformation was well under way in Europe. Have the students keep a time line of the saints. Significant historical events should be included so that the students may better integrate their religious tradition with the rest of history.

2. Martin de Porres was a close friend of Rose of Lima. Have the students find out more about St. Rose and compare and contrast the two saints. Ask them to write essays on what they think friendship really means. Encourage them to submit their essays for publication in their school newspaper.

3. Have the students compose ballads or poems about Martin de Porres. More creative students may wish to add music to their compositions. Or have the students draw a mural illustrating Martin's life in action.

4. Pope John XXIII canonized Martin. Encourage the students to find out more about this popular pope, who initiated the Second Vatican Council.

5. Explain or have students explain the term "mulatto." Discuss how racial prejudice is built on ignorance and fear. This same ignorance and fear can keep people from reaching out to others even in their own classroom or neighborhood. Discuss ways the students can become more alert to preju-

dice of any kind and how they themselves can be more hospitable to others.

6. Martin did great things without leaving the area of his birth. Let the students list ways they can be more caring in the situations in which they find themselves now.

7. Martin was especially devoted to the Holy Eucharist. Remind the students to make frequent visits to the church and before the Blessed Sacrament when they are able. Remind them also to prepare well to receive Christ in the Eucharist, and to spend time in prayer of love and gratitude.

NOVEMBER 4: ST. CHARLES BORROMEO

Charles Borromeo was born on October 2, 1538. He was highly gifted and rather serious for his age. By the time he was twenty-one, he had received his doctorate degrees in civil and canon law. Within the year, he was called to Rome by his uncle, Pope Pius IV, and made a cardinal and administrator of Milan. The list of his duties and responsibilities at that time is long and impressive. As secretary of state at the Vatican, Charles was in charge of all the papal states. He also worked closely with his uncle at the Council of Trent, when many topics were discussed that led to heated arguments. Several times it seemed as though the council would break up and everyone would return home. But Charles, working behind the scenes, helped keep people together.

When he was twenty-five, his older brother died. Usually this meant that the next boy in the family would take over as head. But Charles decided instead to be a priest. Shortly after he was ordained, he was made the bishop of Milan. Although his uncle wanted him to remain in Rome, Charles felt the need to be with his flock in Milan. It was in Milan that his talents and his holiness really became apparent, for more than any other individual at the time, he tried to make the decrees and changes of the Council alive in his diocese.

He traveled throughout his diocese constantly, even into the hills and mountains of Switzerland. He set up orphanages, hospitals, homes for neglected women, seminaries, and colleges. He sought to reform the lives of the clergy and the religious orders of the day. He started a group of priests called the Oblates of St. Ambrose (now the Oblates of St. Charles) to help him in his work. In 1576 a plague broke out in Milan, and with it came famine. So many people were ill and dying that even the city officials fled the area. But Charles did not. He stayed with the sick and ministered to them. He himself ate very little and slept only a few hours a night on hard boards. He sold all he had and even borrowed large sums of money so that he could continue to feed the 60,000 to 70,000 people who came to him for help.

When he was 46 years old, Charles died, worn out from caring for others and bearing the burdens of his position. Although Charles Borromeo demanded much from the priests and religious he worked with, he never asked of them anything he himself was not willing to do. Sometimes it is easier for us to see what should be done or how others can improve than it is for us to make the effort ourselves. Today, like Charles Borromeo, let us try to do what we know is right and not judge those around us.

SUGGESTIONS

1. When people try to do the right thing, they may find opposition to their efforts. Charles Borromeo once attempted to reform a religious order called the Umiliati. They were so angry that they hired an assassin to kill him. An attempt was made on his life during his evening prayers, but he was not injured. Have the students list the challenges and dangers of being a true leader: a leader in school, at home, in the neighborhood, on teams, or in clubs. You might refer to Archbishop Romero of El Salvador as one who faced opposition with others.

2. Borromeo was attracted to certain devotions. Discuss a devotion that you or your parish likes. Show a filmstrip or video about a devotion. Encourage students to bring in articles about devotions.

3. Borromeo had many interests as a young man. He enjoyed hunting; he played the cello; he liked chess. Have the students compose a prayer based on any of these activities or on an activity in which they are personally involved. The following may give them some ideas:

Dear Lord, help me be a good sport in the game of life. When the bases are loaded and I am in a tight spot, give me the courage to go in with a clear eye and keep swinging. When the strikes are against me, help me to blame no one else. And when the game is in my favor, teach me to be kind. I know that it doesn't matter what position I play in life as long as I stay on Your team. Amen.

4. Writers tell us that Charles Borromeo had a slight speech defect, so he spoke seldom and in very low tones. This did not stop him from becoming a great spiritual leader. Encourage the students to read biographies of other leaders who had handicaps. Point out that everyone has some kind of handicap — physical or otherwise. What matters most is how we use what we have.

5. Although there have been schools of Christian doctrine since the earliest years of the faith, it was not until the Council of Trent that the need for a formal organization was recognized. This organization became the Confraternity of Christian Doc-

trine (CCD). Charles Borromeo is credited with doing much to get this work started in the parishes. Have the students do an investigative study of the CCD in the parish, often called today the PSR (Parish School of Religion).

How many students are enrolled in the CCD?

When do they meet? Where?

Who are the teachers?

When did the CCD program begin in the parish?

What activities do they sponsor?

Have the students present their findings to the class.

6. Charles Borromeo was instrumental in establishing what has come to be known as the "Forty Hours" devotion. Although various aspects of this devotion can be found as early as the thirteenth and fourteenth centuries, it was not until November 25, 1592 that formal recognition was given to it and the churches of Rome were commanded to observe it. Traditionally, the forty hours represents the time Christ's body is believed to have rested in the tomb. The devotion used to include the idea of making reparation and petitioning for peace. Today more emphasis is given to it as a means of honoring the Blessed Sacrament, and we do not refer to "Forty Hours Devotion," but rather to "Solemn Annual Exposition" (CF. *Instruction on Eucharistic Worship*). Have the students find out how this devotion is adapted or observed in their parish. Or have them prepare their own vigils and prayer services honoring the Blessed Sacrament.

7. Charles Borromeo, who worked on the catechism used in his day, is the patron of catechists. Let the students write letters of gratitude to those people who have helped them come to know and love God better. Make it a special day of prayer for all catechists.

NOVEMBER 9: DEDICATION OF SAINT JOHN LATERAN

In the earliest days of Christianity, those who believed in Jesus and followed His way met in private homes to hear His teachings and to celebrate the Eucharist. It took a long time before public meeting places could be used or churches could be built. When the Christians were no longer persecuted for their faith, they used their talents to the full and built beautiful churches honoring God. Sometime before the fourth century, a palace owned by a noble Roman family named Laterani had been built. It eventually became the property of the Emperor Constantine. Constantine had recognized Christianity as the religion of the empire and he donated the palace and other buildings on the site to the Church. This became Rome's oldest church. It was given the title the Basilica of the Savior, but later was dedicated to John the Baptist. It was then known as St. John Lateran.

We normally think of St. Peter's and the Vatican as the traditional home of the popes, but this was not always so. It was St. John Lateran that was the home of the popes — the center of the Catholic world for many years. Twenty-eight popes were buried there and it is still considered first in rank of all the basilicas. Although our pope now lives at the Vatican, St. John Lateran is considered his cathedral as the bishop of Rome. The dedication of this basilica is a happy occasion for all the Church because it reminds us of our beginnings, our roots, our unity. It stands as a monument to God and all that He does through His Church.

On this day it is good to be grateful for our own parish church and the cathedral of our diocese. A good way to express our gratitude is to spend some quiet, prayerful time in church.

SUGGESTIONS

1. Technically a basilica is a large rectangular building with supporting columns and a roof. In ancient times these buildings were used as meeting halls, etc. Now, however, only certain structures may be designated as religious basilicas. Have the students research basilicas. Contact local libraries or art museums to secure pictures of famous basilicas.

2. There are four major basilicas in Rome: St. John Lateran, St. Peter (Vatican), St. Paul (outside the city walls), and St. Mary Major (founded by Pope Liberius). Ask the students to report on each of these. Part of St. John Lateran (what had been the palace) is now a museum.

3. Discuss with the students the importance of contributing to the support of the parish community. Invite the pastor, associate, or parish council chairperson in to explain how the Sunday collection is used.

4. A cathedral is the main, or mother, church in a diocese, where the bishop presides, preaches, teaches, and leads in prayer. It does not have to be the largest church in the diocese, but it is the church where the bishop carries out a major part of his ministry. Take the students to the cathedral. Suggest they try to sketch it. Have them note the position of the bishop's chair (the "cathedra") and any significant artistic symbols. Contact the cathedral ahead of time to see if brochures are available and if a guide can accompany the group. Encourage the students to discover more about their own parish church and its history. Recommend that they find and interview older members of the parish about the history of the church as they know it.

5. Have the students design and build replicas of their cathedral or the parish church, or design a new church. Let them use any materials: cardboard, wood, clay, sugar cubes, styrofoam, etc.

NOVEMBER 10: ST. LEO THE GREAT

There are only two popes who have earned the title "Great" — Gregory I and Leo I. Leo was born in the beginning of the fifth century, probably in Rome. We know very little about his early life. He was a deacon, and in that position he had many responsibilities. Already other church leaders looked to him for advice and for explanations of the mysteries of the faith. Leo was even sent to settle arguments between commanders and leaders. He was in Gaul on just such a mission in 440 when Pope Sixtus III died and Leo was elected the new pope. There was much work awaiting him, but Leo went right to the task. He helped the Church stay united at a time when it was being attacked inside by false teachers and outside by warring tribes.

In 452, the Huns, led by Attila, marched toward Rome, ready to destroy it. Pope Leo himself went out to meet Attila and was able to stop him from entering and destroying the city by agreeing to pay tribute to him every year. Three years later another tribe marched on Rome — the Vandals led by Genseric. Again Leo met with this warrior. But this time Leo was only able to stop them from burning the city. For two weeks the Vandals pillaged and looted Rome while the people sought shelter in the churches. Leo helped rebuild the city after the invaders departed and he sent missionaries to Africa to minister to those who had been captured by the Vandals.

Leo is often remembered for his famous writings and explanations of the faith, especially during the Council of Chalcedon in 451. His words were so powerful that the 600 bishops gathered there felt they had heard St. Peter speaking through Leo. Pope Leo the Great died in 461.

As we look back at some of the earliest popes, we see that everyone turned to them for leadership. As leaders of the Church, they were also leaders of peace, leaders for truth. Today we see leaders of other countries, leaders of world-wide organizations, believers and non-believers alike, listening to the teachings of the pope. Christ continues to care for His people in truth and peace.

SUGGESTIONS

1. Pope Leo was regarded as a true pastor, a real shepherd of the flock, whose sermons dealt with everyday needs and problems. Let the students select an ordinary problem or need and write advice about it in the form of a sermon. Also recommend that the students send supportive letters to their own parish priests on this day.

2. Leo was pope for twenty-one years, one of the longest and most significant reigns in the early Church. Have students look up the reigns of the popes. Whose was the longest? The shortest? What names appear most often? etc.

3. Prudence is a virtue often associated with Leo. Ask the students to define prudence and list an event in the life of Leo where this virtue was evident.

4. Declare the day "Pray for the Pope Day" in your class.

5. Suggest that the students draw a picture of the meeting of Leo and Attila the Hun and/or Genseric and the Vandals.

NOVEMBER 11: ST. MARTIN OF TOURS

Goodness cannot be hidden. It can't be locked behind monastery walls or disguised by rough and shabby clothing. Martin of Tours was a good and holy man, and people from far and wide could recognize this. He was born around the year 316 in what is today known as Hungary. He was raised and educated in Italy. His parents were pagans, and his father was an officer in the army. Because he was the son of an officer, Martin was expected to join the army, too, which he did when he was fifteen years old. But at the same time, he had been drawn to Jesus and His teachings and had become a catechumen — one studying and preparing to become a Christian.

A famous story is told about Martin, one that has been captured in paintings and statues for hundreds of years. When Martin was eighteen and stationed in Amiens (France), he was making his rounds one cold winter evening. As he entered the city gates, he saw a poor naked beggar. Having nothing else to give, Martin cut his own cloak in two and wrapped one half of it around the frozen beggar. That night in a dream Martin saw it was Christ Whom he had clothed. Martin was baptized soon after that.

But being both a Christian and a soldier did not appeal to Martin. He could no longer seek to hurt anyone in war or battle. When he was twenty-three, he refused to arm himself for battle. This came to the attention of the emperor. Martin was accused of being a coward and was thrown in prison. He was soon released, however, since the enemy in the meantime had sent a messenger seeking peace. Now Martin was free to give His life to the true battle — the battle against evil. He went to study under St. Hilary, the bishop of Poitiers. He returned home and converted his mother, although his father never converted. He fought heresy and was beaten and driven out of towns for trying to teach the truth. But he never gave up.

Eventually he returned to Gaul (France) and founded a monastery, probably the first one there. He lived there for ten years, but his reputation for goodness and holiness had grown so much that when the bishop of Tours died, the people there would not be satisfied until Martin was made their bishop. Reluctantly he was ordained bishop in 371. He traveled much to meet and help the people, teaching them and curing them. He destroyed pagan temples and the sacred groves. But he also sought the quiet of a prayerful community. So he founded another monastery at Marmoutier. There he trained priests who would also take the Gospel to the poor.

When Martin died in 397, he was honored immediately as a saint. He is one of the first who was not a martyr to be so honored. So popular is this saint that his shrine at Tours is one of the most visited places of pilgrimage in all of Europe. He is known as the Apostle of Gaul, one of the patron saints of France, the patron of soldiers and, at the same time, a true patron of peace.

The goodness and holiness of Martin was real. It was there even when he was called a coward, even when he was beaten for trying to spread the truth. When life's battles get too big, it is a good time to call on Christ through the intercession of St. Martin.

SUGGESTIONS

1. Much of what we know about Martin of Tours comes from a biography of him written by his close friend Sulpicius Severus. True friends are able to see both strengths and weaknesses in each other. Ask the students to write up an event in the life of one of their friends that shows one of the best characteristics of that friend — one that could even qualify him or her as a "candidate for goodness." Share these stories.

2. Martin was a catechumen. If the parish is involved in the Rite of Christian Initiation of Adults, ask a representative to explain the catechumenate to the class.

3. There are many symbols associated with Martin of Tours:
   • a tree (from a legend concerning a tree that would not fall on him)
   • armor (symbol for the soldier-saint)
   • a cloak (from the story of the cloak he cut in two to clothe the beggar)
   • a beggar
   • a goose (from the legend that while he was hiding because he did not want to be made bishop of Tours, his pet goose kept honking and giving away his whereabouts)

Have the students depict one of the events in Martin's life in a diarama.

4. Some say it was Martin who first conceived of the organization of settlements into parishes. Find out how much the students know about their parish: its

founding date, past parish priests, pastoral team, population, active organizations, parish councils, bordering parishes, etc.

NOVEMBER 12: ST. JOSAPHAT

A martyr is a person who gives public witness to his or her faith — even if it might bring death. Josaphat was a bishop who tried to work for unity in the Church. He gave his life trying.

Josaphat was born John Kuncevic in the Ukraine around 1580. He worked as a merchant until 1604, when he became a monk of the Ukrainian Order of St. Basil. It was as a monk that he took the name Josaphat. Five years later he was ordained a priest in the Byzantine Rite. It did not take long until his reputation for holiness grew. People came to him for spiritual advice. They were moved by his preaching and by the example of his life, for he fasted often and was faithful to the prayers, traditions, and customs of the people. He was only in his thirties when he was made bishop of Vitebsk and then archbishop of Polotsk.

But he found the diocese in terrible condition, and he found much unrest among the people. For although Josaphat had been raised in the Byzantine culture and molded his spiritual life and prayers on those traditions, he was faithful to the rule of the Church of Rome. There were strong groups, however, who opposed Rome and Latin rule. These people joined together and named their own bishop. Disturbances broke out all over as people took sides in the confusion. Josaphat felt he had to do something, so he decided to go to the city of Vitebsk himself. He knew this would be dangerous since that city was the center of the disturbance. While Josaphat was there, a priest named Elias kept shouting insults at him. A deacon had the priest locked up. When the mob heard this, they rioted and demanded the release of Elias. The priest was released, but the angry mob did not stop. They broke through all barriers until they made their way to Bishop Josaphat. They beat him and then shot him to death on November 12, 1623. The man who had worked for unity all his life was killed by a violent mob. People were shocked at the news, and much honor and reverence were paid to his memory.

We may never be beaten for our faith, but there will be times when being a strong Catholic will be uncomfortable and difficult. Yet when we stand strong in faith, we build a martyr's heart, a martyr's spirit. It is the kind of spirit that the world needs so much. It is the kind of spirit loved by Jesus.

SUGGESTIONS

1. There is room in the Church for various customs, traditions, and rites. In addition to the Roman (Latin) Rite, there are four other major rites in the

Church, which grew out of these centers: Alexandria, Antioch, Constantinople, and Armenia. In the United States, the Eastern Rites are: Byzantine-Ruthenian, Byzantine-Ukrainian, Maronite, Melchite, Armenian, Byelorussian, Chaldean, Romanian, and Russian. If there is a church of another canonical rite in the area, arrange for a field trip there so that the students may come to know and appreciate the richness of the various rites. Ask them to do research on the rites.

2. Traditions and customs are very important to people. Let the students share some of their family and/or nationality customs. Ask volunteers to prepare Ukrainian food as a treat for the day in honor of St. Josaphat.

3. Josaphat was the first Eastern saint to be formally canonized (1867). Suggest that the students watch their Catholic diocesan newspapers for announcements of any other saints awaiting canonization.

4. One of Josaphat's favorite devotions was the Jesus prayer. Pray it with the students and encourage them to repeat it often throughout the day: "Lord Jesus Christ, Son of God, have mercy on me."

NOVEMBER 13: ST. FRANCES XAVIER CABRINI

If you've ever moved to a new city or a different state, then you probably know how lost and alone you can feel until you get settled and make new friends. Imagine what it is like for the hundreds of thousands of immigrants who make their way to other countries each year, hoping to find a brighter future in a new land. But many of these people have their hopes dashed and they lose their way. It was to people such as these that Mother Frances Cabrini came. Francesca Cabrini was born in northern Italy on July 15, 1850. She was the youngest of thirteen children. Her parents, Agostino and Stella, owned a prosperous farm. They were a loving family and deeply religious. In the evenings Mr. Cabrini would read stories to the children about the work of the missionaries. Francesca enjoyed these stories and hoped to become a missionary herself.

After completing school and receiving a teacher's certificate, Francesca applied for admission to a convent, but she was turned down because she was so frail. She taught for awhile and was then asked to take over a nearby orphanage, House of Providence. Although the orphanage was eventually closed, it was there that Francesca took her vows and gathered around her the small group that would soon become the Institute of the Missionary Sisters of the Sacred Heart. She chose as patrons of the community Saints Francis de Sales and Francis Xavier. Her hope was to travel to China and the East. She went to Rome for approval of her order and it was there that Pope Leo XIII blessed her and her work and told her, "No, not to the East, but to the West." Already the people in Italy had heard of the hard times that had befallen the Italians who had journeyed to the United States and South America looking for jobs and prosperity. And so Mother Frances Cabrini set sail for New York with six other sisters on March 23, 1889. When they arrived there, they discovered that they had no place to stay. They were to find themselves without money or lodging often. But somehow God always provided. Soon hospitals, schools, and orphanages were being established by Mother Cabrini and her sisters. They went to the places where Italians gathered, the "Little Italys" found in many of the major cities. They taught them skills, cared for their needs, and comforted some of them in prisons even as they awaited death. In thirty-five years, Mother Cabrini founded nearly seventy institutions for helping the needy, the poor, the abandoned, and the ill in over eight countries. In 1909 Mother Cabrini became a naturalized citizen of the United States of America.

She continued her work at an amazing pace. She had crossed the ocean thirty times, bringing more sisters and establishing other homes. She was visibly worn out with all her labors, but she felt she could go on as long as God provided her with the strength. In the late fall of 1917, Mother Cabrini was in her hospital in Chicago wrapping presents and helping with plans for a Christmas party for the children. She came down with malaria and died rather suddenly on December 22. She was sixty-seven years old.

Usually it takes quite a while before a person can be canonized, but in the case of Mother Cabrini, this honor came quickly. She was canonized a saint, the saint of immigrants, on July 7, 1946, by Pope Pius XII. We in America may take special pride in the fact that she is the first United States citizen to be canonized a saint. Let us pray.

> God our Father, you called Frances Xavier Cabrini from Italy to serve the immigrants of America. By her example, teach us concern for the stranger, the sick, and the frustrated. By her prayers, help us to see Christ in all the men and women we meet. Amen.

SUGGESTIONS

1. Frances Cabrini was inspired by the stories she heard as a child. Have the students select short stories, biographies of the saints, or other religious literature to read to younger children. Set up a story-sharing time with the younger students so they, too, can learn to dream of serving others in Christ's name.

2. Suggest that the students send letters or personally designed greeting cards to the sick or elderly at home, those in hospitals or nursing homes, or any shut-ins of the parish. Make arrangements to visit

an orphanage, bringing games and prizes for the children there. Sponsor a clothing drive for the needy.

3. What do missionaries do today? Have the students research the missionary efforts in the Church today, particularly any under the care of their own diocese. If there are any Missionary Sisters of the Sacred Heart in the area, invite them in as guest speakers. The chief characteristics of their community are devotion to the Sacred Heart, a spirit of prayer and reparation, intense missionary activity, and obedience to the Holy See.

4. When Frances Cabrini was a young girl, she used to make paper boats and fill them with tiny violets. These represented the missionaries she hoped to send all over the world. She would sail these little boats down the canal near the home of her uncle. Have the students illustrate this event or others in the life of Frances Cabrini.

5. Encourage the students to pray and sacrifice for the success of the Church's missionary efforts.

NOVEMBER 15: ST. ALBERT THE GREAT

There is only one saint who was also a leading scientist of his day, and that is Albert the Great. So devoted to God and such a seeker of truth was he that he saw the whole created world before him, waiting to be discovered, recorded, and taught. Albert the Great is the patron of scientists, philosophers, and students.

Born in 1206 in Swabia, Germany, Albert came from a noble military family. He studied at the University of Padua. It was there that he became acquainted with the Dominican Order. After some hesitation, he became a Dominican — even though his family was against it. He continued his studies and went on to become a famous and gifted teacher. One of his most famous pupils was St. Thomas Aquinas. Albert seemed to be into everything: biology, chemistry, physics, astronomy, geography, economics, politics, logic, mathematics — all of this plus theology, Scripture, and philosophy. But nonetheless his life was not centered on science; it was centered on God. For Albert, all these different areas displayed most beautifully the wonderful plan and providence of God.

Albert was named the provincial superior of the Dominican Order in 1254. Three years later he resigned his post so that he could devote more time to study. Then he was appointed bishop of Regensburg in 1260. After two years he was able to go back to writing and teaching until his death in 1280. For Albert, life was filled with wonders to discover — whether it was the life cycle of a spider or developing the theory that the world was round. If creation is so wonderful, how much more wonderful is the Creator!

Albert the Great is the model of the kind of scientists and faith-filled men and women the world needs today.

SUGGESTIONS

1. If your school sponsors a science fair, have it renamed in this saint's honor, e.g., Albert the Great Expo.

2. Let the students enjoy a nature walk. Or devote extra time to the care of the environment: planting trees, picking up debris, preparing a bird feeder, etc.

3. In 1256, Albert the Great was called to Rome to offer a defense of the mendicant orders. Have the students find out more about mendicant orders and the names of some of them.

4. As bishop, Albert traveled throughout the diocese on foot and so became known as the "Bishop with the Boots." He was also known as the "Universal Doctor" by his contemporaries because of his great learning. Albert might have been inspired by Jesus. Have the students find sections in the Gospel of Luke where Jesus shows an awareness of nature, ministry to others, patient love, etc.

NOVEMBER 16: ST. MARGARET OF SCOTLAND

Some people feel they have done enough for the poor and needy when they have given money. But for Margaret of Scotland — a wife, a mother, and a queen — giving money was never enough. She was there with the poor, washing their feet and making sure they had food to eat and clothes to wear. Only after all the others were cared for would she eat and rest herself.

Margaret was born sometime around 1045. She was raised in the Hungarian court, for she was from the line of nobility. When she was twelve, she was sent to the English court of Edward the Confessor. There she was further educated. But when the Normans conquered England, Margaret, her mother, brother, and sister tried to return to Hungary. Their ship was blown off course and they landed in Scotland. They were warmly welcomed by King Malcolm III of Scotland. It was not long before he fell in love with the beautiful and gentle Margaret. They were married at Dunfermline Castle in 1070.

Scotland was a rough country and although Malcolm was a good man, he was more of a soldier than a scholar or courtly gentleman. But Margaret helped him become a virtuous, gracious leader. They had eight children: two girls and six boys, and all of them grew to love the poor and care for them just as their parents had before them.

Margaret was prayerful. She gathered a group of women together to study and discuss the Scriptures and to embroider vestments and fine altar cloths. She was always surrounded by beggars, and she gave them money and clothes. She helped ransom the English who had been captured, and she set up homes and hospitals for strangers, the sick, and the poor. She and her husband would go to the church in the middle of the night during Lent and Advent. On the way home, they would wash the feet of six poor people and give them money. At home, Margaret would feed nine orphans who were brought to her daily. Then she fed and supported others before she herself would eat. Her concern was for all her people. She brought a love of the arts and education to the people, and they loved her in return. So well did her children learn to love God from her that they are believed to be primarily responsible for two centuries of progress and peace in Scotland.

Margaret died four days after her husband in 1093. In 1250 she was canonized and later declared patroness of Scotland. People today still look to her example. She saw Christ in the poor and did not wait for someone else to take care of their needs. She was there — and led others to loving service as well.

SUGGESTIONS

1. It was recorded that when Margaret went to church, she was quiet and extraordinarily reverent. Remind the students of the respect and awareness of God's presence appropriate as they enter a church. Review with them the use of the blessing with holy water and reverent genuflection.

2. The power of family training and love was evident in Margaret and Malcolm's family. Margaret's youngest son, David, was acclaimed a saint by the people. Encourage the students to spend more time with their families. Have them make a "My Family" booklet, describing the members of their families, their family schedule, mealtime at home, holiday customs, etc. Suggest that the students also recommend ways their families can grow spiritually.

3. Conduct a courtesy and good manners campaign. In this way the students can show by their actions that they understand and appreciate the respect due others as creatures of God.

4. Margaret did much to educate the Celtic clergy and the people. She encouraged the meeting of synods there and helped bring back a proper understanding of the Lenten fasts, the need to receive Holy Communion, and the proper marriage laws. Review with the students the Precepts of the Church (Duties of a Catholic Christian).

NOVEMBER 16: ST. GERTRUDE

The most important thing we know about St. Gertrude (1256-1301) is that she loved God and was very aware of God's love for her. When she was five years old, Gertrude was placed in the care of the nuns

at Helfta. Later she became a nun there herself. When she was twenty-six, she began having deep mystical experiences which she later wrote down in book form. Her life from that point on revolved around the study of Scripture, prayer, spiritual reading, and the liturgy of the Church. Gertrude carried her love for Christ to others through the prayers that she wrote and through the journal of her mystical experiences.

SUGGESTIONS

1. One of Gertrude's deepest experiences was the love of the Sacred Heart. The heart and seven rings (symbol of her union with Christ) are her symbols. Review with the students the meaning of devotion to the Sacred Heart, the symbol of the great love of Christ. Have the students make heart-shaped love trees, and on each heart write one way they will show love today.

DIRECTIONS

1) Have the students fold an 8½" x 11" piece of paper in half. On the fold, have them trace three half-hearts, with the hearts becoming progressively larger.

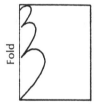 

2) Cut out the outlined hearts.

3) Design the edges of the hearts. In the middle of each of the three hearts, have the students write ways they will show love today.

4) Attach the heart structure to pink or red construction paper, 4¼" x 5½", and add stem, leaves, and base with markers or additional paper. The students might print on the base the words "Letting My Love Grow and Grow."

2. In the Bible, the heart has been understood as the center of the whole life of a man or a woman. Have the students read these sections and reflect on them by writing in their journals: John 15:9; John 13:34; Matthew 12:35.

3. Gertrude is the patroness of the West Indies. Let the students locate the islands on a map and pray for the people who live there.

NOVEMBER 17: ST. ELIZABETH OF HUNGARY

One of the spiritual works of mercy is to bear wrongs patiently. Few people have understood what that means more than Elizabeth of Hungary. Elizabeth was born in 1207. Her father was Alexander II, the king of Hungary. Her marriage had been arranged when she was just a child, and at the age of four she was sent to Thuringia for education and eventually marriage. When she was fourteen, she married Louis of Thuringia. They loved each other deeply and theirs was considered an ideal marriage. Even at so young an age Elizabeth showed a great love for God and the poor. Louis, too, supported her in all she did to relieve the sufferings of the poor and sick. But Louis' mother, Sophia, his brother, and the other members of court resented Elizabeth's generosity. Elizabeth dressed in simple clothes rather than the royal robes expected of someone in her position. She was taunted and mocked by the royal family. But she was deeply loved by the common folk. Louis loved her and defended her. During their time together they had three children.

In 1227, after six years of marriage, Louis went to fight in the Crusades. He died on the way. When Elizabeth heard of his death, she was grief-stricken. Together they had served God. Together they had formed a family. Together they had helped the poor. Now she was without him. At the same time her in-laws at court mistreated her, accused her of managing the finances of the kingdom poorly, and finally forced her and her children out of the palace. They were left homeless and poor. For a while they found refuge only in barns. Finally Elizabeth and her children were taken in by her uncle, the bishop of Bamberg. When her husband's friends returned from the Crusades and saw Elizabeth's plight, they helped restore her to her rightful place in the palace. But rather than just enjoying the comfort and ease of royal life, Elizabeth increased her service to others. She was only twenty-four years old when she died in 1231, tired and worn from always caring for others. So much did the people acclaim her that she was canonized a saint only four years later.

She had suffered much, but she had loved much, too. As a wife and mother she was devoted. Her life is a beautiful example of all the Gospel calls us to be: loving, caring, and forgiving.

SUGGESTIONS

1. Elizabeth is the patroness of the Franciscan Third Order and of all Catholic Charities. a) Have the students research the purpose of Third Orders. Ask them to find out how people become members of these orders. b) Catholic Charities are important in any diocese. Tell the students to find out what services are offered through Catholic Charities and how they can help.

2. It is not easy to bear wrongs patiently. Let the students give examples of how they may be called to do this in their own lives.

3. Elizabeth is often pictured with red roses filling her cape. According to legend, she went out ladened down with loaves of bread to feed the poor. Her husband saw her and took hold of her cape to see what she was carrying. What he saw was roses rather than bread! For this story she is also known as the patroness of bakers. Elizabeth is symbolized with a triple crown — for her roles as a member of the royalty, as a mother, and as a saint, crowned in heaven. Have the students prepare bookmarks using these or other symbols in their design.

NOVEMBER 18: DEDICATION OF THE CHURCHES OF PETER AND PAUL

The basilicas of St. Peter and St. Paul are important because they honor the tomb or place of martyrdom of these apostles, and also because they give the people of God a sense of what Christianity is all about. Peter and Paul gave their lives to spread the Good News that God has redeemed His people. Century after century, saints and sinners alike have found peace and joy in the Church and in her sacraments. Today as we celebrate the Eucharist in our parish churches, we are united with the community of believers all over the world. There is but one Lord, one faith, one Baptism — and we rejoice that we are one people of God.

SUGGESTIONS

1. The largest basilica in Christendom today is St. Peter's. Select a few volunteers to go to the library, find pictures of this basilica, and then use the pictures as they point out to the class interesting details of the structure, including mention of some of the various statues inside. If any of your students have been to Rome, they may have pictures or slides to share with the class.

2. Both basilicas, Peter's and Paul's, were completed in the fourth century under Popes Sylvester and Siricius. Both were later destroyed and reconstructed. Have the students launch a beautifying program for the parish church and grounds. Let them clear out and arrange storerooms, polish church materials, plant flowers, etc.

3. The basilica of St. Peter was erected over the tomb of St. Peter, and St. Paul's on the Ostian Way honors the place where Paul was martyred. Have some students research the excavations under St. Peter's, which indicate the place of Peter's burial in an old Roman cemetery. Discuss with the students the custom of decorating cemeteries as a sign of respect for those who have died. Encourage the students to pay such respect when their families make memorial visits to the grave sites of deceased relatives and friends.

4. Invite the pastor or an associate to give the history of the parish church. Many parishes keep photos or parish annals available for such presentations.

Also see Supplement for November 18.

NOVEMBER 21: PRESENTATION OF MARY

This feast of the presentation of Mary dates back to the sixth century in the East and the fifteenth century in the West. It is based on an ancient tradition that says Mary was taken to the temple in Jerusalem when she was three years old and dedicated to God. What we spiritually celebrate on this day is the fact that God chose to dwell in Mary in a very special way. We, too, become temples of the Holy Spirit at Baptism. We, too, are invited to be as open to God, as dedicated to God, as Mary was. Let us turn to her often today and ask that she help us remain close to God all our lives.

SUGGESTIONS

1. The feast of the presentation of Mary is closely associated with the dedication of the church of St. Mary in Jerusalem. Recommend that the students choose some special way to honor Mary today, e.g., pray the rosary or act of consecration, read the nativity account according to Luke, pay a visit to church for silent prayer, etc.

2. Mary was holy, full of grace. She cared about the needs of others. Encourage the students to place the needs of others before their own, to listen to what others have to say in conversation, to give others first place in line or at lunch, etc., in imitation of Mary.

3. Today sing a Marian hymn with the class.

NOVEMBER 22: ST. CECILIA

We really know very little about St. Cecilia, although stories abound. She lived in the second century during the time of great persecutions. In one story dating back to the fifth or sixth century, we are told that as a young girl Cecilia wanted to give her life to God. Her parents forced her to marry a nobleman named Valerian. In time, she converted him and his brother Tiburtius to the faith. All three of them died as martyrs. Cecilia is often pictured with a musical instrument — a small organ, a harp, or a viola. An account of her wedding says that while the musicians played, Cecilia sang to the Lord in her heart. In the later middle ages, she was pictured playing the organ and singing aloud. We are not sure why this is so, but it is a reminder that the Church has always recognized the value of music and song. Some thoughts and feelings are best expressed in music. We recall that Jesus and His disciples sang on the night before He died (Matthew 26:30).

SUGGESTIONS

1. Sing one of the psalms.

2. Have the students look up information on the catacombs where St. Cecilia's remains were found. Her remains were taken to Rome, where a basilica was built in her honor.

3. Since Cecilia is patroness of music, schedule a band concert or sacred music assembly. Have the students compose their own songs on their patron saints or other liturgical feasts.

NOVEMBER 23: ST. CLEMENT I

Saint Clement I was the fourth pope of the Roman Church after Saint Peter. Very little is known about him. He succeeded Cletus as bishop of Rome around the year 92 and his reign lasted until 101. Even though we have few biographical facts about Clement, we do know that he wrote a very important letter to the Corinthians while he was pope. The city of Corinth had a large Christian population, but it also had a number of problems. During Clement's time a group of people in Corinth refused to follow the legitimate church authority there. They split off from the main group of believers. But when part of the Church is divided, the whole Church suffers. Clement, as the shepherd of the Church, wrote to the people explaining the role of authority, the role of the people, and encouraging peace and harmony. He begged them to stop their jealousies and quarreling. So powerful and clear was the letter that in some places in the early Church it was ranked next to the accepted books of Sacred Scripture. It is one of the earliest Christian documents we have outside the New Testament. Clement was martyred for the faith.

SUGGESTIONS

1. After Peter's martyrdom, the Church was ruled by Linus, then Cletus, and then Clement. Have the students find and memorize the names of the early popes or those of this century. Secure photos of the past several pontiffs and let the students write summaries of their lives. Appoint a group to bring in any and all articles about the travels and work of our pope today.

2. Corinth was a city of problems. Some of these are recorded in 1 Corinthians 1:11-16. Ask the stu-

dents to read this section and explain what the problems were. Paul answered by reminding the people there is only one Christ, and so factions are out of place. Clement, too, had to deal with the problem of factions. Let the students discuss how they would handle the problem of groups of Christians opposing one another. Discuss with them the problems connected with forming cliques in schools and neighborhoods.

3. Have the students draw mosaics of the symbols of the pope:

   a tiara: a beehive-shaped circular headpiece of three crowns, one above the other, with a cross on the top and two lappets hanging down the back

   a triple cross: the papal cross has three crossbars

   a church

   a papal coat of arms

   a miter: the ceremonial headdress worn by bishops that is similar to the tiara

4. Clement is the patron of marble-workers, stonecutters, and mariners. One story about him relates how he made a miraculous spring of water flow for some convicts with whom he worked. Another story states that an anchor was tied around his neck and he was drowned, but the sea opened up to reveal the angels burying him in a marble tomb under the seas. From these stories we have received the spring and anchor as symbols for Clement. Suggest that the students read a biography of the present pope and decide what items would best symbolize him.

NOVEMBER 23: ST. COLUMBAN

Zeal is a word we often associate with missionaries and people enflamed with the love of God. Zeal can win many followers for Christ. It can also stir up enemies — people who do not want to hear how their lives must change. Columban, one of the greatest Irish missionaries who labored in Europe, was a man filled with zeal. He came to know the joy and hardships of working for Christ.

Columban was born in Ireland before the middle of the sixth century. He entered a monastery and led a life of prayer and study for thirty years. Then in the year 591, he and twelve companions were sent to Europe as missionaries. They made their way through France, Switzerland, and eventually Italy. Everywhere they went, they established the monasteries that were to become the centers for Christianity, learning, and prayer throughout Europe. Columban wrote a strict rule for these monasteries, and he tried to reform the lives of the clergy, the nobility, and the lay people. He attacked abuses and evil wherever he saw them. He spoke out loudly against the immorality that was so common among the royalty.

Finally he was exiled for pointing out the sins of the king and for criticizing the local bishops because they did not speak out against him, too. While Columban was being deported, he was shipwrecked and ended up in Italy, where he was befriended. While he was there, he founded a monastary in Bobbio and it was there that he died in 615. We can learn much about zeal for God from the life of St. Columban.

SUGGESTIONS

1. Columban is known for the strict monastic rule he composed. Have the students compose ten or so rules for Christian living or try to write the rules for living together as a Christian community.

2. Saints are not born saints. Nor does holiness guarantee that one will make no mistakes. Even St. Columban made some mistakes. Have the students discuss the positive aspects of making mistakes. Discuss the obligation the students have to study, pray, form Christian consciences, and then live faithful and true lives.

Also see Supplement for November 23.
See Supplement for November 24.

NOVEMBER 30: ST. ANDREW

He was a fisherman. He was an apostle. He not only followed Christ himself, he went out of his way to bring others to Jesus. His name — Andrew.

Andrew was the brother of Simon Peter, and they were both fishermen on the Sea of Galilee. Andrew had been a follower of John the Baptist and he was one of the first to follow Jesus. But he seemed to take a special delight in bringing others to Jesus. It was Andrew who noticed a boy in the crowd with "five barley loaves and two fish" — and that was the beginning of a meal that fed over five thousand. It was Philip and Andrew that the Greeks approached when they wanted to see Jesus. Although we do not know much more about Andrew from Scripture, these few events indicate he was a man who was easy to approach, a man faith-filled and loyal — the kind of man you could trust. Tradition tells us that later Andrew preached in northern Greece, Epirus, and Scythia (what is now the southern part of Russia), and that he was probably crucified at Patras in Greece around the year 70. Andrew is the patron saint of Russia and Scotland.

The name "Andrew" is a Greek name meaning "courageous" or "manly." As one who gave his life and his all to follow Christ, he would certainly live up to his name. Through his intercession, may we live up to our names and calling as Christians.

SUGGESTIONS

1. Have the students write out scripts and act out those scenes from Scripture in which Andrew is

mentioned: Mark 1:16-18 and Matthew 4:18-20; John 1:35-45; Mark 1:29; John 6:1-15; John 12:20-33; Mark 13:1-4.

2. In the fifteenth century, artists began picturing Andrew with the saltire or x-shaped cross which has become his traditional symbol. The fish and the fisherman's net are other symbols of his. Each apostle has a specific identifying symbol. Review these with the students (See *Christ Jesus, the Way*, Theme 7).

3. Andrew and Simon Peter were from Bethsaida in Galilee. Let the students locate Bethsaida on a map. Point out to them the three geographical areas: Galilee (northern), Samaria (middle), and Judea (southern). If slides or photos of these areas are available, show them to the students. Each area can be recognized by its land and vegetation, from the fertile greenness of Galilee to the barren rockiness of Judea. Some students may wish to make a clay or plaster of paris model of these areas.

CHRIST THE KING

Can you imagine a wheel without a center? A center is necessary for balance and for smooth running. Some people, however, try to live without a center. The feast of Christ the King reminds us that Jesus is our center. He is the beginning and the end. This feast comes on the last Sunday of the Church year, right before Advent. We celebrate Christ not only as King of the world and nations, but as King of our families and of our hearts. The kingdom of Christ is within each of us. Every time we try to make something else the center of our lives, we get thrown off-balance. Jesus, the Shepherd-King, loves us and is always ready to guide us.

SUGGESTIONS

1. Have the students draw a crown of thorns and a kingly crown and use them as part of a prayer service in honor of Christ the King.

2. The feast of Christ the King was established by Pope Pius XI in 1925 to worship Christ's lordship over all the universe. At that time, it was celebrated on the last Sunday of October. Now, it comes on the last Sunday of the Church year. Point out to the students that since the Church is living and growing, it can change in some respects. Suggest they interview parents, grandparents, or others about how the Church has changed and how it has remained the same.

3. With Christ as our King, we all belong to one family. Involve the students in mission activities so that they may share in the responsibilities, as well as the blessings, of this worldwide family.

4. Sing songs from the missalette or parish song book for Christ the King.

5. The feast of Christ the King somewhat duplicates the feast of the Ascension, where Christ is crowned in glory and honor. Have the students pray the second Glorious Mystery of the Rosary in preparation for this feast.

DECEMBER 3: ST. FRANCIS XAVIER

What does it mean to be an apostle? The word comes from a Greek word meaning "to be sent." Jesus called twelve men to be His apostles and sent them to bring the message of salvation to all. He called Paul of Tarsus to be His apostle to the Gentiles. Later — in the sixteenth century — Jesus called another man, Francis Xavier, to be an apostle to India and Japan.

Spain was the birth place of Francis Xavier, the youngest son of the chief counselor of the kingdom. The private tutoring he received as a boy highlighted his great intelligence. Eventually he studied at the University of Paris, where he became a teacher of philosophy. He began a career that would bring him prestige and honor, and he accompanied it with an active social life. Ignatius Loyola, who was a retired artillery captain, was a student at the same university. Ignatius recognized the many talents that Francis possessed. He saw the fiery ambition that made Francis a great athlete, as well as a good teacher. He saw Francis's natural ability for leadership, his strong pride, and his extravagant generosity. For his part, Francis did not like Ignatius and mocked him for his life of sacrifice. Ignatius's response often came in the form of a question: "What, then, will a man gain if he wins the whole world and ruins his life?" (Matthew 16:26).

Gradually Francis saw that all the energy, ambition, and talent he was using to further his own career could be better used to teach people about the love that God has for them. He struggled with himself for a long time, trying to choose between a life of popularity, prestige, and pleasure and a life of dedication, sacrifice, and love. Finally, with five others, he agreed to join Ignatius, who started the Society of Jesus (Jesuits). With the other men, Francis took the vows of poverty, chastity, and obedience. These men wanted to serve the Church wherever there was a need. At this time, there was a need for missionaries in the East Indies, and the Holy Father mentioned that a trading ship was leaving. Ignatius assigned two of his men to go. Before the ship sailed, one of the men became ill and Francis Xavier was sent as a last minute replacement. On the five month journey across the ocean, Francis was constantly sea-sick. The food spoiled, and the precious clean water they had became contaminated with disease.

When Francis finally arrived in India, a new part of his life opened up — his life as a missionary. As he worked in this foreign land, he began to develop a system of evangelizing. Francis would always start with the children first — not the influential, the busy, the intellectual. He would go down the street, ringing a bell and gathering the children so that he could tell them stories and teach them religious songs. Then he would go to the poor, the sick, the overworked, and the prisoners. He would become acquainted with them, live among them, and gain their confidence. By the example of his everyday life, Francis introduced them to the teaching and life of Jesus. Then, when he preached, they understood his message. Francis converted thousands in India before his zeal drove him to bring Christianity to Japan.

Francis Xavier faced many problems and physical hardships during his years as a missionary. The letters he wrote speak of his busy schedule and of his loneliness. He begged for news of his brethren. In addition, many of the Christians he worked with had been robbed, butchered or carried off as slaves by pagan leaders. The foreign merchants, with their greed and cruelty, also had caused problems for Francis. But Francis continued undaunted. His zeal for Christ moved him to consider China as the next place to take Christianity. China was a cultural center, and Francis felt his life would be complete if he could also spread the Good News of Jesus to the people there.

However, God had other plans. Enroute to China, Francis developed a high fever and the sailors on the boat became frightened. They took him off and laid him on the sandy shore of a nearby island. The island was so close to the mainland of China that Francis could see it. But he was never able to get there. A fisherman found him as he lay dying, alone and abandoned, and took him to his hut. Francis died there on December 3, 1552.

His missionary spirit had been like that of the apostle Paul, who wrote: "It makes me happy to suffer for you, as I am suffering now, and in my own body to do what I can to make up all that has still to be undergone by Christ for the sake of his body, the Church" (Colossians 1:24). Francis Xavier was canonized by the Church in 1622 and declared copatron of the missions, with St. Therese of the Child Jesus, in 1927.

SUGGESTIONS

1. Invite a missionary to speak to the class about his or her experiences, or show a mission film. Permit the students to ask questions afterward, then have them discuss the following:
   • What ideas or insights on missionary life did you gain?
   • Compare missionary work now with that of Francis Xavier.
   • Have you considered a missionary life style for yourself? Why or why not?

2. Bring mission magazines to class. Have the students read through them and list the organizations they might like to support. Have the class choose one project and decide on something to make and sell (stuffed toys, stationery, cookies, etc.) to raise funds. Send the money to the organization that was chosen.

3. Have the students trace Francis's missionary journeys on a map. You might want them to compare Francis's journeys with those of Paul, the Apostle to the Gentiles.

4. St. Francis Xavier's favorite prayer was, "Give me souls." Ask the students to share their favorite prayers with the class. A prayer corner could be arranged, displaying copies of favorite prayers, small banners, and candles.

5. Write this quote on the board: "What, then, will a man gain if he wins the whole world and ruins his life? Or what has a man to offer in exchange for his life?" (Matthew 16:26). Have the students paraphrase these questions, putting them in their own words. Then have them each compose an essay, giving examples as they answer the second question.

DECEMBER 4: ST. JOHN DAMASCENE

Young John Damascene grew up in the rich, luxurious court of the Moslem ruler of Damascus. His father was a wealthy Christian court official. In order to make sure John had a good solid Christian foundation, he secured Cosmos — a brilliant Sicilian monk, who was a war captive — to train John. Cosmos schooled the boy in science and theology, in the Greek and Arabic languages, and in the culture of Islam. Then John was ready to assume a high place in the government, which he did. But since the spirit of the Moslem rulers was turning against Christians, John left his post in the government and became a monk in Jerusalem. The date of his death is uncertain. Some think he might have lived to be 104 years old.

St. John Damascene's contributions to the Church have been in the area of writing. His most famous work was called the "Exposition of the Orthodox Faith," and it told about the Greek Fathers of the Church. In his writings St. John also explained the mysteries of the Christian faith such as the Trinity, the Incarnation, the Real Presence in the Eucharist, and Mary's Assumption. St. John based many of his ideas on those of the earlier Fathers of the Church. St. John Damascene was also a poet and hymn writer. Some of his songs are summaries of the truths of faith.

St. John Damascene is most famous for his opposition to the heresy of the Iconoclasts. The Iconoclasts were a group who rejected as superstitious the use of religious images and advocated their destruction. This group was supported by the Eastern Christian Emperor Leo III. St. John wrote three defenses of the use of sacred images, explaining that the respect given them is really given to the person they represent. For all his efforts to defend the faith, St. John Damascene was made a Doctor of the Church in 1890.

SUGGESTIONS

1. To help the students understand St. John Damascene, assist them in looking up information on the Eastern churches in communion with Rome. If there is an Eastern Catholic Church in the area, have someone come in to explain this tradition.

2. The use of sacred images, which St. John Damascene defended, has always been practiced by the Church. Ask the students to take a survey in their homes to see which statues or religious articles they own. Have them ask their parents why these were chosen for their home. Discuss the place of religious art in the home.

3. Let the students listen to songs from a religious record to see how religious song writers include messages from Scripture to instruct people in their faith.

4. St. John Damascene had a great devotion to the Blessed Virgin. Pray the Hail Mary at the end of class.

DECEMBER 6: ST. NICHOLAS

Many people have chosen St. Nicholas for their patron. Greece, Sicily, and especially Russia claim him as the patron of their countries. His image appears in stained glass windows, frescoes, and carvings, and about 400 churches in England alone are named for him. Parents name their children Nicole, Nicola, Nicolette, and Nick in his honor. He is one of the most popular saints in the Church.

What is actually known about St. Nicholas? Very little. He was a fourth century bishop in Lycia, which was southeast of Turkey. How could he become so popular for so many years in so many different countries if there is so little known about him? Good question! The saints were men and women who had learned to live like Jesus by showing special love for the poor and reaching out to them. The many stories that are told about St. Nicholas usually have him helping the poor. In one he frees three unjustly imprisoned officers, and in another saves three innocent boys from death. One of the best known stories concerns a poor man who was unable to provide the usual dowries for his three unmarried daughters. Knowing they might be forced to prostitution, Nicholas devised a plan to save the situation. One night he took a bag of gold and threw it through an open window into the room where the

man was sleeping. Then he hurried away so that no one would know who had given the gold. Not long after this, Nicholas heard that the eldest daughter had gotten married. Twice after that, Nicholas tried his secret trick, and each time one of the daughters was able to marry. But on the last night that he threw a bag of gold through the window, the poor father caught him and thanked him over and over.

In the Netherlands, Germany, and Switzerland, children put out their empty shoes on the eve of St. Nicholas's feast in hopes that they will receive presents. They believe that St. Nicholas fills them. In America and England, the legend of St. Nicholas has been adapted to the modern day Santa Claus, who brings presents on Christmas Eve. How can you imitate this famous saint? Start now by secretly doing acts of kindness for others, especially for the poor.

SUGGESTIONS

1. Ask the students to make a list of acts of kindness that could be done in secret either at school or at home. Have them try to do one hidden act of kindness each day for a week in imitation of St. Nicholas.

2. Have the students research the history of St. Nicholas and Santa Claus. They may write reports or display pictures and share their findings with the class.

3. Suggest that the students make a card or bring in a treat for children in a lower grade. Then at recess time, let the students put these surprises on the children's desks.

4. Make a set of St. Nicholas cookies, or give another type of treat to your class in honor of St. Nicholas.

DECEMBER 7: ST. AMBROSE

Ambrose could give courage to bishops today! He was a zealous pastor, liturgist, champion of the poor, teacher of the faith, and a practical, fatherly priest. He had to rebuke emperors, defend his cathedral against attack, write long letters to uphold the faith, and write his own music for the Church.

Ambrose was born in Trier, Germany of a wealthy Roman family. His father was a chief officer in the Roman military. True to family tradition, he received the finest education in Rome. He must have lived in a good Christian household, because his sister soon became interested in religious life and became a nun. Ambrose decided to follow in his father's footsteps and enter political life. In 370 he became governor, with his headquarters in Milan, Italy. Ambrose administered strict and fair justice. His conduct was blameless, and he was considered a courageous leader. He was strong in his Christian faith also. Following the custom of the times, he became a catechumen preparing to be baptized as an adult.

It happened that the bishop of Milan died, and according to custom the new bishop was to be elected by the people. Ambrose attended the election for two reasons. He knew there might be disagreements in the voting, and as governor he felt responsible for keeping peace. Since Ambrose was a catechumen, he was interested in who would become the new bishop. During the election, fighting broke out — just as Ambrose had suspected. No one could agree on who the bishop should be. Ambrose stood and pleaded for peace in the assembly. During the middle of his speech, a voice cried out, "Ambrose for bishop!" Ambrose was shocked. The crowd took up the cry, shouting, "Ambrose for bishop!" Ambrose begged them not to elect him, because he hadn't been baptized nor was he a priest. But he could not silence them. Within several months he was baptized, ordained, and consecrated bishop.

Ambrose turned his attention from political government to church government. Immediately he gave a share of his family's money to the poor, and encouraged others to do so as well. He organized the bishop's household into a more simple life style and freed the place of expensive and ornate finery. He did not hide himself behind the bishop's desk. He was a pastor to his people and took a firm stand in controversial matters of Church and state. Ambrose believed that the Church was supreme in the area of morals. As bishop, as pastor of Christ's flock, he must help the people of the Church and state obey moral laws. He told the people, "The emperor is in the Church, not above it." Even the emperor must obey the laws of God.

This was not easily accepted. Ambrose was successful in opposing the group who wished to place a pagan statue of victory in the senate's court. But young Emperor Valentinian's mother, Empress Justina, was afraid that Ambrose was more popular than her son. She also supported the heretic Arius, who taught that Jesus Christ was not God. Empress Justina ordered Ambrose to give up one of his churches to the Arians for their services. Ambrose refused. "A bishop cannot give up a temple of God," he told her. The empress sent soldiers to force him. The people stood by their bishop. Soon a riot broke out as the people defended their church, and Ambrose had to be called in to bring peace.

Humiliated by her defeat, the Empress Justina did not give up. A few weeks later she sent more troops to take Ambrose's own cathedral. Ambrose refused this ridiculous request and again the scene was repeated. Again the Empress had to withdraw her troops, and she made her final try at the bishop. Ambrose received a summons to appear in court to debate the Arian bishop, but instead he stayed in the church with his people. While the soldiers who came to get him stormed about the outside, he encouraged the people to be brave and taught them songs he had written. Not one soldier dared to approach the entrance of the church. Ambrose had won again.

The succeeding emperor, Theodosius, protected the Church and got along well with Ambrose. However, when several imperial officers were brutally murdered, the emperor lost his temper and in uncontrollable grief ordered that the town be destroyed. Seven thousand innocent men, women, and children were massacred. Ambrose wrote a strong letter to Theodosius warning the emperor that he would be excommunicated if he did not do public penance. People were astounded that Ambrose did this. Would the emperor listen to the bishop? They were speechless to see Theodosius kneeling at Ambrose's feet, humbly accepting forgiveness. Never once did Ambrose glory in his victories over royalty. He accepted each person with fatherly concern. His sermons were learned, but practical enough for all to understand. Augustine, who later became a saint, was impressed by the preaching of Ambrose and was led by him to a new understanding of the Christian faith. Ambrose's writings were pastoral lessons on Baptism, Confirmation, and the Eucharist. The amount of writing he did was especially admirable in light of the busy life he led.

When Ambrose died at age sixty, he was given one of the greatest compliments a bishop could receive. He was missed by his people because he had been loved by them. Ambrose had been like Christ, a shepherd of souls.

SUGGESTIONS

1. Through the homilies of St. Ambrose, St. Augustine was led to the faith. St. Ambrose knew the importance of the Sunday homily for teaching the people about God. Encourage the students to listen closely to the Sunday homily and write down the major points. Discuss how the priest or deacon of the parish taught the people about Christ.

2. To honor St. Ambrose's feast and his skill at composing church hymns, have the class select a favorite religious song. Sing this hymn at the close of the day.

3. St. Ambrose loved the Blessed Virgin and spread devotion to her. Distribute a copy of the Act of Consecration to Mary.

> My Queen, my Mother! I give myself entirely to you, and to show my devotion to you I consecrate to you my eyes, my ears, my mouth, my heart and my whole being. Wherefore, loving Mother, as I am your own, keep me, guard me, as your property and possession. Amen

Encourage the students to pray it daily.

4. St. Ambrose insisted that the Church was supreme in morals. He spoke out in defense of the Church. Have the class give examples of issues in which the Church today must defend Gospel values. (Examples: abortion, euthanasia, human rights, marriage and the family, morality of war, racial prejudice, etc.)

5. St. Ambrose was a catechumen in the Church before he was baptized. Explain to the students that in those days some people were not baptized until they were adults. Introduce the students to the place of catechumens in the Church today, according to the Rite of Christian Initiation of Adults.

DECEMBER 8: IMMACULATE CONCEPTION

A patron is a saint or angel chosen by a person, a group, or by the Church as a protector of individuals, groups or special activities. If you received a saint's name at Baptism, the saint is your patron saint. The saint whose name you will choose at Confirmation will also be your patron saint. Patron saints show us by their example how to be open to the Lord and how to follow Him more faithfully. Countries have patron saints also. Here is a little quiz.

Who is the patron saint of Ireland? (St. Patrick.)

Who is one patron saint of Russia? (St. Nicholas.)

Who is the patron saint of the United States of America?

If to the last question, you answered, "Mary, the mother of Jesus," you are right. The people of the United States, through their bishops in 1846, asked Mary to watch over them and their country in a special way. They have chosen one particular title and feast of Mary — her Immaculate Conception.

Like a finely-cut diamond that acts as a prism, separating the sunlight into an array of brilliant colors, so Mary's life, reflecting God's grace, shows many beautiful privileges and God-given gifts. In response, she offered to God an obedient, loyal love — giving us an example to imitate.

The title chosen by the people of the United States, the Immaculate Conception, emphasizes her privilege of coming into the world free from sin. Through the power of Jesus' death and resurrection, every human being can be freed from sin at Baptism. But through that same power, Mary was always free of sin, even from the very first moment of her life. She never turned from God to do anything that He would not want. Because she always chose to do His will, she allowed herself to become a channel of His love to everyone she met throughout her life. Remembering this special privilege given to Mary, people in the United States gather together to celebrate Mass on December 8. At the liturgy, they thank God for all the blessings He has given to the people of their country. We all thank Mary for watching over and protecting our people. We pray that she will lead us to her Son and keep us faithful to His teachings. Knowing that we have a special bond with her, we pray:

> Father,
> you prepared the Virgin Mary to be the worthy mother of your Son . . . Trace in our actions the lines of her love, in our hearts her readiness of faith. Prepare once again a world for your Son who lives and reigns with you and the Holy Spirit, one God, for ever and ever. Amen.

SUGGESTIONS

1. Write to the National Shrine of the Immaculate Conception, Fourth and Michigan Avenues, Washington, D.C. 20017 for information on the shrine. Also available on loan is a 16mm film describing the shrine and its ministry: "To Him She Leads," narrated by Helen Hayes.

2. Since Mary is patroness of the United States, have the students write petitions for the needs of the country, especially for the rights and dignity of every human being. Have them make their petitions through the intercession of Mary and use them in the daily prayer.

3. Have the students cut out the capital letter "M," decorate it, and post one next to every classroom door on this feast as a reminder. They might also read the above account of the feast over the public address system.

4. Have the students design a Marian candle, using symbols of Mary such as a lily or an "M." The candle should be white to symbolize Mary's freedom from sin.

5. Ask the students to look up Scripture readings for the feast of the Immaculate Conception: Genesis 3:9-15,20; Ephesians 1:3-6,11-12; Luke 1:26-38. Have them discuss why these particular readings were chosen.

See Supplement for December 9.

DECEMBER 11: ST. DAMASUS I

Being a leader is not easy. Damasus I was elected pope at a crisis-filled time in the Church. As supreme pontiff, he tried to make progressive decisions when the situation called for them and to hold to tradition when that seemed best. While in this position of leadership, he accomplished much and suffered much.

His many projects included encouraging missionaries to spread the Good News, getting architects to restore and build churches, and developing the papal chancery. He reformed the liturgy, making Latin the official language for worship (it had been Greek), commissioned St. Jerome to revise a translation of

Scripture, and fiercely fought heresy. Devoted to the early martyrs, he restored and decorated their tombs in the catacombs.

His suffering began soon after his election. After he had been chosen, a minority elected another man, Ursinus, to be pope. Finally Ursinus was exiled, but a few years later he returned with his followers and carried out a plot to get Damasus accused of a serious crime. Only by defending himself both in civil court and in front of the forty-four bishops at a Church synod did he finally prove himself innocent of the crime.

The struggle of Damasus I reminds us that Jesus promised His followers the same kind of treatment that He received and the same final victory through His Spirit. Damasus's faith in the Risen Jesus shines out from the epitaph that he wrote for his tomb:

> He who walking on the sea could calm the bitter waves, who gives life to the dying seeds of the earth; he who was able to loose the mortal chains of death, and after three days' darkness could bring again to the upper world the brother for sister Martha: he, I believe, will make Damasus rise again from the dust.

SUGGESTIONS

1. Have the students research the terms *catacombs*, *papal chancery*, and *synod*, with attention to their historical development and modern day use. Ask them to share their findings with the class.

2. Ask the students to read John 15:18-27 and John 16:1-4 to find out what Jesus said would happen to His followers. Have the students discuss how Christ's words apply to the life of St. Damasus I.

DECEMBER 12: OUR LADY OF GUADALUPE

On the feast of Our Lady of Guadalupe, the Church celebrates Mary as patroness of the Americas. On December 9, 1531, a fifty-seven-year-old Indian, Juan Diego, saw the Blessed Mother on a hill in Mexico City. She told Juan to have a church built in her honor. When Juan went to ask Bishop Zumarraga about this, the bishop did not understand his dialect. He did not believe in his visions. Three days later Mary appeared again and instructed Juan to return bringing the bishop flowers. When he was admitted into the bishop's room, Juan opened his cloak and out dropped roses. On the cloak was an image of Mary. The bishop believed, and today a shrine is erected in Mary's honor. Our Lady appeared in ancient Indian robes to bring love and compassion to an oppressed group of people, the Indians. Mary had heard the prayers and pain of these people and she came to give them hope.

When people show devotion to Our Lady of Guadalupe, they proclaim her intercessory power — especially for the suffering and the poor. It was Mary

in her Magnificat who praised God because he has put down the mighty, exalted the lowly, filled the hungry, and sent the rich away empty. Mary's visit to Guadalupe is a reminder that God will remember His mercy for all people. People honor Our Lady of Guadalupe because they recognize her motherly concern for them.

SUGGESTIONS

1. Obtain a picture of Our Lady of Guadalupe and post it in the classroom so the students can appreciate an Indian painting of Mary. Pictures and materials may be obtained from: Our Lady of Guadalupe Foundation, 2912 Richmond Lane, Alexandria, VA 22305.

2. Mary showed through her appearance at Guadalupe that Christ brings salvation to those who are poor in spirit and live according to the beatitudes. Give the students drawing paper and have them illustrate the beatitudes as they might live them today. (Matthew 5:3-10)

3. Pope Pius XII stated that the Virgin of Guadalupe was queen of Mexico and patroness of the Americas. Have the students find out about special celebrations and customs Mexicans have to honor feasts of Mary.

4. Invite a missionary speaker to explain the missionary work being done in Latin America today and the help the Catholic Church has given the Indians.

DECEMBER 12: ST. JANE FRANCES DE CHANTAL

The feast of St. Jane Frances has been changed to August 18.

St. Jane Frances de Chantal could be considered patron of the second career. In her first career, she had been a faithful wife and mother. When her husband died, she founded a religious community. The tragedy of death that brought Jane much suffering finally led her to begin a new life of complete love.

Jane Frances Fremyot came from nobility. Her father was president of parliament at Dijon; her brother became an archbishop. Visiting tutors came to her home to instruct her in reading and writing. She easily learned to play musical instruments, and she became an excellent hostess. Since Jane's mother had died when the girl was young, Jane was expected to take on added responsibilities in society. She was mature, intelligent, and beautiful. Her personality was charming. Her life seemed almost like that of a legendary princess. She fell in love, married Christopher de Chantal, and went to live in a castle at age twenty-one. The whole household at the castle eagerly welcomed the young bride. Everything she did showed how much she loved her husband. Easily she persuaded him to have daily Mass for the servants, workers, and members of her household. Jane was an active and capable housekeeper, so she had extra time in her daily schedule to include works of charity. Not only did she care for her home and her four children — three girls and a boy — but she also nursed the sick and cared for the aged near her home. Beggars were never turned away from her kitchen.

Then Jane's ideal life was shattered. Her husband was killed by another man in a shooting accident. The couple had been married for only seven years. The loss of her husband seemed an unbearable grief to Jane, and for a while she lost interest in everything. In an attempt to get over her depression, Jane hunted for a spiritual director. Unfortunately the priest she found gave harsh penances and failed to understand her. Then her father-in-law demanded she come and manage his estate. If she didn't, he threatened to take away her inheritance. What choice did she have? The young widow took her children and her belongings to her father-in-law's house. The seventy-five year old man was tyrannical. It took humility to listen to his endless orders without complaining. Jane prayed patiently for hope and strength. She kept busy, too! During the day she would gather the children of the castle together in her room and teach them to read, count, and sew. She also told them about God and taught them their prayers.

Relief from Jane's suffering came after seven years. Her father suggested she spend Lent with her own family. A well-liked bishop, Francis de Sales, was giving a series of talks in that diocese. She went eagerly. At Dijon she could relax. In the leisurely afternoons she found time to listen to her new spiritual director, Francis de Sales. Francis was amazed at Jane's deep faith and courage. God had led her far in prayer. Francis encouraged her to seek God in a way of love, gentleness, and humility. When Jane returned home, she had a more positive outlook on life. Francis de Sales had helped her to get over her sorrow. Now she could seek reconciliation with the man who had accidentally caused her husband's death. She had been afraid to meet him before this.

As time went on Francis de Sales shared with Jane his dream of a religious community of women who would give their lives to prayer and helping the poor in the cities. Jane enthusiastically agreed to found such a community. Her family was raised and she was free to give her life to God in a different way. After much prayer, Francis and Jane decided to ask permission of the pope to start such a group. On June 6, 1610, they opened the first convent that would allow sisters to blend a life of prayer with charitable works. Jane and the twelve other women who had joined her called themselves the Visitation of Holy Mary. Jane had many times reflected on the scene of the Visitation of Our Lady's life. Mary had spent three months with her cousin Elizabeth, helping with the household tasks and planning for the birth of John the Baptist. During that time, Mary had grown in her love of God as she contemplated the child in her womb. Jane's sisters would live a life like Mary's. They would give themselves wholeheartedly to prayer. They would go into the streets and care for the poor, shelter the homeless, nurse the dying, and comfort the neglected.

At first the plan thrived. But when Francis de Sales and Jane decided to open a second convent, Cardinal Marquemont in Lyons, France, protested. He disapproved because at that time in history all sisters were cloistered and did not leave their convents to go into the world and serve. They prayed for the world. The Church was not ready for this new way of life for sisters. The cardinal did not feel people would put up with this. Jane and Francis were disappointed, but they they were willing to do as the Church asked. They had to radically change their plans and make the Visitation sisters cloistered. Eighty convents were founded before Jane's death. Jane directed her convents with the same sensible and compassionate spirit she had shown in directing her home. She had been a devoted mother to her husband and children. Now she would be a devoted mother to her spiritual daughters.

SUGGESTIONS

1. St. Jane Frances de Chantal understood what it meant to be a mother. Suggest to the students that they find a family photo album and spend some time sharing with their mothers stories of the family.

2. St. Jane Frances de Chantal had the courage to change her plans when God asked her to. Close the religion class with a prayer that all in class may see God working in everyday events. Have the students pray that they may be aware of God guiding their lives even when their plans are changed.

3. St. Jane wanted to give her energies to the poor and sick. Provide each student with a small paper that will serve as a link for a chain. Have the students write down how they can help someone in their class, neighborhoods, or families. Link the chain together. Hang it on the bulletin board to remind them of how they can help!

4. Assist the students in constructing collages of the corporal and spiritual works of mercy.

5. Read the story of the Visitation in Luke 1:39-56 as a part of a shared prayer experience with the class. Encourage students who wish to share how they think Mary and Elizabeth felt at this time and to relate it to their own lives in prayer.

DECEMBER 13: ST. LUCY

Do you remember the parable of the ten bridesmaids who waited for the bridegroom to come? Five of them brought just oil lamps and five others brought oil lamps with flasks of oil for refills. The ones who were able to keep the light burning were permitted to enter the wedding banquet with the bridegroom; the others were not permitted to enter.

Lucy, whose name means "light," kept the light of her loyal faith burning through the experience of death, and is now enjoying the eternal wedding banquet. She was martyred for being a Christian in 304 A.D. during the persecution of Diocletion. The fact that she is still mentioned in the first Eucharistic Prayer of the Mass indicates the great respect that the Church has for her.

One story about her portrays Lucy as a young Christian struggling against the pagan influences of her friends and of society. Because of her deep longing for Jesus, Lucy vowed to remain unmarried. When her fiance found out, he reported her to the government for the crime of being a Christian. She then had the opportunity to prove her faithfulness to Christ by giving her life for Him.

Lucy's feast comes during the season of Advent, when we wait for the coming of Christ our Light. Various customs have developed around her feast. In Scandinavian countries, young girls dress in white dresses with red sashes (symbolizing martyrdom). They carry palms and wear crowns of candles on their heads. In Sweden the girls dressed as Lucy carry rolls and cookies in procession as songs are sung. A Hungarian custom is to plant a few grains of wheat in a small pot on St. Lucy's feast. By Christmas there will be little green sprouts — signs of life coming from death. It symbolizes the fact that, like Lucy, we really enter new life — an eternal wedding feast — when we die.

SUGGESTIONS

1. Lucy's feast comes during the season of Advent. Have the students research Advent customs from around the world and report on them.
2. Let the students prepare and celebrate a short Advent light service. Use Scripture readings, prayers, and songs on light, and let each student light a candle.

DECEMBER 14: ST. JOHN OF THE CROSS

"Where there is no love, put love and you will find love." This statement was written by a man who loved and forgave those who had locked him in a cell six-feet-wide and ten-feet-long for nine months, with no light except that which filtered through a slit high up in the wall.

Let us look more closely at the life of this man, John of the Cross. John's wealthy Spanish father had been disowned by his family when he married a poor weaver rather than a woman of equal economic status. Living in poverty proved to be too much for him, and he died shortly after John was born. John spent much time in an institution, where he was clothed, fed, and given an elementary education. At the age of seventeen, he found a job in a hospital and was accepted into a Jesuit college. In 1563, he entered the Carmelite Order. Eventually he enrolled in another university, where he did so well that he was asked to teach a class and to help settle disputes.

When he met Teresa of Avila and learned from her about the reform of the Carmelite Order, John decided to help with it. As part of this decision, he wore sandals instead of shoes and lived very simply in prayer and solitude. In 1577 the attitude toward the reform shifted. John was caught up in a misunderstanding and imprisoned at Toledo, Spain. During those months of darkness in that little cell, John could have become bitter, revengeful, or filled with despair. But instead, he kept himself open to God's action, for no prison could separate him from God's all-embracing love. During this time, he had many beautiful experiences and encounters with God in prayer. Later, he would describe these experiences in poetry. In 1578, He escaped to southern Spain to join the southern Carmelites. There he held leadership positions and wrote reflections on his experiences which showed his deep spirit of prayer. In September, 1591, he became ill and had to move to another place. He chose to go to Ubeda where no one knew him. It was there that he died.

SUGGESTIONS

1. St. John of the Cross knew how to change painful situations into blessings by his reactions. Have the students consider some painful situations in their lives and the ways they have responded to them. Ask them if their general response has been to:
   - defend themselves
   - blame others
   - hold in anger and ignore the situation
   - acknowledge their faults
   - apologize for failures
   - ask God to show them possible causes and creative ways of responding

   Have the students prayerfully reflect on how they can respond to painful situations in the future. Conclude with the Sign of the Cross.

2. St. John of the Cross was involved in reform, in renewal. Ask the class to plan a renewal day for young teens. Have them discuss:
   - What are the goals of a renewal?
   - What are the needs of young teens?

- What could the theme be?
- What topics could be chosen for talks, discussions, or films?
- Who would be a good speaker?
- What activities would match the theme?

3. St. John was known for his deep prayer. Pass out Bibles to the students and have them spend some silent prayer time in church.

DECEMBER 21: ST. PETER CANISIUS

When you open your religion books today, think of St. Peter Canisius who wrote one of the first catechisms. Peter's father intended him to marry well and follow a legal career. But after making a retreat under the direction of Peter Faber, one of the first Jesuits, Peter Canisius decided that God was calling him to serve as a Jesuit — a member of the Society of Jesus. Peter entered the order and began his studies for the priesthood. He was a brilliant student, who easily mastered his subjects. His gifts of preaching and teaching were soon recognized, and his first appointment was rector of a college. Though Peter's gifts were mainly intellectual, he was a man of incredible physical energy. He was often seen visiting the sick or prisoners in his free time.

Bigger tasks were awaiting him at this time when the Reformation was splitting the Church. By 1552, parishes in Vienna were without priests. There had been no ordinations for twenty years, and monasteries were empty. Peter was sent to Germany, where his work for the Church won him the name "the Second Apostle of Germany" after Boniface. Peter worked tirelessly, teaching, diplomatically handling the problems of the Church, and bringing back Catholics who had fallen away from the practice of their faith. He showed gentleness and zeal in caring for the sick during the great plague. People loved him so much that he was offered the position of archbishop. Peter refused, but administered the diocese for one year.

Peter felt the need to strengthen the faith of the people. He did much scholarly writing to defend the faith. He became the advisor to Pope Pius IV, Pius V and Gregory XIII. He attended two sessions of the Council of Trent. But one of his greatest concerns was that the middle-class and the poor understand the Gospel and the teachings of the Church. For this reason, he wrote a catechism that was done in a question-answer style and included a calendar of saints and feast days. The faith was explained in a way common people could understand. Eventually this catechism was translated into fifteen different languages. Peter valued Catholic education and the Catholic press as important means for spreading the faith. His enthusiasm for the apostolic work of the Jesuits drew many vocations. He saw the need for strong, faithful priests and worked hard so that the clergy received a better education and were carefully selected. Some of his letters to Catholic leaders who showed little interest in the Church were stern and critical, yet genuinely positive. Peter lived in an age of confusion within the Church, yet he never despaired or became discouraged, because he was constantly united with Christ. When he suffered a paralytic seizure, he continued to write religious books for six more years with the aid of a secretary. For his contribution to catechesis he was made a Doctor of the Church.

SUGGESTIONS

1. St. Peter Canisius was a promoter of Catholic education. Have the students interview their parents about why they think a Catholic education is important. Let the students write up their interviews and read them to the class.

2. Have the class report on why the Jesuits are known for their high standards of education. Have them list Jesuit institutions in the area.

3. St. Peter Canisius was remembered for his writings, especially for his catechisms. A religion textbook is a way to learn about God and a tool to strengthen faith. Have the students make bookmarks for their religion books and design them with religious symbols or Scripture quotes.

4. St. Peter Canisius loyally supported the Holy Father throughout his life. Have the class include a special prayer for the Holy Father before one of their classes.

DECEMBER 23: ST. JOHN KANTY

There is a story told of the generosity of St. John Kanty. Robbers stopped him and demanded his money. He gave them all. When they left, he realized he still had two coins sewn in his cloak. John ran after the robbers and gave them the coins. The thieves were so shocked that they returned all they had taken. The story is certainly strange, but the generosity described is not. St. John Kanty was loved for his spirit of generosity.

John grew up in Poland and became a priest and teacher at the University of Cracow. He was a serious man, who taught well and quietly exercised very strict discipline upon himself. He ate no meat, slept on the floor, and rested little. Though John was hard on himself, he was patient and kind to his students — who respected and loved him in return. There were some members of the faculty who were jealous of John and had him removed. John was sent to do parish work, but he was not acquainted with these duties and felt the burden of the responsibilities. Although the people liked him for his generous and energetic spirit, John was not successful as a parish priest.

Again John returned to the university to teach Scripture. The material he taught the students was not remembered as much as the holiness of his life. Everywhere he was known for his humility and spontaneous generosity. He gave everything to the poor and kept only the clothes he most needed. Four times he made a pilgrimage to the Holy Land, carrying his luggage on his back. When John died at age eighty-three, people already claimed he was a saint.

SUGGESTIONS

1. St. John Kanty is declared patron of Poland and Lithuania. Remind the students to pray for these countries.

2. St. John Kanty was noted for his almsgiving. He knew that Jesus wanted people to give time, talents, and material goods — even to the point of sacrifice. Suggest that the students contribute money to the missions.

3. St. John showed that a person's life speaks louder than words. Encourage the students to spend extra time at home helping to build family unity just by their presence and selflessness.

DECEMBER 25: CHRISTMAS

God, Who loves us so much and Who wants our love in return, sent His Son to become Man and to make visible His love for us. He wanted so much for us to be with Him that he became one of us.

Everyone knows the story of the first Christmas — of Mary and Joseph searching for a place to stay in Bethlehem, of Jesus being born and laid in a manger, of His birth being announced by angels and indicated by a special star. His love shows itself in His becoming like us in our weakness, and in suffering all the limitations of being human. The real depth of His love, though, was manifested in the mission he came to accomplish — to suffer and die for our sins so that we might be free.

It is God's great love that the Church celebrates with sparkling lights, color, and song during this season. His love leads people all over the world to forgive, to give and receive gifts, to rejoice at being home with their families, to sing Christmas carols. People who understand this feast want to make God's love more visible in their lives. They want to be more welcoming to strangers, more caring about family and friends, more forgiving of past hurts. The angels' message of joy and peace from that first Christmas is true even today.

> Listen, I bring you news of great joy, a joy to be shared by the whole people. Today in the town of David a savior has been born to you; he is Christ the Lord.
>
> Glory to God in the highest heaven, and peace to men who enjoy his favor.
>
> (Luke 2:10-11, 14)

SUGGESTIONS

1. Have the students study the lyrics of popular, religious Christmas carols and compare them with the Gospel accounts of the first Christmas. Direct them to make a list of carols and Scripture references that match.

2. Discuss with the students spiritual (non-material) ways to celebrate Christmas.

3. Let each student prepare a scrapbook which his or her family can use during the Christmas holidays. Pages may be labeled and decorated on the edges. Possible titles for pages may include the following: Advent Events, Christmas Preparations, Family Favorites (which include the favorite cards, cookies, carols, ornaments, and gifts of each member of the family), Christmas Day, What Christmas Means to Me, How Jesus Comes through the Kindness of Others. Allow room on the pages for written paragraphs, photos, Christmas cards, and drawings.

4. Direct the students to find out how to say "Merry Christmas" in different languages. Have them share family or nationality customs for celebrating Christmas.

DECEMBER 26: ST. STEPHEN

After Pentecost, the small group of Spirit-filled Christians began preaching the Good News of Jesus and converting people throughout Jerusalem. At this time, there were two groups of Christian converts from Judaism. In one group were the Palestinian Jews who decided to follow Christ. In the other group were the Greek-speaking Jews, called Hellenists, who decided to be Christians. In the daily distribution of funds or food, the Hellenist widows felt that they were treated unfairly. The apostles really didn't have the time to take care of this problem, because they had been commissioned to preach the Gospel.

To solve the problem, they called the disciples to a meeting and had them choose men to be in charge of the daily distribution. The apostles prayed over these men, who would become the first deacons, and laid hands on them. This delegation of work freed the apostles to care for the spiritual needs of the people. At this point Stephen, a man filled with the Holy Spirit and with faith, began to attract attention. Besides his job as administrator, serving the poor, he also worked miracles and preached. As a Christian Hellenist, he worshipped in the same synagogue with the Jewish Hellenists. This group strongly resented

Stephen's preaching about salvation through Jesus. Perhaps they were resentful because he spoke so forcefully with the power of the Holy Spirit, and they always seemed to lose any argument with him. In any case, the situation became so tense that they found witnesses to falsely testify that Stephen had committed blasphemy.

Stephen was arrested and brought before the Sanhedrin. He knew that the group he stood in front of had a great deal of power and that the odds seemed to be against him. But Jesus had said, "Beware of men: they will hand you over to Sanhedrins . . . . But when they hand you over, do not worry about how to speak or what to say; what you are to say will be given to you when the time comes; because it is not you who will be speaking; the Spirit of your Father will be speaking in you" (Matthew 10:17-20). Stephen believed that he would be helped by the Holy Spirit and he wasn't afraid. His witness might also help some of the listeners to turn to Jesus.

Stephen made two major points in his speech. First, he showed that God can be found everywhere, not just in a single place like the temple and not just in a single person like Abraham. Second, he demonstrated how from the beginning the Israelites had consistently rejected God's messengers, the prophets, and God's chosen servants. And now they rejected and killed God's Son Who had been sent to them.

Those who were listening to Stephen were blinded by an anger so strong that they didn't even wait for the normal court proceedings. They rushed toward him, sent him out of town, and stoned him. His last words were, "Lord, do not hold this sin against them" (Acts 7:60).

Stephen was the first person to be killed for Christ. After his death, a bitter persecution started and many Christians fled from Jerusalem. Saul, who had approved of Stephen's death, became very active in persecuting Christians. Perhaps it was the courageous example of Stephen which eventually enabled Saul to find the strength to turn to Christ and follow Him.

SUGGESTIONS

1. The name *Stephen* means "crown." Stephen won the crown of martyrdom by being killed for speaking the truth about Christ. As he died, he forgave his enemies — following Jesus' example. Have a Forgiveness Day. Here are a few possible activities for the students:

   • Decide to say a kind word or do a kind deed for someone who has hurt them.

   • Consider if there is anyone in their lives from whom they need to ask forgiveness — someone they have hurt. Encourage them to work for reconciliation.

• Pray that they may become channels of forgiveness as Jesus and Stephen were. Write their own prayers or use this one.

   Jesus, help me to imitate You and St. Stephen. Every hurt that I have ever experienced — heal that hurt with Your love. Every hurt that I have ever caused to another person — heal that hurt also. I choose to forgive and be forgiven. Remove any resentment or bitterness from my heart and fill the empty spaces with Your forgiving love. Thank You, Lord. Amen.

2. Have the students work in groups to make mobiles of the various scenes mentioned in Stephen's speech.

3. Using Chapters 6 and 7 from the Acts of the Apostles, have the students write a skit about Stephen's life and death.

4. Show the film "Stephen, the First Christian Martyr" from *Paul and the Early Church*, Episode 2 (Roa).

DECEMBER 27: ST. JOHN THE EVANGELIST

> Something which has existed since the
>   beginning,
> and we have seen with our own eyes;
> that we have watched
> and touched with our hands:
> the Word, who is life —
>   (1 John 1:1)

St. John the Evangelist had the experience of living with Jesus — walking at His side, watching Him perform miracles, listening to His teaching, asking Him questions, sharing experiences with Him, and receiving signs of His great personal love. After Jesus had ascended to His Father, John had many memories to pass on to others.

According to Matthew's Gospel, John was sitting in a boat mending nets with his older brother James and his father Zebedee when Jesus came by and called them to follow Him. John and his brother James said yes to the call. As with so many men and women down through the ages who have welcomed the invitation to friendship with Christ, John's "yes" was the beginning of a great adventure, a truly life-changing experience.

Much of what we know of John's life comes to us through the Gospels. John and his brother James were called Sons of Thunder, possibly because of their fiery tempers. One example of this came when the people in a Samaritan town would not accept Jesus. They wanted to call down fire from heaven to destroy the town. Jesus had to correct their thinking. At another time, the two brothers secretly asked Jesus for a favor. They wanted to have the highest rank in the kingdom he was forming. They wanted more power than any of the other apostles. The other apostles were upset with them when they discovered their plot. Jesus explained to them that real greatness comes to those who serve others, not to those who act important and put themselves above others.

John was favored and allowed special privileges of being with Jesus at crucial times. With Peter and James, John was permitted to watch the miracle of Jairus's daughter coming back to life. With the other two, he witnessed the glory of Jesus' transfiguration. Jesus also invited these three to be closer to Him than the other apostles during His Agony in the Garden, when it was night and there was no show of miracles or glory.

After Jesus had sent the Holy Spirit upon the apostles, we read in Acts how John continued to respond to the challenge of Jesus' call. One day, he and Peter cured a lame beggar in the name of Jesus and were promptly arrested and kept in jail overnight. The next day the religious leaders listened to their message about Jesus' resurrection and were amazed that these uneducated fisherman were so confident and could speak so convincingly. When the leaders warned them never to teach in the name of Jesus, both Peter and John said, "You must judge whether in God's eyes it is right to listen to you and not to God. We cannot promise to stop proclaiming what we have seen and heard" (Acts 4:19-20).

At another time, Peter and John returned to Samaria to pray that the Holy Spirit would come down upon the Samaritans. This was quite a different request from the one he made earlier to call down fire to destroy a Samaritan town. Friendship with Jesus really changes a person, and John had been learning to live like Jesus all those years.

SUGGESTIONS

1. Like the other apostles, John had a close relationship with Jesus. Have the students think about their relationship with Jesus. Ask them to write a letter to Him in their journals, sharing recent experiences they've had and their feelings about them.

2. St. John used the dark/light theme in his writing. Have a light prayer service. Darken the room. Light a large candle in the center of it. Have each student hold an unlit taper. Have a student read the Prologue (Chapter 1) of St. John's Gospel slowly. At each line, have one student walk up and light his or her taper from the large candle. Open and close the service with a few verses of an appropriate song, such as "What You Hear in the Dark" from *Earthen Vessels* (NALR), "The Light of Christ" (Word of God), "Something Which Is Known" from *Go Up to the Mountain* (Weston Priory).

3. There is a story handed down from St. John. When he was very old, the people had to carry him to

where the Christians had assembled to worship. And each time he preached, he gave the exact same homily: "Little children, love one another." The people grew tired of hearing the same thing each time and they asked him if he could talk on a different topic. But he said that this is the Lord's Word, and if they really did this, they would do enough.

Have the students find quotes about love from the writings of John. Instruct them to copy one quote on drawing paper, decorate the edges, and use it as a banner. They may glue or tape yarn on the back of the paper so that it can be hung. Suggest to the students that they hang their love banners on doorknobs or other appropriate places in the school or in their prayer corners at home.

DECEMBER 28: HOLY INNOCENTS

One of the most mysterious martyrdoms in history is that of the Holy Innocents. It was well known that King Herod had a number of his family killed because he feared they might replace him. St. Matthew's Gospel gives the account of how far his persecution extended. When the Magi told Herod of the birth of the new king and how they planned to do Him homage, he was anxious to eliminate His rival king. He ordered to be killed all the male children in Bethlehem who were two years old or younger. The child Jesus was not found because an angel had warned Joseph in a dream to take the child and His mother, Mary, to Egypt. Part of Matthew's intention in telling this story was to parallel the birth of Jesus with that of Moses. Pharoah's persecution of Hebrew children is the blueprint for Herod's action. Matthew takes pains throughout his Gospel to depict Jesus as the New Moses, the giver of a New Law.

The children who were killed were called Holy Innocents. We do not know the exact number of little boys in Bethlehem when this took place. This feast of the first martyrs for Christ has been celebrated since the fourth century. The Church traditionally holds that these children were martyrs not because they died professing Christ, but because they died instead of Christ. This feast can be a consolation to any parent who has lost a child in death. It can remind them that their child shares in the glory of Jesus.

SUGGESTIONS

1. Pope Innocent III said, "He who prays for a martyr does him an injury." Discuss the meaning of this statement with the students.

2. Read the story of the Holy Innocents aloud (Matthew 2:1-18). Then read the account of Pharoah's killing of Hebrew male children (Exodus 1:15-22). St. Matthew wrote the story of the Holy Innocents because he remembered that just as God

broke the power of the Pharoah who persecuted the Israelites, so would God frustrate the plans and power of Herod. Discuss the following questions:

- Why was it important to the Jewish people that Scripture related these two stories?
- How do both of these stories show God's providence?
- When have you experienced God's providence?

3. Some children suffer because their lives are in danger from sickness. Have the students make get-well cards for children in nearby hospitals.

4. Tell the class that the Holy Innocents gave witness not by words but by their lives. Ask them to pray that they may be given the strength to witness both in word and action.

DECEMBER 29: ST. THOMAS BECKET

A deep religious experience can so change our minds and hearts that we turn from one way of life to a new and better way. Thomas Becket must have had such an experience, for he turned from being an extravagant chancellor to being a fearless archbishop. Thomas's life shows that when a person is challenged with the responsibility of serving God, he or she can and will change direction in life.

Thomas was a tall, handsome, intelligent young man who had been a legal clerk. He had a magnetic personality and made friends easily. His remarkable memory and capability in doing business attracted the eye of Archbishop Theobald, who brought him to Canterbury. Since Thomas was ambitious, he worked hard to win the trust of the bishop. More and more the archbishop noticed the outstanding qualities of the young cleric. He found him to be a master of speech and debate, and able to solve complicated problems with practical solutions. The archbishop felt he would be an able match for England's Henry II, who was a self-centered man of energy and ability. At the recommendation of the archbishop, Thomas was made chancellor of England. Thomas loved it, for he never refused an opportunity to do good. He lavishly spent his money on clothes, entertainment, hunting, and good times. The king genuinely liked his chancellor. A strong personal friendship, based on mutual respect, developed. Thomas, in his role as chancellor, exercised his duties efficiently, thoroughly, and energetically, especially in those cases involving the Church.

Henry II had one ambition in life: complete control of his kingdom — which included the Church. His genius for leadership and organization helped unite England. But he also wanted to take some powers away from the Church, and he needed a leading archbishop who would support him. Henry believed Thomas was the man who could do this. Thomas would then be Henry's ally when it came to controlling the power of the Church. When Thomas heard of the plan, he protested, saying, "If you make me archbishop, you will regret it." But Henry was king and Henry had his way. Unwillingly Thomas took up the bishop's miter as archbishop of Canterbury.

Henry did not know Thomas's conscience. Faced with the responsibility of leading the people of God, Thomas drastically changed his manner of living. To Henry's surprise, Thomas resigned as chancellor. He sold his mansion and went to live in a monastery. He sold his rich clothes and furnishings and distributed the money to the poor. The faithful servant of the king became the faithful servant of the pope. He would be a loyal archbishop at any cost. Many were amazed to see him adopt a simple and holy life style. His commanding personality was the same, but more noticeable was his generosity and determination to protect the Church. Thomas opposed Henry's taxation of the Church. He refused to allow Henry to make Church appointments that suited him and stopped any claim that the king made to control the Church.

The king had expected their friendship to continue. Now the hurt and embittered king turned on the archbishop and threatened death and imprisonment. Thomas fled to France and took refuge in a Cistercian monastery. He stayed there for six years. Both Thomas and the king appealed to Pope Alexander III. The pope tried to find a solution, but was having his own problems with the emperor and the antipope. The pope condemned some of Henry's demands, and Thomas felt he had to return to England. This was where God wanted him to defend the truth, even if it would cost him his life.

For a while there was a superficial peace between the Church and the state. Then the king again asserted his power. Henry had the bishops who supported him crown his son — an infrigement of the rights of the archbishop of Canterbury. The pope excommunicated these bishops and Thomas upheld the pope's decision. One night, in a rage, the humiliated king begged his knights to rid him of the archbishop. Four knights rode to the monastery where Thomas lived. An argument took place, but Thomas refused to change what he believed was his obedience to the pope. When the archbishop went into the cathedral to pray, the monks begged him to lock the doors. But Thomas insisted the doors remain unbolted. The knights entered the cathedral and murdered Thomas near the high altar by the bishop's chair. Thomas's last words were, "I accept death for the name of Jesus and for the Church."

The news of the murder shocked Europe. People called Thomas a saint and Henry II was forced to do public penance. Miracles were reported to occur at Thomas's tomb and many pilgrimages were made to his gravesite.

SUGGESTIONS

1. It is interesting that 400 years later another King Henry and a chancellor named Thomas should disagree over the state's interference with the Church. Have the students compare what occurred between St. Thomas Becket and Henry II with the disagreement between St. Thomas More and Henry VIII. Discuss with them what each controversy was about and its outcome for the saints and the Catholic Church in England.

2. Chaucer in his book *Canterbury Tales* immortalized the Shrine of St. Thomas Becket as a place of pilgrimage. Faithful Christians have often made pilgrimages there to petition or praise God. Discuss with the class what the purpose of a pilgrimage is and how it is made. Organize a pilgrimage to a shrine or church near by. Prepare a prayer service to use when visiting.

3. When Thomas Becket was converted, he lived according to his conscience as enlightened by the Gospels and the teachings of the Church. Have the class write down four Gospel values they feel teenagers should live. Let them keep these in a private place. Encourage them to read these as an examination of conscience daily to renew themselves in living the Gospel.

DECEMBER 31: POPE SYLVESTER I

The Edict of Milan (313) had just been issued. After years of persecution, Christians were able to practice their religion freely. The edict recognized Christianity, ended persecutions, and tolerated all religions. The Emperor Constantine was responsible for maintaining it. But Constantine did not just conduct affairs of state. He considered it his duty to also oversee the Church. He heard the complaints of bishops, summoned councils, settled Church disputes and looked upon the pope sympathetically. It took a wise man to work with such an overpowering ruler. Pope Sylvester I held office during this crucial period in history. He had to keep the Church independent of the state, and at the same time keep a precious peace with the Emperor Constantine.

Pope Sylvester I had to work under the handicap of advanced age, which prevented him from travel. To deal with the error of the Donatists, he had to send delegates to a council at Arles. He watched the aggressive Emperor Constantine call the first ecumenical council — the Council of Nicaea — in 325. Pope Sylvester I asked Bishop Osius and the priests Vitus and Vincent to attend the council in his place. This council of bishops was to discuss the Arian heresy and correct the Arians for falsely

teaching that Christ was not God. It was at this council that the Nicene Creed was formed. (The Nicene Creed as used today is based on two councils — Nicaea, 325 and Constantinople, 381 — so it is really the Creed of Nicaea-Constantinople.) **It is said that the Lateran Palace was given to Pope Sylvester I by Constantine and that he converted it into the cathedral church of Rome. Now that Christianity was practiced openly, the pope also built other churches: St. Peter's, Holy Cross, and St. Lawrence's.**

The people of Rome had a high regard for Pope Sylvester because of his pastoral concern for them. At one ceremony it was recorded that he ordained forty-two priests, twenty-five deacons, and sixty-five bishops. Later, when Christians of the Middle Ages heard that Pope Sylvester led such a hidden life, they wrote stories about him to create a more glorious image. They pictured him baptizing Constantine, curing the emperor of leprosy, seeing visions of Peter and Paul, or debating a rabbi. For all their good will in doing this, they missed the real grandeur of the man. Pope Sylvester I was a saintly Holy Father who understood the conflicts his bishops suffered in maintaining loyalty to Rome and to Constantine, humbly accepted the limitations of age and illness, and persevered in his pastoral care of the Church as bishop of Rome. His great trust in God won him his crown of victory.

SUGGESTIONS

1. Pope Sylvester I approved the Nicene Creed. Provide each student with a missalette or copy of the creed. Have the class prayerfully read the creed together. Allow the students to underline the truths that proclaim each Person of the Trinity divine.

2. Pope Sylvester I was also an architect. Help the students find pictures of the basilicas of Rome. Let the students construct these out of sugar cubes, styrofoam or cardboard. Display the finished constructions.

3. The pope promoted peace between the Church and the Roman Empire. Have the students listen to and reflect on the song "Peace Prayer" from the album *Dwelling Place* (NALR).

SUNDAY AFTER CHRISTMAS: FEAST OF THE HOLY FAMILY

A family is a special gift of God to us. A family is a result of His love made visible through the special love of a man and woman for each other. Everyone is born into or adopted into a family. We need family. We need to accept the support and love given by family members, and we need to share our support and love with them. On the feast of the Holy Family, we celebrate the family life of Jesus, Mary, and

Joseph. These three people lived for God and loved and supported each other. The Holy Family is a model for all Christian families.

The Scripture readings for the Gospel on this feast occur in a three-year cycle, which means that one of three Gospels is read on this feast. Each of the Gospel accounts has a message for today's families. The first one shows the obedience of Joseph to the angel's command to leave for Egypt, and the obedience of Mary to her husband. Just as these two parents showed fidelity to each other, so all Christian parents should live in fidelity and mutual support.

The second reading shows Joseph and Mary bringing Jesus to the temple to present Him to the Lord. There Simeon prophesies that Jesus came for both Israel and the Gentiles. Just as Joseph and Mary showed Jesus to the world, so all Christian families by their living example should give witness to Christ. The third Gospel reading tells of Jesus at age twelve coming with his parents to the temple, but not returning with them. When his parents finally find Him, He returns to Nazareth with them and lives obedient to them. In a Christian family, all family members should cooperate in a loving way. On this feast it would seem fitting for each person to take a new look at his or her own family — a look of appreciation for its strengths and a look of understanding for its weaknesses. Our attitude toward our families can be expressed in these words: "My family is my family, special to me. I want to find ways to support and encourage the members of my family."

SUGGESTIONS

1. Have the students think about what they would want most for their families. Suggest they write a prayer in their journals asking God to help their families. Close with a litany for families. The response may be, "Bless my family, Lord."

> Because they accept me just as I am, bless my family, Lord. Because they rejoice at my success and comfort me in failure, bless . . . . Because they encourage me when I'm discouraged, bless . . . . Because they share their love with me, bless . . . . Lord, I am not always grateful for my family. But today, I thank You for each one [pause to name each member] and ask you to bless their lives. Amen.

2. Suggest that during the next week the students try to spend some time with each member of their families to get to know each one better.

3. Have the students rate themselves according to the following checklist:

Scale: 1 never   4 often
        2 seldom   5 every day
        3 sometimes

1) I pray that the members of my family will grow in love for one another.

2) I do my share of the work at home.

3) I speak respectfully to the other members of my family.

4) I thank the other members of my family for the things they do for me.

5) I praise the other members of my family for the things they do well.

JANUARY 1: SOLEMNITY OF MARY, MOTHER OF GOD

When the bishops met in Ephesus in 431, Cyril of Alexandria conducted the assembly. Its purpose was to correct the errors that Nestorius was falsely teaching about the Catholic Church. Bitter controversy had raged among teachers of the Church concerning Mary's role. Who is she in God's plan? Cyril and 150 bishops opened the Council and debated the issue. They declared two things. Mary is really the Mother of Jesus and Jesus is really God. So it must be said that Mary is the Mother of God.

The Council of Ephesus declared that Mary has received the greatest privilege possible. She gave birth to Jesus, the Son of God and Savior of the world. Jesus was able to enter human history because Mary made an unconditional gift of herself to God in faith. The Solemnity of Mary, Mother of God, celebrates her faith and trust in God alone. This feast honors her because she was the faithful, believing daughter of the Kingdom of God.

The oldest Christian greeting of Mary was announced when Elizabeth called her "Mother of my Lord." When Elizabeth welcomed Mary, she proclaimed Mary's great faith. No one heard the Word of God and believed it more than Mary. For centuries Mary has been praised because she believed. She is Mother of God because of her faith in God. The Church wants us to call on Mary, Mother of God, and ask her to help strengthen our faith. She will listen and answer our prayers. The Church wants us also to imitate her faith. As we honor Mary in today's Eucharist, we rely on her to help us grow in faith and trust in her divine Son.

SUGGESTIONS

1. One of the earliest prayers to Mary is from the fourth century. A revised version of this prayer is called the Memorare. Have the students make a copy of this prayer. Encourage them to memorize it.

> Remember, O most gracious Virgin Mary, that never was it known that anyone who fled to your protection, implored your help, or sought your intercession was left unaided. Inspired by this confidence I fly to you, O virgin of virgins, my Mother. To you I come, before you I stand, sinful and sorrowful. O Mother of the Word Incarnate, despise not my petitions, but in your mercy, hear and answer me. Amen.

2. January 1 is recognized also as a day of prayer for world peace. Help the students to understand that they can work for world peace by beginning with themselves. Encourage them to make a class resolution to be kind and considerate to others at home, on the playground, and in the cafeteria.

3. The Islamic authors have always honored Mary as the mother of a great prophet. Have the class pray today to Mary, Mother of God, that she may help reconcile the wars and suffering in the Islamic nations.

4. Have each person bring in a picture of Mary. Display these on a table. Let the students appreciate how people have visualized the Mother of God.

5. When we celebrate Mary as Mother of God, we celebrate the privilege of motherhood and family. January 1 is the first day of the year. Have the students start family scrapbooks of pictures, letters, and memorabilia from family events. Tell them to add to the books throughout the year. Suggest they each write a prayer to Mary, Mother of God, to help their family and paste it in the front of the scrapbook.

JANUARY 2: ST. BASIL THE GREAT AND ST. GREGORY NAZIANZEN

Did you ever hear of a family whose members all became canonized saints? It happened in St. Basil's family; his grandmother, father, mother, two brothers and a sister became saints. Of all of them, Basil is the one most recognized. Basil received the best education possible in Caesarea, Constantinople, and Athens. He was an active man who needed projects to challenge his organizational abilities and who enjoyed a stimulating university life. It was there he met Gregory Nazianzen, a quiet and scholarly man. Basil and Gregory became close friends.

Basil had an opportunity to travel through the East and study the different types of monastic life. As a result, he decided to form his own monastic group with his own rule. Gregory gladly accepted the invitation to join him. From their frequent theological discussions, Basil was able to compose a rule of life for monks. He emphasized a community life in which time was divided between liturgical prayer, study of Scripture, and manual work. He allowed room in his rule for monks and nuns to operate hospitals, guesthouses, and do other good work outside the community if necessary. His rule was so well constructed that his principles still influence Eastern monasticism.

The two friends lived the monastic life for only about five years. Then Gregory had to return home to care for his aging father, who was a bishop. It was not unusual in those times for priests to be married. (Nor is it unusual today among the Eastern Rites.) When Gregory got home, he was ordained a priest, although he did not think himself worthy of this position. But in charity he took on the duties of the priesthood and watched over his father's diocese. In the year 374, Basil was made Bishop of Caesarea. The Church called on Basil to refute the Arian heresy, because he was a leader of great courage. The Emperor Valens had promoted the heresy, which claimed that Jesus was not God. The minute Basil took office, he went into action. He firmly believed the Church must remain independent of the Emperor and spoke out boldly in defense of the Church. He taught the truth by preaching both morning and evening to large crowds of people. He was one who practiced what he preached. When the famine struck, he divided up his money and gave it to the poor. He organized a soup kitchen and served the people himself. Basil even went so far as to build a town, which included a church, a hospital, and a guesthouse.

Busy as he was, Basil kept up his letter writing. He chose who would be ordained, assisted with prison reform and warned leaders when their punishments were too harsh. He corrected priests and bishops who were giving scandal and advised his relatives as to what subjects to take in school. He continued to write for the Church, to oppose the Arian heresy, and to clarify the doctrine of the Trinity and the Incarnation. Basil realized that if truth was to triumph over heresy, there would have to be faithful bishops in every diocese. When one town, known for its fighting and intrigue, was falling away from the faith, Basil turned to his friend Gregory for help. He ordained Gregory bishop and sent him there. Gregory went unhappily because he was a man who disliked conflict. This appointment caused a rift between the two friends, but they were later reconciled.

When the Emperor Valens died, the Arian power was weakened, but it had had a serious effect on the Church. Constantinople was a city that had been under Arian leadership for thirty years. The bishops of the surrounding areas begged Gregory to come and restore the community of faith, and again he went dreading the task. While there, Gregory transformed his house into a church and preached powerful and inspiring sermons on the Trinity. The people called him "the theologian." Gradually he brought back the true faith.

Basil and Gregory worked unceasingly for peace and unity in the Church. Both were misunderstood and misrepresented, but in spite of this, they rebuilt the faith. When Basil died at age forty-nine, he was mourned even by strangers and pagans. Gregory resigned from Constantinople because of the opposition against him and spent his last years reading, writing his autobiography, and enjoying his gardens.

SUGGESTIONS

1. Both Basil and Gregory were defenders of the faith. List on the board the following words and ask the students to explain a little about each.

Incarnation	Catholic Church
Theological Virtues	Creed
Prayer	Ten Commandments
Heaven	Trinity
God the Father	Beatitudes
Jesus Christ	Sacraments
Holy Spirit	Blessed Mother
Rosary	

   Praise the students' efforts at recognizing some of the basic teachings of their faith.

2. Show the students that the Church still defends the faith. The pope writes encyclicals. The bishops publish pastoral statements. Bring in some of these publications and display them. Even though they may be too difficult for the students to understand, it is good that they know about them.

3. Basil and Gregory loved their faith and were willing to suffer for it. Have the students write a personal act of faith on good paper and design the page. Hang these in the classroom.

4. Read this selection from Basil's writings to the class:

   > The bread you do not use is the bread of the hungry; the garment hanging in your wardrobe is the garment of him who is naked; the shoes that you do not wear are the shoes of one who is barefoot; the money that you keep locked away is the money of the poor; the acts of charity that you do not perform are so many injustices that you commit.

   Have a time of silent prayer to reflect on this. Then discuss its meaning with the class.

JANUARY 4: ST. ELIZABETH ANN SETON

Who was the first person born in the United States to be declared a saint? Who opened the first American Catholic parish school and established the first American Catholic orphanage? Who founded the first native American religious community of women? The answers to all of these questions are the same — Elizabeth Ann Bayley Seton.

Born two years before the signing of the Declaration of Independence and the Revolutionary War, Elizabeth Bayley grew up in exciting times. Her parents handed on to her their own convictions. Her father, a prominent New York physician, did not attend church, but by his example he taught his daughter to love and serve the poor. Her mother and later her stepmother were devout Episcopalians who communicated to Elizabeth the value of prayer, Scripture, and nightly examination of conscience.

Elizabeth's education and training also prepared her for life in New York high society. So it wasn't surprising that at the age of nineteen she married a handsome, wealthy business man, William Seton. Furs and satins, frequent parties and plays, an abundance of friends and money — all were a delightful part of the young couple's married life together. But their relationship was not a superficial one. Will and Elizabeth were very much in love and deeply devoted to each other. They loved their five small children — three girls and two boys.

Everything went well until 1803, when Will Seton's business went bankrupt and his health failed. The Filicchi family in Leghorn, Italy invited Will, Elizabeth, and their oldest daughter Anne to visit, so that Will could recuperate in the warm, sunny climate. The other children were able to stay with relatives.

The boat trip over was rough, but no one expected that the landing would be even rougher. Because there had been a yellow fever epidemic in New York before the Setons left, the police in Italy took the Setons to an old fort that was being used for sick people. The Italian government stated that if after six weeks in the fort the visitors did not come down with yellow fever, they would be allowed to enter Italy. Will, Elizabeth, and Anne were taken to a single stone room with a tiny window, a small fireplace, and a mattress in the corner. Will Seton, already very ill, had to lie in the cold damp room day after day. Elizabeth, with the help of a Filicchi servant, nursed him as much as she could. She watched helplessly while the man she loved and had shared so much of her life with grew more and more ill. Besides Will, she had to keep Anne healthy and busy. Finally they were released, but in a few weeks Will was dead.

Elizabeth, widowed at thirty years of age with five small children and many medical bills to pay, returned to New York. If she ever needed help from her relatives, now was the time. But there was a conflict. While she was in Italy, the Filicchi family had taught her much about the Catholic faith. Back in New York she began to attend St. Peter's, the only Catholic church in the city. Her relatives were very upset with her actions. They felt that Catholics were uneducated, poor, lazy, and ignorant — not a group with which they wanted Elizabeth to associate. But Elizabeth felt that she should become a Catholic, and in 1805 she made her profession of faith and was welcomed into the Catholic Church. When she chose to become a Catholic, her family and many friends turned against her, and she found herself on her own.

Having received from her father the belief that every individual has many riches which can be brought out through education, Elizabeth tried to start a school. After a few dismal attempts, she finally opened a girl's Catholic boarding school in Emmitsburg, Maryland. Women with the same vision, the same ideals, came to help Elizabeth, and the school grew. In 1812 Elizabeth Ann Seton and these other women made vows and became a religious community, the Daughters of Charity of St. Joseph. They chose to wear the mourning dress of a widow as their habit. From this time on, the Daughters of Charity have been expanding — serving in hospitals, homes for the aged, orphanages, homes for the mentally handicapped, and in schools.

What became of Elizabeth's children once she became a religious sister? Elizabeth realized that God had given her the children to cherish and raise, and she continued to guide them. Her two sons entered the navy, Anna became a nun but died at an early age, as did Rebecca. Catherine eventually became a Sister of Mercy, working with those in prison.

On September 14, 1975, Pope Paul VI declared Elizabeth Ann Bayley Seton a saint of God. She who had been a wife, mother, widow, and consecrated nun was one who gave an authentic and dynamic witness to future generations that being a saint is still possible.

SUGGESTIONS

1. Have the students research the Daughters of Charity of St. Joseph to find out about their apostolate and their growth. Encourage the students to read one of the many books written about the life of Mother Seton.

2. Show the filmstrip "Mother Seton" (Don Bosco) or "Elizabeth Ann Seton" (OSV) and let the students discuss it.

3. Divide the class into groups. Give each group several strips of long paper, two inches wide. Have each group divide up the events of Elizabeth Seton's life and create their own filmstrip on the saint.

4. Have the students make a mobile using symbols for the different experiences and roles that Elizabeth Seton had, and for the places she lived. Ask students to take one finished mobile to each class in the building and explain the story of Elizabeth Seton's life. Or have the students take their mobiles home and explain her life to their families.

5. Elizabeth Ann Seton always considered herself a mother. She never stopped praying for her children or trying to help them. Have the students interview their mothers on being a mother. Give them time in class to brainstorm for possible interview questions, such as

• What's it like to be a mother?

• What goals do you have for your children?

• What do you see as a mother's role in passing on the Christian faith to her children?

JANUARY 5: ST. JOHN NEUMANN

He was short. People called him the stubby priest and laughed when they saw him riding his horse, because his feet did not touch the stirrups. He was not very good-looking — a square face, a square body. He was quiet, not a man with a vivacious personality, not one to charm a crowd or draw attention to himself. He was not the type of Church leader who pleased influential people. But John Neumann was a man of God who was also true to himself, and he did the best job he could do.

Born and educated in Bohemia, John was interested in botany and astronomy as well as Church matters. By the time he was twenty-five, he knew six languages and was a trained seminarian. Since there were many priests in his country, and since he longed to be a missionary in America, John came to the United States in 1836 — with one suit of clothes and one dollar in his pocket.

The bishop of New York ordained John and sent him to the hardworking German-speaking people who were clearing the forests around Niagara Falls. He traveled on horseback from mission station to mission station, visiting the sick, teaching catechism, training teachers to take over when he left. He was busy with his many responsibilities, but very lonely at times. He felt the need for the fellowship of community life and for the spiritual challenge that living with other priests might bring.

So John entered the Redemptorist Order. As a novice, he was sent to different places so frequently that he wondered if the superiors really wanted him. Finally they allowed him to make his vows, and he became the first Redemptorist to be professed in the United States. He helped in parishes until he was made the superior of the American branch of the order. While John felt very unqualified in this position, it was due to his direction that the Redemptorists became leaders in the parochial school movement. He served as a parish priest in Baltimore until he was made bishop of Philadelphia in 1852. There was great opposition to his appointment.

The influential, wealthy Catholics wanted someone who would make a good impression: one who would speak eloquently and act the part of a refined and polite gentleman. They wanted a bishop who would look the other way when he saw their unchristian practices. The Irish wanted a bishop who was Irish, who was one of their own kind. Those who were unhappy with John did not seem to care that he was a prayerful, sincere follower of Jesus. They did care that he spoke with a thick Bohemian accent in a plain style. They cared that he was very quiet and strict and did not have the graciousness of the wealthy. He received a very cold reception when he went to Philadelphia. While it hurt him deeply, John decided that he would just be himself and do the best job he could. He knew that God would not ask any more than that. But his resolution did not make the criticism stop.

He also found himself confronted by the Know-Nothings, a powerful political group. This group was determined to deprive foreigners and Catholics of their civil rights. To achieve their goals, they burned convents and schools. Between the Catholic and the non-Catholic attacks, John became so discouraged that he wrote to Rome requesting to be transferred to a smaller diocese. He thought that maybe someone else could do a better job in this position. But the highest Church authority in Rome told him to stay at his job — which he did! He stayed and contributed a great deal to Catholic education. In eight years, Philadelphia grew from two Catholic schools to a hundred schools. He organized the Catholic schools on a diocesan basis. Every year he made a visit to each parish and mission station, hoping to start a Catholic school in each place. He brought in many teaching orders of sisters and Christian brothers. For the German immigrants, he published two catechisms and a Bible history in German. He wrote many articles for Catholic newspapers and magazines.

In 1863, he died of a heart attack while walking down the street. After his death, people publicized his many hidden virtues and penances. This short, unassuming, often unpopular man who worked so hard for God was declared a saint on June 19, 1977.

SUGGESTIONS

1. John Neumann lived in the United States between 1836 and 1863. Have the students research other developments in the Catholic Church at this time, especially the Catholic school system in other parts of the country. Tell them to look for significant historical events that may have influenced the growth of Catholic schools. Then allow them time to share their information with the class.

2. John Neumann would not have been an effective leader or an honest person if he had tried to live up to the unrealistic expectations of others instead of being true to himself. He used his own gifts and talents in the best way he could without being envious of other people's talents. Suggest that the students make a list of all the things that others expect of them. Have them put a check next to the ones that would make them more like Jesus.

3. John Neumann started the Forty Hours Devotion (now known as Eucharistic Devotion) in the parishes of the United States. Have the students find out how their parish celebrates the Eucharistic Devotion and how they can take part in it.

4. John Neumann's major contribution to the Catholic Church was in education. Let the students make posters or write essays that explain

how their school is giving them a good Catholic education — helping them to learn Christ's message, live in a faith community, and serve others as Jesus did. The posters may be displayed in the school hall or parish church on Sundays. The essays might be published in a newsletter to the parents.

JANUARY 6 OR THE SUNDAY BETWEEN JANUARY 2 AND JANUARY 8: EPIPHANY

The solemnity of the Epiphany of the Lord is considered to be one of the oldest feasts of Christianity. It was celebrated as far back as the second century in the Eastern Church. In the East, the feast meant the adoration of the Magi, the baptism of Christ, and the miracle at Cana. At each of these events, there was some manifestation of Christ's divinity. This is what Epiphany means, "manifestation, revelation." In the West, the feast came to mean the visit of the Magi. Here it refers to God being made known in the person of Jesus to the Magi, who represent all nations. St. Matthew records the event in his Gospel. Some astrologers — advisors to Eastern kings — traveled to Jerusalem from the east. They followed a star that they believed would lead them to an infant who would be King of the Jews. When they found the child with His mother, they fell on their knees and offered Him gifts of gold, frankincense, and myrrh. The Fathers of the Church later interpreted these gifts to be symbolic of the royalty (gold), divinity (incense), and Passion (myrrh) of Christ.

The readings for the feast emphasize the universality of God's power, love, and presence to all people. Jesus is Light of the Nations — all nations. Jesus has come for all because there are no limits to His love, and He will bring all people to His Father.

The feast reminds us that we are responsible for sharing the Church's gifts, especially the gift of Christ to the world. Our outlook is to be ecumenical. We are to reach out in prayer, sacrifice, and active charity with the vision that God's kingdom is for everyone.

SUGGESTIONS

1. Matthew's Gospel contains themes of proclamation (God is with us!), acceptance (God is welcomed!), and rejection (God is rejected!). Let the students read the account of the Magi (Matthew 2:1-18) and show how these themes are carried out.

2. Let the students sing songs about the Magi: "As with Gladness Men of Old," "We Three Kings," "Shepherds and Kings," "Do You See What I See?", "Winter, Cold Night," "Come Weal, Come Woe," or "Song of Good News."

3. Share crown-shaped cookies as an Epiphany treat.

4. It was a custom in the Middle Ages to remember the feast of the Epiphany by writing the date with blest chalk above the doorways. You may wish to have a priest do this over the classroom doorway. Have the students look up Epiphany customs used around the world and share this information with one another.

5. At first the early Church considered Epiphany a day to celebrate three feasts: Adoration of the Magi (Matthew 2:1-18), the Baptism of Jesus (Mark 1:9-11), and the Miracle at Cana (John 2:1-12). Let the students read each of these accounts. Give the students each three circles and have them attach the three circles together. Post the "Epiphany" symbols.

6. Encourage the students to see Carlo Menotti's "Amahl and the Night Visitors" (the Magi), which is usually on television during the Christmas season.

SUNDAY AFTER EPIPHANY: BAPTISM OF JESUS

Have you ever attended an inauguration or seen this ceremony on television? When a president of the United States has been newly elected, he participates in a formal ceremony of inauguration and presents an inaugural address. In this speech, he explains his role in leading the country and shares his hopes and his plans for the future. Jesus' baptism was similar to an inauguration. One day Jesus was standing in a crowd listening to John the Baptist. John always challenged his listeners to turn their backs on their sinful way of life and turn to God. A sign that a person really wanted to live according to God's way was his or her public baptism by John. When a person stood beside John in the water, everyone in the crowd expected that person to change for the better. After all the people had come forward that day to be baptized, Jesus came forward. This was confusing to John the Baptist. He knew that Jesus did not need to change the way He was living. But the Gospel records that when Jesus was baptized, a very important thing happened: some signs showed that the Father and the Spirit were in intimate connection with Jesus.

Jesus was anointed for His mission just like Isaiah had written: "The spirit of the Lord has been given to me, for Yahweh has anointed me" (Isaiah 61:1). Jesus used the rest of that quote to explain His mission when He spoke to His neighbors at Nazareth:

> He has sent me to bring the good news to the poor, to proclaim liberty to captives, and to the blind new sight, to set the downtrodden free, to proclaim the Lord's year of favor.
>
> (Luke 4:18-19)

Jesus, Who did the work of the Father, was always one with the power of the Father and the Holy Spirit. After His rising from the dead, Jesus sent the Holy Spirit upon His apostles and disciples at Pentecost. Then, under the Spirit's power, their work of spreading the Good News of Jesus began.

Jesus' baptism by John was His inauguration for His mission to save all people from their sins. This mission would result in Jesus' passion and death on the cross, to be followed by His resurrection from the dead. The Gospel records that on His way to Jerusalem, He spoke about His passion and death as a baptism. "There is a baptism I must still receive, and how great is my distress till it is over!" (Luke 12:50). The source of grace received in Christian baptism is the death and resurrection of Christ Jesus. Through the power of the Holy Spirit, we have been baptized into Christ's death (the death that saved us) and have become God the Father's adopted children. As baptized members of the Christian community, we also have a mission — to spread the Good News of Jesus by the way we speak and act. When we celebrate the feast of Jesus' baptism, we can also celebrate our own initiation, our own baptism.

SUGGESTIONS

1. Have the students write "eye-witness" accounts of Jesus' baptism, using one of these Gospel accounts as a basis: Matthew 3:13-17; Mark 1:9-11; Luke 3:21-22. Have them choose to be a particular person at the event: John, sinner, passer-by, newly-baptized.

2. Ask the students to discover as much as they can about their own baptismal day. Have them design a poster or collage which illustrates the important facts and the interesting details of their special day. Have them bring in pictures and other remembrances. Take time for each person to share his or her findings with the class.

3. Have the students list the symbols used in the rite of Baptism: signing on the forehead, candle, water, oil, (catechumen and chrism) white robe, etc. Discuss with them the significance of the symbols. Finally have each student design a prayer card for a newly baptized person, using the symbols of baptism and the words: "You have been baptized in Christ."

4. At the end of the lesson, let the students renew their baptismal promises, following the formula used at the Easter Vigil or at the Mass for Confirmation.

5. The Rite of Christian Initiation for Adults (RCIA) is gradually being reintroduced into the life of the Church. This rite was originally used in the early Church as a process of conversion and preparation

for Baptism, Confirmation and Eucharist. To familiarize the students with this rite:

- Assign different students to research and report on the various rites of the catechumenate: entrance, exorcisms and blessings, rite of election, etc.
- Ask students to find examples of different baptismal fonts in pictures or in actual churches. Discuss what the design and decoration say about the Church's understanding of Baptism.
- Have students discover how their particular parish meets the needs of those who wish to join the Catholic Church.
- Have students interview someone who has been involved in the RCIA to discover more about it. Allow them to share their findings with the class.

6. Show the filmstrip "The Sacraments of Christian Adult Initiation" from *Signs and Sacraments* (ROA). Have the students share new information or insights.

See Supplement for January 6.

JANUARY 7: ST. RAYMOND OF PEÑAFORT

Religious vocations sometimes come late in life. Raymond entered the Dominican Order at age forty-seven. He already had achieved a career as a successful lawyer, university teacher, and vicar of a diocese. This brilliant man, who already had given example to priests with his zeal and charity to the poor, now became a beginner, a novice, in the Dominican Order. Raymond was serious about his new life and begged his superiors to give him a penance to make up for any sins of pride he may have had in his earlier career. He was surprised at their response. They made him a writer! The Dominicans asked him to compile a thorough coverage of the correct administration of the Sacrament of Penance. It was an enormous task. It took Raymond about the length of four books to write it. His writing covered sins committed against God and neighbor, and it gave examples of how to handle questions of conscience. This book became a valuable resource book for priests.

But Raymond longed to do more for God with his life. One of his desires was to be a missionary and convert the many Jews and Moors living in Spain at the time, but his life was not to go that direction. Pope Gregory IX noticed his abilities and called him to Rome to be his confessor. He also asked Raymond to collect all the decrees of popes and councils from the past eighty years together into one volume. This book was called the "Decretals," a book that contained material similar to Canon Law. Raymond's work was accurate and valuable to the Church. The pope was so pleased he told Raymond that he was going to be made an archbishop. The shock of this news was so great to Raymond that he became ill. He pleaded with the pope to let him return to Spain as an ordinary friar to study, pray, and preach. The pope agreed, and Raymond returned to his Dominican friary in Spain.

Three years later he was surprised to learn that his own friars had elected him the third master-general of the order. This time he had no choice but to obey. While in office, Raymond revised the rules of the friars and made them clear. He also visited all the houses where the Dominicans lived.

After two years he asked to resign. Finally he was able to spend the next thirty-five years in an apostolate to the Moors and the Jews. He lived to be nearly one-hundred years old. It was through his writings on Church laws that he had the greatest influence.

SUGGESTIONS

1. From Raymond of Peñafort we get an appreciation of Church law. Have the students list and explain the duties of Catholic Christians.

2. Pope Gregory IX, the pope Raymond advised, wanted to make sure no heresy infected the Church. He had the Dominicans set up an organization called the Inquisition. Have the students look up this organization and discuss its advantages and some of the problems it raised in the Church.

3. Raymond of Peñafort was the third master-general of the Dominicans. The Dominicans have a special role in Christ's Church. They are especially dedicated to prayer, study, and preaching. Have the students look through the Church calendar to find names of other saints who are Dominicans.

4. Raymond of Peñafort contributed much to the understanding of the Sacrament of Penance. Have the students find different acts of contrition the Church suggests for the Sacrament of Penance. Let them pick their favorite one and copy it. Encourage them to pray it before going to bed at night.

5. Raymond was able to influence Pope Gregory IX to receive, hear, and take care of the petitions of the poor. Point out to the students that by setting an example of generosity, they can help others to become more aware of the needs of the poor.

JANUARY 13: ST. HILARY

When Hilary was born to pagan parents of Poitiers, France in 315, no one would have labeled him "disturber of the peace" or realized he would be exiled. After a thorough training in the classics and philosophy, Hilary married. He and his wife had one daughter, Afra. All who knew Hilary said he was a friendly, charitable, and gentle man. Hilary's studies led him to read Scripture. He became convinced that there was only one God Whose Son became man and died and rose to save all people. This led him to be baptized a Christian, with his wife and daughter.

The people of Poitiers were impressed with the example of Hilary and chose him to be their bishop in 353. He was a scholar, an administrator, a pastor and a bishop who spoke out against Arianism. He warned the people of this heresy that denied the divinity of Christ. When the Emperor Constantius II wanted him to sign a paper condemning St. Athanasius, the great defender of the faith, he refused. The emperor was furious and exiled him to Phrygia. In exile he did even greater good through his preaching, writing, and suffering. During this time, he even asked to debate the Arian bishops. Fearing Hilary's strong arguments, Arian's followers begged the emperor to send Hilary home. The emperor, believing Hilary was also undermining his authority, recalled him. Hilary's writings show that he could be fierce in defending the faith, but in dealing with the bishops who had given in to the Arian heresy, he was very charitable. He showed them their errors and helped them to defend their faith.

Though the emperor called him "disturber of the peace," Saints Jerome and Augustine praised him as "teacher of the churches."

SUGGESTIONS

1. St. Hilary guided Martin of Tours. A holy person can bring another person to spiritual greatness. Have the students share experiences in which their actions have strengthened another or another has strengthened them.
2. Love of his faith directed St. Hilary's life. Have the students make banners on faith, using appropriate Scripture texts and symbols.
3. St. Hilary had strong faith convictions and defended the faith fearlessly. Ask the students to read what St. Paul teaches Timothy about the faith in 2 Timothy 1:6-14.
4. Review with the students who their bishop is. If you have a picture, show it to the students. Discuss the good things the bishop of their diocese has done.

JANUARY 17: ST. ANTHONY

God calls each person to follow a particular way to holiness. To some the life style of St. Anthony may seem unrealistic and uninviting. But Anthony's example and message are still important for anyone who wishes to know God.

Anthony was born in Egypt, 250 A.D. He disliked school and its social atmosphere. At age twenty, when his parents died, he did not welcome the thought of taking care of a large home and property. He had

heard the Scripture reading, "Go sell all you have and give it to the poor," and had decided to take the advice literally. First Anthony made sure his younger sister's education could be completed in a community of holy women. He then sold all his possessions and left for a life of complete solitude in the desert. There Anthony found an elderly hermit who taught him about a life of prayer and penance. For twenty years, he lived in isolation. Anthony wanted to know God deeply. He did penance by taking only bread and water once a day at sunset. The devil appeared to him in many terrible shapes to tempt him during these years. But Anthony had developed great confidence in God, Who has power over the evil one. Anthony's unusual life did not make him harsh, but instead made him radiant with God's love and full of caring and compassion.

Stories of Anthony's holiness spread, and people began to come to come to the desert to learn from him how to become holy. There was a freshness of spirit and energy to his teachings. Many stories and sayings grew up around this desert monk, and they were written down to teach people how to live holy lives. One story was about three men who would go and visit Anthony every year. Two would discuss their hopes, their future, and their spiritual life with Anthony. The third never said anything. After this went on for many years, Anthony said to the third man, "You often come here to see me, but you never ask anything." The man replied, "It is enough to see you, Father."

Some admirers who came wanted to stay, so Anthony — at age fifty-four — founded a type of monastery consisting of scattered hermitages near one another. Anthony wrote a rule that guided the monks in a life of silence, prayer, and manual work. Later when Anthony heard of the persecutions of the Christians by the Emperor Maximinus, he wanted to die a martyr. At age sixty, he left the desert to minister to the Christians in prisons, fearlessly exposing himself to danger. While doing this work, he realized that a person can also die daily for Christ by serving Him in ordinary ways with great love. So he returned to the desert to his life of prayer and penance. However, his life of solitude was again interrupted when at age eighty-eight he had a vision in which he saw the harm Arian followers were doing to the Church by denying the divinity of Christ. To refute this heresy, Anthony left for Alexandria to preach against it. During this time Anthony worked miracles and won converts.

When the Emperor Constantine wrote Anthony asking him to pray for him, people were impressed — but Anthony wasn't. He explained, "Don't be surprised that the emperor writes to me. He's just another man as I am. But be astounded that God should have written to us, that He has spoken to us by

His Son." At age ninety, another vision sent Anthony searching the desert for St. Paul, the first hermit. Together these two holy men met and spoke of the wonders of God. Anthony is said to have died peacefully in a cave at age one hundred and five. The impact he left on the world is tremendous. Anthony taught us that through solitude and penance we do not move away from those in the world, but come closer to them.

SUGGESTIONS

1. Anthony reminded the world of the need for solitude. Plan a "hermit time" for the class. Take the students to church for a silent fifteen minutes. Allow them to read from the Scriptures, write in their journals, or read the life of a saint. Encourage them to share what they learned from their solitude.

2. It is said that Anthony triumphed over the power of the devil many times by just making the Sign of the Cross. Explain to the students the value of the Sign of the Cross. We make the Sign of the Cross before we pray to compose ourselves and let our minds and hearts think of God. In temptation we make the Sign of the Cross to be strengthened. It is also a sign of blessing that God may sanctify us. In addition to professing our faith in the Trinity, Incarnation, and Redemption, the sign is an act of offering ourselves to God: we give Him our intellect (forehead) and will (breast or heart) — the two powers of the soul — and our entire body. Ask the students to be conscious of these things when they make the Sign of the Cross. Encourage them to slowly make the Sign of the Cross immediately on waking each morning. Have them make it reverently at the end of class.

3. Anthony found out that God doesn't want everyone to die in persecutions. God sometimes asks the daily martyrdom of hidden, unrewarded kindnesses and sacrifices. Remind the students to quietly offer up any difficulties for love of God.

4. Anthony found that as he would stop during his manual work to think of God, his love of God grew stronger. Teach the students several ejaculations, such as, "My Jesus mercy," "My God I trust in You," "Jesus, Mary, Joseph." Encourage them to pray one silently during the day.

JANUARY 20: STS. FABIAN AND SEBASTIAN

Persecution in one form or another touches people in all walks of life, of all age groups and backgrounds. Fabian was a pope and Sebastian, supposedly, was a soldier in the civil army. What do they have in common? Both were faithful followers of Christ, faithful until death.

The traditional story told about St. Sebastian is that he was an army officer who was condemned to death for his belief in Jesus. His fellow soldiers shot him with arrows. Surviving this, he was clubbed to death. The only actual fact we have is that Sebastian was an early Christian martyr under the reign of Emperor Diocletian. More is known about the life of St. Fabian, who was pope in 236 when the political situation was very unstable. Philip, an ambitious and ruthless man, killed Emperor Maximus and made himself emperor. Later he regretted his own violent behavior, and changed the government policy from persecution of Christians to tolerance for Christians. He even gave Fabian permission for Church authorities to own property. For the first time, being a Christian was officially legal. But this easy life for the Christians did not last long.

Philip was killed by his own lieutenant, Decius, who became the next emperor. Decius believed that his empire could be saved only if the pagan customs of ancient Rome were restored. He reversed Philip's policy by sending an edict which commanded the death penalty for all who would not give up their following of Christ. Pope Fabian quickly showed to whom he gave his loyalty by eagerly dying for the faith. Following his example, many Christians died as martyrs. However, the years under Philip had softened the dedication of many of Jesus' followers. In a moment of terror, many denied their faith in Christ.

Decius was pleased. He hoped that without a pope and with so many Christians defecting, the Church itself would disband and then disappear. But he didn't realize that a power stronger than the power of human beings was protecting the Church. Jesus said, "And know that I am with you always; yes, to the end of time" (Matthew 28:20).

SUGGESTIONS

1. The early Roman persecutions produced many martyrs for the Church. Have the students make word searches or word puzzles using the names of martyrs. Let them switch puzzles with one another and work them.

2. Have the students choose roles and act out a scene form the life of St. Fabian. Choose students to be Fabian, Emperor Decius, the emperor's messenger who announces the edict, faithful Christians, soldiers who arrest Christians, unfaithful Christians, and soldiers who question and intimidate the Christians. Include a scene in which the Christians try to encourage one another in being loyal to Christ.

3. Ask the students to imagine that they are living during a time of persecution. Have them consider what their response would be if they were arrested

for being a follower of Christ. Tell them to write a short story about the situation and their response. Let them share the stories with the class or post them.

JANUARY 21: ST. AGNES

Love is stronger than death. One of the most famous and well loved martyrs showed this. St. Agnes, a thirteen-year-old girl, gave her life willingly for Christ in the third century. She preferred death, so that she could remain a bride of Christ.

The traditional story of Agnes assures us that holiness does not depend on age. Agnes was beautiful, and many men wanted to marry her. She refused each one because she had decided to remain a virgin. One of her suitors was so angry he reported to the governor that she was a Christian. The governor summoned Agnes to the palace. He threatened her with punishment and showed her the tortures they would use on her body. Agnes looked at the instruments of torture with heroic calmness. The governor had her sent to a house of prostitution to be tempted. All of the men who saw her courage were afraid to touch her. One who looked at her lustfully was struck blind, but Agnes prayed for him, and he regained his sight. The governor seeing that she could not be persuaded had her condemned and executed. St. Ambrose wrote that she went to the place of execution more cheerfully than others go to their wedding.

SUGGESTIONS

1. St. Agnes is often pictured with a lamb at her feet. Ask the students to find out what symbols their saints are pictured with. Have them enlarge these symbols and display them in the classroom or at home.

2. St. Agnes has her name in the first Eucharistic Prayer. There are six other women listed with her. Have the students look in the missalettes to find the names of the other saints. Encourage them to do some research on these women to find out why they are honored as saints also.

3. It is said that the blood of the martyrs brought life to the early church. Persecutions spurred growth. St. Agnes' courage helped strengthen the courage of others. Have the students write on cards how they can grow in Christian courage and place these cards by the Bible. Then let them plant a seed in a pot and place it by the Bible. As the class checks the seed's progress, point out that the slow, steady growth of the plant symbolizes their slow, steady efforts to grow in Christian courage.

4. St. Agnes, one of the most popular saints, has always been regarded as a special patron of purity. Encourage the students to pray to her in times of temptation.

JANUARY 22: ST. VINCENT

The traditionally told story of St. Vincent is unexplainable, and to some people it sounds impossible. But for Vincent all that he suffered was possible because of his great love for God. St. Augustine praised Vincent in one of his sermons, and centuries later the glorified accounts of his sufferings were gathered to form this story.

Vincent was trained and ordained a deacon by Valerius, Bishop of Saragossa, Spain in the third century. These were dangerous times to be a Christian, for the Roman emperors had written edicts which made being a Christian punishable by death. When the Emperor Dacian discovered Bishop Valerius holding Christian services, he had him imprisoned. Vincent, too, was caught visiting the bishop and put in prison. The emperor refused to give food to either of them. Both men were so cheerful and strong in suffering imprisonment that the emperor banished Bishop Valerius and had Vincent tortured on the rack. Vincent accepted and endured this suffering for love of Christ. Seeing that the torturers had failed to weaken Vincent's courage, Emperor Dacian ordered the torturers to be beaten.

Dacian then told Vincent he would spare his life if he would hand over the sacred books to be burned. Vincent refused, and in fury Dacian ordered Vincent to be roasted on the gridiron. Again Vincent suffered this patiently and survived. It is said that Dacian wept with rage and had Vincent thrown in a dungeon filled with broken pottery. Vincent was so calm and heroic that he converted the jailor. The emperor, at his wits' end, finally had Vincent confined to a regular prison. Friends of Vincent came to console him, cleanse his wounds, and pray with him. Vincent died there in the bed his friends had made for him. From the story of Vincent's sufferings and death, we can learn much about the spirit of Christian courage. Here is a man who welcomed pain, suffering, and death as a chance to show his love for Christ. We can pray to St. Vincent for the grace to love Jesus Christ as he did.

SUGGESTIONS

1. Vincent served as a deacon. Invite a deacon in to explain his role in the Church.

2. Have the students read Acts of the Apostles 6:1-7 to discover the role of deacons in the early Church. Make a chart comparing their role with the role of deacons today.

3. Encourage the students to write a cheerful, understanding letter to someone they know who is suffering or lonely.

4. Suggest that the class imitate St. Vincent and try to suffer patiently and uncomplainingly any difficulty they meet during the week.

JANUARY 24: ST. FRANCIS DE SALES

Francis de Sales was a man who knew how to multiply his efforts. In a variety of circumstances, he used fresh ideas and creative approaches to spread the kingdom of God to the widest number of people in the most effective way. Francis, the eldest of thirteen children, was born into a family of nobility. His father, who wanted him to be a man well versed in the arts, sent him to study at the University of Paris. After six years, Francis was intellectually competent in many different areas. Besides his studies, Francis was a skilled swordsman who enjoyed fencing, an expert horseman, and a superb dancer. Once he returned home, he realized that his father wanted him to study law and choose a career with the state.

So Francis studied at the University of Padua and received a doctorate in civil and canon law. When his studies were finished, he discovered that his father wanted him to marry. But through his studies, Francis had gradually grown in a life of prayer and desired to share the love that he had for God with other people by being a priest. His father finally consented that Francis become a priest when a cousin arranged for the bishop to give Francis a priestly position of dignity. Francis was ordained to the priesthood in 1593.

Francis and his cousin Louis, who was also a priest, volunteered to work among the people in Chablais, where religious wars were taking place. They visited homes, preached the Word of God, and sought new converts. The work went so slowly that after four months Louis became discouraged and left. Then Francis needed to multiply his efforts. Trying a new tactic, he began to write and distribute a weekly essay, explaining some doctrines of faith. For two years, he and his friends had these essays printed and they passed them on to as many people as they could. Why was this a new tactic? It is difficult to understand when we realize how much printed material on religious matters we have today. In Francis' time, however, the printing press was thought to be mainly a means of preserving the best thoughts of the past. It only gradually occurred to people that it could be used to evangelize, to bring new ideas to the people and to encourage them to follow Christ in the Catholic Church.

Another talent that Francis began to utilize was his gift for public speaking. He preached with power and charm in a simple, clear language. His gentleness and love were so appealing that he drew many hearts to God. The final result of his printing and preaching was that the majority of the Chablais inhabitants accepted the Catholic faith.

When Francis was appointed bishop of Geneva, he discovered other ways to multiply his efforts for the Lord. First, he did much for the formation of priests. He not only wrote for and encouraged the active priests, but he also took an interest in candidates for the priesthood. He even conducted the preordination examinations to see if the candidates were fit for this vocation. By working with the priests, Francis helped form good leaders who in turn would guide the people of God to a greater dedication to their Christian calling. Second, he gave lay people an active part in spreading the kingdom. When visiting each parish, he instructed the people, administered the sacraments, and set up catechism classes for the young people. The classes would be held every Sunday and holy day, and he trained lay people for the role of teaching them. To help people grow in their relationship with God, Francis often had individual conferences with them and gave spiritual guidance.

In 1610 Francis helped St. Jane Frances de Chantal found the Visitation convent, where religious women found a way to pray and sacrifice for God's kingdom. Once again his efforts were multiplied, this time by all the sincere women who joined that order.

To reach more people, Francis wrote a book called "The Introduction to the Devout Life." This book, written in a simple, clear style, shows that everyone can grow in holiness — not just priests and nuns. Among his other writings is another very important book called "Treatise on the Love of God," which is his own story, the history of his own love for God.

For his writings, Francis was declared a Doctor of the Church and the patron of journalists and writers. He is also well known for the gentleness and patience that he showed to everyone, no matter how tired he was or how bothersome the person was. In his many dealings with individuals, he followed the words of Jesus: "Shoulder my yoke and learn from me, for I am gentle and humble in heart. . . ." (Matthew 11:29).

SUGGESTIONS

1. St. Francis de Sales is the patron of Catholic journalism. Have the students bring in a variety of Catholic periodicals, newspapers, and pamphlets. Encourage them to research various organizations involved in the ministry of publishing Catholic material. Allow the students to make a display of current Catholic literature.

2. St. Francis is the patron of writers. Have the students compose a class prayer to St. Francis which they could recite before they begin their daily English composition class. Have them make copies to put in their composition notebooks.

3. Francis was creative at multiplying his efforts for the spread of the kingdom of Christ. Ask the stu-

dents to think of a way they haven't tried yet. Encourage them to share their ideas and to try one of them soon.

4. Francis once wrote, "You can get more flies with honey than you can with vinegar." Have the students paraphrase this quote and then think of examples that prove it to be true.

JANUARY 25: CONVERSION OF ST. PAUL

"And for anyone who is in Christ, there is a new creation; the old creation has gone, and now the new one is here" (2 Corinthians 5:17). Paul was able to write about a person being caught up in a new creation because he himself had a life-changing experience. He encountered the Risen Christ, and his whole life was transformed by that one meeting.

Paul, who was also called Saul, had two names because he belonged to two societies. As a Roman citizen, he was given the name Paul. He lived in Tarsus, which was a bustling city and a center for Greek culture. The Greek influence appears in Paul's letters when he writes about wrestling, military drills, parades, and games. As a Jew of the tribe of Benjamin, he was called Saul. Under the watchful eye of his Jewish parents, Saul learned the strict traditions of the Pharisees. At the age of five, he probably knew the basic content of the law. At the age of six, he may have started school in the synagogue and studied the Scriptures. If he followed the usual pattern, he went to the temple college in Jerusalem at the age of fifteen and studied under an excellent teacher. Most rabbis then married and learned a trade. While Paul never had a wife, he did learn the work of tent-making and used it later on in life.

Because of his strict Jewish upbringing, Saul viewed Christianity as an evil force, the enemy of Judaism. After he watched St. Stephen murdered for his faith, Saul became a leader in the movement to stamp out Christianity. He never did things halfway. He was given spies, temple soldiers, and legal authority. Zealously he went into homes and dragged Christians to prison.

Then one day, when he set out from Jerusalem armed with letters to harass Christians in the Damascus community, a strange thing happened. As he was journeying on the road, a great flash of light appeared and he fell to the ground. He heard a voice say, "Saul, Saul, why are you persecuting me?" "Who are you, Lord?" he asked, and the voice answered, "I am Jesus, and you are persecuting me" (Acts 9:4-6). At this moment, the resurrection of Jesus overwhelmed him. Jesus is alive! He is risen from the dead! And somehow Jesus is present in His Church and in the Christians whom Saul was persecuting. Saul had planned to enter Damascus powerful, commanding, and strong. He actually entered Damascus led by the hand of one of his companions because he had been blinded by the experience. He came helpless, and then followed the Lord's orders to find Ananias, a man who would arrange for his baptism and cure him of his blindness.

Paul, now a Christian, still did not do things halfway. For three years he lived in the Arabian desert. This was a period of training for him. It was a time during which he went through the process of letting go of his old way of thinking and allowed the new life of Christ to be built up within him. Intellectually and emotionally, the process of conversion continued and his knowledge of the mystery of Christ deepened.

From Arabia, Paul returned to Damascus to preach that Jesus was the Son of God. The Jewish community was confused because they knew Paul's reputation. They had expected help in destroying Christianity. Seeing that he was a traitor, they plotted to kill him. Discovering the plot, Paul had the disciples lower him in a basket over the city wall so that he could escape!

Then he went to Jerusalem to meet the apostles, but they were afraid of him. At first they thought he might be playing a trick to find out about the Christians before he would try to destroy them. Barnabas bravely welcomed Paul and introduced him to Peter and the other apostles. Now they decided to trust him, and Paul stayed there — preaching fearlessly in the name of Jesus.

This account is only the beginning of the mission which St. Paul accomplished in the Church. From the Acts of the Apostles and his letters, we can gain an idea of the scope of his journeys, the extent of his writings, the intensity of his suffering and his joy. Throughout his Christian life, Paul lived up to the words that the Lord had said about him at the time of his conversion, ". . . this man is my chosen instrument to bring my name before pagans and pagan kings and before the people of Israel" (Acts 9:15).

SUGGESTIONS

1. Let the students rewrite the incident of Paul's conversion, putting the story in a modern setting. Or they may write the story of the conversion of someone they know or someone they have read about.

2. Have the students fold a sheet of paper in half. On one side, have them write two diary entries that might have been written by Paul before his conversion experience. Post the results.

3. Have the students think about any times in their own lives when they received a "mini-conversion," a new insight into God or themselves, e.g., after celebrating penance, during a tragedy, while praying quietly. Suggest they write about the experience in their journals.

4. Let the students dramatize the story of Paul's life up to and including his conversion. Or have some students prepare a dramatic reading of Paul's conversion (Acts of the Apostles 9) and present it to the class.

5. Have the students choose a scene from the story of St. Paul and illustrate it. Cut out the pictures and mount them on a frieze.

JANUARY 26: STS. TIMOTHY AND TITUS

Reading the Acts of the Apostles and letters of Paul is like sitting back and watching a dramatization of the growth of the early Church. Bishops were ordained, customs were established, conversions occurred, and guidelines were set down. Saints Timothy and Titus lived in the early Church around the time when the apostles were dying and the Gentile Christians were beginning to take roles of active leadership.

Both Timothy and Titus knew St. Paul well and were his travelling companions. They were bishops of newly converted communities, but the role of bishops was not so clearly defined as it is today. They were not specifically attached to just one community; rather they administered a large area and travelled in and out of a number of the Christian communities.

Timothy was from a "mixed" marriage. His father was a Gentile and his mother was Jewish. Timothy had studied the Scriptures as a young man and was converted by Paul, who was on a missionary journey to Lystra in Asia Minor. Paul was in need of a travelling companion at the time because Barnabas and Mark had just left him. Timothy was willing to help and did important work for Paul. He was ordained to the ministry and sent as a representative of Paul's to the Thessalonians, Corinthians, and Ephesians. Acting as envoy for Paul was difficult, because he sometimes met trouble in the communities. However, Timothy proved himself capable enough for Paul to make him bishop of Ephesus. Paul wrote several pastoral letters to Timothy, but he also praised Timothy's enthusiasm and example. It is in the letters of Paul to Timothy that some description of a bishop's role is given. Timothy was told that as a bishop he was to correct innovators and teachers of false doctrine. He was the one to appoint bishops and deacons.

Timothy must have been a good friend of Paul because Paul begged him to come to comfort him in prison in Rome. Seeing Paul's courage in suffering must have been a consolation to Timothy because he was later to undergo martyrdom himself. Timothy opposed pagan festivals and was killed by the pagans with stones and clubs.

The other young bishop and companion of Paul was Titus. A mention of Titus is found in one of Paul's letters to the Corinthians. He tells that he had gone to Troas and was worried because he did not find Titus there. He then went to Macedonia where there was trouble among the Christians. Paul writes, "But God comforts the miserable, and he comforted us, by the arrival of Titus . . ." (2 Corinthians 7:6). There was a depth of friendship and an apostolic bond of preaching the Gospel that Paul had with this Gentile Christian, Titus. Paul's trust in Titus's competence as a peacemaker and administrator was evident. Titus restored obedience and smoothed out difficulties between the Corinthians and Paul. He organized the Church in Crete as its first bishop. He corrected abuses, appointed bishops, and seemed to carry out his work for the Church in an energetic, efficient, and decisive manner. Titus died in Crete when he was ninety-three.

Both of these bishops were given instructions by Paul for teaching and governing the Christians. Under their fatherly guidance and example, the early Church grew stronger. Their feast is fittingly celebrated the day after that of their great friend, Paul.

SUGGESTIONS

1. Let the students look up the following descriptions Paul gives of his traveling companion, Timothy: 1 Corinthians 4:17, Philippians 2:19-20, Romans 16:21, and 2 Timothy 1:4-5.

2. Have the students read the letters of Paul to Timothy and Titus. Ask them to list the characteristics of a good bishop.

3. Have the students write an imaginary "unwritten" chapter of the adventures of St. Paul, which include Timothy and Titus.

4. Let the students make book jackets for the letters of Timothy or Titus. Have them write a short summary on the back of the jackets.

5. Conduct a class discussion of how the roles of bishops are the same or different from the time of Timothy and Titus.

JANUARY 27: ST. ANGELA MERICI

"Convert the woman and one converts the family," said St. Angela Merici. Her goal was to help the Church and society by restoring strong Christian family life through good education of future wives and mothers.

Angela did not have a perfect family life herself. She was orphaned early in life. She lived for some years with her uncle's family and grew into a simple, charming woman of good looks and capable leadership abilities. Her faith led her to become a member of a Third Order, to dedicate herself to good works and to prayer. Angela received a vision in which it was revealed, "Before your death, you will found a society of virgins at Brescia." For ten years Angela waited patiently for God to help her know what to do. A sign came when the Patengoli family invited her to Brescia to keep them company because they had recently lost two sons in death. After she lived in Brescia for a short time, her eyes were opened to the needs of the city. Deprived girls were unable to get an education, for only rich people and nuns were educated. This distressed Angela. She began catechetical work for these girls, but the task was overwhelming for one person.

At fifty-seven years of age, she formed a religious group of twenty-eight women who thought as she did. Angela decided to call her group the Company of St. Ursula. St. Ursula was the patron of medieval universities, and Angela had great devotion to this saint who was a leader of women. The work Angela undertook was difficult because women in religious communities at that time were not permitted to leave their convents to teach or nurse except in emergencies. Men's communities such as the Dominicans and Franciscans already were actively engaged in such charitable works, but women's orders were not. Angela's dream was to use education as a means for building up the faith and for social reform. Christian education would lead to strong Christian families, and the good moral values of these families would help the Church and society.

To accomplish her dreams, Angela's sisters received permission from Rome to live in their own homes and devote themselves to every type of corporal and spiritual work of mercy, with emphasis on education. They would teach young girls to read and write, and prepare them for what they needed to know about a Christian home and marriage. Her sisters wore lay clothes and met once a month for a day of prayer and discussion on their ministries.

Forty years later St. Charles Borromeo asked the sisters to become a religious community and to live together in a convent rather than in their own houses. Gradually they began to wear distinctive habits and were known as the Ursulines. St. Angela was the first to form a religious order of women that served God outside the cloister. Her vision of serving God in an active manner was followed by many groups of religious women who teach, nurse, and minister for the kingdom.

SUGGESTIONS

1. When St. Angela first formed the Company of St. Ursula, they were not a religious community. Today they might be called a secular institute. Have the students look up the meaning of "secular institute" and find out what these groups do for the Church today.

2. Today there are many communities of women who actively minister in the Church. Have the students list the names of the communities they know and the ministries in which they engage.

3. If there is an Ursuline community in the area, invite a sister to speak to the class about the life and spirit of St. Angela.

4. Let the students find out about a Third Order and the requirements for membership. *The Official Catholic Directory* would have information about local groups.

5. Have the students make a list of all the birthdays and anniversaries in their families. Encourage them to post this list in their bedrooms and remember to do something cheery for each family member on his or her special day.

6. St. Angela's goal was the re-Christianization of family life. Have the students check the Sunday bulletin to see what their parish does to strengthen family life.

7. Review with the students the spiritual and corporal works of mercy. Ask them to select one that they could practice in their families that week. Suggest they write in their journals how they practiced this work of mercy.

JANUARY 28: ST. THOMAS AQUINAS

The name St. Thomas Aquinas brings to mind one of the world's most intellectual, scholarly, and influential theologians. Yet St. Thomas was the first to insist that his learning was due more to prayer than to genius.

St. Thomas came from a wealthy, ruling family. At age five he was sent to a Benedictine monastery at Monte Cassino in hopes that someday he would be abbot. But King Fredrick II was having military troubles and sent his troops to occupy the monastery as a fortress. Thomas then transferred to the University of Naples. It was there that he came into contact with the Dominicans. Their life style of prayer and study fascinated him and he was determined to join them. His family was shocked that Thomas, who was a nobleman, would join a group of poor friars. His mother sent his brothers after him, and they pursued, kidnapped, and imprisoned him for over a year at a family castle. Nothing would shake his resolution to enter the Dominicans. Finally his family gave up and in 1244 he joined the order. For the next years, he gave his energies to studying, teaching and writing.

Thomas first studied under Albert the Great, and he profited immensely from the scientific precision of Albert's studies. But he preferred theology. Thomas is well known for his writings in philosophy and theology. His most famous work, "The Summa Theologica," contains five volumes of Thomas's thought on all the Christian mysteries. It is said that no one has equalled the depth of understanding and the clear reasoning that Thomas showed. He was a brilliant man and had extraordinary powers of concentration. He reportedly never forgot anything he read, and he had the ability to dictate to four secretaries at the same time on different subjects. But this intellectual giant of a man was very humble. He prayed often and acknowledged that all his gifts came from God. While saying Mass on December 6, 1273, he received a revelation from God. After that, he stopped writing completely. Thomas said that all he had written was so much straw after what he had seen.

This great man of God died at age forty-nine on his way to the Council of Lyons, France. Pope Gregory X had asked him to come. He had been an advisor to kings, a writer of masterpieces, a counselor to popes and a teacher of classics. But most of all, Thomas was a servant of God.

SUGGESTIONS

1. Pope Leo XIII declared St. Thomas patron of Catholic schools. Have the class compose a prayer to St. Thomas and read it over the PA as a morning prayer at school.

2. Some organizations have an Aquinas talk. A speaker will present a talk on faith or Scripture. Invite a member of the parish or the parish priest to come to talk to the class.

3. Encourage the students to pray to St. Thomas to help them in their studies.

4. St. Thomas is a Doctor of the Church, often called the "angelic doctor." Have the students find out why he is called this.

5. Ask the students to find out why the discipline of study is a characteristic of the Dominican Order. Why did St. Dominic believe this was important?

JANUARY 31: ST. JOHN BOSCO

With the industrial revolution in Europe came a major change in society. Hundreds of orphaned or destitute boys flocked to the cities in hope of finding work. They lived poorly — six or seven of them crowded in a small room. They were paid little and worked long hours. With the absence of family or religious training, these boys often turned to petty thievery. John Bosco could have lived like that if it hadn't been for his hardworking and devout mother.

John was the youngest son of a peasant family. His father died when he was two, so he was brought up by his mother. The family lived in extreme poverty and there was no possibility for higher education.

Once when the family went to hear special sermons for the Holy Year, a priest, St. Joseph Cafasso, noticed John's intent face as he listened to the homily. The priest questioned John and discovered he had a remarkable memory. When he heard that John wished to be a priest, he encouraged him to enter the seminary. John was excited, and with shoes and clothes provided by charity, he arrived at the major seminary in Turin. The seminary proved to be a perfect place for John's charismatic personality to emerge. John was a natural leader and gifted with initiative.

St. Joseph Cafasso and one of his friends saw John's talent for working with youth. They showed him the jails and slums of Turin and encouraged him to use his gifts to keep the young people out of trouble. During this time John met a poor orphan, sixteen-year-old Bartholomew Garelli. He gently questioned the boy to discover if he had been to Mass. Bartholomew didn't even know what it was. John had a talk with the boy and asked him to come back and bring some friends.

This is how John Bosco's famous Sunday expeditions began. John felt that poor city boys needed contact with God's creation. He would gather a group of young boys together on Sunday and take them into the country. The day would start with Mass, which was followed by breakfast and outdoor games. The afternoon would include a picnic, a catechism lesson, and closing evening prayers.

The groups grew larger because the young men loved him. They could tell he genuinely loved the boys. His fatherly manner of dealing with them made each boy feel needed and important. John had a gift for handling difficult boys without corporal punishment. He respected every boy as a person and used gentle effective discipline. He wanted the boys in an environment that would help them to be good. He felt faith should be the framework in which they studied, worked, and prayed — so Sundays were not enough.

In 1850, after overcoming numerous difficulties, John was able to get a house for himself and forty boys. His sensible and generous mother was persuaded to be the housekeeper. John Bosco opened workshops to train boys to be shoemakers and tailors. He believed every boy should know a trade and be proud of it. By 1856 there were 150 boys in residence. At John's oratories, places where the boys lived, John made sure every boy got a religious education. He encouraged them to receive the sacraments often. Because he understood how active teenagers are, he taught them to play musical instruments, to perform in plays, and to engage in sports. Often when John would go into the villages to preach and celebrate the Sacrament of Penance and the Eucharist, he would take along boys to provide entertainment in the evening. His reputation as a preacher became well known. He wrote and printed books on Christian faith for boys, using his own printing press.

John lived during times of political trouble in Italy, when the state did not favor the Church. For four years, assassins were after him. Once they tried to shoot him while he was teaching, and at other times tried to poison him and attack him on the street. But so successful and honest was John's work with boys that even those who were enemies of the Church changed their minds and supported him.

In 1859 John started a religious congregation that would serve the Church by helping poor boys. John Bosco admired Francis de Sales so much that he named the group the "Salesians." By the time of his death, this group had grown to over 1000 members serving in Italy, France, England, Argentina, Uruguay, and Brazil. Today there are two provinces in the United States. No matter how urgent the demands of the immense projects John Bosco had started, he remained calm, unhurried, and gentle. He was never impatient, but always ready to talk to a boy, hear a confession, or leave in the middle of the night to go to a sick bed. He could do this because John had a realistic approach to life combined with a deep trust in Providence.

When John Bosco died, 40,000 people came to his wake. He is often called the patron saint of boys.

SUGGESTIONS

1. The Salesian fathers are an international community, as are the Salesian sisters. Have the students find out if the work of these priests and sisters is similar to that of John Bosco.

2. John Bosco believed in the power of Catholic journalism. There is a company which publishes audio-visuals with this aim in mind. View one of the Don Bosco filmstrips from the series *Famous Men and Women of the Church.*

3. St. John Bosco always considered himself a friend of youth. Conduct a John Bosco hour. Have the students invite a younger class over to their classroom for games or a student dramatization of a life of a saint. Perhaps a treat could be provided.

4. St. John Bosco had a devotion to Mary, Help of Christians. He had a basilica built in her honor. When the contractor started to build the church in 1863, John made his first payment. "Here is all I have," he said, "but Our Lady will provide what is necessary for the church." He put in the man's hand forty cents. The rest of the money came. John's trust in Mary and in God's Divine Providence led him to do great things. Have the students dedicate their day to Mary, Help of Christians, by singing a song in her honor.

5. When John Bosco was in the seminary, he started a club called the Cheerful Club. No one was allowed to say or speak in an unchristian way. Each one had to do his studies and be cheerful. Try John Bosco's club in the classroom for one week.

FEBRUARY 2: PRESENTATION OF THE LORD

Forty days ago we celebrated the feast of Christmas, the birth of Jesus. According to the law of Moses at the time of Christ's birth, for forty days after the birth of her son, a woman was excluded from public worship. Then, on the fortieth day, she would bring an offering of a pigeon or a turtledove to the temple. It was also customary to bring an offering of thanksgiving and praise to God for the safe birth of the child. This offering would be a young lamb or, if the couple was poor, another pigeon or turtledove could be substituted. And so we read that when Mary and Joseph went to the temple for the purification, they took the child Jesus to "be consecrated to the Lord," and they offered a pair of turtledoves or two young pigeons, the offering of the poor. They were careful to observe all that the law required. This ceremony was an act of deep love for them. In the Gospel of Luke we read that there was a man named Simeon in the temple of Jerusalem at that time, a man "upright and devout . . . . It had been revealed to him by the Holy Spirit that he would not see death until he had set eyes on the Christ of the Lord" (Luke 2:25-26). When Simeon saw the child Jesus, he took the child into his arms and prayed, "Now, Master, you can let your servant go in peace, just as you promised; because my eyes have seen the salvation which you have prepared for all nations to see, a light to enlighten the pagans and the glory of your people Israel" (Luke 2:29-32).

A light for all to see. The coming of Jesus was like a light breaking upon a dark, sin-weary world. Another name for this feast is Candlemas. Candles are blessed on this day, and the liturgy suggests that after the blessing there be a candlelight procession representing the coming of Christ as the Light of the World. Today is a good day to remind ourselves that we, as Christians, are to be lights in this world.

The name of this day's feast has gone through several stages. In the fourth century in Jerusalem, the feast was celebrated on a different date and was called simply "the fortieth day after the Epiphany." By the sixth century, it was known in the Eastern Church as "the meeting of Jesus and Mary with Simeon." By the seventh century in Rome, it was named the "Purification of Mary." But the central act of the feast brings it the current title of the "Presentation of the Lord in the Temple." At the present time throughout the world, today's feast celebrates Jesus' offering of Himself to His Father as the Savior of all people. The symbolism of the Jewish feast, emphasizing the purifying of the mother and the buying back of the child, has been given a greater meaning. As the chosen one of God, Mary did not need the rites of purification. As God's Son, Jesus did not need to be "consecrated" or ritually "redeemed." But by the mystery of God's plan, Mary and Jesus showed obedience to the Mosaic laws.

SUGGESTIONS

1. Discuss with the students the difficulties involved in obedience. Point out that in Jesus and Mary, we have a clear example of obedience.

2. Have the students participate in the blessing of the candles and in the procession in the parish if possible. Recommend that they check to see if their families have any blessed candles available at home. If not, encourage them to get some for the family.

3. Remind the students that this feast is also recalled in the fourth Joyful Mystery of the Rosary. Pray it together with the class.

4. Have the students read and act out the Presentation from Luke 2:22-40.

5. Inform the students about the many customs that surround the celebration of this feast. In Europe, if the weather is bad and the skies are cloudy on Candlemas, it means summer will come early. If the sun shines for most of the day, then forty days of cold and snow are expected to follow. In America, the weather predictions associated with Candlemas have been ascribed to Ground Hog Day, also occurring on February 2.

6. Have the students decorate large candles for the blessing. They might use flowers, holy pictures, or liturgical symbols. The decorations can be glued onto the candles, or, if the students are making their own candles, the decorations can be sealed right into the wax.

7. Sing songs written about Christ the Light: "We Are the Light of the World," "Christ Is the World's True Light," "The Light of Christ," "I Am the Light," "The Lord Is My Light."

FEBRUARY 3: BLASE

If you are already familiar with St. Blase, it is probably through the blessing of throats — a tradition on his feast. Various stories about St. Blase and actual episodes in his life have been woven together to form the picture we have of him.

Blase was the bishop of Sebaste (now in central Turkey). He was martyred sometime around 316, under the persecutions of the Emperor Licinius. About four hundred years after his death, various stories began to be told about him — especially in France and Germany, where he became very popular. According to tradition, Blase had been a doctor before he was ordained a priest and later a bishop. When the persecutions broke out, he fled to the mountains and lived the life of a hermit. Here he cured and tamed the wild animals. One day, hunters discovered Blase and took him back to the Governor Agricolaus, who sentenced Blase to death. Many people came out to see him on his way to prison. A woman ran up to Blase and pleaded with him to cure her son, who was choking to death on a fish bone. Blase prayed over the boy, who was cured. Later in prison, Blase was condemned to darkness, but a friend secretly brought him some candles. (The candles used for the blessing of throats remind us of these wax tapers smuggled to Blase in prison.) Blase was cruelly tortured and finally beheaded.

Blase is the patron of those with throat diseases. He is also invoked to protect animals against the attacks of wolves. In fact, he is patron of wild animals, woolcombers, and wax makers. In some areas, people pray to him for fair weather, too.

We are often concerned about our physical ailments. But there are spiritual ailments that should be of great concern to us, too. If we call on St. Blase to protect us from sickness of the throat, let us also call on him to help us speak the truth at all times. Today and always, let our words be true and kind, reflecting the goodness and kindness of God our Father.

SUGGESTIONS

1. Blase is one of the Fourteen Holy Helpers. This list of "helpers" originated sometime during the Middle Ages and contains patrons for almost every aspect of life. Have the students look up these Fourteen Holy Helpers. Then have them choose two or three saints they want to have as their personal friends on earth. Ask them to write an explanation of why they chose the particular saints and how these saints will be good "helpers."

2. In Europe there is a custom of giving blessed bread on this day. This bread is referred to as St. Blase sticks. According to custom, a person eats a piece of this bread when experiencing a sore throat. Today, rather than having students share bread, encourage them to donate money so that bread or other foods may be purchased and given to the poor.

3. The blessing of the throats with two candles fixed together to form a St. Andrew cross began during the sixteenth century. After providing an explanation of the purpose of the blessing, have the

students receive the blessing of the throat. It is important that the students understand that a blessing demands an openness of faith on their part.

FEBRUARY 3: ST. ANSGAR

You don't have to be considered successful to be a saint. Some saints, like Ansgar, whose feast we celebrate today, worked very hard, but lived to see their work destroyed and their efforts proved apparently fruitless. Ansgar was born in France around the year 801. He entered the Benedictine Order and became a powerful preacher and teacher. He was sent as a missionary to Denmark, where for three years he worked and ministered to the people — but with little success. When Sweden asked for missionaries, Ansgar again set out, this time with another monk. On the way, the missionaries were captured by pirates and suffered many hardships before they finally reached Sweden. Less than two years later, Ansgar was recalled and made bishop of Hamburg. For thirteen years, Ansgar worked and prayed in Hamburg. He was known for his excellent preaching, his great love of the poor and the sick, and his humble, prayerful life. He gave his all to his people, leading his flock to Christ. But he was to know yet another suffering. In 845 Hamburg was invaded by the Northmen and burned to the ground. Ansgar then saw the people return to paganism. But still he continued.

Ansgar was a true missionary, who knew his call was to preach the Good News and to care for the people — even if his efforts never seemed to be rewarded. Ansgar was appointed archbishop of Bremen in 848 and in 854 he began new missionary work in Sweden and Denmark. Deep in his heart, he carried the desire to give his life for his faith, to show his love through martyrdom. But he died peacefully at Bremen in 865. After his death, Sweden again returned to paganism.

Many people can look at the life of Ansgar and see one defeat after another. Yet God does not look at life that way. God reads the hearts of us all. He knows the love we have and the reasons we act as we do. Ansgar was a winner in all the things that really matter in life — in love and devotion, sacrifice and prayer, in the giving of self to God and to others. May we remember the life of Ansgar, the "Apostle of the North," and be winners in Christ.

SUGGESTIONS

1. Point out to the students that there are various spellings of this saint's name: Ansgar, Anskar, Anschar. Those wishing to do additional research may need to check these alternate spellings.

2. Have the students locate Denmark and Sweden on a map. Ansgar was made the papal legate for the Scandinavian missions in 832.

3. Ask the students to recall a time in their lives when they seemed to be unsuccessful at something for which they had worked very hard. What did they learn from the experience? Review with the students the meaning of Divine Providence, God's loving concern for us that brings good out of all that happens. Help the students discern this Providence in their own lives through reflective prayer.

4. Have the students reflect on those things that really matter in life by reading Matthew 25:31-40.

FEBRUARY 5: ST. AGATHA

She is the patroness of nurses, foundrymen, miners, jewellers, and even Alpine guides. She is invoked against fire, earthquakes, famine, thunderstorms, and volcanic eruptions. In Italy her feast day is celebrated with firework displays. Who is this saint? St. Agatha.

Many stories are told of Agatha. According to these, she was born of noble parents. Her reputation for loveliness and kindness was widespread and came to the attention of Quintian, governor of Sicily. Quintian put her into prison for being a Christian, and there she underwent extreme tortures that finally killed her. Popular art represents her as holding a plate, a candle, or a house in flames.

We know for certain that Agatha was a martyr. She probably suffered death during the persecutions under Decius from 240 to 251. Although Agatha lived in Sicily, devotion to her was so widespread and so fervent that her name came to be included in the canon of the Roman Mass. We know that she has long been honored for her great courage in suffering and in remaining pure for the sake of Christ.

We, as Christians, need the example of others. We need to see those around us living according to the faith. We need to see people who love Jesus so much that they are ready to carry their own crosses for Him. And if we need to see others do all this, then they, too, need to see us do it. God chooses the weak so that we may rely on Him and let Him work through us. Like Agatha, may we be strong followers of Christ.

Students may be curious about pictures of St. Agatha or about popular accounts of her life. Teachers should, therefore, know some of the details connected with her martyrdom. All the stories make mention of her tortures:

1) She was forced to live in a house of prostitution.

2) Her breasts were cut off.

3) She was rolled in hot coals.

In many pictures, she is holding a plate on which her severed breasts are lying. To understand the kind of tortures suffered by St. Agatha, it is helpful to know that Roman Law forbade the killing of virgins. Before death, they had to be subjected to attacks on their virginity. The Church names them virgins because of their firm determination to remain pure for the love of Christ.

SUGGESTIONS

1. Discuss with the students the importance of remaining pure and of understanding the role of modesty in this regard.

2. People have always feared natural disasters: fires, earthquakes, floods. On St. Agatha's day in the Middle Ages, especially in the southern part of Germany, people would have blessed those important items that could be destroyed by fire: bread, fruits, letters. Candles were also blessed on this day. Ask the students to list the five things they would most desire to save from destruction. After their lists have been made, compare them. Help the students to try to understand what their priorities are in life according to their lists.

3. Lead the students in a prayer:

Lord,
You have promised us the power
  To rise above our littleness —
  Not by grasping power or wealth
  Nor by basking in the light of others' glory,
  Nor by seeking glory of our own.
But, by realizing how well loved we are —
  Your own cared-for children,
  Heirs with Jesus to your kingdom,
  Brothers and sisters of the risen Lord.
Free us, Lord, from our worldliness.
                    Amen.

FEBRUARY 6: ST. PAUL MIKI AND HIS COMPANIONS

Nagasaki, Japan: it is the city on which the second atomic bomb was dropped. But over three centuries ago, it was the scene of another kind of tragedy, for there, on the top of a windy hill, twenty-six men were crucified for being Christians. These are the Nagasaki martyrs, Paul Miki and and his companions.

By the 1500's the Church had been well established in Europe. But the far East had remained mission territory. Japan had closed its doors to foreigners, and it was not until 1549 that missionaries, like Francis

Xavier, were able to bring the Good News of Christ to these people. Many of the people became Christians, including the Shoguns, the commanders or lords of the various areas. When the first missionaries arrived in Japan, they were welcomed. But when the leader Nobunaga died, Hideyoshi took command in place of the emperor. At first Hideyoshi tolerated the presence of the missionaries and Christians. But then he began to grow suspicious. He sensed a spirit of unity among the Christians, and he feared they would try to take control of his government.

Hideyoshi issued a decree on July 25, 1587, banishing all missionaries. Some of the missionaries left; others went into hiding and exchanged their priestly clothes for the clothes of the people, so that they could continue to minister to the Christians. In the meantime, Hideyoshi had many of the churches destroyed. Later Hideyoshi eased some of his demands and rules, and the missionaries continued their work. It was always under the watchful and suspicious eyes of Hideyoshi, however.

On December 8, 1596, Hideyoshi arrested and condemned the friars of Miako. Among the condemned men were three Japanese Jesuits, six Franciscans (four of them Spanish), and seventeen Japanese laymen. They were condemned to death by crucifixion. The charge: attempting to harm the government. But the real reason was the fact that they were Christians. Among these Christians were young men: Louis, age 10; Anthony, age 13; Thomas, age 16; and Gabriel, age 19. The best known of these martyrs is Paul Miki, a Japanese of aristocratic family, a Jesuit Brother, and a brilliant preacher.

The twenty-six men were tortured and then forced to walk more than 300 miles from Miako to Nagasaki through the snow and ice and freezing streams. But all along the way, they preached to the people who had come out to see them. They sang psalms of praise and joy. They prayed the Rosary and told the people that such a martyrdom was an occasion of rejoicing, not of sadness. Finally on February 5, they reached Nagasaki where the twenty-six crosses awaited them. It is said that they ran to their crosses, singing. They were bound to the crosses with iron bands at their wrists, ankles, and throats. Then they were thrust through with two lances. Many people came to watch the cruel deaths. Hideyoshi and his soldiers had hoped the example would frighten other Christians. But instead, it gave them the courage to profess their faith, too.

Hideyoshi died in 1598, and for a few years the persecutions stopped. But by 1612, they had begun again. Some Christians were beheaded, some burned, some drowned, and some tortured. There are some 3,135 known martyrs from these years of persecution. It is believed there were thousands of others. By the middle of the seventeenth century, Japan closed its doors to all foreigners again. Surely all of Christianity would die there. But in 1858, after France and Japan had signed a treaty — in part permitting Christianity in Japan — the returning missionaries found thousands of Christians still in Japan, especially around Nagasaki. For two hundred years they had carried on the faith in secret.

Today we celebrate the twenty-six martyrs of Japan. There are 205 other martyrs of Japan who have been beatified and await canonization. But the land of Japan still has few Christians. And the missionary cry of the Church continues.

SUGGESTIONS

1. Paul Miki was born in Japan around 1564. He was educated by the Jesuits and joined the order in 1580. He was known as an excellent preacher. He was one of the three Jesuits martyred at Nagasaki. From his cross, he forgave his persecutors and told the people to ask Christ to show them the way to be truly happy. The other martyrs included teachers, doctors, carpenters, acolytes, priests and brothers. Suggest that the students do research on the individual martyrs of Nagasaki.

2. These martyrs sang and prayed, loudly and joyfully. Ask the students to compare their enthusiasm for song and prayer with that of the young men of Nagasaki. Encourage the students to proclaim their faith by participating wholeheartedly in the liturgy.

3. Some of the history of the persecutions has been recorded on Japanese tapestries and silk drawings. Have the students find out more about Japanese culture. What particular difficulties might they encounter as present-day missionaries to the East? Or have the students draw pictures of current religious practices in their own parish that could one day be used by others as recorded history of their church.

4. One way to identify Christians during the persecutions was the "tread" picture. These pictures were plates depicting the crucifixion of Jesus, the nativity, or other mysteries of the Church. Suspected Christians were ordered to walk on — tread on — the pictures. Those who refused to show such disrespect for the articles were condemned. Remind the students of the respect to be shown to religious articles because of the sacred persons or objects they represent.

5. For the Japanese Christian, the cross and the passion of Jesus were powerful symbols and meditations for their faith. Display the cross prominently in the classroom. Have the students make crosses out of twigs and wire (or yarn) and then exchange them with other students as reminders that we are all to share in the cross of Christ.

6. So that they may become more aware of the Church's needs and pray for missionaries, have the students write to the Office of Evangelization to find out the distribution of Catholics in the world today.

FEBRUARY 8: JEROME EMILIANI

Jerome Emiliani was born in Venice, Italy in 1486. He had been a soldier, but was captured during a battle and imprisoned in a dungeon. During that period, he had time to think about his life. He tried to "change his heart"; he wanted to get his life on the right path. After he escaped, Jerome returned to Venice. He took care of the sick and the poor in the hospitals in Venice. He also studied for the priesthood and was ordained in 1518. Some time later, in 1528, the plague broke out, and with it came famine. Jerome dedicated himself to caring for the sick, and he became more aware of the many children left orphaned, homeless, and abandoned. So deeply touched was he by their pain that he decided to devote his life to the care of these children. From city to city he travelled, and he founded three orphanages, a hospital, and a shelter for penitent women. Jerome himself set up an educational program for the children — similar to the vocational training classes offered today. Jerome used the question-and-answer method to teach Catholic doctrine.

Around the year 1532, Jerome and two other priests founded a congregation specifically for the care of orphans and for the education and training of priests and children. It began as the "Society of the Servants for the Poor," but eventually became the "Clerks Regular of Somaschi" (the Order of the Somaschi) — named after the mountain hermitage built by Jerome in Somaschi. Jerome stayed close to the people always. While he was caring for the sick, he himself contracted the disease of his patients and died in 1537. His congregation was approved by Pope Paul III three years later. Jerome was canonized by Pope Clement XIII in 1767, and in 1928 Pope Pius XI named him the universal patron of orphans and abandoned children.

SUGGESTIONS

1. The spirit of Jerome Emiliani's religious congregation is best described as love of charity. But Jerome also included imitation of the suffering Christ and devotion to the guardian angels and the Blessed Virgin. Jerome tried to live out the law of love in all he did. In our times, Mother Teresa of Calcutta is known for trying to respond concretely

to the needs of others and the law of love. Read parts of her biography or show the film "To Works of Love" (Ikonographics). Discuss ways of showing charity and imitating the suffering Christ today.

2. If there is a children's home or hospital in the area, have the students design cards or table favors for the patients. They could also plan visits.

3. Jerome found ways to teach little children. Plan a Mass with the primary and junior high students. Or have the older students prepare games for the younger children — crossword puzzles, word-search games, or outline-pictures to color — all on religious topics or aspects of doctrine appropriate to the age level. Run off copies of the work for distribution throughout the school. This is a good way to work together within a school.

4. Declare the day "Kindness to Brothers and Sisters Day." Have the students make cards of appreciation, plan to do something extra-special for their brothers and/or sisters, or prepare "Glad You're You" passes:

> Because I'm GLAD YOU'RE YOU,
> I want to make this day special for you by
>
> _____
>
> _____
>
> Signed,

5. Prepare a Giving Tree. Find out the needs of the sick and poor in the area. Write these out on individual slips of paper and attach them to a tree (or a large branch potted in sand) in the hall or church. Encourage the students, their families, and other parishioners to take the slips, supply the need, and return the slip with the items to be delivered to the needy. Names and addresses should not appear on these slips, but should be kept on a master sheet at the rectory, office, or parish center.

FEBRUARY 10: SCHOLASTICA

Sometimes we can learn big lessons from small events. Although we know very little about St. Scholastica, we do have one recorded event that teaches us much. Pope Gregory the Great wrote a collection of stories and events about the saints called the "Dialogues." He devoted his entire second book of the Dialogues to St. Benedict. It is from that collection that we learn of a simple and loving event in the lives of St. Scholastica and St. Benedict. St. Scholastica was the twin sister of St. Benedict.

Benedict had spent some time studying in Rome, but then decided to devote all his life to the search for God. He first organized several cluster-like community dwellings, but finally established a very important monastery at Monte Cassino. Scholastica founded a community of religious women at Plombariola, about five miles south of her brother's monastery. Benedict directed the progress of these women, so Scholastica must have been the abbess there.

Scholastica and Benedict visited together only once a year. They would go to a small house near their monasteries, for no women were permitted at Monte Cassino. On one occasion, Benedict, with several of his monks, met Scholastica at the house. They spent the day praying and speaking of God and the spiritual life. After they had eaten, they continued their conversation late into the night. When Benedict said he had to return to his monastery, Scholastica begged him to stay and talk a while longer. Benedict refused, saying that his rule required that the monks be in the monastery at night. Heartbroken at his refusal, Scholastica folded her hands, put her head on the table, and quietly wept and prayed. While she was praying, a terrible storm began, a storm so terrible that no one could venture out into it. "God forgive you! What have you done?" Benedict exclaimed to his sister. She explained that since he had refused the favor she asked, she had turned to Almighty God instead and He said yes. What more could Benedict say? They continued their conversation and prayer until morning, and then Benedict and his monks left. Three days later, Scholastica died. They had enjoyed their final conversation. Benedict told the monks that he saw her soul, like a dove, ascend toward heaven. He had her buried in the tomb he had built for himself.

We may not know much about Scholastica's early life, about her penances or powerful virtues, about her hopes and her dreams. But we do know that she valued people more than things. She knew it was important to listen to and care about others. And she also knew how to pray. So complete was her trust in God that she turned to Him often. She placed her problems and her hurts in His loving heart. And that made all the difference. From this small event, we know all we need to know to become saints: love God, love others.

SUGGESTIONS

1. Scholastica offered a short prayer, an ejaculation of sorts, to God. These tiny prayers offered often throughout the day help keep us aware of God's loving presence and concern for us. They help keep our minds, hearts, and wills on Him. Teach

several ejaculations to the students. Write them out and post them around the room so that the students may recall them in prayer throughout the day.

My Lord, my God, my all!

Be near, Lord Jesus!

I love You, my God!

2. Have the students find the following short prayers in Scripture and pray them often. Recommend that they keep a special notebook for recording such prayers or for writing their own.

Matthew 8:8	Luke 22:42
Matthew 9:27	John 6:68
Matthew 14:33 or 16:16	John 11:27
Matthew 15:25	John 20:28
Mark 9:24	John 21:17
Luke 1:38	

3. One lesson Scholastica teaches us is the importance of being available to people when they are in need. Suggest that students make special efforts to be aware of the needs of others throughout the day, to take time to listen to people and just be with them.

4. Benedict and Scholastica were close to each other and close to God. Much of their warmth may have been due to their family experiences. Give the students pages from the current calendar (the current month). Have them write the name of a family member in each block on the calendar. On the respective day, the students should offer special prayers for that relative, and they should call or send greetings. Parents, brothers, and sisters should be included often. The students might wish to continue this practice throughout the year. To extend this project to the entire school, a large general calendar could be posted with the families of all the students represented.

FEBRUARY 11: OUR LADY OF LOURDES

Each year, over two million people make their way through the mountainous country of southeastern France to Lourdes. They come seeking cures, hoping to find answers, believing, and praying. There at Lourdes, these pilgrims pray in the church, wash in the baths from the flowing stream, and walk, sing, and pray in the processions. There the people recall the Lady dressed in white, with a blue sash, yellow roses at her feet, and a rosary in her hand — Our Lady, the Blessed Virgin Mary, the Immaculate Conception.

It was a cold day on February the eleventh, 1858. Bernadette Soubirous, fourteen years old, her sister, and a friend had gone out to collect firewood. Being weak and sickly from childhood, Bernadette fell behind the other girls. She came to a stream and was preparing to cross it when she heard a strong wind. As she looked around, she saw a young woman, not much taller than herself, dressed in white, carrying a rosary on her arm. Bernadette was frightened at first, but the kind smile and gentle manner of the Lady assured her there was nothing to fear. Bernadette began to pray the Rosary, and the Lady joined her in praying the Glory Be at the end of each decade. When the Rosary ended, Bernadette told the two girls what she had seen. At home, Bernadette was questioned about her experience, and it was clear that her parents were upset. But she was permitted to return to the spot, and the lovely Lady appeared to her again — eighteen times from February 11 through July 16.

News of the girl from Lourdes who had seen a vision spread, and crowds began to form whenever Bernadette returned to Massabielle, the place where she had first seen the Lady. At one time nearly 20,000 people were present. Yet no one saw or heard the Lady but Bernadette. The Lady told her many things. She assured Bernadette that although she would not find happiness in this life, she would have it in heaven. She told her to do penance and pray for sinners. She instructed Bernadette to tell the priests that a chapel was to be built at the site, and processions were to be held. When Bernadette sought to know the Lady's identity, she replied, "I am the Immaculate Conception." The Blessed Virgin, through Bernadette, had come to call sinners to a change of heart. She touched the hearts of the people deeply, inspiring them to reach out and care for the sick and the poor — and all those who were losing hope.

On February 25, 1858, the Lady told Bernadette to dig in the dirt and drink of the stream. Bernadette began to dig and, after several attempts, she was able to find the water to drink. The water continued to flow from where she had dug with her hands until it was producing over 32,000 gallons of water a day — as it still does. A week later, a blind man was cured in those waters. From that time till the present, there have been over 5,000 cures recorded, several hundred of which have been declared miraculous by the Church. They are declared so only after a very exacting ecclesiastical review and a medical review by a board of international doctors, some of whom are not even Christian.

Bernadette eventually entered the Sisters of Charity and Christian Instruction, seeking to get away from the fame and the crowds. She lived a short life, was greatly misunderstood, and at times even harshly treated. After suffering painfully with tuberculosis, she died on April 16, 1879, at the age of thirty-five. But while Bernadette retired to the background, more and more people turned to Mary, the Immaculate Conception, and made their way to

Lourdes, France. There are daily reports of cures, but most people know that the greatest blessings of Lourdes happen not to the body but to the soul, the spirit, the very heart of the people who go there. And so today we celebrate the feast of Our Lady of Lourdes. We may never travel to France or go to Lourdes to join in the processions, but we will know always that we have a Mother to help us in our weakness and lead us to her Son, Jesus. And so we pray to her:

> God of mercy,
> we celebrate the feast of Mary,
> the sinless mother of God.
> May her prayers help us
> to rise above our human weakness.
>
> We ask this through our Lord Jesus Christ, your
> Son,
> who lives and reigns with you and the Holy
> Spirit,
> one God, for ever and ever
> (Opening Prayer, Proper of Saints,
> February 11)

SUGGESTIONS

1. The song "Immaculate Mary" is known also as the Lourdes hymn, used in procession at the shrine. Have the students sing this song as a closing prayer.

2. There are many fine books about Bernadette Soubirous. Encourage the students to read more about this simple, pert, and straightforward saint.

3. Bernadette (1844-1879) was canonized by Pius XI on December 8, 1933. One message to her from the Virgin Mary was to pray the Rosary. Review the Rosary with the students. Then pray the Glorious Mysteries together with the class.

4. The dogma of the Immaculate Conception had been defined by Pope Pius IX four years previous to the first apparition at Lourdes. Review with the students the significance of the Immaculate Conception, i.e., that (in view of the role she would have in salvation history) Mary was free from original sin from the moment of her conception.

5. There are many facets of Bernadette's life that could inspire young people. Point out some of these to your students:

   - When the lovely Lady of the apparitions asked Bernadette to return each day for fifteen days, Bernadette answered that she would *if* her parents would permit her to do so. She remained obedient to her parents.

   - Bernadette was questioned, and at times threatened, by lawyers, doctors, police, civil authorities, priests, religious, her teachers, friends, relatives, bishops. They were finally convinced of the truth of her story because of her steady honesty, the sameness of her account, her evident humility and straightforwardness. Honesty is its own reward.

   - Bernadette was slow to learn to read and write, and she always had difficulty with her catechism questions. But she knew how to love and how to suffer. She knew the healing waters of the grotto would never help her, yet she did not let that stop her from showing kindness to everyone. Bernadette knew what was really important in life.

6. When asked to describe the Lady, Bernadette said that she looked nothing like the images and statues she had seen in the church. The Lady was so much more beautiful and natural. Have the students bring in their favorite pictures, drawings, holy cards, statues, and/or medals of Our Lady. If they have background information on any of their items, ask them to display that also.

FEBRUARY 14:   CYRIL AND METHODIUS

It is hard to keep going when many people seem to be against you. Some people just give up once things become difficult — but the real saints in the world do not give up. That is one lesson we can learn from the lives of Saints Cyril and Methodius.

Cyril (whose name was Constantine before he became a monk) and Methodius were brothers, born in Thessalonika, Greece. Cyril (825-869), a brilliant philosopher, studied at the university in Constantinople. He was ordained a priest. His brother Methodius (826-884), for five years the governor of a Slavic section of the empire, later became a monk. In 861 these two brothers were sent as missionaries to one of the regions of Russia. They learned the language of the people before they went and were able to lead many people to Christ.

Later, in 863, Cyril and Methodius were sent to Moravia, which is in Eastern Europe. How well they prepared for their work — and how much love and respect they showed for the people! With their knowledge of the Slavonic tongue, they began translating the Gospels into the language. To do this, Cyril devised a special alphabet (still used in Russia and in some Slavonic countries) and so he also helped promote Slavonic literature in general. Cyril and Methodius ministered to the people as one of them, and they celebrated the Mass and gave homilies in Slavonic. But some German bishops at the time were suspicious of these two from "the East." They accused the missionaries of many things, so that in 869 Cyril and Methodius were called to Rome to defend their actions. So well did they do this that not only were they told to continue preaching and using Slavonic in the liturgy, but they were also to be consecrated bishops and given their own sections. They could then ordain to the priesthood the candidates they had helped. Cyril died before he could be consecrated bishop; Methodius was consecrated, and then he returned to Moravia. There some German bishops continued to hurl accusations at him until he was deposed by a German synod and imprisoned. Methodius was released two years later by the order of the Pope, but the tensions continued. Again, in 878, he was called to Rome to defend his actions, and again he was approved. For the rest of his life, Methodius was to endure the anger and misunderstanding of the German clergy.

Something deep within Cyril and Methodius kept them going. Love of God, love of the people, love and knowledge of the Scriptures they had worked so hard to translate — all of these played a part in their determination. At Baptism, we, like Cyril and Methodius, received many gifts through the power of the Holy Spirit dwelling within us. One of those gifts was fortitude — courage. It made all the difference in the lives of Cyril and Methodius. It could make all the difference in our lives, too.

SUGGESTIONS

1. Today it is considered a normal thing to have the Mass celebrated in your own language. But it was not always that way. In fact, when Cyril and Methodius began to celebrate the Mass and give homilies in the language of the people, they were suspected of being heretics. It has taken quite a while for the vernacular (native tongue, language of the people) to find its rightful place in worship. There is, however, a value in knowing a common language, one that can be understood by everyone. In the Church, Latin is that type of language. In large multi-national gatherings (such as you would find at Lourdes or the Vatican), common prayers are often said in Latin. Teach the students the Our Father, the Hail Mary, and the Glory Be in Latin so that they can identify with this universal ecclesial language.

THE LORD'S PRAYER

Páter nóster, qui es in cáelis:
sanctificétur nómen túum;
advéniat régnum túum;
fíat volúntas túa, sícut in cáelo, et in térra.
Pánem nóstrum cotidiánum da nóbis hódie;
et dimítte nóbis débita nóstra,
sícut et nos dimíttimus debitóribus nóstris;
et ne nos indúcas in tentatiónem;
sed líbera nos a málo.

THE HAIL MARY

Áve, María, grátia pléna: Dóminus técum: benedícta tu
in muliéribus, et benedíctus frúctus véntris túi, Jésus.
Sáncta María, Máter Déi: óra pro nóbis peccatóribus,
nunc et in hóra mórtis nóstrae. Amen.

GLORY BE

Glória Pátri, et Fílio, et Spirítui Sáncto,
Sícut érat in princípio, et nunc et sémper:
et in sáecula saeculórum. Amen.

2. Cyril and Methodius are called the apostles of the Slavs and are honored by Russians, Serbs, Ukranians, Bulgarians, Czechs, Slovaks, Croatians and many others. Have the students locate these areas on the map and see the extent of their influence.

3. Cyril is credited with developing a Slavonic alphabet. His alphabet is called Glagolithic. The Cyrillic alphabet often associated with him was developed by his followers, who continued his work after his death. Let the students find out more about this alphabet and the translations of the Bible Cyril made.

4. Cyril and Methodius exemplified some of the best procedures in missionary work: trying to understand the people and their particular culture rather than imposing on them a foreign culture or tradition. It is easy to want others to change rather than to accept them as they are. Discuss with the students the importance of loving and accepting people as they are.

5. Review with the students the gifts of the Holy Spirit they received at Baptism and which are sealed and strengthened in Confirmation. How did Cyril and Methodius use their gifts? How can people today use their gifts?

FEBRUARY 17: SEVEN FOUNDERS OF THE ORDER OF SERVITES

Some people are content to complain about the evils in society. Some people feel called to actively fight such evil. And there are still others who fight, but in a silent way. These are the people who examine their own lives and resolve to live lives of witness to eternal values. There were seven such men in Florence, Italy in the mid-thirteenth century. They were wealthy, well-known merchants. But they found themselves in a society in which many people had come to disregard God's law. Riches and the "easy life" had come to mean more to these people than love of the poor and service to the needy. So these seven men decided to withdraw from the city. They chose to lead lives of prayer and penance. They chose to turn their lives totally over to God and give witness to all that is good and true. At first, so many people came to see them on the outskirts of the city that it was necessary for some of them to move to the quieter slopes of Monte Senario.

This group of men fostered special devotion to the Blessed Virgin, particularly in her seven sorrows. They came to call themselves the Servants of Mary, or Servites. Although they began as monks — living apart from the world and devoted to a contemplative lifestyle — they gradually became more like friars, more involved with helping other people in an active apostolate. The order was recognized in 1259, and approved by Benedict XI in 1304. Only one of the original founders, Alexis Falconieri, lived to see this final approval. In 1888, these seven founders were canonized by Leo XIII.

We may not found an order or move to the slopes of a mountainside for prayer, but we all must find a way of answering God's call. We all must find a way of witnessing to what we believe in, of witnessing to Christ. We live in a society that is confused, but as Christians we must witness to eternal values, to love of the poor and service of the needy. Let us pray for God's help:

> Lord,
> fill us with the love
> which inspired the seven holy brothers
> to honor the mother of God with special
> devotion
> and to lead your people to you.
>
> We ask this through our Lord Jesus Christ,
> your Son,
> who lives and reigns with you and the Holy
> Spirit,
> one God, for ever and ever.
> (Opening Prayer, Proper of Saints,
> February 17)

SUGGESTIONS

1. Have the students research the difference between monks and friars. You might wish to schedule a trip to a monastery or friary, if one is located nearby.

2. On July 27, 1274, the Second Council of Lyons issued a decree directed at limiting the number of religious orders in the Catholic Church. Critics of the Servites urged that the new order either be abolished or absorbed by one of the older orders, such as the Dominicans, Franciscans, Carmelites, or Augustinians. Have the students find out more about mendicant orders in general and the specific orders listed above. Let them find out about the work of these orders today and how the members witness to eternal values.

3. The names of the seven founders were Bonfilius Monaldi, John Bonagiunta, Gerard Sostegni, Bartholomew Amidei, Benedict dell'Antella, Ricoverus Uguccione, and Alexis Falconieri. It took great courage for these men to leave their prosperous businesses and seek the solitude of prayer and penance. They had been leaders in society, so their decision to change their way of living certainly caused a stir and inspired others to rethink their values and make some changes in their own lives. Discuss with the students the importance of example and the responsibility of

the leaders in society to live according to principles. Have the students list current leaders and indicate what their values appear to be from the type of lifestyle they lead. Discuss the power of good example to inspire others.

4. Before founding the order of Servites, all seven men had been members of confraternities. Ask the students to find out which confraternities exist in their diocese and in their parish. Invite representatives of various confraternities to speak to the class about the purpose of their groups.

5. The Servites are especially devoted to the Blessed Virgin. Have the students review the seven sorrows of Mary (See *Saints and Feast Days*, September 15). Lead the students in prayer to Mary. The response is in italics after each line.

LITANY OF MARY, MOTHER OF THE CHURCH

Lord, have mercy.
Lord, have mercy.
Christ, have mercy.
Christ, have mercy.
Lord, have mercy.
Lord, have mercy.
God our Father in heaven,
have mercy on us.
God the Son, our Redeemer,
have mercy on us.
God the Holy Spirit,
have mercy on us.
Holy Trinity, one God,
have mercy on us.
Holy Mary,
pray for us.
Mother of God
pray for us.
Woman of faith,
pray for us.
Most honored of all virgins,
pray for us.
Joy of Israel,
pray for us.
Honor of our people,
pray for us.
Model of prayer and virtue,
pray for us.
Incentive to trust,
pray for us.
Temple of the Holy Spirit,
pray for us.
Spouse of Joseph,
pray for us.
Mother of Jesus,
pray for us.

Faithful follower of Jesus,
pray for us.

Mother of the Church,
pray for us.

Image of the Church at prayer,
pray for us.

Our Lady of Guadalupe, patroness of the Americas,
pray for us.

Mary Immaculate, patroness of the United States,
pray for us.

Advocate of life,
pray for us.

Guide for the young,
pray for us.

Friend of the single,
pray for us.

Companion of the married,
pray for us.

Voice for the unborn,
pray for us.

Mother of mothers,
pray for us.

Support of the family,
pray for us.

Comforter of the sick,
pray for us.

Nurse of the aged,
pray for us.

Echo of the suffering,
pray for us.

Consoler of the widowed,
pray for us.

Strength of the broken-hearted,
pray for us.

Hymn of the joyful,
pray for us.

Hope of the poor,
pray for us.

Example of detachment for the rich,
pray for us.

Goal of pilgrims,
pray for us.

Resort of the traveler,
pray for us.

Protector of the exile,
pray for us.

Woman most whole,
pray for us.

Virgin most free,
pray for us.

Wife most loving,
pray for us.

Mother most fulfilled,
pray for us.

Queen of love,
pray for us.

Lamb of God, you take away the sins of the world:
have mercy on us.

Lamb of God, you take away the sins of the world:
have mercy on us.

Lamb of God, you take away the sins of the world:
have mercy on us.

(St. Bernard)

ALL:
Remember, O most loving Virgin Mary,
that never was it known
that anyone who fled to your protection,
implored your help, or sought your intercession
was left unaided.

Inspired with this confidence, we turn to you,
O Virgin of virgins, our Mother.
To you we come, before you we kneel,
sinful and sorrowful.

O Mother of the Word Incarnate,
do not despise our petitions,
But in your mercy hear and answer us.
Amen.

(Service written by Rev. Medard P. Laz
and James E. Wilbur)

FEBRUARY 21: PETER DAMIAN

It takes a special kind of person to be a reformer, and Peter Damian was such a person. Born in Ravenna (Italy) in 1007, he knew hardships as a child. His older brother, however, made sure he had a good education. Having been a good student, Peter later became a successful teacher — but only for a short time. He was ordained to the priesthood, and in 1035 he entered the Benedictine monastery at Fonte Avellana.

The monks lived in small hermitages, with two monks in each one. It was a strict, demanding life, and Peter devoted himself totally to it. He was known for his fasting and acts of penance and for the long hours he spent in prayer. In 1043 he was elected abbot (prior) of the monastery. As abbot, Peter began reorganizing the practices and rules of the order. He believed that only by going back to the original spirit and purpose of the Benedictine order could the monks really witness to others and praise God. Many candidates were drawn to the monastery, and eventually Peter started five other foundations.

But Peter's talents and zeal did not remain confined to the monastery. In 1057 he was made cardinal and bishop of Ostia. Soon he was called upon by the Church at large to settle disputes, to attend synods, to fight abuses. Painfully aware of the many problems of the time, Peter believed that the best way to reform society was to reform society's leaders. So he devoted much energy to helping the clergy, as well as the leaders of the empire. By letters, biographies, sermons, stories, and poems, he encouraged others to restore discipline to their lives.

Throughout all his travels and diplomatic missions, Peter Damian remained a monk at heart. Drawn to prayer and solitude, he served the Church as he was asked and as best he could. He died on February 22 in 1072 and was declared a Doctor of the Church in 1828. From Peter Damian, we learn that the best way to reform others is to reform ourselves first!

SUGGESTIONS

1. Peter Damian preferred to teach principles through stories, anecdotes, and examples, rather than by long arguments and debates. The story form (parable) was used by Jesus Himself. Have the students write short stories showing Christian virtues in action. Encourage them to illustrate their stories.

2. Peter Damian fought hard against simony and clerical marriage. He also tried to get religious to simplify their lifestyles by cutting out needless travel, violations of poverty, and luxurious living. Today, too, many people are concerned about simplifying their lifestyles. Have the students brainstorm ways to simplify their lives. Here are a few suggestions:

   • Make gifts instead of purchasing them.
   • Start a vegetable garden and learn about home canning and preserving.
   • Repair and recycle toys and games for the needy.

3. It is said that Peter Damian spent many nights in prayer, and that eventually he developed a severe case of insomnia. Other sources tell us that in his old age Peter made wooden spoons and was involved in making other artifacts. Point out to the students that the lives of the saints are not solely occupied with huge concerns or activities. In every life, there are joys and sorrows, little surprises and inconveniences, but all of these can help us grow closer to God, sharing with Him our daily "ups and downs." Have the students write in their journals, sharing with God the ups and downs they experienced today.

FEBRUARY 22: CHAIR OF PETER

Whenever the pope, the bishop of Rome, speaks out on an issue or delivers a teaching, his words are recorded, printed, and even meditated. Whenever the pope, the servant of the servants of God, cautions world leaders, pleads for peace, or condemns discrimination and social injustice, people listen and prepare some kind of response. The pope travels where other leaders would not dare to go; he speaks freely about issues which others would be too fearful

to discuss. What is it that makes the world so often stop and listen to this particular shepherd of Christ's flock? Why is his ministry so much more far-reaching than that of other bishops, other shepherds?

The answer lies in Scripture and it lies in tradition. If you were to look through the New Testament, you would find that one apostle heads the list: Peter. He is named first among the followers and apostles of Jesus; he was often the spokesman and leader for the others; he was the first to preach after Pentecost, the leader in defending Christ and His message to those rulers who opposed Him. Peter was there at the Transfiguration; he was there in the garden. Peter proclaimed, "You are the Christ," and Christ in turn singled out Peter:

> Jesus looked hard at him and said, "You are Simon son of John; you are to be called Cephas" — meaning Rock (John 1:42).

> "So I now say to you: You are Peter and on this rock I will build my Church. And the gates of the underworld can never hold out against it. I will give you the keys of the kingdom of heaven: whatever you bind on earth shall be considered bound in heaven; whatever you loose on earth shall be considered loosed in heaven." (Matthew 16:18-19)

Jesus prayed for Peter:

> ". . . I have prayed for you, Simon, that your faith may not fail, and once you have recovered, you in your turn must strengthen your brothers." (Luke 22:32)

And Jesus gave Peter a three-fold commision of love and ministry:

> After the meal Jesus said to Simon Peter, "Simon son of John, do you love me more than these others do?" He answered, "Yes Lord, you know I love you." Jesus said to him, "Feed my lambs." A second time he said to him, "Simon son of John, do you love me?" He replied, "Yes, Lord, you know I love you." Jesus said to him, "Look after my sheep." Then he said to him a third time, "Simon son of John, do you love me?" Peter was upset that he asked him the third time, "Do you love me?" and said, "Lord, you know everything; you know I love you." Jesus said to him, "Feed my sheep."
>
> (John 21:15-17)

From the beginning, the specialness, or "primacy," of Peter has been recognized. It is a sign of the tender love Christ has for His Church, for those who follow Him. It is a sign of Christ's special presence and protection, too.

And so when we celebrate the feast of the Chair of Peter, we really celebrate our unity as a Church. We celebrate that love, presence, and protection of Christ for us, the Church. The title of the feast, the Chair of

Peter, calls attention to the fact that the actual chair from which a bishop presided and from which he gave homilies was a symbol of his authority. When the title refers to St. Peter, it recalls the supreme teaching power of the Prince of the Apostles and his successors. It is from the chair, from the pastoral power given him, that the pope teaches, guides, and shepherds the flock of Christ. As we celebrate this feast, let us remember to pray for the Church and to pray especially for our pope, _____, that God may protect him and give him the strength, courage, and wisdom he needs to guide us.

SUGGESTIONS

1. Two letters were written by St. Peter. This might be a good time to introduce the students to these letters and to all the letters referred to as "universal" or "catholic" because they are not addressed to any specific church: James, 1 Peter, 2 Peter, 1 John, 2 John, 3 John, and Jude. Provide some time during the day for the students to quietly read one or two of these letters.

2. Show the students pictures or slides of the Vatican.

3. Have the students bring in articles on the pope, his travels, his teachings, and his interests. You may wish to encourage them to read biographies of the recent popes.

4. Help the students plan and conduct a prayer service for the pope, the bishops, the priests, and the deacons. Make it part of a vocation-awareness day. The students might wish to write letters to the clergy, expressing their prayerful support.

5. Have the students locate Scripture references relating to Peter. What qualities of a leader does Peter have? What other qualities did he have to overcome in order to give better witness to Christ? Suggest that the students act out a scene from Peter's life as found in the Acts of the Apostles.

6. Ask the students to find out the meaning of the term "Holy See." Recommend that they consult the *New Catholic Encyclopedia* for the information.

7. Peter is often represented in art with a set of keys, with a ship or fish, with a cock (representing his denial of Christ), dressed in a toga or as a pope or bishop, or as being crucified upside down. Have the students find pictures with these representations or have them draw their own.

8. Tradition indicates that Peter was the bishop of Antioch before he went to Rome, where he was martyred. Have the students locate Antioch on a map and do research on why it was an important city in the early Church.

9. The words inscribed on the base of the dome of St. Peter's are from Matthew 16:18. Ask the students to study their parish church for symbolism and for Scripture references.

FEBRUARY 23: POLYCARP

Polycarp was born sometime around the year 60. Although we know few details about his life, we know a great deal about the story of his martyrdom. It is the earliest recorded account of a Christian martyr.

Polycarp was a disciple of St. John the apostle. While still quite young, he became the bishop of Smyrna (now in Turkey) and, as such, was one of the most respected leaders in the first half of the second century. St. Ignatius of Antioch and St. Irenaeus spoke highly of him, and the people loved him very much. Polycarp was a Christian leader in a pagan world. He spoke with clarity and simplicity, fearless in his love for and defense of Christ, even though persecutions raged around him. He sought only to hand on the message he had been given by John, who had seen and heard and really followed Jesus Christ. Even as Polycarp himself prepared for martyrdom, his joy and his confident trust were evident to all those around him.

Polycarp was seized for being a Christian. He was threatened and pressured in many ways, yet he explained to his captors that he had followed Christ for eighty-six years. Persecution and death would not tear him away from Jesus now. So Polycarp was led into the Stadium of Smyrna. The crowd demanded that he be left to the lions, but instead he was sentenced to death by fire. He was finally killed by the sword on February 2, 155, and then his body was burned. A group of Christians took his remains and buried them.

The community of believers celebrated the anniversary of his death with great joy, for in Polycarp they had seen an outstanding example of love and patience. He had held strong and had won — not an earthly treasure that could rust or corrode but, instead, he had won the treasure of eternal life. Polycarp, along with Ignatius of Antioch, Clement of Rome, and a few others, is remembered as an Apostolic Father — one who was a disciple of the apostles, one who bridges the gap between those who lived with Jesus on earth and those who would know and love Jesus by faith. We may not live in the "time of Jesus," but we know He is present with us. We may not see Him in the flesh, but we see Him with eyes of faith. Like Polycarp, we are called to hand on the tradition of giving Christian witness — joyfully, no matter what the cost.

SUGGESTIONS

1. Polycarp was so highly respected that he was sent as the representative of the churches in Asia Minor

to Rome to discuss with Pope Anicetus the date for the celebration of Easter. East and West had chosen separate dates for the celebration of this major feast. When a compromise could not be reached, Pope Anicetus did not demand Polycarp's agreement, nor did the Bishop Polycarp encourage any schism or division between the groups over the issue. They sought in charity to leave the two separate dates for the time being, and then together they celebrated the Eucharist. Their acceptance of diversity and respect for differing customs are lessons for us all today. Challenge the students to evaluate how they solve disagreements among themselves, or how well they accept the customs and styles of other people.

2. In his letter to the Church at Philippi, Polycarp stressed patience (after the example of Christ), the following of the Gospels, almsgiving, and prayer for kings, rulers, enemies, and persecutors. Have the students write and include petitions related to these areas in their prayers. Encourage them to make a special effort to pray for their enemies and for those who ignore or hurt them in any way.

3. Polycarp helped fight against the Gnostic heresies, especially those expressed through Marcion and Valentius. Challenge the students to do additional research on this early heresy and on the heresies of contemporary society.

4. People are usually interested in knowing what it was really like in the time of Christ. Books and movies have sought to capture the spirit and customs of that time and the beginning of the early Church. Many people have also searched to find the true likeness of Christ. Many images of Christ have been collected throughout the centuries — most of them symbolic. A fascinating area of additional study is the iconography of Jesus Christ. Suggest that students do research in this area and display any reproductions they may find.

See Supplement for March 3.

MARCH 4: CASIMIR

Saints are seldom found in palaces or castles. But St. Casimir, prince of Poland, was an exception. Much of Casimir's strength of character can be ascribed to the influence of his exceptional teacher, John Dlugosz. John was a Polish historian who was quick to note in Casimir the natural gifts of leadership and idealism. The great teacher instilled in Casimir a desire to love God's divine law and to live by his conscience. Casimir was highly disciplined and eager to learn. By the time he was thirteen, his virtue and integrity were so well known that the nobles in Hungary, dissatisfied with their king, wanted Casimir as ruler. Casimir's father equipped him with an army and sent him to

the Hungarian border to take over the country. As young as Casimir was, he discerned the problems facing his troops. Their pay was low and soldiers were deserting. As Casimir surveyed the situation, he saw he was clearly outnumbered by the enemy, and the battle would be a waste of lives. Moreover, he learned that Pope Sixtus IV had sent an embassy to his father to deter him from the expedition. So Casimir returned home with no kingdom to his name. Casimir's father felt angry and disgraced. To punish his son, he banished him to a nearby castle for three months. The boy went as directed and continued to study and pray. During this time, he made a serious resolution never again to be involved in wars; instead, he would govern by peaceful means. Casimir also decided to remain unmarried. This decision frustrated his parents when he refused to marry the daughter of the Emperor Frederick III. Casimir briefly governed the Polish empire while his father was on a tour of Lithuania. But he died at the age of 26 of a lung disease. Casimir loved Our Lady very much and every day repeated the hymn "Daily, Daily Sing to Mary." He requested that this song be buried with him.

Casimir's life reminds us how important it is to have a well formed conscience and to live by our convictions. Casimir saw that his first duty was to God. We should pray to know our responsibilities to God and to be strong enough to fulfill them — even at the cost of risking our lives.

SUGGESTIONS

1. Casimir loved the Mother of God and sang her hymns on the way to battle. Sing a Marian hymn at the end of class today.

2. After Casimir had witnessed the horrors of the battlefield, no amount of persuasion could make him fight again. He resolved to rule by peace. Help the students answer the following questions:

   1) How does the Church view war?

   2) What has Pope John Paul II taught us in his letter to the United Nations (*L'Osservatore Romano*, June 21, 1982), which examines the moral principles surrounding war and peace in the nuclear age?

   3) What do your families believe about war and peace?

   4) How can you become a more peace-loving person?

3. Casimir is the patron saint of Poland and Lithuania. These countries were once behind the Iron Curtain, where the free exercise of the Catholic religion was severely restricted. The Cathedral of Vilna, where Casimir was buried, has been turned into a museum and art gallery, and his remains

have been transferred to a parish church. But the people of these countries still honor him. Have the students locate Poland and Lithuania on a map and pray for Catholics who live there, that they may have the courage to witness to their faith.

4. Casimir's love of peace should make us more aware of our own quest for peace. Have the students write this prayer in their journals and encourage them to pray it often.

> Lead us from death to life,
>   from falsehood to truth.
> Lead us from despair to hope,
>   from fear to trust.
> Lead us from hate to love,
>   from war to peace.
> Let peace fill our hearts,
>   our world, our universe.

5. Casimir's love and respect for the Mother of God encourage us to ask the following questions of the class:

- Do you carry a rosary with you and pray it at times?
- Do you ever pray a part of the rosary when you go to bed?
- Do you have a statue or picture of Our Blessed Mother in your house?
- Do you pray to Mary for your family?
- Do the words, "Mary, Mother of God," evoke honor and respect in your house?

MARCH 7: PERPETUA AND FELICITY

Have you ever read the journal or diary of a famous person? Diaries and journals written by people like Pope John XXIII, Anne Frank, and Dag Hammarskjold are published so that others may be encouraged, comforted, and inspired. St. Perpetua wrote a diary during her last days, while she awaited execution. Her diary, along with an eye-witness account of her death, is one of the oldest, most reliable histories of a martyr's sufferings. This account was passed down generation after generation to encourage other Christians to witness to the world with their lives — to teach others that wealth, popularity, convenience, pleasure, and power are not the most important things in life. What is greater than life itself is knowing Jesus and being loyal to Him.

Perpetua's account records the events that took place in Carthage, Africa in the year 202, when the Emperor Severus issued an anti-Christian edict, forbidding anyone to be baptized and thereby to become a Christian. At that time, the twenty-two year-old Perpetua was a catechumen, studying to become a Christian. Perpetua was arrested along with four other catechumens, including Felicity, her slave woman, who was about to give birth to a child. All were tried and sentenced to be thrown to the wild beasts in the amphitheater during a national holiday. Their deaths would be scheduled along with sports events and various games.

During the days before their execution, their teacher Saturus voluntarily joined the catechumens so that he might die for Christ with them. Perpetua's father, a wealthy pagan, endeavored to make his daughter change her mind. He pleaded with her to offer sacrifice to the pagan gods so she could be freed from imprisonment, but she refused. While they were awaiting death, Perpetua and her companions were baptized. Shortly before the scheduled execution, Felicity gave birth to her child and was free to join her companions in the arena. During childbirth, Felicity had cried out in pain, and when someone asked her how she would ever endure the suffering of martyrdom, she replied, "Now it is I who suffer what I am suffering; then, there will be another in me who will suffer for me, because I will be suffering for Him."

On the day of their execution, the martyrs left their prison "joyfully as though there were on their way to heaven" and entered the amphitheater, where they were killed before the cheering crowd.

What enabled these Christians to face death so courageously? What made them so happy, so cheerful? St. Paul explains their joy in this way to the Colossians: "You will have in you the strength, based on his own glorious power, never to give in, but to bear anything joyfully, thanking the Father who has made it possible for you to join the saints and with them to inherit the light" (Colossians 1:12).

SUGGESTIONS

1. When her father was pleading with her to deny her faith in Christ, Perpetua said, "Father, do you see this water-jar, or whatever it is, standing here? Could one call it by any other name than what it is? Well, in the same way I cannot be called by any other name than what I am — a Christian." Have the students consider how their Christian faith should permeate their lives. Suggest that they choose a situation they will be facing in the next few days, a situation in which they will have an opportunity to act as Christians. Have them picture the place and the persons involved, and visualize their response to the situation. Explain that when people know they are going to face a difficult situation, it sometimes helps if they go through the coming event mentally and decide on the Christian response they want to give.

2. Perpetua and Felicity were arrested because of a law against Christians. Ask the students to imagine they are living under a government which refuses to allow Christians to practice their faith, and they

are on trial for doing this. Have them write what they would say to prove that they are living as Christians.

3. Perpetua's mother and one brother were already Christian, and another brother was a catechumen. In her family, Perpetua found support for her own faith. Let the students tell ways their families support and encourage them in their efforts to live Christian lives. Ask them to also consider how they can assist the other members of their families. Put two columns on the board, one labeled *From the Family* and one labeled *For the Family*. Have the students, as a group, compile a list of ways that families help the members.

4. Perpetua, Felicity and their companions went to martyrdom rejoicing. Have the students look up Scripture passages that refer to the joy of suffering for Christ. Then have them choose a quote, print it on a piece of heavy construction paper, and decorate it appropriately. Post these papers around the room to remind the students that they also can offer their sufferings for Christ in joy. Some references are:

2 Corinthians 12:9-10	Philippians 4:13
Galatians 6:14	Colossians 3:4
Philippians 1:30	1 Peter 1:6-7
Philippians 3:8-10	1 Peter 4:13

5. After Perpetua had been attacked by a wild beast, but while she was still alive, she said to her Christian brother who was watching from the crowd, "Stand firm in the faith, love one another, and do not let our sufferings be a stumbing-block." By her own words and example, Perpetua wanted to encourage her brother to be strong. Ask the students to think of someone who has recently given them a good example. Have them write a note of appreciation to that person.

6. "All baptized in Christ, you have all clothed yourselves in Christ, and there are no more distinctions between Jew and Greek, slave and free, male and female, but all of you are one in Christ Jesus" (Galatians 3:27-28). Perpetua was a wealthy free woman and Felicity was a slave. However, both women realized that in Christ they were one, and each was as important as the other. Consider with the students the various types of prejudice in the world and in the students' own environment. Have them discuss Christian ways to combat prejudice.

7. "[Be] strong in faith and in the knowledge that your brothers all over the world are suffering the same things" (1 Peter 5:9). Let the students research countries where governments have tried to suppress Christianity. Have them find out how the people are keeping their faith alive under such conditions. Ask them to share their findings with the class.

MARCH 8: JOHN OF GOD

Life begins at 40! For John of God, these words are particularly appropriate. As a Spanish soldier, he had given up religion and turned away from God. The wild life he led gave him a scandalous reputation. When he left the military at age 40, he returned to the work he did as a boy — shepherding on the mountains in Spain. This left him much time to think about his past life. Believing he was a miserable sinner, John decided to make a radical conversion in his life. He vowed to go to Moslem North Africa and free Christian slaves. He imagined himself gloriously dying as a martyr. It took his confessor some months to convince John that this plan was not wise. Gradually, John settled on a more prudent plan: to open a religious book store in Granada, Spain. This project he successfully managed, but he was still not content; his spirit was restless.

One day John went to hear John of Avila preach, and the sermon struck home. John's impetuous nature again showed itself, for he felt he must do something at once to show the world he had converted. John began publicly beating himself in remorse for his sins; he ran through the streets tearing his hair, behaving wildly; he gave his books away so frantically that people threw stones at him. This man, who felt his need for God so deeply, was committed to a mental institution. When John of Avila heard the effect his homily had had on John of God, he hurried to the hospital. The preacher calmed John and persuaded him that rather than going to such extremes, he should spend his great energy caring for the sick and poor. This idea seemed reasonable to John, who wanted to love God. He left the hospital and rented a house near Granada. Out into the streets he went to find the penniless and the uncared for. What a hospital he had! The lepers, the lame, the insane, the paralyzed, those who were dumb and deaf found a shelter.

At first John went begging to find enough money to support these poor, but soon people gave him money, food, and supplies because they were so impressed with his charity. John led a life of total giving and constant prayer. Once when a fire broke out in the house, John ran back into the burning building countless times, carrying the sick out on his back. When unemployed men came to his back door, he found them work. When the archbishop called John to his office because people complained that John kept tramps and immoral women in his hospital, he was silenced by John's humility. For John fell on his

knees, saying, "I know of no bad person in my hospital except myself, who am unworthy to eat the bread of the poor." His ceaseless energy and wholehearted goodness attracted so many helpers, he soon had a flourishing hospital. Later these helpers formed a religious community called the Brothers Hospitallers.

After a life of complete dedication to the poor and destitute, John of God died from a disease contracted while saving a drowning man. When John realized that he was dying, he went carefully over all the hospital accounts, revised the rules and time tables of his staff, and appointed a capable leader to take his place. He died kneeling before the altar in his hospital chapel. John's lifelong conversion encourages each one of us never to give up trying to love God more deeply. John shows us that it often takes many personal struggles to live the Gospel, but perseverance can bring a heavenly reward.

SUGGESTIONS

1. The origin of John's title is interesting. The bishop of Puy once invited John to supper. The bishop was so impressed by John's humility that he called him "John of God." Pass out half sheets of paper and have the students design their name and a title as a plaque. Encourage them to choose titles of a religious nature. Have them write the reasons for their choices on the back of the paper. A sample follows:

Front

Joe the Charitable

Back

Jesus showed us how to love His Father and others. I want to be like Him.

2. Share with the students this famous story about John of God. Once, as a bookseller, he was travelling home after an exhausting day of work. Along the road, he saw a child whose feet were bleeding because it had no shoes. John picked the child up and carried the little one to the next town. All the while, his burden was getting heavier and heavier, until finally he was forced to rest. Suddenly the appearance of the child changed and it was the Christ Child, Who held out to him a halved pomegranate, saying, "John of God, you will find your cross in Granada." Explain to the students that the Spanish word *granada* means "pomegranate." If possible, bring in a picture of

John of God. Have the students note that he is usually pictured holding a pomegranate surmounted with a cross.

3. John of God is the patron of hospitals. Have the class visit a hospital in the area. Perhaps the students could prepare songs or skits for the children and present them at a prescheduled time.

4. John of God was a promoter of religious books. Today there are many interesting books on the lives of holy people who love God. Have the students select a saint from whom they would like to learn, and read a section of his or her biography to them every day.

5. St. John of God is a good saint to imitate for peace and justice. His spirit of charity is reflected in these words: "It [my hospital] receives the elderly and children, pilgrims and travellers. We offer them fire and water, salt and cooking vessels. We receive no payment, but Christ provides. When I see so many of my brothers and sisters suffering beyond endurance or oppressed in body and spirit and I cannot help, I grieve indeed but I trust in Christ, for my heart is sure of Him." Have the students pray to John of God for the unemployed, the suffering, and the destitute.

6. Suggest that the students interview someone who works in a hospital to find out why this person serves and cares for people. Have them write up their interviews for publication in the school newspaper.

7. For ten years, St. John of God hid the fact that he was suffering. Finally Lady Anne Ossorio, who was his spiritual friend and benefactress, asked the bishop if she could care for him. John was unhappy to leave his work and be cared for, since he wanted to go on serving God to the last minute. Discuss why a person who has done much in the service of God and neighbor would not want to give up such work in spite of old age or illness.

MARCH 9: FRANCES OF ROME

When Lorenzo Panziano of Rome brought Frances, his beautiful bride, to the altar, his family and the wealthy of the city of Rome were in awe. Not only did he marry one of Rome's most charming and gentle maidens, but one who was virtuous and holy as well. Frances, who was thirteen when she was married, was known to be different from the other rich girls of her time. Her mother had taught her how to pray and love the poor as well as how to manage a large household.

Though she had wished to be a nun, Frances married and went obediently to live with Lorenzo and his family. She was young and spirited, and dressed herself in the silks, velvets, and jewels of the family to please her husband, who dearly loved her. She also loved him and willingly took care of her duties at the castle, but Frances was sometimes lonely and yearned to serve God in the poor. One day her sister-in-law Vanozza discovered Frances crying and confided that she, too, had the same desires. Together they made a plan: they would faithfully live their married lives, but they would also care for the poor. Frequently Frances and Vanozza left the palace in simple dresses and veils to care for the sick in the hospitals and to distribute goods to the poor. But their plan was not secret for long. Lorenzo's family and relatives were horrified when they found out what the two noble women were doing. The wealthy, proud aristocrats ridiculed and insulted the young women.

But Frances persuaded Lorenzo to allow her to continue to serve the needy. He could not resist her pleas. Frances was a marvelous mother to their growing family. She personally supervised the education of her children, and spent long hours caring for them. When her mother-in-law died, Frances efficiently took charge of the castle. She treated the servants so well that they did their work more carefully and even attended church more often. Though Frances spent long hours in prayer, she always cared for her family first.

Some people might think that it was easy for Frances to be so generous to the poor since she was well off and had time to waste. But Frances met with many trials also. When floods and famine crippled Rome, Frances opened her house as a hospital and freely distributed food and clothing. Her father-in-law was outraged at her behavior and took away the keys to the supply rooms. But he relented when he saw the corn bin and the wine barrel miraculously replenished after Frances finished praying. Natural disasters were followed by wars. When Rome was invaded by enemies, Frances endured the kidnapping of her husband and the death of three of her children. The wars brought plagues and hardships. Again Frances opened her home as a hospital and drove her wagon through the countryside to collect wood for fire and herbs for medicine. She was seen everywhere, burying the dead, nursing the sick, serving the poor, and patiently taking upon herself the hardest most disagreeable work.

When at last the wars were over and Frances's husband had returned, she founded an order of sisters called the Oblates of St. Mary. This was a congregation of women who lived in their own homes and served the poor. Later the Oblates decided to live a community life, but Frances did not join them until after her husband had died and her children had been reared. The charity of Frances was a ray of hope and joy during the disasters that struck Rome in the early 1400's. To the city she was another

Christ. The advice of Mother Teresa of Calcutta to her sisters might be words Frances would choose for us: "Let Christ radiate and live his life in you" (*Something Beautiful for God*).

SUGGESTIONS

1. For twenty-three years, Frances had an archangel as her companion. Visible only to herself, the angel companion was the protector of Frances on her charitable missions. Remind the students to pray to their guardian angels to protect them and their families from all harm.

2. The kind of service Frances gave is now called pastoral ministry in the Church. If the parish has a person involved in this work, invite him or her to speak to the class. Have the class list the main roles laypersons can take to become involved in the Church today.

3. Mother Teresa of Calcutta is often compared to Frances of Rome. Have the students read about the lives of both women and write a report on how each served God through the works of mercy.

4. Frances suffered much from her son's beautiful but violent-tempered wife, who scorned Frances for her love of the unfortunate. But when this daughter-in-law fell seriously ill, it was Frances who nursed her back to health and converted the girl by her kindness. Ask the students to remember to speak lovingly and patiently to those who irritate them.

5. Frances loved her family and reared her children to be good Christians. Encourage the students to do something to give extra rest to their mothers when they are especially tired or not feeling well.

6. Frances began a soup kitchen to aid the poor. During Lent, especially, the students could have a soup lunch. The money saved by having soup instead of a regular meal could be given to the missions.

7. Review the corporal and spiritual works of mercy. Original skits about each work of mercy could be performed for the younger students in the school.

8. Have the students read Genesis 22:1-19. Then tell them that when Frances's husband was kidnapped, the captors demanded his son as ransom. Frances was frantic. She prayed and wept. Then she felt she must act as Abraham did and give up her son. However, God answered her prayers, and the horse that was to carry the boy away would not budge. The superstitious driver gave the boy back to his mother, and her husband returned safely also. Ask the students to share stories of occasions in their lives when God called them to act as Abraham did and then rewarded them.

MARCH 17: PATRICK

Patrick was a model missionary, and his methods of evangelization can be a guide for missionaries today. He helped the people of Ireland not only to keep their beautiful history and culture, but also to add to their heritage the richness of Christianity.

Patrick's early life was his best schooling. The son of a Roman military officer stationed in Britain, Patrick grew up more interested in a career than in religion. At the age of 16, however, he was captured by Irish pirates and taken to Ireland. For six years he worked as a shepherd, suffering from cold and near-starvation. Even more than these physical pains, Patrick suffered the loss of his freedom. All alone among the hills, he finally turned to God — his only hope as he looked for a way to return to Britain.

Eventually he was able to escape aboard a German vessel, paying his way by taking care of a pack of stolen dogs the crew planned to sell. His family was delighted when he returned home — but they were surprised to find a new Patrick. He had changed a great deal, and now had a goal and a vision to serve God. Patrick studied for the priesthood and zealously fulfilled his duties.

When the Church began to discuss the possibility of evangelizing Ireland, Patrick struggled to decide whether or not he should volunteer for this work. He wanted to go, but he remembered his former days of slavery with distaste. When Palladius, the first bishop of Ireland, died, Patrick expressed his desire to become a missionary to that land. He had had a dream in which he heard the voices of Irish people calling to him, "We beg you come and walk with us again." Now Church officials had to decide whether or not to send Patrick, for he was not well educated. However, Pope Celestine I saw in him the extraordinary qualities of a missionary. Patrick understood the people of Ireland because he had lived among them; he knew their language; and already he had spent fifteen years in parish ministry. Most of all, Patrick had a firm belief in his vocation. At the age of forty-two, Patrick was ordained a bishop, and the Pope sent him to northern and western Ireland — where the gospel had never been preached.

Bravely Patrick and several missionary helpers faced the new land. The people of Ireland lived in tribes and clans and worshipped pagan gods. Druids, who were magicians and wizards, kept the people away from any other type of religion. Patrick understood the situation, and knew he would have to convert the chief of a clan before he could win the people. As a man of action, Patrick courageously started with the most powerful clan: Tara. Immediately the chief respected Patrick, who was the son of a military official, who spoke the chief's language well, and who explained his beliefs with sincerity. The chief was converted, and Christianity began to take root in Ireland. Patrick faced personal danger often, for the Druids carefully plotted to do away with him. But Patrick continued to preach the faith, ready for death at any time. He always remembered that he had been a slave, so he showed compassion for all classes of people. He set up monasteries and convents, established parishes, adapted Irish celebrations to Christian feasts, and worked to abolish paganism. His deep prayer kept him calm when British priests criticized his way of ministering or when enemies disgraced his name.

It was in response to his critics that Patrick wrote his Confessio, a kind of autobiography, in which we find the facts of his life. Today Patrick is the patron saint of Ireland, but his feast is a worldwide day of celebration. When we see a picture of St. Patrick, we should remember the joy he found in serving God. We should also remember that we, too, have a mission to witness the Gospel to the ends of the earth. For us, this may mean witnessing in our classrooms, in our homes, on the bus ride home from school, and in the places we go for recreation with our friends.

SUGGESTIONS

1. As the prayer to end class, pray the morning prayer of praise called the "Breastplate of St. Patrick" or the "Lorica." It was probably written down after Patrick died, but best expresses Patrick's love and trust in God.

BREASTPLATE OF ST. PATRICK

I bind unto myself today
The power of God to hold and lead.
His eye to watch, his might to stay,
His ear to listen to my need,
The wisdom of my God to teach.
His hand to guide, his shield to protect,
The word of God to give me speech.
His heavenly messengers to be my guard.

Christ be with me, Christ within me,
Christ behind me, Christ before me,
Christ beside me, Christ to win me,
Christ to comfort and restore me,
Christ beneath me, Christ above me,
Christ in quiet, Christ in danger,
Christ in the hearts of all who love me,
Christ in the mouth of friend or stranger.

I bind unto myself the name,
The strong name, of the Trinity
By calling on the same,
The Three in One, the One in Three,
From whom all nature has creation:
Eternal Father, Spirit, Word.
Praise to the Lord of my salvation.
Salvation is of Christ the Lord. Amen.

2. The principal cathedral in New York is dedicated to St. Patrick. Because so many Irish immigrants had settled in that city, an Irish bishop was appointed and the cathedral dedicated appropriately. Have the students research the founding of their own parish church to discover why the particular title was selected.

3. St. Patrick's day has inspired many colorful customs. Have the students share some of the ways their families and friends celebrate the day.

4. The Irish had an oral culture. They passed on their history and heritage in poems and songs. Among their legends are many stories about St. Patrick. Have the students find out about these stories and relate them to the class. A common story describes St. Patrick expelling all the poisonous snakes from Ireland.

5. When St. Patrick came to Ireland, he did not find barbaric people. Though their culture was not as highly developed as that of the Romans, the people of Ireland were skilled craftsmen. When Christianity was adopted on the island, the people used their artistic talents to make chalices and religious articles. The Celtic (Irish) Cross was very popular. Show the students an example of this art.

Celtic

6. Many statues show St. Patrick holding a shamrock. Ask the students to find out the story behind this representation.

7. St. Patrick is said to have preached in the strife-torn city of Ulster in County Down. Ask the class to bring in articles that discuss what is happening in Northern Ireland today. Show how this religious division is far from the unity Patrick worked to build. Have the class pray for reconciliation and peace in Northern Ireland.

8. St. Patrick, one of the most beloved saints, suffered many personal hardships. A friend in whom he had confided his struggles and former failings supported Patrick through school and in the discussions over his becoming a bishop. Later that friend turned against Patrick and publicly ruined his name. Patrick was tempted to despair. Yet his confidence in God remained unshakable. Have the class discuss reasons why we protect others' reputations and why we keep secrets.

MARCH 18: CYRIL OF JERUSALEM

Being well-liked is not a requirement for being a saint. In fact, Cyril's case was just the opposite. His brother bishops exiled him three times, he was accused of heresy, and another bishop sent to help Cyril administer his diocese left because the situation seemed hopeless. Such was the life of Cyril of Jerusalem. Such was the making of a great saint.

Cyril was born in 315 in Jerusalem and was educated in the city where he would someday be archbishop. He was well acquainted with the Scriptures, and after he became a priest, his bishop, St. Maximus, put him in charge of the preparation of those to be baptized. The Church was facing a new situation. There were so many to be baptized that individual instruction was impossible. Cyril became well known for the clear, understandable catechesis he prepared for the baptismal candidates.

When Maximus was near death, he feared for the future of Jerusalem, "Mother of all the Churches." The heresy of Arianism, which denied the divinity of Christ, was speading so fast and so far that even bishops and the emperor believed in it. Maximus wanted a successor who would be strong enough to stand up for the Church's teaching against heresy. No doubt Cyril was a good person for the position. Cyril was ordained a bishop in about 349 and began at once to bring law, order, and peace to Jerusalem. However, there was a staunch believer in Arianism in the neighboring diocese — a man named Acacius — who felt that the young bishop could be easily manipulated. When Acacius discovered he could not persuade Cyril to support Arianism, he became angry. Now Cyril faced years of trouble. First Acacius and his friends accused Cyril of heresy. When Cyril remained firm in his faith, his enemies summoned him before a council of bishops, saying he had sold church property to feed the starving poor of the diocese. When Cyril refused to appear at the council, the group charged him with disobedience, and Cyril was exiled to Tarsus in southern Turkey. In exile, he won the hearts of the people with his preaching.

When Cyril was finally allowed to return to Jerusalem, the Holy City was violent with heresy, schism, fighting, and crime. Even St. Gregory of Nyssa, who was sent to help Cyril, left because conditions were so bad. Twice again before his death, Cyril was exiled over Arian disputes. He died in 386, at the age of seventy. Fifteen hundred years later, in 1822, Cyril was completely vindicated and was declared a Doctor of the Church.

Ten years after Cyril's death, the abbess, Lady Etheria, made a pilgrimage to the Holy Land and wrote in her letters that she found a peaceful Christian community celebrating the liturgy and serving the poor. This period of peace was the result of the efforts of Bishop Cyril, who personally suffered to heal the wounds Arianism had inflicted on the

Church. The example of Cyril teaches us to be like the Divine Healer, bringing peace where there is misunderstanding and disagreement.

SUGGESTIONS

1. Cyril of Jerusalem is remembered for the sermons he wrote instructing those to be baptized. This section of Cyril's instruction to the catechumens emphasizes his deep reverence for Baptism. Read it to the class and thank God together for the gifts of Baptism.

> My brothers, this is truly a great occasion. Approach it with caution. You are standing in front of God and in the presence of the hosts of angels. The Holy Spirit is about to impress His seal on each of your souls. You are about to be pressed into the service of a great king.

2. Have the students ask their parents the date of their Baptism and then mark it on their calendars. Let them each decorate a candle to be lit on the anniversary of their Baptism. The following are directions for decorating a large white candle:

   1) Cover the candle with a coat of shellac and allow it to dry.
   2) Apply decorations with acrylic paints.
   3) Cover with another coat of shellac.

3. Cyril was influential at the Council of Constantinople, where the Nicene Creed was accepted. This council of bishops was especially strong in accepting and affirming the Holy Spirit as a divine Person in the Trinity, and in opposing the Arians. Have the students read the Nicene Creed. Tell them that creeds were written to teach doctrine, and ask them to find the many doctrines included in this creed.

4. Jerusalem was called the "Mother of Churches" when Cyril was bishop. Post pictures of Jerusalem which you and the students have collected. Ask the students to recall the importance of this city in salvation history and to name events that occurred there.

5. Cyril was a peacemaker. Suggest that the students try to bring reconciliation to a situation involving their family or friends.

MARCH 19: JOSEPH, HUSBAND OF MARY

When was the last time you looked through your family photo album? What type of "photo album" would Jesus have had? Who were the people with whom He lived in His early years? What were the qualities He saw lived out in the people around Him? As we look to the home at Nazareth, we can guess what He must have seen and experienced with Mary, His mother, and with Joseph, His foster father. Neither Mary nor Joseph appear on a great many pages in Scripture, but the beautiful pictures we do find there help us to reconstruct Jesus' "photo album." Let us consider the pictures of His foster father.

The Gospels of both Matthew and Luke present Joseph as the gentle but strong protector of Mary, the Mother of Jesus. When Matthew traces Jesus' human ancestry, it is Joseph's family that is given (Matthew 1:16), emphasizing his relationship to the House of David. St. Luke's introduction of Mary identifies her as the betrothed of a man named Joseph, of the house and family of David (Luke 1:27). This "just man" does not know of the miracle that has been worked in Mary, who is to be the Mother of God, and so he is faced with a terrible dilemma when he realizes that the woman he loves and to whom he is engaged is to bear a child (Matthew 1:18-25). Through a dream, Joseph is informed of the tremendous event that has occurred, and his loving protection of Mary is deepened. As the time for Jesus to be born draws near, Mary and Joseph must go to Bethlehem — not only to be enrolled among the members of the House and Family of David, but also to have the Messiah born in the city of the Great King, as prophecy has foretold.

At the birth of Jesus, Joseph guards Mary and her Child (Luke 2:4-20). Joseph is present also, giving Mary protection as her legal husband, when the Child is circumcised and when He is offered to His Father at the Presentation. With Mary, Joseph hears the prophetic words of the aged Simeon regarding the sufferings to be endured by Mary and her Child (Luke 2:21-35). Through the harrowing years when the life of the Child is in danger because of the hatred of King Herod, Joseph guards and provides for his family in Egypt until he can safely take them back to Nazareth (Matthew 2:13-23). During one of the keenest sufferings of her life, Mary has Joseph's strength and courage to rely upon. When Jesus is lost in Jerusalem, Joseph and Mary together seek Him and take Him back to Nazareth with them (Luke 2:41-52). After this episode, Joseph slips out of the Scriptures, except for a few scattered references to Jesus as the "carpenter's son" (Matthew 13:55; Luke 3:23; John 1:45; John 6:42). It is thought that Joseph died before Jesus began His public life.

These scriptural pictures of Joseph describe him as a "just man," one to whom revelations are made in dreams. He is an obedient man, a guide. We usually refer to Joseph as a carpenter, but the word used in Scripture concerning his trade can actually mean an artisan or craftsman, a worker in stone, metal or wood.

For many centuries after St. Joseph's death, little attention was given to him. His life after death remained as hidden as it had been before. But soon people began to consider his role, his virtues, his trials and his courage. Public veneration of St. Joseph was already found among the Eastern Copts in the fourth century. The Church began to celebrate his feast in the sixth century. St. Ignatius of Loyola and St. Theresa of Avila (fifteenth and sixteenth centuries) were some saints who looked to St. Joseph's example. The devotion to him grew steadily and was given worldwide recognition in 1870, when Pope Pius IX proclaimed St. Joseph the Patron of the Universal Church. Since then, St. Joseph has been named patron of different groups and countries. In 1955, Pius XII named May 1 as the feast of St. Joseph the Worker. In 1961, Pope John XXIII proclaimed Joseph the heavenly protector of Vatican Council II. In 1962, the same Pope included Joseph's name in Eucharistic Prayer I of the Mass.

The feasts may multiply as we become more aware of the greatness of St. Joseph's mind and heart, but he will always remain the silent saint of the Holy Family. His life speaks so powerfully of obedience and love that few words were necessary to preserve for all time the picture of this "just man."

SUGGESTIONS

1. "Abba" is the Aramaic equivalent of the term "Father." Play a recording of "Abba, Father" and have the students think of the influence that a father has on his children. Then let them think of the great love of the Heavenly Father for us, His children, and of the influence He has on our lives.

2. Have the students write thank-you letters to their fathers, grandfathers, uncles, brothers, or other significant father figures in their lives. You may wish to schedule a similar activity later (perhaps in May) for writing to mothers, grandmothers, aunts, sisters, or significant mother figures in their lives. Encourage the students to write letters to their parents or present their parents with homemade gifts on the celebration of their own birthdays, since the event was of special significance to their parents, too!

3. Have the students examine the statue or picture of Joseph in the parish church. Let them note how he is represented and what characteristics the artist portrays. Perhaps you could display some of the famous art pictures of the Holy Family or of Joseph alone. Have the students note how representations of St. Joseph have changed with the times.

4. Sometimes Joseph is pictured as an old man — apparently to safeguard Mary's virginity. However, the custom of the times would indicate that a man should marry between the ages of 13 and 19 and the girl should be between the ages of 12 and 16. Since Joseph was a "just" man, law-abiding, he would most likely have observed the customs of the day. Clarify this fact with the students, since apocryphal stories still abound.

5. Joseph is described as "just." The Biblical notion of "just" is very broad and includes such ideas as law-abiding and holy — one transformed by God and open to His will. Have the students read the description of the just man as given in Ecclesiasticus 45:1-6. Then ask them to write about any person they know who seems to fit this description. Tell them to explain why they chose the person they did.

6. By papal documents, Joseph has been made patron of prayer and the interior life, the poor, those in authority, priests and religious, travelers, and devotion to Mary. He is also the patron of Mexico (1555), Canada (1624), Bohemia (1655), the Chinese missions (1678), Belgium (1689), and the Church's campaign against atheistic communism (1937). Joseph is also known as the patron of the fathers of families, bursars, artisans, procurators, manual workers, carpenters, and all those who desire a happy death (a widespread devotion since the seventeenth century). Acquaint the students with these titles. Have them choose the title that means the most to them and write short prayers to Joseph under that name.

MARCH 23: TURIBIUS OF MOGROVEJO

No one was smarter than Turibius. This member of a wealthy Spanish family had won scholarships to college; he was a brilliant professor of law at Salamanca University. He was a sharp enough judge at the court of the Inquisition, prudently and moderately dispensing justice. His responsibility and keen insight were praised by Philip II, King of Spain.

Unexpectedly this layman received a notice that the pope had appointed him archbishop of Lima, Peru. The news upset and shocked Turibius. He frantically cited all the rules and regulations that forbade making laymen bishops. He was not a priest! He hadn't volunteered! He had never been to South America! But the pope, the king, and his friends knew that protestations were useless. Turibius was an unusual person. His genuine holiness and courage showed in every decision he made. God needed a man who would bring Christ's teachings and His peace and justice to the Church in South America. Greedy Spanish conquerors had taken over the land and the people of Peru. Those wealthy landlords were guilty of every type of oppression. In some cases, priests had also forgotten their responsibility to love and serve the poor and had joined the Spanish in neglect of the people. It certainly was a bleak and critical situation that Turibius faced when he rode into Lima, Peru in 1581.

But Turibius was an energetic and zealous man, who lived by strict principles. Immediately upon his arrival, he began the visitation of every parish and mission in his diocese. This effort took him seven years. He travelled thousands of miles along the coastland, up mountains, and through jungles. His journeys were doubly dangerous because he went without a companion through vast unknown areas plagued by wild animals and tropical diseases. Sometimes he was two or three days in a place without food or a bed. The condition of the Indians horrified Turibius. Thousands of these poor, uneducated, baptized people had little idea of Christianity because there were no catechisms or Bibles in their language and no priests for their missions. The rich Spanish conquerors disregarded the poor. They lived in mansions and were only interested in making fortunes. When he saw such outrages practiced in the name of Christianity, Turibius resolved to make some changes!

At the end of his seven-year visit, Turibius went into action. He gathered the bishops for the Third Council of Lima. Together they decided to print catechisms in the Indian language, to set up classes for the poor, to regulate the administration of the sacraments, and most of all to reform the priests. This last point was met with outraged protests from those priests who were content to serve the rich and not the poor. But Turibius was firm, though understanding. He set an example by learning the Indian language himself, so he could speak to the people when he visited them. He spent himself in baptizing and confirming, in building hospitals, and in establishing the first seminary in the new world. He took his office of bishop seriously. Courageously and unhesitatingly, he spoke out against the way the Spanish treated the poor — even expressing his concerns to the king. He was unusually effective because he loved Christ and did not work for his own interests.

Turibius died as he lived. He was an old man, visiting a mission when he felt sick. He dragged himself into a church and begged for the Sacrament of the Anointing, then he died in that little mountain town. The work of Turibius may have been only a fraction of what was needed for the Church in South America, but he was the kind of witness a bishop should be. According to Vatican Council II, "Since, like St. Paul, he [the bishop] is in duty bound to everyone, he should be eager to preach the Gospel to all, and to spur his faithful on to apostolic and missionary activity" (*Dogmatic Constitution on the Church* #27).

SUGGESTIONS

1. The life of Turibius may seem unusually heroic. But his efforts to bring justice, peace, and mercy are not unlike the efforts of Archbishop Oscar Romero of the twentieth century. Have the students compare the lives of these men.

2. Let the class compile a scrapbook of Central and South American saints. The students could bring in pictures of these saints or pictures of the places where they lived and served. St. Turibius, St. Rose of Lima, St. Martin de Porres, and St. Peter Claver are some saints they will want to include.

3. Pope John Paul II made several trips to Latin America. Have the class find out about the journeys of the pope and why he traveled to this part of the world. His trips include the following: Mexico, 1979; Brazil, 1980; Argentina, 1982; Central America and Haiti, 1982. Read from the books published after the pope's travels to Latin America, quoting his talks to all classes of people. The Daughters of Saint Paul have the most complete list of these books available at reasonable prices.

4. Turibius of Mogrovejo was given the diocese of Lima, Peru to shepherd. Locate Lima on a map. Point out that the majority of the population was Indian. Have the students look up information on Peru to find out the answers to the following questions:

   1) Who first brought Catholicism to the natives of Peru?

   2) Why did the Spanish conquistadors come?

   3) If there were so many baptized Indians, why were there no priests to care for all the missions?

   4) Why was the poverty these Indians faced not the same as the poverty of the spirit praised by Jesus in the Bible?

   5) What changes did the Spanish conquerors make in their style of living after having been made aware of the problems they caused?

5. Turibius had the courage to speak up for the suffering, even though he became unpopular. Remind the students to take advantage of an occasion when they can stand up for the right thing.

6. Help the students become aware of the gifts of the Spanish and Latin Americans to world culture. Play music and show art from these countries to the class.

MARCH 25: ANNUNICIATION OF THE LORD

"I have some good news for you!" If someone gave you this message, what would be your response? Would you be cautious? Curious? Excited? You probably would want that person to tell you the news immediately. John's Gospel tells us the good news that "God loved the world so much that he gave his only Son, so that everyone who believes in him . . . may have eternal life" (John 3:16).

At a moment in time which we now call the Annunciation, God revealed this good news to Mary. She was the first to hear the good news and to believe that God would do what He promised. Her faith told her that nothing is impossible for Him. Mary also heard God's invitation calling her to be the virgin mother of His Son. This call meant that her life in the future would be different from what she might have expected. This call meant that Jesus would be formed in her womb, and that she, as His mother, would nourish and care for Him. This call meant that she had a special place in God's plan for salvation. She would be able to bring Christ to everyone she met.

Mary heard this word of God and responded, "I am the handmaid of the Lord . . . Let what you have said be done to me" (Luke 1:38). In her "yes" response, Mary agreed to God's plan because she wanted what He wanted. She was willing to accept all the joy and pain, all the unexpected events which would help her and guide her. She was willing to bring Christ to a waiting world.

In our lives, let us, like Mary, listen to God's word and believe in His promises. Like Mary, let us be ready to say yes to God's plan for our lives. Let us try by our words and actions to become so much like her Son, Jesus, that we bring Him to everyone we meet.

SUGGESTIONS

1. Slowly read Luke 1:26-38, the account of the Annunciation. Ask the students to jot down words or phrases which strike them during the reading. After the reading, have them draw symbols which capture the meaning of the words or phrases. Let students share their reflections and symbols with the class. Point out that a single Scripture passage can be very rich in meaning.

2. The call that Mary received from God was a call to a way of life. Have the class list the various calls, or vocations, a person might receive: married life, single life, priesthood, diaconate, consecrated life as a brother or sister. As a class, have the students compose a prayer, asking God to lead each one of them to know his or her vocation in life.

3. Remind the students that the Angelus is a traditional prayer about the mystery of the Incarnation and is usually prayed each day in the morning, at noon, and in the evening. Have the students pray the Angelus at the end of the class.

4. Post various artistic representations of the Annunciation. Discuss with the students the way each artist portrays Mary. Have them choose the picture that best matches the way they understand her.

5. In the account of the Annunciation, the angel refers to some qualities that Mary's child will have. These qualities were first mentioned in the Old Testament. Have the students match up the qualities and the Scripture references.

1) Isaiah 41:14	Son of the Most High
2) Daniel 6:28	great
3) Psalm 48:1	Holy One
4) Exodus 15:18	king (who has a throne and who rules)
5) Genesis 14:19-20	savior (meaning of name, Jesus)

Answers:
1) Holy One
2) savior
3) great
4) king
5) Son of the Most High

6. Divide the Annunciation account of Luke 1:26-38 into nine sections as follows: verses 26-27, verse 28, verses 29-30, verses 31-33, verse 34, verse 35, verse 36, verse 37, verse 38. Then, with the class, pray the First Joyful Mystery of the Rosary, while a volunteer reads a section from the gospel account after the recitation of each Hail Mary.

7. Mary brought Christ to others. Have the students plan ways to bring the story of the Annunciation to a younger class through booklets, oral reports, skits, an announcement over the public address system, etc.

8. The feast of the Annunciation is celebrated as a Marian feast. However, in Matthew the angel of the Lord appears to Joseph rather than to Mary. Have the students read Matthew 1:18-25 and explain why the feast is also a feast of St. Joseph.

APRIL 2: FRANCIS OF PAOLA

When Francis was only thirteen, he made a pilgrimage to Rome and Assisi with his parents. He was so impressed by what he saw that he went home and did an unusual thing — he became a hermit in a cave overlooking the sea. By the time Francis was twenty years old, other men who had heard of his holiness had joined him. After still others entered the group, they took the name Hermits of St. Francis of Assisi, or the Franciscan Minim Friars. Minim meant they were "the least in the household of God." Like Francis, most of the friars were charitable, uneducated men who wanted to do much penance for love of God. Francis felt that a person had to do heroic mortification in order to grow spiritually. To the vows of poverty, chastity, and obedience, Francis added a fourth vow: a perpetual Lenten fast. Interestingly, this order attracted many candidates, and the whole countryside praised God for the gifts of prophecy and miracles that Francis possessed.

Though Francis loved the contemplative life of prayer and penance, he later felt God was calling him to an active life of defending the poor and the oppressed. Francis was fearless and did not hesitate to scold King Ferdinand of Naples and his sons for their wrongdoing. The fame of Francis spread far and wide. In 1482, when King Louis XI of France was dying after an apoplectic seizure, he begged that Francis come to cure him, promising the saint money and favors. Francis at first refused, but Pope Sixtus IV ordered him to go to France, care for the king, and prepare him for death. When the king saw Francis, he fell on his knees, pleading for a miracle. Francis reprimanded him, saying that the lives of kings are in the hands of God, and Louis ought to let God cure him. Francis did not settle into the ease and luxury of the court life; rather, he influenced the fate of nations, restoring peace between France and Great Britain by advising a marriage that united the families of the ruling parties. Francis also helped bring peace between France and Spain.

Francis died in the French court. Though his miracles were numerous and well known, he was canonized for his humility and discernment in blending the contemplative life with the active one. He is a good example for the busy people of today.

SUGGESTIONS

1. Because most of Francis' miracles were connected with the sea, he was named the patron of seafarers by Pope Pius XII. Encourage the students to pray for those whose occupations involve work on seas, lakes, and rivers.

2. Among the many famous artists who have depicted St. Francis are Murillo, Velazquez, and Goya. He is even the subject of Franz Liszt's sonata, "St. Francis Paola Walking the Waters." Have the students find out about other saints who have had songs or poems written about them, or who have been painted by famous artists. (A clue: articles in the *New Catholic Encyclopedia* give this kind of information.)

3. Though Francis was an uneducated man, people said that his words were so wise that it was as if the Holy Spirit were speaking. Have the students use an index to their Bibles to find passages where Jesus praises the simple and lowly. Let them design bookmarks from these quotes.

4. Francis believed bodily mortification was a help to spiritual growth. Fridays are prescribed days of penance for Catholics. Tell the students they have the choice of either abstaining from meat on Friday or performing some equivalent form of penance. Also recommend that they give up snacks between meals on one or two days a week. Let them share their experiences of spiritual growth from fasting.

5. Francis knew the real tension between work and prayer. Remind the students that no matter how busy their day is, they should still remember the need for prayer. Help them become conscious of morning and evening prayers.

APRIL 4: ISIDORE OF SEVILLE

If you had known Isidore of Seville as a boy, you might have wondered just how he would turn out in the future. He sometimes didn't do his homework and even skipped his studies. After the death of his parents, Isidore was cared for by his elder brother Leander, a monk who later became the archbishop of Seville and was venerated as a saint. Leander wanted his younger brother to become an educated person, but Isidore did not like the hard studies in which his brother tutored him. One day (when he should have been studying) Isidore found an old stone well. He noticed that there were grooves in the stone walls where thin wet ropes had worn the stone away. He was fascinated by the discovery that such thin rope could alter very hard stone. Then he found a parallel to this situation in his own life. Just as the rope could wear away the rock by consistently cutting a little bit at a time, so he might become successful at his studies if he tried consistently. Isidore kept his resolution to persevere in his studies, and in later years he became known as the most learned man of his era. His influence was felt in the political, historical, educational, and religious fields of his times.

Politically, Isidore presided over the council of Toledo in 633. This council helped settle the differences between the reigning king and a usurper to the throne. This council also decreed that Jews be given the freedom to keep their religion rather than being forced to become Christian.

Historically, Isidore wrote biographies and a history of the world from creation to his own times. This work is useful even today as a source book on Spanish history.

Educationally, Isidore worked to establish in each diocese a college to instruct seminarians. This action shows dramatically the change in attitude which Isidore experienced since his early youth. Also in the area of education, his principal work was a brand new idea in the seventh century. He wrote an encyclopedia which contained all the secular and religious knowledge available at his time: from astronomy to geography, from monsters to household utensils. What an undertaking! In the area of religion, Isidore worked hard to renew the Church in Spain. He greatly encouraged the reading of Sacred Scripture. Some of his theological works helped shape the spiritual outlook of the Middle Ages. For all of this, he was declared a Doctor of the Church in 1722.

At this point you might be wondering why this highly successful man is declared a saint. It is not because he wrote an encyclopedia, founded a college, or helped a king. Isidore is a saint because he worked hard at being open to God's love and grace. He was also outstanding for helping the poor. It was his love for God and others which gave Isidore his lasting success in heaven!

SUGGESTIONS

1. To help the students appreciate the almost limitless range of knowledge open to them, have each one choose a topic from the *New Catholic Encyclopedia* and prepare a one-minute summary. Then have the students share their findings with the class.

2. Isidore found that consistent effort made the difference. Have the students think of one goal they have been trying to achieve — a personal habit that needs changing, a family relationship that needs improving, etc. Encourage them to make a one-week plan, thinking of something they can do each day to achieve their goal.

3. Isidore had difficulty with his homework. Suggest that the students make a resolution to do all their homework this week in honor of St. Isidore.

4. Considering his poor start in education, Isidore did quite well academically. Have the students think about the elements they appreciate in their Catholic education: the Christian atmosphere, the encouragement of teachers, the good example of classmates, the emphasis on prayer and Scripture, etc. Suggest that they write one paragraph on their appreciation of their own school. The opening sentence can be similar to the following: "Catholic education at (*name of school*) is outstanding in three ways."

5. The thin wet rope wearing away the thick stone wall was an image which paralleled for Isidore the way that he should work at his studies. Have the students think of an image which would demonstrate how they can work in school or at home. In their journals, have them write about the image or draw a picture of it.

APRIL 5:   VINCENT FERRER

To understand the saints, we must also understand the time in which they lived. In the 1300's and 1400's, the Catholic world was in havoc. Three different men claimed to be pope. Kings, princes, priests, and lay people fought one another to support the different men who claimed the Chair of Peter. This state of chaos in the Church led to the Western Schism. During these confusing years, God raised up a Dominican priest, Vincent Ferrer, to heal the Catholic world by his preaching and to prepare the way for union in the Church under one head.

Vincent was a man with a fiery spirit, and when he joined the Dominicans, he zealously practiced penance, study, and prayer. After his solemn profession, he taught philosophy, though Vincent's greatest gifts were not in teaching. Naturally gifted as a preacher, he was well liked by the people — who called him the "mouth-piece of God." What made his preaching so effective was his saintly life. The subjects of his preaching were judgment, heaven, hell, and the need for repentance. He had to preach in the open air in France, Spain, and Italy because no church was big enough to hold the crowds. So convincing were his words and actions that he made many converts.

But the schism in the Church distressed Vincent most of all, and he wanted to heal this division. Unfortunately, even the holiest of people can be misled. Pope Urban VI was the real pope and lived in Rome. But Vincent and many others were persuaded to think that Clement VII and his successor Benedict XIII, who lived in Avignon in France, were the true popes. Using his gifts of eloquence and learning, Vincent passionately convinced kings, princes, clergy, and almost all of the people of Spain to give their loyalty to Clement and Benedict. After Clement VII died, Vincent tried to get both Benedict and the pope in Rome to abdicate so that a new election could be held. It hurt Vincent to see that Benedict's stubbornness and pride refused peace.

Gradually Vincent came to see the error in Benedict's claim to the papacy. Discouraged and ill, Vincent begged Christ to show him the truth. In a vision, he saw Jesus with St. Dominic and St. Francis commanding him to "go through the world preaching Christ." For the next twenty years, Vincent spread the Good News throughout Europe. He rarely stayed in one place longer than a day. He fasted constantly, he preached continually, he worked miracles, and by his enthusiasm for Christ, he drew many people to become faithful Christians. Still Vincent never forgot the sad circumstances of the Catholic Church. Again he returned to Benedict in Avignon and asked him to resign. Benedict refused. Even though he was an old man and worn out, Vincent knew what he had to do for the Church. While Benedict was presiding over an enormous assembly gathered in a prominent church, Vincent, though close to death, mounted the pulpit and dramatically preached an unforgettable sermon. Vincent denounced Benedict as the false pope and encouraged everyone to be faithful to the one, true Catholic Church in Rome. Benedict fled for his life, knowing his supporters had deserted him.

Later the Council of Constance met to end the Great Western Schism, but Vincent refused any part in the Council, fearing that it, too, might cause more division. Fortunately the Council resolved the problem in the Church. Vincent, ever faithful to Christ and His teachings, died soon after. On his death bed, he asked for the Passion to be read. Vincent serves as a model of fidelity to the Church; despite confusion and tension, he always sought to defend the truth.

SUGGESTIONS

1. St. Vincent was favored with the gift of tongues. It is said that when preaching in his own language, he was understood by Germans, Hungarians, Swedes, and others. Have the students read what St. Paul has to say about the gifts of the Spirit (1 Corinthians 12:1-11). Discuss the purpose of the gifts of the Spirit and why they are given.

2. St. Vincent prepared all his homilies at the foot of the crucifix. He told others, "Never begin or end your study except by prayer," and at another time, "Let devotion accompany all your studies and study less to make yourself learned than to become a saint. Consult God more than your books; ask Him with humility to make you understand what you read." Recommend that the students pray before doing their homework, asking God to guide all their study.

3. The need for reconciliation was a theme of St. Vincent's preaching. Stress with the students the importance of the need for conversion, and

encourage them to make use of the Sacrament of Penance frequently. Read and discuss the two eucharistic prayers for reconciliation.

4. Have the students look up facts about the different popes of the Western Schism to understand how the schism started and how it was finally healed. The three popes at the time of the Council of Constance (1414), when the schism ended, were Benedict XIII (anti-pope), Gregory XII (true pope), and John XXIII (anti-pope who died in 1419 after the Council of Constance). It might be valuable to point out that our late Pope John XXIII, who reigned from 1958-1963, took this name to fill up the vacancy left by an anti-pope.)

5. Remind the students to pray for the present pope, who bears the responsibility for the Church.

APRIL 7: JOHN BAPTIST DE LA SALLE

In his early years, John Baptist de La Salle, patron of school teachers, had little interest in education for everyone. In seventeenth century France, education was reserved for the rich, and only by special providence did La Salle become interested in schools for poor boys. Born into a powerful, wealthy family, La Salle as a young man had different ambitions, since his background and early training for the priesthood prepared him for high offices in the Church. When La Salle was ordained a priest, his good looks, polished manners, intelligence, and wealth set him apart from the poor.

By chance, La Salle met M. Nyel, an innovator in education, who was establishing charitable schools for poor boys. La Salle disliked the rough behavior of the poor and the smells and the sights of the slums, but he sympathized with their poverty. Moved by charity, La Salle helped open a school for poor boys. He secured five school teachers and rented a home for the boys. As La Salle checked on the progress of his school, he witnessed shocking conditions. The teachers were often brutal, beating and insulting the children. Frequently the teachers themselves could neither read nor write, and they spent their nights in taverns, drinking or playing cards. Because they received very little salary, they had little motivation or self-esteem.

No matter how he hated the idea of becoming involved, La Salle decided he had to bring order, discipline, and efficiency to the school. He planned to upgrade the standards of the teachers and train them to be religious educators. La Salle discussed the problems of the school with his staff and worked to give them a strong sense of self-respect. Achieving his goal seemed a hopeless task. His teachers quit. But soon men of better quality, who took their places, thrived under La Salle's training in faith, prayer, order, and discipline. Gradually, La Salle was becoming aware of the call of God. He began to see that he must identify with his teachers, so he gave away his fortune and dedicated himself to education.

The education of the poor was an urgent need of the times, and La Salle realized the value of a religious congregation of men to fulfill this ministry. To answer the need, he founded the Brothers of Christian Schools. This religious group was different from all the other orders of the time. In La Salle's community, no member would be a priest. The main purposes of the congregation were to train teachers and to provide religious education for the poor. La Salle's extraordinary leadership enabled him to influence education in three ways: the teachers all taught in the native language of the people (not in Latin); individual instruction was replaced by classroom teaching under well-prepared teachers; the students had to be silent while teaching took place; and the teachers kept the students occupied with work. "The more religious a school is, the more successful it is," was La Salle's philosophy. So his boys attended daily Mass, were taught the catechism and prayers, and had religion integrated into other subjects, as well as taught in separate classes.

By motivating the students to prepare for a career and guide their lives by Christian principles, La Salle helped them become self-confident and strong Catholics. His schools soon became so successful that he attracted boys from fee-paying schools. La Salle's teachers were in demand everywhere, and his schools were overflowing. Other instructors became jealous, criticized his methods, and tried to bring lawsuits to ruin his work. But his efforts were praised by the people. Even King James II of England, in exile in France, sent fifty young gentlemen from his court to be educated at La Salle's school. La Salle's work was growing and expanding. He opened boarding schools for poor boys and gave them courses in practical skills. He founded schools for delinquents from wealthy families so the young boys would not be sent to prison.

When La Salle died on Good Friday, 1719, he was praised by all as a man who lived and taught genuine love, just as Christ, the Master Teacher, had shown love for all. John Baptist de La Salle is a saint to whom we can pray. He had a heart for all students and wanted them to feel needed and important.

SUGGESTIONS

1. John Baptist de La Salle believed the main purpose of a Catholic school was to help young people grow in becoming good Christians. Hold a class discussion on what makes a school Catholic.

2. Plan with the students a "Teacher-Appreciation Day" for the school. The day could open with a P.A. announcement expressing gratitude to the teachers for their work in religious education. Perhaps students could prepare baked goods as a special treat for the teachers or plan simple programs in their honor.

3. Help the students prepare a special issue of the school newspaper to explain the advantages of a Catholic school, its projects, and some of the religious activities the school promotes.

4. Encourage the students to think of ways they can promote a more religious atmosphere within the school. Have them list these suggestions on a large sheet of paper and then choose one each week as a special project in which the whole school can join.

5. Work with the class in planning a special liturgy on the theme of Catholic education. The liturgy could include songs, petitions, and, perhaps, a slide presentation that fits the theme.

Note: If there is a school nearby operated by the Christian Brothers, the members of La Salle's order, have some of the boys visit it to find out its main purposes.

APRIL 8: JULIE BILLIART

Looking at a statue cannot possibly give one a true impression of this dynamic woman, because a statue is cold and immobile. If we could see St. Julie in action, we would see a woman with children tagging after her on her way to church, a woman bargaining at the market place, a woman praying late into the night, or a woman traveling the backroads of France on foot.

Julie Billiart, the founder of the Sisters of Notre Dame, was born into a peasant family in 1751 in Picardy, France. Her father ran a small shop and owned a handkerchief-sized piece of property. As a child, Julie learned to do the ordinary things: read, write, count, sew, and memorize the catechism. When Julie was in her teens, her father's store was invaded by robbers, who took most of its stock. Later an enemy planning to take her father's life shot at him in the room where Julie was also sitting. No one was hurt, but gradually the shock of the event affected Julie's nervous system and she was struck with paralysis.

Life in France was not easy for Julie, now an invalid. The French Revolution was over, but the Church was still suppressed. Julie was firm in her faith and she gathered children to her bedside to speak to them about God and to tell them stories from the Bible. Julie was a delightful person from whom to learn, and the children loved her. Soon, however, people who did not love God reported to the government that Julie was teaching religion. To avoid arrest, Julie had to be smuggled from house to house. Such moving about was painful for Julie. Finally a room was found for her at the home of a wealthy woman,

Francoise Blin de Bourdon. It was to Francoise, who became a close friend, that Julie confided her dream of founding a community of women who would teach the faith to children. How could she accomplish such a dream? She was penniless. For more than twenty years, she had been an invalid. Julie and Francoise prayed.

One day, after a novena to the Sacred Heart, the priest who was Julie's confessor commanded her: "If you have any faith in the Sacred Heart of Jesus, walk." And Julie stepped forward! She was cured! Now at the age of 53, she began her active life. Together with Francoise, who gave her money to the project, Julie founded the Sisters of Notre Dame to care for orphans, to educate poor girls, and to train Christian teachers. What John Baptist de La Salle had done for poor boys about a hundred years earlier, Julie and Francoise now began to do for poor girls.

Julie's energy, joy, and holiness were visible. The deepest lesson she had learned during her years of pain and sickness was "God is good." Soon other companions joined Julie and Francoise in their work to spread the good news of the goodness of God. One day, Julie had a vision of sisters in religious habits, standing around the cross of Christ. A voice said, "Here are the daughters I will give you in the institute marked by the cross." Indeed, this was true. Julie's work was marked by the cross. The government had no use for Catholicism. Some of Julie's own sisters betrayed her, people withdrew financial support from her schools, bishops were skeptical about her work. But through all this misunderstanding, Julie's confidence grew. With great hope, she started schools, trained teachers, and performed countless works of charity.

When she died, Julie did not know that her sisters would one day be speading the Good News of Christ around the world. Julie's story gives courage to all Christians. In all her difficulties, she blessed Christ, rejoiced in the cross, and never ceased repeating: "How good is the good God!"

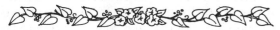

SUGGESTIONS

1. St. Julie is called "The Smiling Saint" because she was cheerful and hopeful even when experiencing great pain or sorrow. Julie knew that everything God permitted was good. Have the students remember to greet everyone with a smile, even when — especially when — they are not feeling happy.

2. As a teacher, Julie showed genuine love and concern for her students. Because she wanted the classroom to be a pleasant place, she gladly helped those who had difficulties. Have the students plan to do something especially nice for the class today.

3. In the beginning of their apostolate, the Sisters of Notre Dame taught only girls, but now they teach both boys and girls. Find out the names of schools where the Sisters of Notre Dame teach. Some of the girls could visit there to ask about the work of the sisters. Or the class could invite a Sister of Notre Dame to speak on St. Julie and the work her sisters do in the world today.

4. St. Julie had special devotion to the Sacred Heart. Bring a suitable picture (not saccharin or pietistic) of the Sacred Heart of Jesus to be enthroned in your classroom. Tell the students about the love of Christ for each of us. Some of the students could research the history of the apparitions of the Sacred Heart of Jesus and report to the class.

5. St. Julie wanted all children to know about the life of Jesus and to practice their faith. Have the class make a book with stories and illustrations about the ministry of Jesus. Some of the students could share the book with students in a lower grade.

APRIL 11: STANISLAUS

In 1072 the people of Cracow, Poland were without a bishop, and they begged Pope Alexander II to give them Stanislaus as their spiritual leader. Stanislaus was a legend in his own day. This well-loved leader, who was so enthusiastically acclaimed, was generous to the poor and the needy. His courage proved itself when he opposed King Boleslaus II for unjust wars, violence, cheating the poor, and abducting a nobleman's wife. King Boleslaus pretended repentance, but his virtue was short-lived. Soon he returned to his old ways of corruption. And Stanislaus, in his outspoken way, tirelessly preached the ways of God to the monarch. Enraged by Stanislaus' reprimands, Boleslaus accused the bishop of various crimes.

One story reports that a man named Knight Peter had given an estate to the bishop. Later Peter died. Boleslaus accused Stanislaus of not paying for the property. Stanislaus fasted for three days, ordered the grave of Peter opened, raised him to life, and brought him to court. Peter upheld the good name of the bishop. Still Boleslaus behaved like a tyrant, and Stanislaus had no choice but to excommunicate him. Now the anger of Boleslaus knew no bounds. The king entered the cathedral where Stanislaus was officiating, and services were suspended. Stanislaus, pursued by the king, fled to a chapel outside of town. The king ordered his guards to enter the church and kill the bishop. When they refused, the king boldly marched into the chapel and slew Stanislaus with his own sword.

Stanislaus, a brave witness for Christianity, is patron of Poland. He defended Christ and His Church and spoke the truth, even if it meant his death. Stanislaus was not a man who would lie just to please the authority, the king. Pray often to him that you may love your faith enough to witness it even to the point of sacrifice.

SUGGESTIONS

1. Centuries after the time of Stanislaus, the diocese of Cracow was served by the future Pope John Paul II as its bishop. Have the students find out how Pope John Paul II has courageously witnessed his faith, as did Stanislaus.

2. St. Thomas More wrote, "Men desire authority for its own sake that they may bear a rule, command and control other men, and live uncommanded and uncontrolled themselves." Discuss the meaning of this statement with the class. Also consider why those in authority or in the government have a responsibility to set a good example.

3. Have the students locate Poland on the map. Ask them to find out how Poland is governed. Remind the students that in Poland the faith was tolerated under a Communist regime.

4. Suggest that the students read about the life of St. Maximilian Kolbe, a Polish saint who gave his life as a witness to Christian charity. (Canonized in 1983.)

5. Tell the students that Boleslaus finished his life as a penitent in a Benedictine abbey. Point out to the students how God always forgives even the greatest of sins. Encourage the students to use the Sacrament of Penance.

APRIL 13: MARTIN I

Sometimes God asks a person to be a martyr by witnessing to the faith in prison and in chains. That was the sacrifice asked of Pope Martin I at a time when the Church in Constantinople was very influential.

The future Pope Martin I had been a lector and deacon in his youth. He was elected pope in 649. Martin was aware that a heresy called Monothelitism was causing confusion in the Church. This doctrine held that there was one nature in Christ — the divine nature — and that Christ had only one will. It therefore denied our redemption by Christ. Because this group was slowly splitting the Eastern Empire, many eastern Catholics attempted to compromise with the group. In an edict called the "Typos," the Emperor Constans II practically accepted the heretical doctrine by forbidding any further discussion of the wills in Christ. Pope Martin, fearing that the truth about Christ would not be taught, called a council at the Lateran. One hundred and five bishops attended the council, which condemned Constans' "Typos" and published an explanation of the doctrine of the two natures in Christ. The council did not blame the emperor, but emphasized that he had been misguided by his advisors.

The council and its results angered the emperor, who had Martin arrested and taken on a long, difficult voyage from Rome to Constantinople. The pope suffered terribly because he was given little food, was forbidden for forty-seven days to wash even in cold water, and was denied all help. When Martin arrived in Constantinople, he was insulted by the people and accused in an unjust trial, not for defending the faith, but for being a traitor. Publicly, the emperor had Martin stripped of his episcopal robes, which were ripped from top to bottom. Then Martin was condemned to death. Worn out from his sufferings and from neglect, the pope wrote sadly to a friend that he had been abandoned by all, even by the Church in Rome. The verdict of death was changed to exile when the repentant, dying patriarch of Constantinople wrote to the emperor, interceding on Martin's behalf. Martin was then exiled to Crimea, where he died, neglected and forgotten.

Martin is an example of what it means to suffer persecution for justice's sake. He willingly gave up his life for the faith because his love for God was stronger than death.

SUGGESTIONS

1. Direct the students to research why a pope calls a council. When did the last council occur? Why was it called?

2. When Pope Martin I was condemned to death, the Church elected a new pope. Martin, exiled and neglected, wrote that he prayed for the safety of the faithful in Rome and especially for the guidance of the new pastor now placed over them. Martin was a man who refused to become bitter, but trusted in God even when he felt abandoned by all. Have the students read the Passion of Jesus Christ to see how Jesus suffered the abandonment of His followers and how He endured great pain for our salvation.

3. On the board, have the students list the responsibilities of the pope. Have them write essays on what they believe is the pope's most important witness to Christ.

4. Pope Martin I was the last pope to be venerated as a martyr. Have the students look up the word *martyr* in the dictionary or in an encyclopedia to discover the root meaning of the term. Let them discuss how Christians of the twentieth century can be martyrs.

5. Help the students understand how the pope shepherds the Church. Encourage them to bring in articles from newspapers and magazines that report the pope's travels, addresses, and fulfillment of responsibilities. Compile a scrapbook of these articles.

APRIL 21: ANSELM

When Anselm was a young boy in Aosta, Italy, he thought of becoming a priest. His father, angered by this desire, introduced his son to court life. This easygoing life, with few responsibilities and many pleasures, made Anselm forget about his vocation. But in 1060, after the death of his mother, Anselm became interested in Lanfranc, the popular spiritual leader of monasticism in Normandy, France. Lanfranc's monastery at Bec was said to be the best school at the time, and when Anselm entered it as a monk he quickly made friends with Lanfranc. Three years later, Anselm became prior, and at the request of his community began to publish his writings on the existence of God.

In the monastery, Anselm was known for his great virtue and his teaching skill. He kept exceptional control of his temper, and the monks praised his patient, sensitive way of dealing with people. It was not surprising that he was unanimously elected abbot in 1070, when Lanfranc was made bishop of Canterbury in England. William the Conqueror had just gained control of England in 1066, and was reorganizing the government and the Church under the Norman heads. When Lanfranc died in 1089, the English clergy wanted Anselm as their bishop; however, Rufus, the son of William the Conqueror, would not approve. For four years, there was no Bishop of Canterbury. Then, suddenly, a mysterious sickness made Rufus mortally ill. In fear of being sent to hell for all the scandal he had caused, Rufus appointed Anselm archbishop of Canterbury. Knowing he would come into conflict with Rufus over the Church, Anselm at first refused the appointment. The pope, however, ordered him to accept.

As suddenly as Rufus had become ill, he recovered. Once well, Rufus fell into his former sins again: taking Church lands and attempting to appoint his own bishops. Anselm told the bishops · that their obedience demanded they be loyal to the pope and ignore the king's interference in Church matters. Frightened over this conflict between the archbishop and the king, the bishops and priests abandoned Anselm. The king then exiled him. In exile, Anselm was not idle. He wrote treatises and took part in the Council of Bari (1098), where he spoke eloquently on the Holy Spirit. After the death of Rufus, who was killed in a hunting accident, Anselm returned to England. Henry I, brother of Rufus, was now the king, but he continued to rule as his predecessor had done.

Henry also wanted power to appoint bishops, and Anselm refused to accept his appointment from the king. Again Anselm was exiled to Rome. It was Pope Paschal who worked out a compromise between the king and the bishop. The pope made the rule that only the Church could invest a bishop with the ring and the crozier, but the king would have some power in the selection of bishops. Until his death in 1109, Anselm remained in England defending the faith. His holiness, patience, and love of the Church were so well respected that Canterbury came to be recognized as the major see in England. In 1720 Anselm was given the title Doctor of the Church and Father of Scholasticism because he analyzed and taught the truths of the faith by the aid of reason. The Church encourages the faithful to live as Anselm did — loyal to God at whatever cost.

SUGGESTIONS

1. St. Anselm had great compassion for the sufferings of Christ on the cross. The Cistercians promoted much of this spirituality, and it was through this movement that we got the familiar representation of Christ on the cross. Before this period, Christ had been represented as crucified but glorified. Have the students bring in crosses or crucifixes they have at home and display these in the classroom. Speak to the students about reverence to the cross and its importance. Today, not all crosses have the corpus (body of Christ crucified).

2. Anselm did not spend all his energies dealing with kings; he had great concern for the poorest of the poor. Anselm was the first in the Church to oppose slave trade. It was through his efforts that the National Council at Westminister (1102) passed a law prohibiting the sale of men. Discuss with the class what bishops do today to promote Christ's teachings through social justice.

3. Anselm's correspondence was phenomenal: 475 letters giving spiritual direction to popes, royalty, monks, nuns, and laity. This showed how much he cared about others. In his spirit, have the students write a letter to a friend or relative they have not seen for awhile.

4. A biographer of Anselm records a famous speech he gave at the abbey of Cluny on the fourteen happinesses of heaven. To Anselm, the greatest happiness was to possess God. Have the students write about fourteen happinesses they possess or look forward to. Encourage them to write with a spiritual outlook.

5. Anselm was an excellent teacher, and his students recalled that his oral method of teaching, based on parables drawn from life, showed the richness of his spiritual character. Share with the students today something from your life that has drawn you close to God.

6. Anselm was an original and independent thinker. The nineteen prayers and three meditations he wrote show these qualities. The prayers were written by special request. Have the students write a prayer that asks God's help and praises Him for His goodness.

7. Pope Paschal said that only the bishop may invest a new bishop with the ring and crozier. Have the students find out why the bishop is given these special objects. If they can find a picture of the cross, crozier, and ring worn by their own bishop, have the students make drawings of these special symbols.

APRIL 23: GEORGE

The real story of St. George is heroic enough. George was probably a soldier in the fourth century who courageously and publicly defended the faith and encouraged his fellow Christians. For this action, he suffered martyrdom under Diocletian. For this heroism, he was venerated as a popular saint in the east. By the sixth century, St. George had become the ideal Christian knight, and the story of his slaying the dragon had become immensely popular. In the seventh and eighth centuries, stained glass windows in the Churches of Europe depicted this sixth-century legend. Already St. George had become a popular saint in the west.

Though the story of the dragon is not verifiable, it has become so closely connected with St. George that it deserves a place here. The story tells of a dragon that terrorized the land and poisoned with its breath all who approached it. George slew the dragon and refused any reward, but he made the king promise he would build churches, honor priests, and show compassion to the poor. This act made George so popular he became the personification of all the ideals of Christian chivalry. He was named patron of soldiers, and when the English king Richard I led his soldiers in the Crusades, he placed his army under George's protection. In one famous battle, the opposition was so strong that the Christians were losing. Later the army leaders insisted that in the midst of the battle, St. George rode forward and led the troops to victory. From then on, George became the patron of England. King Edward III founded an order of knights under his patronage, and his feast was kept as a national festival.

Though the stories of St. George seem extraordinarily courageous to us, no one can deny the fact that his real heroism was in dying for Christ.

SUGGESTIONS

1. Often people are not content to let the lives of great people be simple. Glorified stories of their love of Christ are repeated. Have the students dramatize the heroism of St. George's life.

2. Poems have been written applauding St. George's heroism. The following is a stanza from a poem by Edmund Spenser.

> For thou, among those saints whom thou doest see,
> Shalt be a saint, and thine own nation's friend
> And patron: thou Saint George shalt called be,
> Saint George of merry England, the sign of victory.
> (*The Faerie Queene*, bk. 1, canto 10, stanza 61)

Have the students write a ballad on George or on their own patron saints.

3. Direct the students to read about Christian chivalry and the important part it played in the Middle Ages. Have them report their findings to the class.

4. Hold a class discussion on glorified lives of the saints: why such legends become popular. Discuss why such popular tales can inspire people to lead better lives.

5. It is interesting to note that St. George was offered anything he wanted for killing the dragon. He refused all material things, but made the request that churches be built, priests respected, and the poor cared for. Encourage the students to imitate such conduct. Even though the story is probably a legend, they can imitate the example of one who did all for the honor and glory of God.

6. St. George is the patron of soldiers and all who work for the good of their country. Remind the class to pray for the armed forces of our country.

APRIL 24: FIDELIS OF SIGMARINGEN

Born at Sigmaringen, Prussia, Fidelis was a man of many names. Mark Roy was his baptismal name, Fidelis his religious name, and his nickname was "Poor man's lawyer." All his life, Mark Roy was known for his extraordinary generosity. After taking his doctorate in philosophy and law, he tutored young boys from noble families. But his heart was with the poor. He established himself as a lawyer and took only those cases which upheld the cause of the poor and the oppressed. Soon he became disgusted with the corruption and injustice he saw among his fellow lawyers. They cared little about the destitute in Switzerland and Austria. Inspired to search for a deeper, more committed life of serving God, Mark decided to enter the Franciscans. He distributed his wealth among the needy seminarians and the poor, made his religious vows, and chose the name Fidelis. So well did Fidelis live the Franciscan way of life that he was soon chosen by the friars as superior.

While Fidelis was guardian of the monastery, an epidemic broke out in the city, and Fidelis generously opened up the friary to care for the sick. It was reported that he cured many soldiers staying there.

He was so compassionate that it was not unusual for Fidelis to offer the clothes he was wearing to a man or woman suffering from the cold. In 1608, Protestantism had swept through Switzerland. Because Fidelis was a good preacher, he was sent by the Propagation of the Faith to preach to the Swiss people and bring them back to unity with the Church of Rome. Though Fidelis labored hard in preaching and performing acts of charity, people who knew him claimed his best results came from the hours of prayer he spent late in the night.

It was a dangerous mission he had undertaken because the people were in revolt against the Catholic Church and hated anyone connected with it. But Fidelis put his life in the hands of God. At Seewis in 1622, a gun was fired at him as he preached. He escaped unharmed, and a Protestant friend offered him shelter, but he refused. Later he was slain in the church by a group of angry peasants. The life of Fidelis showed that there are no limits for a person who deeply loves God. A Christian can conquer the fear of death and generously perform dangerous tasks when faith is strong enough.

SUGGESTIONS

1. St. Fidelis is considered a martyr for his efforts in evangelization. Have the students find out what the Church is doing today to evangelize.

2. Love for the poor and the sick was a major part of the work of St. Fidelis. Review with the students the significance of living out the corporal and spiritual works of mercy in their lives.

3. When St. Fidelis was a lawyer, he was very much concerned about justice for the poor and oppressed. Honesty and integrity were important to him. Remind the students of the implications of the seventh and tenth commandments. Discuss with the class how Christians can overcome greed in their lives.

4. Mark Roy chose Fidelis as his religious name. Remind the students that they will have an opportunity at Confirmation to chose a new name or to keep their baptismal name.

5. St. Fidelis believed in the power of prayer. He took extra time every day to pray so that his preaching would be effective. Point out to the students the power of prayer. Have them explain when prayer has helped them be more effective Christians in their daily lives.

APRIL 25: MARK

The pioneer in gospel writing was St. Mark (about 65 A.D.). His is the shortest and the oldest of the Gospels. Little is known of Mark except from the New Testament. Mark was not one of the twelve apostles, but rather a member of the first Christian community. It was probably Mark's mother who opened her house as a place of prayer for the apostles during Peter's imprisonment (Acts 12:12). Mark also had firsthand experience of the early church and apostolic life. He was a traveling companion and assistant of Paul and Barnabas on the first missionary journey. Something happened to Mark on that journey — perhaps homesickness — so he returned to Jerusalem. The incident caused a quarrel between Paul and Barnabas. Barnabas, Mark's cousin, was sympathetic to Mark's problems, but Paul would not hear of Mark accompanying them again. Later Paul and Mark must have been reconciled, because when Paul wrote to Timothy during his final imprisonment, he asked for Mark's assistance (2 Timothy 4:11).

Mark's Gospel was his great contribution to the Christian community. It included oral and written tradition concerning the words and deeds of Jesus. He probably secured some of his material from St. Peter and then presented the account of God's saving plan through the life, death, and resurrection of Jesus. Mark shows Jesus as the suffering Son of God. Mark knew that it was easy to be a disciple of the Risen Jesus and anticipate the assured victory of eternal life. But Mark also knew that to accept the Risen Jesus meant to come to terms with the cross. Jesus was glorified because He willingly allowed Himself to suffer death for our salvation. He was taken by His enemies, mocked, misunderstood, humbled, and, through these sufferings, was glorified. Mark writes sincerely that anyone who wishes to come after Jesus must accept the cross.

Mark wrote to proclaim the Good News to a community that had as its members both Jewish and Gentile Christians. His Gospel is direct and simple to read. He speaks to Christians about a Jesus Who understands their difficulties and sufferings and will one day bring them to share with Him eternal joy and glory. He shows Jesus to be the one Who forgives sins and leads people to everlasting happiness.

SUGGESTIONS

1. Let the students discover why artistic tradition uses the symbol of a winged lion to represent St. Mark.

2. Share with the students stories that have been passed down about St. Mark. He is traditionally thought to have been a bishop of Alexandria, and while living there cured a shoemaker and suffered martyrdom.

3. The spirit of Mark's Gospel is willingness to accept the destiny of Jesus as a suffering, dying, and rising Messiah. Have the students look up the following passages from St. Mark and St. Paul. Discuss how these references fit Mark's theme: Romans 8:17; 1 Corinthians 2:1-2; Mark 8:34-38; Mark 10:30; Mark 10:45.

4. Many of the passages of St. Mark's Gospel are also found in Matthew and Luke. But Mark has some sections which are not repeated in other Gospels. One of these passages gives parables on the kingdom of God. Read these aloud in Mark 4:1-32. Suggest that these parables be dramatized.

5. St. Mark records many miracles of the Savior, thus showing Christ's power as the Son of God. Ask the students to define the word *gospel*. Then have them select a part of St. Mark's Gospel to read quietly. Finally, have them write in their journals one thought they had while reading this gospel.

APRIL 28: PETER CHANEL

"No one is a martyr for a conclusion, no one is a martyr for an opinion; it is faith that makes martyrs," wrote John Henry Cardinal Newman. Faith certainly characterized Peter Chanel, who was born of a French peasant family in 1803. The parish priest noticed Peter's unusual intelligence and prayerful spirit, and he helped the young man into the local seminary. After ordination, Peter's first assignment was to be pastor of a parish in a run-down district. Through endless patience and perseverance in showing kindness to the sick and all in need, he revived the parish. But Peter wanted to be a foreign missionary more than anything else, so after three years of parish work he joined the new congregation of the Marist Fathers. (He was only 28 at the time.) Peter was not sent to the missions immediately, but was assigned to teach for five years in the seminary.

At last, after fulfilling his teaching duties, he was sent with Bishop Pompallier and other missionaries to islands in the southern Pacific Ocean (1837). The bishop left Peter and a brother on the island of Futuna, promising to return in six months. But it was five years before circumstances permitted the bishop to return. Peter and the brother were accepted by some of the natives, and their abilities to heal the sick were respected, but conditions were far from easy. Missionary work was difficult; cannibalism still flourished on these islands; the language seemed almost impossible to learn. But Peter continued to work with faith, even though only a few natives came for instructions and baptism. From every viewpoint the mission seemed a failure.

A turning point came, however, when the chief's son asked to be baptized. This conversion made the chief so angry he sent a band of warriors to kill Peter. The warriors surrounded Peter's hut, clubbed him, and dragged his dead body out where others cut it up with knives and axes. Peter was the first martyr of Oceania. The chief had thought that the missionary's death would crush Catholicism on the island. But it had the opposite effect. Peter's witness through martyrdom was the seed of the faith. Within a year, the whole island was Catholic. Peter Chanel's life shows that we can never know how much good we do when we accept our sufferings with faith. Our example can be the source of another person's conversion.

SUGGESTIONS

1. Locate Oceania on the map and point out that Peter Chanel has been named patron of this territory.

2. Invite into the class a Marist priest or brother to explain the apostolic work of this congregation.

3. Have the students decorate empty cereal boxes with pictures, words, and symbols of missionary activity. Let them display these boxes on the lunchroom tables to make the school aware of the foreign missions.

4. St. Peter Chanel labored for the missions in a serene and gentle spirit. But this work was often tiresome and unrewarding. Have each student in the class write on a small slip of paper one action the class can offer in intercession for missionaries. These papers can be put into a box from which the students draw a slip each day. As a class, the students can perform the practice and unite themselves with missionaries throughout the world.

5. St. Peter Chanel won the hearts of the people by his compassion toward the sick. Encourage the students to make a call or send a card to someone who is sick or needs their prayers.

6. St. Francis de Sales once wrote, "You catch more flies with a spoonful of honey than with a jar full of vinegar." It seems Peter Chanel and the brother working with him knew the value of this kind of spirit. Discuss what the statement means.

7. Peter Chanel was always cheerful in spite of hardship. After Peter's death, a lay brother described the missionary's life: "Because of his labors he was often burned by the heat of the sun, and famished with hunger, and he would return home wet with perspiration and completely exhausted. Yet he always returned in good spirits, courageous and energetic almost every day." Ask the students what they believe was the source of Peter's optimism. Discuss how they can overcome depression and moodiness.

APRIL 29: CATHERINE OF SIENA

Catherine's mother was at her wits' end. She had twenty-three children, eleven grandchildren, a small overcrowded house, and now her youngest, Catherine, wanted a room of her own for prayer. It is understandable that her mother demanded that Catherine do her share of the housework, cooking, and washing, and scolded her for locking herself up in her room to pray and meditate. Catherine was a lively, charming, and outgoing girl, and her mother could not understand why she did not want to marry or become a nun. In fact, when her mother repeatedly tried to get Catherine interested in marriage, Catherine protested and cut off her hair. Her mother was frantic. When Catherine would not eat because she was fasting, her mother worried and lectured. It was her father who understood Catherine and calmed his wife. In the end, Catherine got her way, her room, and her peace.

Catherine's home in Siena was in sight of the Dominican friary. When she was six, Catherine saw a vision of Christ above the church. By the age of seven, she was resolved to become Christ's bride and remain unmarried. At sixteen, she joined the Third Order of St. Dominic. Members of the Third Order were women who wore the Dominican habit, spent a life of prayer and good works, but lived in their own homes. What people found puzzling and confusing about Catherine was her confident claim that her vocation was to be a contemplative in her own home.

For three years, Catherine lived in her room at home and left it only for Mass. She ate very little, slept only a few hours, and kept silence. Often after Communion, her body would become stiff and without feeling as Catherine went into a trance. She could not see or hear others around her, because she was having a conversation with Jesus. Of course, her mystical experiences caused much curiosity and conversation among the neighbors. Even though Catherine was uncomfortable when others talked about her, she wanted only what Jesus asked of her. When Catherine was tempted to believe Christ had abandoned her, she would hear Him say, "I am always with you in your heart, strengthening you."

After three years of seclusion, Jesus said to Catherine, "The only way you can serve me, Catherine, is in your service of your neighbor." Catherine then began her works of mercy in her own city. She visited the prisons, encouraging the inmates to repent and receive the sacraments. When a plague spread through Siena, Catherine was seen everywhere, bringing food and clothing, nursing the patients no one else would touch, and burying the dead. Her special gifts of prophetic vision and spiritual guidance became apparent. Three Dominican friars had to be assigned to hear the confessions of those who repented after talking to her. By the time she was twenty-three, Catherine had attracted a group of followers of all ages who accompanied her on her journeys. They were priests, religious, and lay people. She was their spiritual guide, and Catherine affectionately called them "her family." Some of them addressed her as "Mama." There was much criticism about her activities, but Catherine's honesty and genuine charity eventually won the respect of all. A Dominican, Raymond of Capua, served as her confessor, friend, and secretary. Catherine could barely read and write, so she dictated over 400 letters and two books. Sometimes she would speak so fast that Raymond would be worn out and fall asleep.

At this time, Pope Gregory XI, a Frenchman, refused to live in Rome. Rather, he stayed in Avignon and took orders from the French king. This situation confused Christians, but Gregory lacked courage to go back to the Vatican. Catherine was asked to go to Avignon, noted for its corrupt and scandalous lifestyle, and advise the pope. She went, and for four months pleaded, scolded, and encouraged the stubborn Gregory: "Be a man, Father . . . . Make peace with Italy, not war. Return to Rome not with swords and soldiers but with the Cross and Blessed Lamb." The turning point came when Catherine told Gregory of a private vow he had made when he was a cardinal. He had never told this vow to anyone. He had promised that if he ever came to be the pope, he would return the papacy to Rome. Finally Gregory determined to go back to the Vatican. This decision enraged the French, who hated Catherine. It is said that even Gregory's aged father threw himself on the ground in front of Gregory, begging him to stay in Avignon, but the pope remained true to his decision.

Catherine returned to Siena, but her health was failing. While she was dictating her books, she was called again to aid the pope. The Church was having even more severe problems and needed help. Pope Gregory XI had died and Pope Urban VI had been elected in his place. Pope Urban was a determined, strict man, sometimes to the point of being cruel. He saw the terrible need for reform in the Church and often acted imprudently. His manner angered the French cardinals. They did not want Rome as the center of the Church; they rejected the Italian Pope Urban VI (they said they had been forced to elect him); they went back to Avignon and elected a rival pope. The Great Schism had begun. People blamed Catherine for having brought the pope back to Rome, and she lost all her friends.

Now Catherine was broken by worry over the Church; constant pain racked her body; she was often discouraged. Only her faith in Christ crucified could strengthen her. She offered her life for the good of the Church. She died at the age of 33, one of the Church's greatest mystics. What Catherine did in the Middle Ages was unheard of for a woman. She left home, advised popes, had visions, cared for the destitute, and composed books, even though she was uneducated. She shows us that the power of Christ working in us can do infinitely more than we can ask or imagine.

SUGGESTIONS

1. In the solution of two major problems of the Middle Ages, women saints played an important part. Catherine of Siena helped to restore the spiritual power (the pope to Rome) and Joan of Arc worked to restore the temporal power (the Dauphin to become the lawful king of France). Both were mystics. Have the students read the biographies of these two saints and report on their lives.

2. The papacy had been in France almost seventy-five years when Gregory XI returned to Rome. This time was called the Avignon Papacy. Have the students find out why this split in the Church occurred. Discuss with them how political problems were closely related to Church problems in the fourteenth century.

3. Catherine often visited the hospitals and cared for patients no one else would help. The story is told of a woman named Tecca, whose condition was so bad no one would go near her. Tecca rejected Catherine's kindness and spread scandalous gossip about her. Catherine cried when she heard this slander, but Christ appeared to her with a crown of gold and a crown of thorns. He asked her to choose one; the other He would save for her in eternity. Catherine chose the thorns, asking that the wounds remain invisible until her death. One day when Catherine was caring for Tecca, the woman saw Christ instead of Catherine. Overcome by sorrow, she repented. Catherine also bore the stigmata on her body, invisible to all. Have the students find out what the stigmata is. Remind them that the "little sufferings" we bear for love of Christ can be marks of His wounds. Tell them that many paintings of Catherine show her wearing a crown of thorns.

4. St. Catherine of Siena is the co-patron of Italy with St. Francis of Assisi. Have the students compare the lives of these two saints to see how both stressed the importance of Christian living and the power of suffering to transform a life.

5. Catherine had a regular confessor to help guide her spiritual journey. Discuss with the students how going to the same priest for the Sacrament of Penance can help a person's spiritual life. Encourage the students to use the Sacrament of Penance regularly and to talk with a priest about their spiritual life.

6. Review the spiritual and corporal works of mercy. Provide space on the bulletin board for the students to post magazine and newspaper articles describing situations where people carry out the works of mercy.

7. When Catherine went to advise the pope, some people accused her of selfish interests. A group of theologians met with her for twelve hours to test her integrity. At the conclusion of the meeting, the theologians were exhausted, but Catherine was refreshed, calm, and self-assured, because she relied on Christ. Have the students make bookmarks with quotations about honesty.

8. In 1970, along with St. Teresa of Avila (feast, October 15), Catherine of Siena was declared a Doctor of the Church. These are the only two women to bear this title. Have the students look up what is meant by a Doctor of the Church and why this honor has been given to Catherine of Siena.

APRIL 30: PIUS V

When Pope Pius V walked in processions through Rome barefoot, head uncovered, his long beard blowing in the wind, the people said there had never been a more holy pope. This visibly saintly man had come from a poor Italian family and had entered the Dominican order at the age of fourteen. A teacher, a master of novices, a bishop, and finally a cardinal, he was known in all these roles as a strict and honest man, as well as a zealous reformer. He wept when the cardinals informed him in 1566 that he had been elected Pope. The eighteen-year-long Council of Trent had ended just three years before, and he, as Holy Father, had the task of implementing the letter and spirit of that council.

Pius V began his papal reign with immediate changes, and the Catholic world was more than surprised. The previous pope, Pius IV, had been easygoing. At first the people did not like the changes made by the new pope. They complained that the atmosphere of Rome became like that of a monastery. But soon the integrity of the pope's personal character changed the minds of his people. He ordered that the money given at the time of his coronation be sent to hospitals and to those in need. The Church finances were examined and accounted for, the army was reduced, the life-styles of the cardinals and bishops were simplified.

With the help of St. Charles Borromeo, seminaries were established, synods were held, dioceses were organized, and parish priests were called to regular meetings. A new catechism based on the decisions of the Council of Trent was completed, translated into many languages, and widely distributed. Parish priests were made responsible for the Catholic education of the young. The Roman Missal — both a restoration and a revision — supplanted all local and regional missals, and it became the sole Mass book for the Western church (with a few minor exceptions). It came to be called the "Tridentine Missal." After four centuries, it has now been supplanted by the current Sacramentary (1970) and Lectionary (1969). The Breviary or Divine Office was also

revised. The lives of the saints were rewritten to emphasize their essential holiness and to abolish exaggerated stories, and Sacred Scripture was given a more prominent place.

But it was in international affairs that Pius V had many troubles. He was a holy man, but unsuccessful in restoring England to Catholic unity. Queen Elizabeth was determined to complete the separation of the Church from Rome begun by her father, Henry VIII. Pius V's excommunication of the queen opened new persecutions against the Catholics in England. The pope was more successful in his efforts to check the Turks, who threatened to overrun Europe. At the Battle of Lepanto in 1571, the Christian forces successfully crushed the Turkish fleet in a spectacular battle. After only six years as pope, Pius V died of a painful disease of which he had never complained. He was admired for his kindness to the poor and sick, for his self-discipline, his truthfulness, and his unfaltering efforts to make the Church effective in its mission to spread the Good News. Pius V is a good example for us to follow: he was a sincere, dedicated man who lived according to his conscience.

SUGGESTIONS

1. When Queen Elizabeth was excommunicated with all of England, she forbade Catholics to practice the faith. Anyone found participating in Mass was fined or sent to prison in the Tower. Priests were often condemned to die. Have the students read about the brilliant, daring, and handsome Jesuit, Edmund Campion, who heroically worked to keep the faith alive and became an English martyr.

2. Pius V was a scholar and he respected study. During his term of office, Thomas Aquinas was made a Doctor of the Church and a new edition of his works was published. Encourage the students to do their homework neatly, carefully, and with pride.

3. The Battle of Lepanto was said to have been won through the intercession of our Blessed Mother. The feast of the Holy Rosary was established after the battle had been won. Pius V loved Mary and wanted devotion to her to be spread. Have the students set up an altar to Mary in the classroom and ask for volunteers to bring flowers. Place a box and slips of paper near the altar so the students can write petitions to Our Lady. Encourage them to pray the Rosary, perhaps a decade a day.

4. Pius V prayed frequently, fasted, and denied himself many personal comforts because he wanted to show his love for Christ through sacrifice. Encourage the students to make sacrifices to show their love: to sit up straight in class, to pay attention, to avoid distracting others.

5. Bring a Liturgy of the Hours book to show the students and pray part of the Morning Prayer of the Church with them. Point out that priests, sisters, brothers, and an increasing number of lay people pray parts or all of these prayers every day.

6. Duplicate copies of G.K. Chesterton's poem *Lepanto* and have the students read it for oral interpretation. The vivid imagery and the captivating rhythm will help the students imagine the famous battle. Have the students recite or read the poem for another class.

MAY 1: JOSEPH THE WORKER

Joseph. His name is familiar to us. He was protector and provider for the Holy Family at Nazareth. All over the world, you will find churches that carry his name, children named after him, feasts devoted to him. Often, when in need, families will turn to him in prayer, for he understands the struggles of family life — the trials and heartaches — as well as the great joys. Joseph also understands the importance of work. He was a carpenter — a builder — and it is quite possible that he taught Jesus his trade. Perhaps together they worked, hour after hour, trying to make the world a better place in which to live. Through his work, Joseph honored the Father in heaven and continued the act of creation. Joseph earned a fair wage and lived in dignity.

Over the years, workers and people in need of work have turned to Joseph, for Joseph knows how important it is to work. In 1889 a group called the International Socialist Congress decided to celebrate May 1 as a day for workers, a holiday in their honor, a day to celebrate the importance of work. But these people and many Communists like them did not view work as a way to honor God, or as a reflection of human dignity, or as a way to share in God's work of creation. These people did not believe in God. To give workers a patron, the Church turned to Joseph, who had been made the Patron of the Universal Church by Pope Pius IX in 1870 and the model for fathers of families nineteen years later. Joseph was named protector of workers by Pope Benedict XV, and in 1955 the feast of St. Joseph the Worker on May 1 was set aside by Pius the XII.

We know how difficult work can be. Perhaps we all know, too, how satisfying it can be. When you have worked hard at a job, you can stand back and admire it, and praise God through it. Whether your work be a cathedral or a sand castle, it can be important and can bring you closer to God.

Let us pray to St. Joseph for his help in all our work and for those many people who want and need jobs, but cannot find them.

SUGGESTIONS

1. Sponsor a Career Day in the school. Invite several parents and parishioners to give short presentations on their jobs and careers. Ask them to point out in their talks how they are able to witness to Catholic Christian values in their particular careers.

2. A number of parishes and communities make use of a "skills bank." People of all ages may register with this skills bank by listing various services they are willing to provide free of cost to those who could not afford to pay for them. For example, a junior high student might register with the bank as being able to mow lawns and do yard work. When an elderly or handicapped parishioner phones in and requests yard service, the junior high volunteer is contacted. Encourage the students to become a part of the local "skills bank," if there is one, or set up such a group within the school itself. Jobs listed could include cleaning up the school yard or parish grounds, helping to set up and clean the classrooms, acting as student aides for a day school or PSR, providing baby-sitting service (particularly during Mass), etc. In this way students can experience the dignity of labor and can witness to Christ through service to others.

3. Display the students' best work — their best papers in a subject area — on May 1.

4. Plan a special Arts and Crafts Day for May 1 to provide the students with an opportunity to be creative.

5. Read the Scripture account of creation and discuss with the students how we are made in God's image. Lead them to see that our gifts of thinking, loving, and choosing enable us to make things.

6. Sometimes a large number of people experience the painful effects associated with being out of work. Lead the students in prayer for these people and their families. Encourage them to become involved in programs that minister to those in such situations, e.g., by serving or doing dishes for free meal programs, etc.

MAY 2: ATHANASIUS

When Christ was on earth, He said that His followers would have to suffer if they wished to live their lives according to His message. In every age since then, the Church has had to endure many hardships — either persecution from without or heresy and schism from within. To balance these evils, great champions have risen to defend the cause of Christ. St. Athanasius is one of these persons.

Athanasius was born of Christian parents in Alexandria, Egypt, about the year 295. As a young man, he spent four years in prayer and solitude in the desert. It was here that he met St. Anthony the Hermit, who had a powerful influence on him. Some years after he left the desert, Athanasius became a priest and was appointed secretary to Alexander, bishop of Alexandria.

Meanwhile, another talented young priest, Arius, had begun to preach against the divinity of Christ, claiming that Jesus was not truly God, that He was only a good and holy man. To answer the false teachings of Arius, the Church held a council at Nicea in the year 325. Two important things happened at this council: Arius and his heretical ideas were condemned, and the bishops composed the Nicene Creed, a profession of faith in defense of Christ's divinity.

Athanasius, who had accompanied Bishop Alexander to the Council of Nicea, was deeply impressed by everything that he had witnessed and, for the rest of his life, he defended all the doctrines of the Church. When he became bishop of Alexandria in 328, it was the beginning of almost fifty years of persecution at the hands of the Arian heretics, who had become very popular among the clergy, the lay people, and even the Emperor Constantine. During these long years, Athanasius was unjustly accused of various crimes and sins, was deliberately misunderstood and humiliated, and was exiled several times.

The last few years of his life were rather peaceful, and he died in his native city in 373. Unfortunately, he did not live to see the Council of Constantinople affirm and expand the doctrines of the Nicene Creed in the year 381. It is this creed which we use as the profession of our faith in the Eucharist on all Sundays and other special days. Athanasius deserves the title of saint, because he defended the faith, but also because of the meekness and charity with which he treated his enemies.

SUGGESTIONS

1. Like Athanasius, men and women still suffer in this day and age because they refuse to compromise the principles of Christ and His Church. Suggest that the students look up information on one of these modern defenders of the Church who has been persecuted for the faith, and then prepare a report for the class: Pope Pius IX, Father Miguel Pro, S.J., Jozsef Cardinal Mindszenty, Aloysius Cardinal Stepinac, and Archbishop Oscar Romero.

2. Have the students make Christ candles and design a Chi Rho on them using acrylic paints. They might also wish to put other symbols of Christ on these candles as a reminder of how St. Athanasius suffered for the Church's doctrines on Jesus Christ. Suggest that the students place their candles on their dining room tables and light them during the evening meal.

3. St. Athanasius was a prolific writer. One of his most popular works, *Life of St. Anthony*, was translated into many languages. This work on St. Anthony, founder of Christian monasticism, inspired many men and women to pursue the monastic life. Have the students look up the definitions of the following terms and then discuss them: monk, monastery, hermit, hermitage, silence, penance, prayer, contemplation, solitude, and desert. Guide the class into realizing that all these terms are vital components of a contemplative life, stressing, however, that "desert" has to be modified to suit modern times.

4. Athanasius spent most of his life defending the faith. Have the class discuss people they know — even fellow classmates — who witness to Jesus Christ by their attitude and actions.

5. Direct the students to write either the Nicene Creed or the Apostles' Creed from memory and then check their version with the one that appears in the missalette (Nicene Creed) or in their textbooks or prayer books (Apostles' Creed).

MAY 3: PHILIP AND JAMES

History records several holy men with the names Philip and James living in the same geographical area during the same period of time. There is no doubt, however, about some things: St. Philip and St. James were both apostles, and both served Christ faithfully during the very early days of the Church.

Philip seems to have been an enthusiastic person. He was the one who brought his friend Nathanael to Jesus, insisting to Nathanael that he had found the one about whom Moses had written. Some years later, it was Philip again who made arrangements, with the help of Andrew, to have a group of Greek gentiles brought to Jesus. Philip the apostle is not to be confused with the Philip of Acts 8, who baptized the Ethiopian, although some writers say that they are the same person. Philip also had a practical, down-to-earth mind. He was the apostle who commented that it would take a considerable amount of money to feed a crowd of more than 5000 hungry men, women, and children. It was Philip who asked to see the Father when Jesus spoke about Him at the Last Supper.

James was the son of Alphaeus and seems to have been born in Caesarea. He is mentioned less frequently in the New Testament than Philip. Sometimes James is called the Less, which might be a hint that he was a short person, or else that he knew Jesus for less time than the other apostle named James.

After Jesus' death, James continued to preach the Gospel, and is believed to have become the first bishop of Jerusalem. Assuming that James and the first bishop of Jerusalem are one and the same person, then he met his death as a martyr in that city about the year 62 A.D. Tradition identifies James as the author of the Epistle associated with his name.

SUGGESTIONS

1. One of the things that we can learn from Sts. Philip and James is that external facts about our lives don't really matter too much. What does count is the way we fill our lives with the love of God, and how we bring His love to others. Encourage each student to do one thing today to make a classmate or a member of his or her family happy.

2. Have the students consult the New Testament to find the list of the twelve apostles and memorize it, because these men are the foundation stones of the Church.

3. Philip is mentioned several times in the New Testament. Tell the students to read one of the following references, all of which involve this saint: John 1:43-50; John 6:1-15; John 14:1-11.

4. Tell the students the ancient story about James that tradition gives us. It says that people respected James so much they called him "James, the Just." He seems to have earned this title from the fact that, since his early years, he drank no wine or strong drink, ate no meat, and was never anointed with oil. He prayed for hours upon end in the temple and was responsible for many converts to Christianity. This again emphasizes the fact that it is the witness of a person's life that counts, not the great things which he or she does.

5. Have the students name persons for whom Philip or James could be patron saints. For example, St. James could be the patron saint of the person who toils quietly behind the scenes to make a project a success; St. Philip could be the patron saint of the friendly person who likes to share his or her friends with other people.

See Supplement for May 10.

MAY 12: NEREUS AND ACHILLEUS

The Church does not know too much about Nereus and Achilleus except that they were among the first martyrs to be venerated as saints. It seems that both men were Roman soldiers who helped in the persecution of Christians until they themselves were converted to Christianity. In order to live their new faith more completely, they resigned from the emperor's army and left Rome. Eventually Nereus and Achilleus were captured and put to death for their beliefs. Some biographers place their martyrdom in the second century.

SUGGESTIONS

1. Even though Nereus and Achilleus died for Christ about 1800 years ago, Christians have still been suffering and dying for their faith in this century in such places as Red China, Communist Russia, Nazi Germany, Mexico, Spain, and Albania. Encourage the students to say a short silent prayer during the day for these modern martyrs.

2. Tell the students that St. Damasus, one of the first popes, wrote the epitaph for the tombstone of Sts. Nereus and Achilleus. In this epitaph, he mentioned that it was love for Christ and a desire to witness to their new faith that inspired Nereus and Achilleus to "throw away their shields, their armour, and their bloodstained javelins" and give up their lives in martyrdom. Encourage the students to consider that if the love of Christ was so strong that two Roman soldiers were able to sacrifice their lives for Him, what would happen in their classroom if each of them would be inspired by such love. Have the students write in their journals one sacrifice they could make out of love for Christ today.

3. Direct the students to the Book of Psalms. Have them find a short prayer for modern-day martyrs from one of the psalms, write it on a small piece of paper, and pray it throughout the day.

MAY 12: PANCRAS (PANCRATIUS)

Even though Pancras was hardly in his teens (at the time of his death, he was either 12 or 14), he had enough courage and personal love for Christ to die as a martyr. His death took place in Rome in the fourth century. Some biographers say that he may have died on the same date, but not the same year, as Sts. Nereus and Achilleus. This is the reason why we honor all three saints on the same day.

SUGGESTIONS

1. When two people love each other very much, they want to do difficult things for each other, because this is one way of saying, "I love you." Pancras said these words to Christ by sacrificing his young life. Ask the class what difficult thing each one of them can do today as a silent way of saying to Christ, "I love You." Have each student write this resolution in his or her journal.

2. Direct the students to 1 Timothy 4:12. After reading this passage, let them discuss why these words could have been an instruction to St. Pancras.

3. Remind the students that they can be an example to their families, even though they are still young. Suggest that they encourage their families to pray grace before meals together and include petitions for each member of the family, for the poor, and for those who suffer unjustly in any way.

4. St. Pancras was martyred, but he rejoiced to suffer for Jesus Christ. Encourage the students to display a crucifix somewhere in their homes as a reminder of the great mystery of salvation: eternal life comes only through death.

MAY 14: MATTHIAS

"I can't believe it! She just told me that Kate is entering a convent next week!" "Have you heard the latest? Dave is going to be a priest! I'm floored!" Sometimes we are astounded by the way God works when He calls certain people to follow Him more closely. It must have been somewhat like that when St. Matthias was elected to take the place of Judas.

The New Testament mentions Matthias only once, and that is in the account of how he was chosen to become one of the apostles. After the death of Judas, the apostles met to elect someone to replace him. Peter presided at this meeting and reminded the others of the qualifications necessary for being an apostle: first, the candiate had to have been a follower of Jesus Christ from the time of Jesus' baptism by John the Baptist until His Ascension into heaven; second, the person had to have been a witness to Jesus' resurrection. Soon the choice was narrowed to two men: Joseph, so good and holy that he was known as Joseph the Just; Matthias, also a very good and holy man. At this point, it would seem as though Joseph had an edge over Matthias, but God's ways aren't the same as our ways. Matthias was chosen by lots. Through the prayerful inspirations of the Holy Spirit, the apostles had chosen Matthias rather than Joseph.

After becoming an apostle and a missionary, Matthias quietly drops out of sight. Tradition links him with the country of Ethiopia, where he is believed to have met his martyrdom. The known facts about the missionary work and martyrdom of St. Matthias are not many. What is known is that he loved Christ and that he lived and died to spread the Good News as far as possible.

SUGGESTIONS

1. Every year, we elect officials of our government. Suggest that the class say a prayer for voters the world over, that these people will pray and study about candidates for public office and then have the insight to vote for the best-qualified persons. Ask the class if they themselves voted for the best-qualified students when they last participated in school or classroom elections.

2. Two saints who seemed to lack some of the qualifications required for their vocations are St. John Vianney and St. Margaret Mary Alacoque. Father

John had a great deal of trouble with his studies; Sister Margaret Mary Alacoque was very impractical. Yet they were both successful in their vocations with the help of God. Suggest to the students that they speak to a priest or a sister if they should be called to the priesthood or religious life but seem to lack the necessary skills or talents.

3. Becoming a priest, a deacon, a brother, or a sister is not a decision made by the candidate alone. The rectors of seminaries and superiors of religious institutions must also decide whether the candidate is suited for that type of life. Have the class say a prayer today for all those persons who must make difficult decisions concerning the young candidates in their charge.

4. It is interesting to find out how Matthias was chosen to take the place of Judas. Have the students read Acts 1:15-26 and then answer the following questions:

- **Why did the place of Judas have to be filled?** (There had to be twelve apostles, according to what King David had said through the inspiration of the Holy Spirit, and Judas had died.)

- **Where were the apostles gathered on this occasion?** (Upper room.)

- **What qualifications did the new apostle have to have?** (The candidate had to have been a follower of Jesus from the time of Jesus' baptism until His ascension; he had to have witnessed to the resurrection of Jesus.)

- **Why did he have to have these two qualifications?** (So that he could spread the Good News of Jesus and of the Resurrection with authority.)

- **How did the apostles learn which person God wished to take Judas' place?** (They prayed for inspiration and then drew lots.)

- **What qualifications do you think a Christian leader should have today?** (Answers will vary.)

MAY 15: ISIDORE THE FARMER

Note to the Catechist: St. Isidore is included here because of popular appeal, even though he does not appear in the revised Roman calendar.

On Ash Wednesday every year, we are powerfully reminded of our strong link to the earth. The ashes placed on our foreheads are a vivid reminder that each of us comes from the earth, is nourished by it during life, and will someday return to it. It's strange, then, that comparatively few people really appreciate the earth and its importance in our lives. Perhaps St. Isidore the Farmer can teach us some valuable things.

Isidore was born in Spain more than 900 years ago, and as soon as he was old enough, he began to work with the soil. Farming was to be his labor for the rest of his life. While he walked the fields, plowing, planting, and harvesting, he also prayed. As a hardworking man, Isidore had three great loves: God, his family, and the soil. He and his wife, who is also honored as a saint, proved to all their neighbors that poverty, hard work, and sorrow (their only child died as a little boy) cannot destroy human happiness if we accept them with faith and in union with Christ.

Isidore understood clearly that, without soil, the human race simply cannot exist too long. This insight may explain why he always had such a reverent attitude toward his work as a farmer.

During his lifetime, Isidore had the gift of miracles, and more than once he fed hungry people with food which seemed to multiply miraculously. He died in 1130 A.D. after a peaceful life of hard manual labor. Today he is honored in Spain as one of her greatest saints, and he is also honored especially in the rural United States.

SUGGESTIONS

1. St. Isidore appreciated the earth because it is the source of most of our food. To honor him today, suggest to the class that they waste no food — either at home or at school.

2. Young Americans who are interested in farming often join the 4H Club. Have the class do research on this organization to see how it helps prepare future farmers of our nation.

3. If St. Isidore were to take a walk through some of our cities, towns, or rural areas today, he would be disturbed by the litter that he would see, because littering is a sign that we do not appreciate the beauty of the earth. Encourage the class to make a resolution not to litter today. Even better than that, suggest that each student resolve to pick up at least one piece of litter today in the school yard and one piece in his or her neighborhood.

4. In the United States, St. Isidore is patron of the National Rural Life Conference. In the state of New Mexico, his statue is brought into the fields on his feast day and also when there is a shortage of rain. Have the students pray for all farmers today that they may enjoy good weather, have fine crops, and reap a generous harvest through the intercession of St. Isidore.

5. St. Isidore was known for his love of the poor. Often he and his wife brought food to poor hungry persons and prayed with them. Encourage the students to participate generously whenever there is a food drive for the poor. Tell them to be alert for any of their classmates who do not seem to have enough to eat at lunch time, and to be thoughtful and generous with them.

6. Suggest that the students plant a garden. The produce may be given to a poor family in the locality.

MAY 18: JOHN I

There have been twenty-three popes named John, but only one of them, John I, has earned the title of saint thus far.

John became pope in 523 A.D., at a time when the Arian heresy was still troubling the Church. In an attempt to stamp out this heresy, the emperor of Constantinople, Justin, began to oppress the Arians. In 526, the Arian king, Theodoric, urged Pope John I to restrain Emperor Justin in his dealings with the Arians. The pope was able to moderate Justin's zeal against the heretics. But Theodoric was angry with the pope, whom he unjustly suspected of favoring the ancient political liberty of Rome. When the pope returned from Constantinople, he was arrested and imprisoned. Subjected to severe privations in prison, he died soon after. We honor John I as both a pope and a martyr.

SUGGESTIONS

1. The Church has had a long, unbroken line of popes. Direct the class to look up in an encyclopedia the list of the popes and answer the following questions:
   - How many popes has the Church had? (John Paul II is #262.)
   - How many popes are honored with the title of saint, blessed or venerable? (85.)
   - Who was the first pope? (St. Peter.) Who is pope today?
   - Which pope reigned longest? (St. Peter.)
   - Which three names have been chosen most frequently by popes? (John, 23 popes; Gregory, 16 popes; Benedict, 15 popes.)

2. The popes have had many serious problems and trials. Our present Holy Father wants and needs our prayers. Ask the students which prayer includes the Holy Father and his intentions. (Morning Offering) Read it to them from page 169 of this book or make copies of it for them. Encourage them to resolve to pray this prayer more fervently each day in order to support the pope.

3. There are many saints with the name John. Have the students match the following saints or holy people with the correct phrase.

   1) John I
   2) John Paul II
   3) John Chrysostom
   4) John Vianney
   5) John the Evangelist
   6) John Neumann
   7) John Bosco
   8) John XXIII
   9) John the Baptist

   a) Wrote the fourth Gospel
   b) Opened Vatican Council II
   c) A pope who was martyred by the jealous Emperor Justin
   d) A Polish Holy Father
   e) Patron of priests.
   f) A prophet who prepared the way for Christ.
   g) A bishop of Philadelphia and an American saint.
   h) A bishop and doctor of the Church whose preaching earned him the title "Golden-mouthed."
   i) A priest who was most concerned about boys; the founder of the Salesian Fathers.

   Answers:
1) c	6) g
2) d	7) i
3) h	8) b
4) e	9) f
5) a	

4. Pope John I suffered martyrdom because of the Emperor Theodoric's envy. Tell the students that if they are tempted to envy, they should try to compliment the person of whom they are envious. If they are the victims of another person's envy, encourage them to say a prayer for the offender and to offer up their suffering for peace among the envious nations of the world.

5. Like Pope John I, Pope John Paul II has suffered much in his lifetime. Have the students do some research on Pope John Paul II to find out things about him which substantiate this statement. Use this information to encourage the students to remember the pope in their daily prayers and sacrifices.

MAY 20: BERNARDINE OF SIENA

What connection can there be between decks of playing cards and the religious symbol IHS? The answer to this question is found in the life of St. Bernardine of Siena.

Bernardine was born on September 8, 1380 in Italy. As a little boy, he lost both parents and was cared for by his aunt. He had a brilliant mind, but when he contracted the plague at the age of twenty, it looked as though he would never have a chance to use his talents for God and His Church. Bernardine did recover, however, and entered the great Franciscan order two years later. The young seminarian was ordained a priest in 1404, and the first few years of his priestly life passed quietly and unnoticed. In time, however, he began to gain fame as a remarkable preacher. Soon he was known throughout all Italy. He could hardly keep up with the many requests for his sermons. Bernardine was a fascinating speaker and had the rare ability to move his listeners to tears and to laughter in the same homily. He had a great devotion to the Holy Name of Jesus and became famous for creating the symbol IHS, which he devised from some of the Greek letters in the name of Jesus.

One of the things which Father Bernardine preached against with a great deal of success was gambling. Once when he was approached angrily by a man whose cardmaking business had suffered as a result of the priest's sermons, the saint suggested that he start making religious cards with the IHS symbol, instead of playing cards. The merchant's first reaction was one of disgust, but he later took Bernardine's advice and became a very wealthy man.

Throughout his life, which ended in 1444, this good priest worked humbly and patiently to spead the Good News of Jesus. He received the power to work miracles and used this gift only to help others. Sometimes St. Bernardine is pictured with three miters at his feet, because three times he refused to become a bishop. (A miter is the tall headdress which a bishop wears.)

SUGGESTIONS

1. St. Bernardine had a great devotion to the Holy Name of Jesus and widely used the IHS symbol. Tell the students to be alert the next time they visit the parish church and discover how many times they can find this symbol used in the church building or furnishings.

2. Some parishes have an organization called the Holy Name Society. The members of this group promote love and respect for the name of Jesus Christ. Have the class find out more about this organization and ask one of the parish priests to assist the class in starting a junior Holy Name Society.

3. Encourage the students to bow their heads today every time the name Jesus is used in prayer.

4. Give the students a copy of the Divine Praises or read this prayer to them. Call their attention to the second and fourth invocations. Have them select one of these short prayers and encourage them to say it silently during the day, especially when they meet difficulties or temptations.

MAY 25: GREGORY VII

It takes courage to tell someone that he or she is doing wrong, but it takes heroic courage to do this when the wrongdoer is a powerful emperor. Pope St. Gregory VII, a Benedictine, had that kind of courage.

Gregory was born in the early part of the eleventh century, at a time when the Church had to battle several internal, evil practices. One of the worst of these was lay investiture. This was the custom by which a lay person, such as a king or an emperor, had the right to appoint churchmen to the office of bishop, abbot, and so forth. This, of course, created many problems for the Church and caused much conflict among the rulers of various Christian nations.

When Gregory became pope in 1073, he began to preach against lay investiture. His chief enemy in this battle was Henry IV, emperor of Germany. The pope asked the Norman rulers of Southern Italy to help him in his fight against Henry. With their assistance, the pope succeeded in having the emperor apologize for his wrongdoing, but this was not a sincere act on Henry's part. In a short time, he again attacked Pope Gregory, who was forced to leave Rome and go into exile at Salerno, Italy. Pope Gregory died in exile, after having been pope for approximately twelve years. Although he had not been totally successful in his battle against lay investiture, Pope St. Gregory VII was responsible for beginning the long fight which eventually managed to do away with this troublesome practice.

SUGGESTIONS

1. Today in Communist countries, civil authorities interfere with Church appointments and elections. Invite one of the parish priests in to explain to the class how a bishop is appointed today or how a pope is elected.

2. In various parts of the globe today, there are men and women who are courageously speaking out against the abuse of power by civil authorities. Encourage the class to remember these men and women in their prayers today.

3. One of the other evils that Pope St. Gregory VII fought against was simony. Have the students read Acts 8:9-24 to get some background on the practice of simony, and then find the definition of this word in a Catholic dictionary or encyclopedia. Call attention to the link between *simony* and *Simon* Magus' name.

4. Pope St. Gregory VII was the advisor to eight popes before he himself became pope. He was often called the "Reform Pope." Have the students look up the definition of the word *reformer* and then discuss what difficulties a reformer might meet in his or her work. Direct them to do further research on other Church reformers: Teresa of Avila, Catherine of Siena, Ignatius of Loyola, Peter Claver, Vincent de Paul, Francis of Assisi.

MAY 25: MARY MAGDALENE DE PAZZI

How many times have you ever had to say, "There's something on my mind, and I'd like to talk it over with you"? If you and I had been acquainted with St. Mary Magdalene de Pazzi, we would never have had to tell her what we were thinking, because God had given her the power to read minds!

Catherine de Pazzi was born in Florence, Italy in 1566. Her family was quite wealthy, and it looked as though Catherine would grow up to be a woman of high society, but she surprised everyone by becoming a Carmelite nun at the age of sixteen. She took the name Mary Magdalene and was soon leading a life of deep prayer, humility, and penance. After a number of years, she was appointed novice mistress and then superior. It was at this time that she was given the ability to read her sisters' thoughts, a gift which she used only for the good of her nuns.

St. Mary Magdalene de Pazzi suffered for three years from a severe illness that finally caused her death in 1607. During this painful period, she was heroically cheerful and kind to everyone around her. It was her deep prayer, her humble use of the talents that God had given her, and the great charity which she practiced toward the other nuns that made this quiet nun such a wonderful saint.

SUGGESTIONS

1. St. Mary Magdalene de Pazzi became a contemplative nun, a woman who spends her entire life in quiet prayer and hidden penance. Encourage the students to make inquiries as to whether there is a monastery of contemplative nuns in the area. If there is one, have a representative of the school visit this monastery to interview one of the nuns when the school observes Vocation Week or has a Vocation Day.

2. Contemplative nuns and monks spend their whole lives praying for the needs of the world and doing penance for the sins of others, but they also need *our* prayers because they are human beings. Tell the students to say a very special prayer today for all contemplative nuns and monks, and for those young men and women who may be considering serving God in such a challenging way.

3. To honor St. Mary Magdalene on her feast day, encourage the students to imitate her great charity by making a resolution to say nothing mean about anyone, either at home or at school, and to say something kind to someone instead.

4. St. Mary Magdalene de Pazzi loved prayer very much. She thought it was so important that she set aside much extra time daily to spend with God. Have the students take a personal inventory of their prayer life. They are to place a check mark in front of the actions which they perform *each day.*

_____ Spend a few minutes in personal prayer

_____ Pray after getting up in the morning

_____ Concentrate on class prayers

_____ Try to make a visit to church

_____ Read the Bible for several minutes

_____ Speak the name of Jesus reverently

_____ Pray to the Holy Spirit for guidance

_____ Participate in meal prayers with the family

_____ Before going to bed, talk over the past day with Christ

MAY 25: BEDE THE VENERABLE

St. Bede said of his life, "I have spent the whole of my life . . . devoting all of my pains to the study of the Scriptures, and amid the observances of monastic discipline and the daily task of singing in church, it has ever been my delight to learn or teach or write." St. Bede's life was as undramatic as that. Here was a saint who worked no miracles, saw no visions, and found no new way to God. He won heaven by living an ordinary Christian life, by doing the will of God moment by moment.

Bede was probably born in 672 in England and by the age of seven was already in the monastery school. At 29, he was ordained a priest. His gifts for writing and teaching were noticed immediately and he devoted his life to these two tasks. He composed forty-five books. Thirty were commentaries on Scripture; others were on the lives of the saints and secular subjects. But his most widely recognized work was the *Ecclesiastical History of the English People.* This book has given us a clear picture of the history of the Church of early England and Ireland. It is objective, historic, and documented from trustworthy sources. Bede's whole life was dedicated to faith and learning. He died as simply as he had lived. When he felt close to death, he summoned the monks to his bed, gave them each homemade gifts, dictated the last line of his book to his secretary, and died singing the Glory Be, his favorite hymn.

We learn from Bede the importance of being faithful to God in every ordinary task. Let us call on his intercession for our present task — our studies.

SUGGESTIONS

1. Before history class today, have the class pray to St. Bede, a patron of historians.

2. St. Bede, a Benedictine, was educated by monks. In the Middle Ages, it was monasticism that zealously kept alive the truths of the faith and carried on the teaching of secular subjects. The

monks preached, healed, labored, and continued to serve in the works of mercy. Invite a Benedictine monk to the class to share some of the history of the order.

3. St. Bede respected the resources of libraries. Today, have the class visit the library, select a good book, and thank the librarian for the services he or she offers.

4. St. Bede was an excellent student, as well as an excellent teacher. Suggest that the students imitate St. Bede by paying close attention in class today and trying to do their work carefully and neatly.

MAY 26: PHILIP NERI

The two favorite books of St. Philip Neri were the New Testament and a book of jokes and riddles. He is a saint especially remembered for his great sense of humor, his cheerfulness, and his ability to bring out the best in people. "Good little Phil," as his family called him, was born in Florence in 1515. The family was poor, but they had planned an ambitious future for Philip. When he reached eighteen, they sent him to be trained as a business man with his uncle in the city. After working there for several months, Philip sent a thank-you note to his uncle, packed his bags, and headed for Rome. There he tutored two boys, attended the university, and lived in a small attic with only a bed, books, and a line where he could hang his clothes. Philip achieved brilliant grades at the university. During his free time, he would enjoy Rome and pray in the churches and catacombs.

Once, while deep in prayer at the catacombs, he had a mystical experience that transformed his life. He went home, sold his books, and for the next thirteen years was a lay minister to the young men of Rome. Philip wanted young men to come to love their faith and practice it. His enjoyable, likeable personality easily helped him to make friends. He encouraged young men to give their lives to prayer and good works. Soon young men, rich and poor, were flocking to be with him. They went to the hospitals, made the beds, cleaned the filth from the floors, and brought food and gifts. Philip was always with them, full of jokes and ready for fun. Philip and the young men would gather in the afternoons for spiritual talks, discussions, prayer, and music. Philip loved good singing. Later he formed these men into a community call the Oratorians.

People noticed Philip's appealing personality, his gift of reading hearts, and his ability to direct people spiritually. They persuaded him to be ordained. His advice was welcomed by all. St. Ignatius Loyola, St. Francis de Sales, St. Charles Borromeo, and St. Camillus de Lellis were saints who had Philip as their spiritual director. Even popes, cardinals, and bishops looked to Philip for guidance.

People enjoyed Philip's good humor and appreciated his humble and simple ways. Philip was opposed to anything that was pretentious or snobbish. He went about in old clothes, big white shoes, and with his hat cocked to the side. When the pope wanted to make Philip a cardinal, he left a cardinal's hat outside Philip's door. Philip used it to play catch with. Another time when people were following him around saying he was a saint, Philip shaved off half of his beard.

After hearing about the great conversions of St. Francis Xavier, Philip wanted to go to the Indies. But a friend of his persuaded him to continue his good works in Rome. He was to become a "Second Apostle to Rome."

Philip teaches us that being holy does not mean being sad. One can be joyful and spontaneous in loving God. God's love impels us to go out and spread the Gospel in charity and service. And when we serve God, people should see smiles on our faces!

SUGGESTIONS

1. St. Philip Neri loved music and singing. He found that the best musicians were those who composed songs based on Scripture and who wrote them in the people's native language. To celebrate Philip's feast, play some music from the "Lord of Light" or "Faith of Life" albums.

2. Tell the following incident to show how Philip taught a young man to be humble. Once a young man, a follower of Philip's, came to him and asked to wear a hair shirt for penance. Philip knew the young man was very proud of his penances. He told him to wear the shirt on the outside of his clothes. Ask the students why Philip felt that it was a great grace to be able to "laugh at oneself." Then discuss how doing the following can help them become better persons:

   • laughing rather than pouting when things don't go your way.
   • cheerfully accepting difficulties.
   • acting enthusiastic rather than indifferent or bored when the class has a project.
   • developing a sense of humor.

3. Philip used his natural gifts — his personality, his humor, his spirit of fun — to influence people to be good. Have the students try to use their natural gifts to give joy and service to others by complimenting others, by readily volunteering to help someone, by doing what is right despite what others are doing.

4. St. Philip Neri's favorite feast was Corpus Christi. Suggest that the students imitate his love of the Eucharist by making a visit to the Blessed Sacrament just to thank and adore Christ.

MAY 27: ST. AUGUSTINE OF CANTERBURY

You don't have to be a hero to be a missionary! This could be a caption for the life of Augustine of Canterbury.

Little is known of the early life of Augustine except that he became a monk and was a friend of Pope Gregory the Great. Gregory respected Augustine's virtues of loyalty and perseverance and appointed him to lead a band of thirty missionaries to evangelize England. At first the trip to England went fine, but as the group traveled on, news reached them of the treacherous English channel they had to cross and the fierce tribes in England. The missionaries were so afraid they persuaded Augustine to return to Rome to ask the pope if they could give up the journey. Gregory encouraged the fearful Augustine and sent him back.

The terrified band of missionaries, who could not speak English, were met by Ethelbert, overlord of Kent. Fortunately the king was married to a Christian princess from Paris, so he gave them a house and allowed them to preach. But he hesitated to give up his pagan beliefs. During his stay in England, Augustine wrote many letters to Pope Gregory asking for advice about his missionary work. It was through the wisdom and direction of Gregory that the missionary efforts in England were profitable. Pope Gregory instructed the men to respect local customs, to not destroy pagan temples (only the idols), and most of all to give witness by their lives of Christianity. The monks did just that. They preached, cared for the poor, endured hardships patiently, lived simply, and prayed much. By 601, Ethelbert and many others were baptized. Augustine was able to write to Gregory pleading for more missionaries. Gregory responded by sending more men and sacred books, sacred vessels, and relics. Augustine built the first cathedral in Canterbury.

Conversion of the people was slow, and Augustine died after only seven years of work in England. He was never able to see the faith take root. Like Augustine, we must have faith and proceed slowly, even if we meet with what we think is limited success in doing God's work. The advice of Gregory to Augustine still holds true today. "He who would climb to a lofty height must go by steps, not leaps."

SUGGESTIONS

1. Relate the following to lead the students to a better understanding of how St. Augustine met failure:

   Not all Augustine's work was successful. The Celtic monks who had brought the faith to England long before Augustine had been cut off from Rome due to distance and poor communication. For example, they had a different date for Easter. They had different ways of baptizing. When Augustine met with the leaders of the Irish church to discuss these matters, he forgot to stand when they came into the room. They were hurt and refused to listen to him, speak to him, or acknowledge him as archbishop. Yet all his life, Augustine patiently worked for reconciliation with them. Ask the students to follow St. Augustine's good example and ask forgiveness today of anyone whom they have hurt.

2. Pope Gregory the Great supported mission work. He brought the faith to different countries by sending groups of missionaries and encouraging their efforts. Discuss with the students how our present Holy Father encourages mission work by his letters, his visits, and his prayers. How does this help the faith of people in mission lands?

3. Augustine has been called "Apostle of England" because of his missionary efforts. Yet he had normal, human struggles. Tell the class that today they should see who can be an "Apostle to (name of your school)" by being neat in the lunchroom, by listening during class, or by helping other students. Stress that good example is a powerful way to spread the faith.

4. Have the class read Paul's letters to Timothy and compare the advice given by Paul to the advice given by Gregory to Augustine. Then have them imagine that they are Augustine and have them each write a fictitious letter to Gregory.

MAY 30: ST. JOAN OF ARC

Note to the Catechist: Joan of Arc is included here because of popular appeal, even though she does not appear in the revised Roman calendar.

In 1431, those who loved Joan of Arc called her the "Maid of Orleans," the "Saint of France," and the "Friend of God." To those who hated her, she was a "heretic," a "cowgirl," or a "witch." To us, she seems to have been an extraordinarily brave young woman, whose holiness and purity made her a radiant witness to Christ.

Joan of Arc was born to a peasant family in Domremy, France. Joan was certainly her mother's pride and joy as a homemaker, because it was said that no young woman could embroider as well as she. Everyone knew Joan as healthy, spirited, and energetic. As a young girl tending sheep, Joan was not aware of the terrible political troubles France was having with England. The Hundred Years War was raging and France was gradually surrendering town after town to the English.

The country had a defeatist attitude and lacked a strong leader. The crown prince, the Dauphin, was too afraid to go through a coronation ceremony. One day when she was fourteen years old, Joan was working in her father's garden. A bright light descended upon her and she heard a voice call her name. Later she heard three voices and had visions of her heavenly visitors, whom she identified as St. Michael the archangel and the virgin martyrs, St. Catherine of Alexandria and St. Margaret of Antioch.

For about five years, Joan kept these voices a secret while they helped her grow in prayer. The voices revealed to her the three-fold mission she was to accomplish. This was to save the city of Orleans from the English, make sure the Dauphin was crowned king of France, and drive the English out of France. But during this time, the people of her village knew only that Joan was more frequent in receiving the sacraments, more gentle in her kindness to the sick, and more generous in her service to the poor.

When Joan was sixteen, the voices became insistent that she tell Robert de Baudricourt, the general of the French forces near her town, of her mission to save France. Her visit to the general proved fruitless. He laughed at the thought of soldiers being commanded by a young girl, mocked her, and sent her home to her father to be whipped. When Joan pleaded with her voices that she could not do the task they asked because she could not read, write, or fight, and because the general had refused her assistance, the voices told her, "It is God who will command the army."

Joan obediently returned to the general. This time he gained her an audience with the Dauphin. The weak Dauphin disguised himself as a servant and hid in the crowd when Joan made her appearance. But Joan unhesitatingly walked up to him, knelt, and said, "Dauphin, I have been sent from God to bring help to the kingdom and yourself." The Dauphin was still skeptical and sent Joan to a board of theologians to be questioned. They declared she sounded authentic and Joan was given the leadership of the French forces.

Joan's positive, hopeful attitude lifted the morale of the soldiers. Just the sight of Joan with cropped hair and white armor, holding the flag with the design of God the Father, the fleur-de-lis, and the words Jesus and Mary on it, rallied the men. They marched to Orleans. Joan had every soldier go to confession and prepare spiritually. The fighting began, but after twelve hours the French were still not successful. Joan had been wounded by an arrow, but after having the wound treated, re-entered the battle and urged the army on to victory. The English were defeated and the French credited Joan and the power of God with the victory. It was the feast of St. Michael.

Joan was impatient to get on with her second task, the crowning of the Dauphin as King Charles VII.

After many difficulties, this finally took place at Rheims, and Joan stood by the new king, clutching her banner. When he was anointed by the archbishop, she knelt at his knees and wept.

Her voices warned her that she would not live long and she must hurry with her mission. Joan's army captured over nine towns, and though her plans were delayed by the indecisive Charles VII, she was winning France back from England. But there were those who were jealous of her, and in Compiegne she was captured by the Burgundians, who sold her to the English. Not one person in France came to her aid. No soldier tried to rescue her. The Dauphin made no effort to gain her release. So the English put her on trial. They mercilessly cross-examined her, trying to get her to deny that her voices were from God. They tortured her. Finally, afraid, abandoned, and exhausted, she was forced to sign a paper denying her voices. But immediately she refuted the document and bravely declared the holiness and truth of her mission. For this the court condemned her to be burned at the stake. As she was led to the stake, an English soldier made her a cross of twigs. She died crying, "Jesus, Jesus." Later, the Church re-examined the trial of Joan and declared that she was innocent and worthy of canonization. Joan of Arc brought hope where others predicted failure. She met political intrigue with integrity. Joan showed courage where others were afraid. We learn from Joan that when we allow God to work in our lives, we can do impossible things.

SUGGESTIONS

1. The life of St. Joan of Arc has often been depicted in plays and novels. Have the students choose portions of her life to dramatize.

2. Religion and patriotism played a central role in the life of Joan of Arc and Catherine of Siena. Both saints lived in the fourteenth century and both ended the two major traumas of the century. Catherine of Siena persuaded the pope to return to Rome, and Joan of Arc persuaded the Dauphin to be king of France. Have the students compare the lives of the two saints and show how God accomplished greatness for the Church through each of them.

3. Encourage the students to find out about the three saints who were Joan's voices: St. Michael the Archangel, St. Catherine of Alexandria, and St. Margaret of Antioch. When they have finished their research, have them tell why they think these saints were good helpers to Joan and France.

4. St. Joan of Arc's greatest gift was her genuinely positive attitude to life. She placed all her confidence in God. Suggest that the students try to face difficult situations in their lives in the spirit of Joan of Arc. Tell them to notice how an enthusiastic, uplifting spirit can make a home or a school a happier place.

5. Show the class a picture of a fleur-de-lis and explain to them that it is a symbol of France and it is also a symbol of Our Lady, a symbol of purity. Have the class draw the fleur-de-lis symbol on napkins to use with their lunch and as a reminder to pray that the people of France always remain strong in their faith.

MAY 31:   THE VISITATION

Have you ever waited for a friend to arrive? You watch at the window, you listen for the phone. And you know the joy you feel when you see your friend appear at the door or hear that person's voice.

Perhaps the greatest visit ever made was the one Mary made to her relative, Elizabeth. This event is called The Visitation. The Gospel of Luke records that after the angel announced to Mary that she was to be the Mother of God, she left at once to visit Elizabeth, who in her old age was to bear a son. What a wonderful visit it must have been, because as soon as Elizabeth saw Mary, her own child leaped for joy within her. She greeted Mary as the Mother of the Lord. And Mary's response was the Magnificat. Mary's whole life was totally filled with the good news that Jesus was coming. The Church has always praised Mary as the Christ-bearer for two reasons. First, by the power of the Spirit, Mary physically brought Christ to the world. Secondly, she brings Christ spiritually to everyone by the holiness of her words and example.

We can love and imitate Mary by bringing Christ to others, too. We can reach out, visit others, and share the Good News of Jesus Christ by our love and concern for them. The more we think about Mary and the message of the Gospel, the more we will be like her in our own lives.

SUGGESTIONS

1. Pray the Second Joyful Mystery, The Visitation, with the class today. Or read the account of The Visitation to them from Luke 1:39-56.

2. Tell the students that Mary visited the elderly Elizabeth because she was concerned about her relative. Encourage them to visit an elderly neighbor or relative, or write to their grandparents on this feast day.

3. Explain to the students that the message of Mary's Magnificat, Luke 1:46-55, has special importance for our times. Mary rejoices because the good news about Jesus means that God has exalted the lowly. The Gospel of Jesus is for those who are poor in spirit. Salvation is for those who trust only in Jesus. Have the students compare the words of the Magnificat to Luke 6:20-26. How are the words of Jesus in this passage saying the same thing?

4. Mary is the example of bringing Christ to others through charity and the spirit of service. Suggest that the students assist their mothers in some service that evening, imitating Mary.

IMMACULATE HEART OF MARY

Saturday following the Second Saturday after Pentecost

"Conquests and empires not founded on justice cannot be blessed by God . . . . Nothing is lost by peace, but everything may be lost by war," wrote Pope Pius XII on August 24, 1939. A week later, Adolph Hitler unleashed his army and opened fire on Poland. The Second World War had begun. On the radio, by letter, and in person, the pope pleaded for peace. Nation after nation entered the war and thousands were killed in battle daily. It seemed the world needed someone whose heart could bear the sorrow of the Church and the world and bring comfort. Who other than Mary? For the Mother of God possesses such a heart of charity that she wishes all people to love her Son and be saved. It was at this time that Pope Pius XII consecrated the world to the Immaculate Heart of Mary and recommended this devotion. But this devotion is not just for times of war; it is for all times.

Mary loves each person, and when we dedicate ourselves to her Immaculate Heart, she will help each of us deepen our friendship with God. By coming to know the love of Mary, we will come to know better the overwhelming love of God. Today, let us dedicate ourselves to the Immaculate Heart of Mary and confide to her all those intentions we have that most need her love and care.

SUGGESTIONS

1. The heart of Mary is mentioned in the Gospel of Luke (2:52). Have the students look up the reference and write in their journals what Mary was "storing in her heart."

2. Suggest that the students read the story of Our Lady of Fatima. Point out that this appearance of Mary reawakened devotion to the Immaculate Heart of Mary.

3. Have the students cut out hearts of different sizes, decorate them, and make a design of them. In the middle of the different hearts, have them write the

names of those people they would like Mary to protect and help. At the top of the hearts, let them print "Immaculate Heart of Mary, pray for them."

IMMACULATE HEART OF MARY, PRAY FOR THEM!

4. Have the class pray to the Immaculate Heart of Mary or sing a Marian hymn to ask Mary to intercede for world peace.

JUNE 1: JUSTIN

"Nobody in his senses gives up truth for falsehood." Would you be willing to say that if a powerful judge ordered you to deny your faith in Jesus Christ or lose your life?

Justin was not afraid to be loyal to his Christian faith. As a young man, he searched everywhere for truth. He traveled to many big cities, where he talked and studied with wise teachers. One day a stranger told Justin to read the books of the Old Testament prophets, who had foretold the coming of Christ. He did this, and it eventually led him to the recognition that the Christian religion taught the truth — that Jesus had brought the truth into the world. He accepted the newfound faith and was baptized.

Justin began to speak and write in defense of Christianity, since some people of the time were attacking what Christians believed and practiced. His books gave us some insight into what this early Church was like. In one of them he described the ceremony of baptism in the Church around the year A.D. 160. It was very similar to the ceremony today. In another place he wrote that the Sunday meetings of the Christian community included readings from Scripture, a homily, offering of bread and wine, and giving communion to the assembled people. Doesn't this remind you of the eucharistic celebration today?

In about A.D. 165, Justin was arrested for being a Christian, but he refused to give up his faith in Jesus and His Church. The judge asked him, "Do you have an idea that you will go up to heaven and receive some suitable rewards?" Justin answered, "It is not an idea that I have; it is something that I know well and hold to be most certain." The judge ordered him to be killed. Justin was a strong and courageous martyr.

SUGGESTIONS

1. Justin was the first to record the beliefs and actions of eucharistic worship. He loved to participate in the Eucharist because he found peace and strength from its nourishment. Write the following list on the board. Have the students copy it and check the ways they can participate in the eucharistic liturgy.

_____ planning the liturgy

_____ playing an instrument

_____ being part of the presentation of gifts

_____ giving to the collection

_____ singing and giving responses at Mass

_____ being a lector

_____ reading the general intercessions

_____ designing a banner for the liturgy

2. Have the class prepare a liturgy for the feast of St. Justin. Allow them to study and discuss the life of the saint and the readings chosen for the Mass. Have them suggest appropriate songs for the liturgy, compose petitions, and choose lectors and those who will participate in the entrance and offertory procession. The whole class could be in the procession, leading the priest celebrant — a sign of unity of priest and people and of our pilgrimage to the promised land of heaven (the altar).

3. Help the students become more familiar with the following terms by having them make an illustrated dictionary:

lectionary	stole
altar of sacrifice	vestment
sacramentary	priest
lector	cross
pew	paten
candle	bread
incense	chalice (cup)
wine	celebrant's chair

4. Justin spent many years searching for the meaning of life. He found his answer when he discovered Jesus. Tell the students they have a rich opportunity every day to study their faith. Encourage them to participate enthusiastically in religion class and to share faith experiences, so that they can help one another to know and love the faith.

JUNE 2: MARCELLINUS AND PETER

Long ago, people hardly ever wrote down the story of a person's life. They did not think it was important to keep track of such things. And besides, there were no printing machines in those days. That is partly why we know so little about the two saints whose feast is today. St. Marcellinus was a good, holy priest who lived about the year 300, probably in Rome.

One day a Christian exorcist named Peter, who was in prison because of his faith in Jesus, asked Marcellinus to baptize the jailer and his family. Peter had converted this family while he was serving his prison sentence. When the governor learned that Peter had been spreading the Christian faith, and that Marcellinus had baptized Peter's converts, he called both men into court. He ordered them to offer incense to the false gods. When they refused, the governor commanded his soldiers to behead them. Of course they were tortured before they were killed, but they took every bit of suffering quietly and joyfully because they loved Jesus and knew He was waiting for them in heaven. Several years later Constantine, the new Christian emperor, had a large church built over the place where these two martyrs were buried.

If it sometimes seems hard to admit that we believe in Jesus and His Church, remembering how brave Marcellinus and Peter were long ago will give us strength.

SUGGESTIONS

1. Tradition holds that Marcellinus and Peter converted the jailer and his family. Have the students read a similar story in Acts 16:25-34. Then let them dramatize the story.

2. Marcellinus and Peter are included as optional in Eucharistic Prayer I. Equip the students with missalettes and have them find which saints are included in this Eucharistic Prayer. Ask them who they are and why they are included.

3. Both Marcellinus and Peter were buried in the catacombs. If possible, show the students pictures of the catacombs. Explain that these were underground burial places built in the first centuries of the Church. On the walls of these underground tunnels are drawings of scenes from the Old and New Testaments, the eucharistic banquet, and Baptism, as well as representations of early Christian martyrs. Discuss the importance of respect for the dead, which Christians have always had.

4. Have the students print the word *courage* vertically on their papers.

C _____
O _____
U _____
R _____
A _____
G _____
E _____

For each letter, let them write words or phrases that describe Christian courage. The same activity can be done with other appropriate words.

JUNE 3: CHARLES LWANGA AND HIS COMPANIONS

Kenya, Uganda, Nigeria. Have you heard these names on TV lately? They are small nations in Africa. Uganda lies in central Africa, just west of Kenya. About 100 years ago, in 1886, a young man named Charles Lwanga was burned to death in Uganda because he would not give up his practice of Christianity.

Charles was probably in his late teens and had begun to live as a page in the king's court. He was a catechumen at that time. The king learned that Mukaso, master of the court pages, and Charles were helping the Christian boys practice their faith. They encouraged the young men to refuse to take part in pagan customs of the country. This angered the king so much that he ordered Mukaso to be killed. That very same night, Charles asked to be baptized. This made the king still more angry. He commanded his soldiers to take Charles and twenty-one of his Christian friends and kill them. Some were burned, some were beheaded. Try to imagine how these brave young men prayed as they walked out to their death. Perhaps they said something like this:

We are warriors now, fighting on the battlefield of faith, and God sees all we do; the angels watch, and so does Christ. What honor and glory and joy, to do battle in the presence of God, and to have Christ approve our victory.

SUGGESTIONS

1. Locate Uganda, Kenya, and Nigeria on a map for the students. Have them pray for missionaries who serve in those countries. Also have them write to the Holy Childhood Association to find out more about mission work in Africa. The address is: Holy Childhood Association, 1720 Massachusetts Avenue, N.W, Washington, D.C. 20036. The Holy Childhood Association provides filmstrips, mission activities, prayer services, and teaching ideas for further mission studies. Contact your diocesan Propagation of the Faith (Mission) office as well.

2. Charles Lwanga and his Christian companions were all under 25 years of age when they heroically gave up their lives for the faith. They declared they wished to remain Christian until death, no matter what torments they were given. The companions of Charles were pages in the king's court, a judge, and a teacher. Tell the students how these martyrs prayed and sang loudly and enthusiastically even at their death. Encourage the students to proclaim their faith by participating in the liturgy and prayer celebrations.

3. These Christian martyrs refused to give in to the homosexual demands of the king. They are saints who respected their bodies and loved the commandments of God. Have the students pray today to be strong in times when they are tempted to sins of impurity.

4. Ask the students to look up the meaning of *catechumen*. Have them find out what place this stage has in the preparation for Baptism and what takes place at this stage. Perhaps they could talk to the parish priest.

JUNE 5: BONIFACE

Let's move backwards in time and pretend. The date is about 754. The place is a small woods in Frisia, a country that is in Holland today. The characters are Bishop Boniface and a crowd of pagan idol worshipers.

Pagan 1: Who is that?

Pagan 2: He is Bishop Boniface, a Christian.

Pagan 3: What is he going to do with that huge ax?

Pagan 1: Maybe he is going to offer a sacrifice to the god Wotan, who lives in the beautiful oak tree.

Pagan 2: No, he is a Christian. He will never offer a sacrifice to our gods.

Pagan 1: Look! He is beginning to chop down our sacred tree!

Several Pagans: Don't do that! Stop him! He must not destroy that special oak tree! The gods will strike him dead.

Boniface continues to chop steadily and firmly. The pagan people watch him, afraid and worried. Finally, the tree falls to the earth with a crash like thunder.

Pagan 3: There! We told him! The thunder god will punish him with death now. Look out everyone!

Boniface: My friends, I have destroyed this tree. Now you can see that no harm has come to me. Listen to what I want to tell you about the one true God and His wonderful, kind Son. His Son came to earth to tell us how to live in order to earn heaven, his home, forever and ever. Just listen.

Before he became a bishop, Boniface, who was baptized Winfrid, was a brilliant and talented monk in a Benedictine monastery in England. He was the head of a monastery school, but he thought God wanted him to be a missionary in a pagan land. He went to Frisia to begin his work. A war in that country forced him to return to England for a few years.

But he did not give up. Next he journeyed to Rome to ask the pope to tell him where to serve. Pope Gregory II changed his name to Boniface, which means "a man who does good deeds." Then he sent him to eastern Germany. For nearly thirty-five years, Boniface traveled all over Germany, preaching, teaching, and building schools, monasteries, and convents. He made another trip back to Rome to report to the pope about his work. While he was there, the pope ordained him a bishop and sent him back to Germany to continue his missionary work. He invited monks and sisters from England to come and help him. The Benedictine monastery at Fulda is probably the most famous one Boniface started.

As a frail, old man, Boniface returned to Frisia to work there among the pagans. One early morning, he was waiting to confirm a group of converts. A band of angry natives rushed into the church and murdered Boniface and about fifty of the new converts. Today St. Boniface is called the patron saint of Germany.

SUGGESTIONS

1. Pope Gregory II gave Boniface his name, which means "a man who does good deeds." Encourage the students to find out the roots of their Christian names. (*A Saint for Your Name* [*Saints for Boys*] or *A Saint for Your Name* [*Saints for Girls*] by Albert Nevins, M.M. Our Sunday Visitor.)

2. St. Boniface is remembered for the great strength of his friendships. He cared for his friends deeply and led them to live holy lives. Ask the students to reflect on the importance of friends and the friendships they have now. Have them write in their journals how they have led their friends to Jesus or how their friends have led them to Jesus.

3. St. Boniface's work planted the seeds of the Catholic Church in Germany. This later became a strong Catholic country, whose patron is St. Boniface. Have the students discover some of the rich religious customs that have come from this country and present them to the class on a special day. Perhaps some students could bake German cookies and serve them to make the day festive.

4. The missionary success Boniface achieved for the Church could not have been possible if it had not been for the nun Lioba and her sisters, who helped him in his preaching and teaching. Tell the students the following story of Lioba, who was loved for her kindness and wisdom. Lioba was educated in an English convent. When Boniface was sent to convert the Germanic tribes, she wrote him letters promising prayers and asked Boniface to pray for her studies. Boniface wrote to Tetta, who was superior of Lioba's convent, asking for help in his work. Tetta sent Lioba and thirty sisters to act as assistants to Boniface. The holiness and gentleness of Lioba encouraged many girls to become sisters also.

5. Have the students find out about the other saintly "teams" in Church history and report on them. A few of them are St. Francis de Sales and St. Jane de Chantal, St. Francis of Assisi and St. Clare, St. Vincent de Paul and St. Louise, St. Jerome and St. Paula, St. Teresa and St. John of the Cross.

6. Boniface is called the "Apostle of the Germans." Though Boniface did not begin mission work until age forty-three, he did give all of his energy, love, and care to the German people. Ask the students to think of where Christ is sending them as apostles. Have them write essays entitled "Me: An Apostle to My Family," "Me: An Apostle at School," "Me: An Apostle to _____ Parish."

JUNE 6: NORBERT

Do you remember how St. Paul was changed from an enemy of Jesus into a strong loyal Christian? Norbert had a similar experience when he was a young man. Norbert was born in Germany, a cousin to the emperor, so he had nearly everything he wanted in life — money, popularity, success. But his carefree life did not make him happy. One day he went horseback riding through the woods. Unexpectedly a heavy storm broke. A sudden bolt of lightning frightened his horse. As the horse reared up, Norbert fell to the ground. When he regained consciousness, he considered the accident a warning from God. Like St. Paul, he wondered, "Lord, what do you want me to do?" Norbert seemed to hear a voice deep within him say, "Give up the foolish, empty life you are leading. Begin to do good to those around you." Norbert took these words very seriously. He sold all his property and prepared to be ordained as a priest.

Once he was a priest, Norbert preached to everyone about the danger of living the way he had lived a few years before. Over the years so many young men wanted to live the way Norbert did that he had to start several monasteries. He tried to build these monasteries in out-of-the-way places, where people did not hear the Word of God very often. Near each monastery, Norbert usually opened a hospice. Here sick people, travelers, and pilgrims could find rest and help. When Norbert died in 1134, he was an archbishop. He had worked very hard to stop heresies and to encourage loyalty to the pope. He had preached with great success to the rich and the poor, to the wise and the uneducated, to believers and unbelievers. Norbert was a man of faith, goodness, and loyalty.

SUGGESTIONS

1. Norbert wrote a rule for his priests to follow. The first sentence begins, "Be of one mind and heart in God." Tell the class this is a good rule to have in the classroom. Have volunteers letter this quote and design it. Then post it above the classroom door. Let this motto inspire the class for the rest of the year.

2. Norbert's life was given to helping parish priests serve in the best possible way. Norbert saw the value of the priestly ministry. Encourage the students to get to know the names of their parish priests and how to spell them. Perhaps they could write letters to the priests telling them how much they appreciate the service the priests give to Christ and His Church.

3. St. Norbert loved to teach about the faith and generosity of the early Christians who had been empowered by the Holy Spirit. Have the students read Acts 4:32-35. Suggest that they resolve to live in the spirit of these early Christians.

4. Respect and reverence for the Holy Eucharist meant much to St. Norbert. Review with the students the importance of being reverent when they receive this sacrament. Remind them not to chew gum or talk when they are at the celebration of the Mass. Have them recall what the eucharistic fast is.

5. Before Norbert reformed, he led a carefree and worldly life. He wastefully spent money on luxuries he did not need. Tell the students the importance of sharing their own wealth with the needy. Have them make a checklist of how they use their personal funds. Suggest they add to the list "Money to be given to the needy." Encourage them to a deeper awareness of giving to others who are not as fortunate as themselves, even if it means personal sacrifice.

JUNE 9: EPHREM

Did you ever think of becoming an author? Authors are an interesting group of people. Some of them write history or science fiction; others write westerns or travel stories. Ephrem was a different sort of author. He wrote poems, hymns, and homilies.

He was born about 306 in the country that today is called Turkey. As a young man, he was ordained a deacon and became a well-known teacher. Years later, the bishop suggested that Ephrem be ordained a priest. Ephrem begged the bishop to allow him to stay a deacon because he thought he was not good enough to be a priest. Although Ephrem never became a priest, he did become a monk. When the Persian army conquered his homeland, Ephrem had to seek refuge. He escaped to the mountains and lived alone in a cave. Once people in the nearby city discovered him, many came to listen to him and ask for help with their problems. At this time Ephrem did a lot of writing. His homilies were very popular, and so were his religious poems. He also took the songs that heretics were teaching and changed the words. He used these same popular melodies to teach the truths of the Catholic faith. Ephrem was one of the first to write songs for the liturgy of the Church. He wrote so many beautiful and original hymns that he has been called "Harp of the Holy Spirit." Quite a few of his homilies and hymns were devoted to Mary, the Mother of God.

Ephrem died about 373. After a very long time, the Church named him a Doctor. The title "Doctor" means that a particular saint's writing or preaching is outstanding in guiding the Christian faithful.

SUGGESTIONS

1. As a young person, Ephrem easily became angry and had outbursts of temper. But gradually, he became outstanding in self-control. Discuss with the students the importance of having self-control in daily life. Lead them to decide on an area in their own lives in which they could improve their self-control. Then, just as Ephrem gained control of his anger by relying on God's help, have the students take time to pray silently for God's help in their own lives.

2. Ephrem was a refugee at one point in his life. Raise the class's awareness of the sufferings of present-day refugees by having the students list the painful situations that refugees might have to face in leaving their homeland. Then have each student compose a petition for refugees. Lead the class in a litany of petitions. The response to each petition could be "Lord, guide Your people."

3. Direct the students to choose one of their favorite hymns and print the words of one stanza on a piece of paper. Then have them write a few sentences on the paper explaining the meaning of those words. Finally, have them illustrate the song or create a border design on the paper.

4. Ephrem wrote many religious poems and songs. Encourage the students to attempt to compose a religious song or poem. To give them some structure for this, you might suggest that they write an alphabet poem. Tell them to print a sequence of letters from the alphabet on the left side of the paper and use each letter as the first letter of a line of the poem. An example is given here.

   Always I praise you, my Creator and Father.
   Because You give me life and faith and friends.
   Can I ever thank You enough?

5. In honor of St. Ephrem, teach the students a new song that could be used in the eucharistic liturgy. Encourage the students to sing with conviction and joy.

JUNE 11: BARNABAS

He was called Joseph at first. When he left his native island of Cyprus, he may have had no idea what life held for him. Soon he became a Christian, perhaps on the day of Pentecost. The apostles welcomed him and changed his name to Barnabas, which means "son of encouragement." Barnabas sold his property and gave the money to the Jerusalem community. Gradually other Christians came to see that Barnabas was a man of deep faith, filled with the Holy Spirit. He was the one who reached out to Paul after his conversion. Barnabas, respected by the members of the Jerusalem Church, trusted Paul and took the risk of defending him. He introduced Paul to the apostles and encouraged everyone to accept him.

For a while, Barnabas and Paul were leaders in the Church at Antioch. There, for the first time, followers of Christ were called "Christians." This name shows that others began to think of Jesus' followers as a religious group separate from Jews and pagans.

When Barnabas and Paul returned to Jerusalem, the Holy Spirit had other plans for them. One day as a few Church leaders were fasting and praying together, they came to see that Barnabas and Paul were to be set apart by the Holy Spirit for special missionary work. Their mission first took them to Cyprus, where they welcomed many Jewish and Gentile converts into the Church. Then they sailed north to the city of Lystra in Asia Minor. There Paul cured a crippled man by telling him to stand up, and the people were astonished. In their native language, they enthusiastically declared Barnabas and Paul to be gods in disguise. Once Barnabas and Paul realized the misunderstanding, they tried to explain that they were only men who came to teach about the living God Who created the world. But the crowds turned against them, so the next day Barnabas and Paul left Lystra and traveled on to other cities to preach the Good News.

In every place where they established a Christian community, Barnabas and Paul appointed leaders to guide the local church. Eventually the two of them separated. Barnabas took the disciple John Mark to Cyprus, while Paul set out on another missionary journey. Christian tradition tells us that Barnabas was martyred, and a handwritten copy of St. Matthew's Gospel was found clasped to his heart. Pictures of Barnabas often show him carrying the Scriptures.

Why is Barnabas called an apostle? He was not one of the first twelve chosen by Jesus, but he played an important part in the early Christian Church.

SUGGESTIONS

1. Have the students read about Barnabas in one of the following passages from the Acts of the Apostles:

Acts	4:36-37	Acts 13:27-30
	9:26-29	13:44-52
	11:27-30	14:1-7
	12:24-25	14:8-14
	13:1-3	14:21-23
	13:4-12	14:36-40

   Then ask them to illustrate their selections and print a title and the Scripture reference on the picture. Have the students post the pictures in sequence.

2. Many scholars agree that the Gospel of Matthew was written in Antioch, the place where Barnabas

did much of his preaching. Have the students pick a passage from Matthew's gospel and copy it in their journals. Then tell them to write an explanation for their choice. Finally have them memorize the passage and recite it to the class.

3. To settle a serious problem, Barnabas and Paul met with Church leaders at the Council of Jerusalem. Through prayer and discussion, they came to a decision. Have the students make a chart in their journals to show how they deal with disagreements. Tell them to draw three columns. In the first column, have them list some recent disagreements they have had. In the second column, have them explain how they handled each disagreement. In the third column, have them write the results of their actions. Then have them put a check next to each disagreement that they handled in a Christian manner. Finally, have the students discuss ways to handle disagreements as Jesus would.

4. Barnabas, an important member of the Jerusalem Christian community, took Paul's part when no one else would take the risk. Ask the students to think of someone they know who seems to be lonely. Challenge them to help that person in some way in the coming week.

5. Barnabas and Paul were once sent to bring relief from Antioch to Christians in Jerusalem who were suffering from famine. Help the students become aware of various Christian organizations that distribute food to the starving in today's world. Then have the class choose one organization and decide on a way of helping that group.

✻ ✻ ✻ ✻ ✻ ✻ ✻ ✻ ✻ ✻ ✻ ✻ ✻ ✻ ✻ ✻ ✻ ✻ ✻ ✻

JUNE 13: ANTHONY OF PADUA

Imagine a statue of a young man dressed in a brown Franciscan habit, holding an open Bible. A very young child is standing on the Bible, talking to the man. Do you know the saint whom this statue represents? The child is Jesus and the man is Anthony of Padua.

Anthony was born of noble parents in Lisbon, Portugal, in 1195. We do not know much about his early life, but we do know that for some time he was in the Order of St. Augustine. His whole life changed when he witnessed the burial of several Franciscan missionary priests in his hometown of Lisbon. These priests had been tortured and martyred in Morocco, Africa. Listening to the heroic adventures of these men lit a bright flame in Anthony's heart. He obtained permission to become a Franciscan and to sail to Morocco to be a missionary. But the African climate was not good for Anthony, and he became very ill. He decided to return to Portugal. God had a very different plan for him, however. His boat was driven off course by a strong wind, and he landed in

Sicily. After a few months, he made his way to Italy, where the Franciscan priests and brothers were holding an important meeting. Anthony attended that meeting and probably met St. Francis of Assisi, who was then a frail old man.

While Anthony was in Italy, it was discovered that he was an expert on Scripture. A story is told that at an ordination Mass, the priest who was to give the homily did not arrive on time. At the last minute Anthony was asked to give the homily. He did, and from that day on his reputation as an inspired preacher spread through Italy and France. Anthony converted so many heretics through his preaching and the works of mercy that he was called the "Wonder Worker."

The very fast pace of Anthony's preaching and teaching finally led to poor health. He died at the age of 36 and was buried in Padua, Italy. His fame spread throughout the world. According to tradition, Anthony had experienced a vision of the Child Jesus. That is why many statues of Anthony show him holding a Bible with the Child Jesus standing on it.

SUGGESTIONS

1. Many customs and devotions are associated with Anthony of Padua. In Italy, there is a fund that is used for the poor. The fund is called St. Anthony's Bread. Have the students share other customs or devotions about St. Anthony with which they are familiar.

2. Anthony was an outstanding preacher. Have the students form groups and make a list of the qualities needed to be an effective preacher of the Good News. Be sure the students include in their lists "being open to the guidance of the Holy Spirit." Then have them think of someone they know who has each of the qualities on the list.

3. Have the students create mini-homilies, following these steps:
   - Choose a Scripture passage.
   - Think of an opening that is related to the Scripture passage and interesting to the people.
   - Decide on one way that Christians could live out this passage.
   - Think of a closing that will inspire those listening to follow Jesus more closely.
   - Practice giving the homily, which should only last between 30 and 60 seconds.

   When the students are ready, have them give their homilies to the class.

4. As a Franciscan friar, Anthony was very poor, and he had a great love for the poor. Have the class evaluate how they have shown love for the poor, the lonely, and the elderly in the last few months. Encourage them to give examples of their own experiences or examples in which the whole class has participated.

5. Early in his life, Anthony learned that what he wanted was not always what God wanted. First he wanted to be a missionary, and then he wanted to return from Morocco to Portugal. Through various circumstances, such as illness and the strong wind that rerouted his boat, Anthony found God's will for him. Have the students write in their journals a prayer for openness to whatever God wants for them in their everyday lives.

JUNE 19: ROMUALD

In 972, when Romuald was a young man, his father killed a relative in an argument over money. This action disturbed Romuald so much that he entered a monastery to do penance for his father's crime.

For many years he lived alone as a hermit. He fasted and prayed a great deal. When he was quite an old man, he began to think about being a martyr. Finally the desire became so strong that he decided to travel to Hungary, where he hoped to be killed for his Christian faith. On the journey, he discovered that he was too old to continue, so he returned to his native land of Italy. Here he again led a hermit's life. His way of living was so strict that at first few people were strong enough to imitate him. But he did start several groups of hermits in northern and central Italy. When he died in 1027, he was probably 75 years old.

SUGGESTIONS

1. Romuald wanted to help his father. He knew that his prayers and his sacrifices would be the best way to help him. Eventually his father repented for the murder and also entered a monastery. Have the students write in their journals a prayer for their own parents. Then allow time for shared prayer, during which the students may offer spontaneous petitions for their parents.

2. Even when Romuald was an elderly man, he continued to do penance and to offer sacrifice to God. Have the students consider times when they have made up excuses to avoid fulfilling their responsibilities, such as washing dishes, caring for the lawn, and doing homework. Then divide the class into groups and have each group make up two skits on this kind of experience. In the first skit, a person makes excuses for not doing a certain job. In the second skit, the person refuses to make excuses and does the same job with courage and enthusiasm.

3. As Romuald advanced in age, the desire to be a martyr grew strong in his heart, and he spent much time in prayer and penance. Many elderly people devote much time to daily prayer and to living for God. Have the students give examples of elderly people they know who come to daily Mass or witness a deep love for God. Share your own examples as well.

4. Often a person's love can be measured by that person's generosity. For most of his life, Romuald made many sacrifices to show his love for God, but his generosity always wanted to do more. Have the students reflect on how generous they are with God by asking themselves these questions:
   - Do I spend time with God each day?
   - Do I speak to Him and listen to Him?
   - Do I take time to thank Him for the good things and to share the hurts I experience?
   - Do I tell Him that I love Him?

5. Have the students read Matthew 16:24. Explain that from the earliest days of the Church, Christians have done penance in response to the Lord's invitation. Ask the students to suggest possible penances that they could do in school, such as choosing not to make a sarcastic remark when it would be funny; taking the time to produce neat written work; taking the middle or last place in a line. Have each student decide on one secret penance that he or she will do during the day.

JUNE 21: ALOYSIUS GONZAGA

When Aloysius Gonzaga was born on March 9, 1568, his parents began planning for his future. His mother wanted him to be a priest. His father was determined to have his oldest son become a military leader or famous political figure — anything but a priest.

At the age of five, Aloysius was sent to a military camp to get started on his career. His father must have been very pleased to see his little son marching at the head of the platoon of soldiers around the camp grounds. His mother and his tutor were extremely displeased when he came home using the rough, coarse language of the camp. At the age of seven, Aloysius received a special insight from God. While other boys were dreaming about being military heroes or heads of wealthy estates, Aloysius thought of other matters. He decided to become a saint, and he began acting on that decision. He prayed long hours at night and fasted several times a week. This was unusual for a boy of his age.

While he was on a visit to Spain with his parents, Aloysius read the lives of saintly Jesuit missionaries, and he decided to become a Jesuit. His father and some other relatives tried hard to change his mind. It was a fierce battle of wills, but after several years, Aloysius won. With his father's permission, he joined the Jesuit Order at seventeen years of age. The novice director, who was in charge of training Aloysius, told him to cut down on his long hours of prayer and to give up some of his fasting and other penances. Aloysius obeyed willingly. He understood that his obedience was better than "doing his own thing."

In 1591 a serious epidemic broke out in Rome. Aloysius volunteered at once to help in the hospital. At that time, hospitals were not the clean, orderly

places that we are familiar with today. It was very easy to "catch" an illness. That is what happened; Aloysius became very ill. No medicine could help him. He died when he was only twenty-three years old. He was not afraid to die. During his life he had focused on doing what God wanted: serving and loving God and His people.

SUGGESTIONS

1. Have the students list on the board the various actions Aloysius chose in order to become holy, which is to become like Jesus: prayed daily, read lives of the saints, chose to do difficult things to gain self-control, and asked advice from a priest. Ask the students to make three-point plans for growing in personal holiness. Direct them to write their plans in their journals.

2. During the time Aloysius was growing up, Renaissance society was filled with brutality, dishonesty, and immoral behavior. It needed the example of saintly people like Aloysius, who was determined to do what God wanted. Today's society, too, needs Christians who rely on God's power and live saintly lives. Direct the students to find three newspaper headlines that reflect needs in our society. Have them cut out the headlines and glue them to a piece of paper. Then have them write something they can do to respond to these needs with Christian attitudes.

3. Aloysius came from a wealthy and famous family. He never used the power that his family had or boasted of his wealth. He would sign his name "Aluigi" or "Luigi" instead of using his formal name. He volunteered to do unpleasant jobs. Have the students listen to the following questions and answer them silently:

- Like Aloysius, do I volunteer for unpleasant jobs?
- Do I avoid boasting of my talents?
- Do I want people to always notice the good things that I do?
- Do I try to be first in line?
- Do I use money to get people to like me and do what I want?
- Do I avoid being with unpopular people because I think they will ruin my "image"?
- Do I put other people down so that I can look good?

Then have the students listen prayerfully as you play a song that reflects the love Christians have for one another.

4. Aloysius showed obedience to his father by going to military camp and by not joining the Jesuits until his father gave him permission. He showed obedience to his novice director by following his

suggestions. Have the students write an essay on the value and challenge of obedience in the life of a Christian. Encourage them to use examples from the lives of the saints and from their own lives.

5. Aloysius had to overcome the habit that he had acquired at military camp of using offensive language. Recall with the students the second commandment: "You shall not take the name of the Lord, your God, in vain." Then distribute copies of the following word search on this commandment. Have the students define the listed words on the back of the paper and locate them in the puzzle.

TERMS:

perjury	profanity
cursing	obscene language
blasphemy	

S	E	T	B	B	L	A	S	P	H	E	M	Y	D	D
W	W	X	A	C	A	C	U	R	S	I	N	G	K	L
O	B	E	D	F	F	B	L	O	B	S	A	T	N	E
V	U	G	A	I	I	D	M	F	S	Y	O	F	M	N
O	P	R	C	R	O	F	P	A	T	Z	U	G	O	T
A	D	A	E	O	I	G	O	N	V	A	B	H	L	M
T	F	L	A	D	U	N	R	I	W	E	C	I	Q	V
H	I	M	P	D	C	H	G	T	M	O	W	S	R	W
S	I	P	E	R	J	U	R	Y	X	I	D	J	S	X
O	B	S	C	E	N	E	L	A	N	G	U	A	G	E

When the students have finished the word search, let them discuss how a person could break the habit of using offensive language.

JUNE 22: PAULINUS OF NOLA

Paulinus of Nola, Spain, who lived in the fourth century, wrote letters to and received replies from St. Ambrose, St. Jerome, St. Gregory, St. Martin, and St. Augustine. He was not only a good letter writer, but also a successful lawyer, a wealthy governor, and a talented poet. He married a rich Spanish noblewoman named Therasia. For some years, the two of them enjoyed the comfortable life of the very rich.

Then in 389, both of them decided to become Christians and were baptized. Later they had a little son, Celsus, who died after only eight days. This event could have led Paulinus and Therasia to withdraw into self-pity. Instead they decided to give their wealth to the poor, as Jesus had said, and to live a very simple, plain life. The people in the city admired and loved Paulinus so much for his Christian witness that they wanted him to become a priest. Eventually he did become a priest and even a bishop.

He and Therasia lived in an old two-story home. Paulinus used the first floor as a place where debtors, wanderers, and the very poor could find shelter.

Paulinus and a few other men lived like monks, using the second floor of the house. Therasia took care of the household.

On June 22, 431, Paulinus died. One of his last acts was to give to the poor fifty silver pieces that he had just received as a donation. To the last day of his life, Paulinus followed these words of Jesus: "Sell your possessions and give alms. Get yourselves purses that do not wear out, treasure that will not fail you, in heaven where no thief can reach it and no moth destroy it. For where your treasure is, there will your heart be also" (Luke 12:33-34).

SUGGESTIONS

1. Early in life, Paulinus was placed under the protection of St. Felix, a saint of the third century. Paulinus wrote a poem in honor of St. Felix every year on his feast day. He also built a basilica in his honor. Have the students do research on their patron or favorite saint. Tell them to prepare a short talk in which they try to convince the class that their saint would be a good patron saint. When they are ready, have each student give his or her talk to the class.

2. At least fifty letters written by St. Paulinus have been preserved. He wrote often in poetry and used many Scripture quotations. Have the students find a Scripture quote and use it in a thank-you note. Direct them to write the note to someone who works in the school: maintenance personnel, cafeteria workers, office staff, street guards.

3. Paulinus and Therasia grew more like Christ after their little son died. They began to reach out to others. Encourage the students to share with the class the story of someone who has grown after experiencing a tragedy. This person could be someone they know personally or about whom they have read or heard. Lead the class in a prayer in which each student offers a petition for people who are suffering from a tragedy. The response could be "Lord, help them." For example:

   For those who are starving because of famine, let us pray to the Lord.

   For parents whose children are ill, let us pray to the Lord.

4. Paulinus and Therasia helped each other to grow closer to the Lord. They were baptized at the same time. Together they distributed their goods to the poor. They were faithful to each other throughout their married life. Have the students nominate from television programs or public life married people that mutually support each other in doing good. List the names on the board. Then have the students vote by secret ballot for the one couple that best shows unselfish love and support.

5. Paulinus and Therasia gave away all their money and property so that they could live a simple life-style. They wanted to be one with the poor and to

help the poor. Encourage the students to reflect on how they can simplify their life-styles. To help them, ask questions similar to the following:

- **Do you borrow and lend records and books or must you own every book and record yourself?**
- **Do you have clothes in your closet that you don't wear, even though they still fit?**
- **Are you careful to turn off lights and water when they are not needed?**
- **Do you ask your parents to buy expensive food or games, or to take you to expensive places?**
- **Do you enjoy activities that don't cost money?**
- **Are you satisfied with what you have or do you always want some thing more?**

After the reflection, have the students compile a list of ways to simplify their life-style. Have them copy the list into their journals and resolve to try to live more simply at home.

JUNE 22: JOHN FISHER AND THOMAS MORE

There are two saints listed for today. They share the same day probably because they were beheaded just two weeks apart for the same "crime" against the King of England.

John Fisher was born in 1469. He was educated at the best schools in England. After he was ordained a priest, he continued his study of religious matters. The royal family recognized him as a holy and learned priest. So he was appointed tutor for the young Prince Henry, later King Henry VIII. In 1504, Fisher became the Bishop of Rochester, a small diocese in England, and also Chancellor of Cambridge University. This last position was a very high and great honor. As a bishop, Fisher visited the parishes in his diocese and paid special attention to the poor. His people knew he was a man of strong, upright conscience — one who would hold tight to the truth and correct action. He wrote eight books against heresy, and Henry, now king, was proud to be his friend.

But all this changed when King Henry decided that his marriage to Catherine, his brother's widow, was not valid. Henry's request for a divorce was refused by the pope, and Bishop Fisher went along with this decision. The bishop foresaw the serious danger he would be in if he refused to agree with the king. But he was strong enough and honest enough to resist signing the document siding with King Henry. All the other bishops of England had already signed it.

Six months later, parliament wrote another document claiming that King Henry VIII was supreme head of the Catholic Church in England. Again Bishop Fisher refused to sign this decree. This act made the king extremely angry. The bishop was sentenced to prison in 1534 on the charge of high treason. Henry became furious when the pope declared the jailed bishop a cardinal. Fisher was kept in prison for fourteen months without any trial. Finally in June, 1535, he was condemned to death by beheading. He had been a noble and saintly man, good to the poor and loyal to the Church and the pope.

Several years ago a play and a movie entitled "A Man for All Seasons" was very popular. It was the story of Thomas More. He was born in 1477, the son of a successful lawyer in London. As a young teenager he studied Greek, French, Latin, and math. At first he planned to become a priest, but he changed his mind and entered law school. His three daughters, one son, and many friends helped make his home a happy, joyful place.

Besides being a keen and shrewd lawyer, he was a charming, witty man, who very soon won the friendship of the king. Henry VIII began his rule of England as a devout and sincere king. He even wrote a book in defense of the Catholic Church. Later great pride, selfishness, and stubborness led Henry into trouble. He argued that the permission from the pope to marry Catherine, the widow of his older brother, was no good. Really, Henry had become tired of Catherine and too much interested in a young, attractive woman, Anne Boleyn.

King Henry asked More to approve of the divorce he wanted. More refused to along with Henry. Of course, the king became angry. He knew that More had studied the problem and weighed both sides. By this time More had become chancellor of all England. This was the position next to the king in importance. Henry wanted Thomas More on his side.

Henry went one step further. He had the Parliament — his Senate and Congress — write a document stating that King Henry VIII would be the head of the Catholic Church in England from then on. Every bishop, except John Fisher, and many important people in the government signed the Oath of Supremacy. Thomas More refused because he believed strongly that the pope was a direct successor of the first pope appointed by Jesus. More resigned his position as chancellor. He retired to his country home, hoping for a quiet life with his family, his friends, and his books.

Henry continued to pester him. Finally, More was sent to prison because he would not give in. He was kept imprisoned for more than a year in a dungeon known as the Tower. The king tried hard to make him change his mind, but Thomas stood firm. He knew this stand would mean certain death for him and disgrace for his family, but he followed his conscience.

Finally, after much suffering in the Tower from hunger, cold, and loneliness, More was led out to his death on July 6. He saw that the masked swordsman was quite nervous. So Thomas said in a joyful way, "Be not afraid, for you send me to God." Then, still a friend to the king, he said to the crowd of people, "I die the king's good servant, but God's first." Can you understand now why the title "A Man for All Seasons" is a perfect title for St. Thomas More?

SUGGESTIONS

1. John Fisher and Thomas More were friends. Both men were loyal friends of King Henry VIII. Ask the students how these men could call themselves friends of the king and still not approve his actions. Lead them to see that helping our friends to choose good and avoid evil is a sign of sincere, unselfish love. Have the students discuss ways they could actually help their friends make good choices. Give them two good rules to follow:
   • Pray for the courage and the right moment to speak.
   • Advise their friends in an honest, respectful way.

2. Both John and Thomas were loyal to God and to themselves in doing what they believed was right. Have the students write a brief essay on one of the following statements:

   Honesty is the heart of friendship.

   Honesty is the best policy.

   Some people are honest/dishonest because _____.

3. Although they were under enormous outside pressure, John and Thomas did not change their minds. Ask the students to write in their journals about a time when the Lord helped them cling to what was right in the face of outside pressure. Then have them thank God and pray for God's help in the future. Pray one of the following prayers with them:

   Saints John Fisher and Thomas More, pray that we may be strong in faith and loyalty.

   Father,
   you confirm the true faith
   with the crown of martyrdom.
   May the prayers of Saints John Fisher and
     Thomas More
   give us the courage to proclaim our faith
   by the witness of our lives.
   Amen.
           (Prayer for the feast of Sts. John Fisher
                       and Thomas More)

4. Thomas More was known and loved for his sense of humor. Even when he was imprisoned in the cold, damp Tower, he would joke with his daughter and the other visitors who came. Have the students tell about people they know who bring joy to others, even when they themselves are suffering. Share with the class the story of someone you know who does this.

5. John Fisher once wrote a book on the penitential psalms in the Bible. Read aloud or have a student

read aloud Psalm 28 or 86. Show the students the pattern the psalmist used for these psalms:

- Address God
- Explain the situation
- Admit that you were wrong and ask for forgiveness or help
- Tell God that you trust Him
- Praise Him

Then have the students choose a situation in their own lives and write a psalm using the same pattern.

6. Encourage interested students to research other people who were martyred under King Henry VIII. The *New Catholic Encyclopedia* lists these martyrs in the article "Martyrs of England and Wales." Have the students compare and contrast the types of professions or careers, the various "crimes," and the types of death of these courageous men and women.

JUNE 24: BIRTH OF JOHN THE BAPTIST

Some athletes who have won Olympic gold medals began their training as early as the age of two. They spend their childhood preparing to achieve their goal of being the best in their sport. John the Baptist seems to have had an even earlier start in preparing for his goal. According to Luke's gospel, Zechariah, John's father, was the first to be prepared for John's birth. While he was offering incense in the temple, the angel Gabriel came with the announcement. The angel said that the baby's name would be John, that he would be his father's joy and delight, that he would be filled with the Holy Spirit, and that he would bring people back to God. Because of his momentary lack of faith, Zechariah lost the power to speak and hear until John was born.

The same gospel also tells of the visit between Mary and Elizabeth, John's mother, before both John and Jesus were born. It tells of the joyful reaction of relatives and neighbors at John's birth. Eight days later, these same people wanted to name the baby Zechariah. However, his father indicated in writing that he wanted his little son to be named John. With this action, Zechariah recovered his ability to speak, and the people were amazed. They began to ask the question, "What will this child turn out to be?" (Luke 1:66). Some years after this event of the naming, Luke's gospel records that John spent his youth in the wilderness, preparing for his mission. What was his mission? His father gave a prophecy on the day that John was named:

> And you, little child,
> you shall be called Prophet of the Most High,
> for you will go before the Lord
> to prepare the way for him.
>
> (Luke 1:76)

SUGGESTIONS

1. Zechariah foresaw that his little son would some day prepare the way for the Messiah, the Savior. At John's naming, he spoke a canticle recorded in Luke 1:76-77. Tell the students that this prayer is called the *Benedictus,* which is the first word of the canticle in Latin. Have students read the canticle aloud. Then have them do one of the following activities:

- paraphrase the canticle, print it on onionskin paper, and design the edges
- make transparencies for various parts of the canticle
- recite the canticle in sections for a choric speech presentation

2. Show the students how the name *John* is written in Hebrew, which may be the language in which his name was originally written.

Showing how "John" is written out in square Hebrew letters — as Zechariah must have written. This name means "Yahweh is gracious."

Then have the students research the name John in different languages. Some forms of the name are given here.

Johannes (Norwegian)	Sean (Gaelic)
Joao (Portuguese)	Evan (Welsh)
Janos (Hungarian)	

3. Have the students read Luke 1:5-25 and write a news report of the events recounted there. Have them print the report on unlined paper and draw an appropriate illustration to accompany it. Display the finished reports.

4. Read to the students the prophecy in Isaiah 40:3-5. Then, in honor of John the Baptist's birthday, have the students listen to an Advent song that mentions the role of John or the Isaian prophecies.

5. Have the students create a repeat-pattern design using Scriptural symbols of John the Baptist. First, direct the students to read Matthew 3:1-11 and John 1:6-8. Next, ask them to think of a symbol that represents John the Baptist or something he said or did. This symbol may be an image that is in the actual Scripture text or an image that could be drawn from the passage. Then give the students styrofoam meat trays, which can be obtained from the meat department of a food store. Have each student carve a design on the back of a tray with a pencil. Instruct the students to press hard but not to carve all the way through the tray. Then have them use a paintbrush or sponge to apply tempera paint to the design. They can then use the tray as a stamp. Have them press repeatedly on a sheet of

paper to make a patterned design. After the paint on the paper is dry, direct them to letter one of the Scripture passages over the design with a black felt-tipped pen.

JUNE 27: CYRIL OF ALEXANDRIA

What would a saint born in the land of camels, pyramids, and the Great Sphinx be like? Cyril was born about 376 in Alexandria, the famous Egyptian center of learning.

Very little is known about his early life. We know he became archbishop of Alexandria when his uncle, the former archbishop, died. During his first years in this position, he was quite strict, sometimes even severe, with heretics and other people who caused trouble for the Christians of his diocese.

As he grew older and had more experience, he became famous for his action at the Council of Ephesus. He tried very hard to make the heretic Nestorius understand that Christ was truly God and Man united as one Person. He defended the teaching that Mary is the Mother of God, and insisted on calling her "Theotokos," a Greek name meaning "God-bearer" or "Mother of God." Several bishops who sided with Nestorius succeeded in having Cyril sent to prison. They called him the heretic. Three representatives from the pope arrived in Ephesus in time to save Cyril from further trouble. Because of his long, hard struggle with heretics, and his forceful writing about doctrine, Cyril was named a Doctor of the Church. He died in 444.

SUGGESTIONS
1. Have the students find out more about the Council of Ephesus. Direct them to research and report on the following:
   - the letters that Cyril and Nestorius wrote to each other
   - the leadership role that Pope Celestine I had in the synod (A.D. 430)
   - the actual meeting of the ecumenical council approved by Pope Celestine in Ephesus (A.D. 431)

2. As archbishop of Alexandria, Cyril had to make important decisions and be responsible for his actions. Every Christian is responsible for making decisions based on Gospel values. Read the following situations to the students. Have them write down the decision they think each person should make. Then discuss their answers.

   1) Miguel must give a speech in class tomorrow. He is very afraid that he'll forget his lines. The last time he gave a speech, he was so fearful that he froze and could not continue. What should Miguel do?

   2) Sally was chosen for the lead in the play. Jan, one of her good friends, really wanted the part. What should Jan do?

   3) Matt overheard some boys and girls talking about his friend offering them marijuana. What should Matt do?

3. Cyril's writings show that he must have reflected on various parts of the Bible. Teach the students the steps for a prayerful reflection on a Gospel story.

   STEPS FOR PRAYERFUL REFLECTION ON THE GOSPEL
   1) See: Have the students visualize the persons, place, setting (circumstances: who, what, where, when, why, and how).
   2) Catch: Have the students look for the message that is conveyed.
   3) Apply: Have the students apply the message to their own lives.

   Then have the students choose a Gospel story and prayerfully follow the steps. Finally, have them write their thoughts in their journals.

4. At the beginning of his life, Cyril was very strict with heretics and others who caused trouble for the Church. Later, he came to grow in the compassion and forgiveness of Jesus. Have the students think about themselves over the last several years and how they have grown in becoming a little more like Jesus. Have them choose one quality in which they have grown and allow time for them to pray silently to God, thanking Him and asking for His help.

5. Have the students work in groups to create acrostics, using either the words "Theotokos" or "Mother of God." Direct them to use other titles of Mary in the acrostic.

JUNE 28: IRENAEUS

How strong is a chain — a watch chain, a tow chain, or even a friendship chain? It is as strong as its weakest link.

Irenaeus was one of the very strong links in the chain that joined the Church at the time of the twelve apostles and the Church of the second century. He was a link because he wrote and taught the faith handed on by the apostles and preserved it when it was attacked. His chief concern was unity among the churches. We do not know very much about St. Irenaeus. He was born about 130 in Smyrna, a port town in western Turkey. For some reason he traveled to Lyons, France, where he was ordained a priest. Eventually he became the bishop of that growing commercial city. He was very much concerned about heretics who were attacking the teaching of the

young Christian church. Irenaeus realized the importance of guarding the teaching of the twelve apostles from false doctrine. Especially strong was his battle against Gnosticism, one of the worst dangers ever faced by Christianity. This heresy claimed that eternal life could be gained only by receiving special knowledge about God, knowledge that was available just to a few chosen people. Irenaeus taught that, according to Scripture, God wished all persons to be saved and to come to know the truth. He and other Christian writers insisted that knowing God, obeying His commandments, and having a close relationship with Him were the important things.

At one time, a group of Christians in Asia Minor, which was Irenaeus' homeland, did not want to celebrate Easter at the time the Church in Rome had decided. Irenaeus explained to Pope Victor I that this was not a matter of faith. The date for celebrating Easter was an old tradition for these people. His pleading for them "saved the day." Some years later the matter was cleared up and the date for Easter was settled. Irenaeus was one of the important writers in the early Church. He was a strong witness to the teaching of the Church as it came from Peter and the other apostles. Perhaps Irenaeus was martyred after a long battle against heretics. We know only that he died about the year 200.

SUGGESTIONS

1. Irenaeus spent much of his life defending the truth. Direct the students to make a "truth" chain by following these directions:

- Distribute one slip of construction paper (8 ½" x 1 ½") to each student.
- Have each student choose one of the following Scripture references and write the quote on his or her link.

Romans 2:20	Galatians 2:14
Romans 3:7	Ephesians 1:13
Romans 9:1	Ephesians 4:21
1 Corinthians 13:6	2 Thessalonians 2:13
2 Corinthians 4:2	1 John 3:19
2 Corinthians 6:7	1 John 4:6
2 Corinthians 13:8	1 John 4:16
Galatians 2:5	1 John 5:6

- Have the students assemble the chain with staples or glue. Tell them to be careful to keep the written quotes on the outside of the chain as they assemble the links.
- Display the chain.

2. Have the students research the controversy over the date of Easter in the early centuries. Direct them to discover what role each of the following saints played: Cyril of Alexandria, Hippolytus, Pope St. Leo, Augustine of Canterbury.

3. The name *Irenaeus* means peace, and this saint was true to his name. Irenaeus worked for peace and promoted respect among Christians. Have the students bring in any items that call for peace: pictures, stickers, buttons, newspaper or magazine articles, etc. Have the entire class make a peace scrapbook or a giant peace collage, using the items that students have brought.

4. Irenaeus safeguarded the truth that had been handed down by the apostles and their successors. Led by the Holy Spirit, he helped to protect the Church through his writings. St. Joseph is a saint who has been designated protector of the Church. Have the students copy the following prayer to St. Joseph in their journals and pray it often for the Church.

> St. Joseph, watchful guardian of the Holy Family, defend the Church. Keep it from all error and sin. Once you rescued the Child Jesus from danger. Now protect God's holy Church from all harm. Help us to imitate your example in life and to die a happy death. Amen.

5. Irenaeus and other Christian writers insisted that obeying God's commandments was very important for the Christian life. Put the numbers from 1-10 on separate slips of paper and place the slips in a box. Have the students draw a slip, recite the commandment that has that number, and give an example of a person keeping the commandment.

6. If the students are not familiar with terms used in this summary of St. Irenaeus' life, have them look up the words in a Catholic dictionary or encyclopedia. Terms to consider are heretics, false doctrine, Gnosticism, and heresy.

JUNE 29: PETER AND PAUL

We have met Peter and Paul several times before this in the Church's calendar. In November, January, and February, we celebrated their feasts. And here they are again. Why four times in one year? Because they are the giants of the early Christian Church, and as giants they deserve some extra attention. When Peter was crucified, he was buried in an old Roman cemetery, probably on the spot where the huge basilica of St. Peter is today. Paul was beheaded in a prison outside the old city walls.

Peter was very likely a middle-aged man when Jesus called him. He was a fisherman from Bethsaida, a village near the Lake of Galilee. Perhaps he was part of a "Fisherman's Co-op" with his brother Andrew and friends James and John. At any rate, Andrew introduced Peter to Jesus. "Jesus looked at him and said, 'You are Simon son of John; you are to be called Cephas' — meaning Rock" (John 1:42).

During the three years the apostles lived with Jesus, Peter showed definite signs of leadership. He was often the spokesman for the Eleven. He answered for all when Jesus asked, "'Who do you say I am?' Then Simon Peter spoke up, 'You are the Christ,' he said, 'the Son of the living God'" (Matthew 16:16-17). It was Peter who objected very strongly to Jesus' stating that he was on his way to Jerusalem to suffer and die. This time Jesus scolded him. Peter is mentioned 195 times in the New Testament. From these references, he appears lovable, impetuous, practical — and sometimes weak under pressure. But Jesus loved him dearly.

Peter became the leader in the early Christian Church. According to the Acts of the Apostles, he was the first to preach on Pentecost Sunday. He arranged for the selection of Matthias to replace Judas. He worked the first public miracle: curing the lame man at the temple gate. He welcomed the first person who was not Jewish into the Church. His reputation became so great that people thought just his shadow passing by would cure the sick and the lame, the blind and the deaf.

Peter was put into prison three or four times. Just as soon as he was released, he began preaching again about Jesus Christ. Finally, in Rome, he was sentenced to death by crucifixion. Out of deep respect for his Master, Jesus, he asked the guards to fasten him to the cross upside down. That was how he died in about the year 64 or 65.

Paul was Peter's spiritual brother, so they share this feast day together. Paul received the very best education as a young boy. Because he was a strict Jew, he thought it was his duty to persecute the "new-fangled" Christians. They were teaching strange new things, and Paul meant to stop it. You will remember how he was converted one day while traveling to Damascus. He was on his way to drag Christians out of their homes and throw them into prison. But Jesus had other plans for Paul.

Once he found Jesus, he never lost sight of Him. Paul became the greatest missionary we have ever known. In the beginning Paul had great difficulty convincing the Jews that the Old Law of Moses did not apply strictly anymore. Jesus came to teach a way of love and service freely given. The Jews who were part of the early Church were also unwilling to accept anyone for baptism who was not Jewish. But Paul argued so skillfully, under the guidance of the Holy Spirit, that he finally won this battle.

Paul worked very hard for about thirty years, traveling around the Roman Empire and preaching Christ. From his letters and from the Acts, he seems to have been an affectionate, loyal, courageous, and dedicated man. He was the right man to build the bridge between the Old Testament Jewish religion and the Christianity of the New Testament.

Worn out with traveling, preaching, and suffering, he was imprisoned and finally beheaded. He was so sure of his call to be a missionary for Jesus that he wrote to the Christian community in Rome: "For I am certain of this: neither death nor life, no angel, no prince, nothing that exists, nothing still to come, not any power, or height or depth, nor any created thing, can ever come between us and the love of God made visible in Christ Jesus our Lord" (Romans 8:38-39).

SUGGESTIONS

1. Have the students present incidents from the Acts of the Apostles, using the flannel board. Divide the class into pairs. Have each pair choose an incident from Acts. Then have them draw figures and scenery fitting to the story on heavy paper. Tell them to cut out each piece and glue a piece of flannel to the back of it so that it will stick to the flannel board. Direct them to practice telling their story and moving the figures on the flannel board. Finally have each pair give their story for a younger class.

2. Direct the students to design triptychs showing Jesus, Peter, and Paul. First have them fold a piece of construction paper into three equal parts. While the paper is folded, have them cut the top of the paper into the shape of an arch.

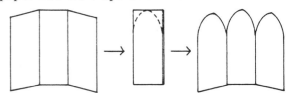

Discuss with the students appropriate symbols for Jesus, Peter, and Paul. On another sheet of paper, have them draw pictures and symbols that represent the three figures. Finally have them glue their pictures and designs on the background, putting Jesus in the center and Peter and Paul on either side.

3. Tell the students to choose an incident about Peter or Paul from the Acts of the Apostles, read it, and make up a ten-point quiz on the passage. Have them exchange quizzes, read the suggested passage, and take the quiz. Or read aloud Acts 12:1-9 and give this oral quiz to the students:

   1) **Did God intervene and save Peter?** (Yes.)

   2) **Was the guard negligent or lazy?** (No.)

   3) **Did the people pray for Peter?** (Yes.)

   4) **Did the guard see Peter leave?** (No.)

   5) **Did Rhoda let Peter into the house immediately?** (No.)

   6) **Were the Christians surprised to see Peter?** (Yes.)

   7) **Did Peter remain in the house of John Mark?** (No.)

   8) **Did Herod excuse the guards for Peter's escape?** (No.)

   9) **Did Herod accept praise in a humble manner?** (No.)

   10) **Did Herod die of a serious disease?** (Yes.)

4. Have the students write questions about Peter and Paul on slips of paper. Then put the slips in a box and have each student draw a question and answer it. You might wish to include the following questions:
   1) What is a quality of Peter's character?
   2) How did Peter receive the call to follow Christ?
   3) In what way did Jesus say that Peter was like a rock?
   4) How did Paul die?
   5) Why are the names of Paul and Barnabas often associated?

5. Encourage the students to memorize the names of the epistles of the New Testament. Then challenge them to recite the entire list in order in a twenty-second time limit, with perfect accuracy and clear speech.

6. Remind the students that Peter and Paul and the other early apostles did not lead lives of fame and glory. Have a student read aloud 2 Corinthians 6:3-10. Then discuss these points with the class:
   - Christians will meet criticism and mockery from people who have values different from theirs.
   - Their own weakness will sometimes block the good they want to do.
   - Christians are not afraid to face suffering for Christ because they rely on God's power and strength.

Conclude the discussion by playing a song that deals with Christian courage in suffering.

JUNE 30: FIRST MARTYRS OF THE CHURCH OF ROME

Nero became the Emperor of Rome in the year 54. About ten years later, he began to persecute the Christians. When a terrible fire broke out in the city, Nero accused the Christians of causing the fire. So he increased his efforts to destroy anyone who was Christian. During the next two centuries, thousands of Christians were put to death. There were so many that no one could possibly keep track of them. All these unnamed and unnumbered martyrs are honored the day after the feast of Peter and Paul.

SUGGESTIONS

1. Martyrdom is the greatest witness of a person's love for God. Have the students copy the Act of Love and memorize it: "O my God, I love You above all things with my whole heart and soul, because You are infinitely good and deserving of all my love. I love my neighbor as myself for love of You. Amen." Have them summarize how the martyrs lived this prayer.

2. On this feast day, no *one* martyr receives special notice. Each individual Christian was generous and brave, but the whole group receives our admira-

tion. One of the antiphons for this feast contains these words:

> The great numbers of martyrs stood firm in their love for one another because they shared the same spirit and the same faith.
> (The Liturgy of the Hours)

Discuss the full meaning of this statement with the students. Then encourage them to give examples of groups whose members have stood firm in their love for one another and their love for good when faced with evil, sin, or social pressure. Have the students use examples from the news, from their reading, or from their personal experience. To begin the discussion, share some examples from your own experience.

3. Tell the students that to become a Christian during a time of persecution was to choose to live in danger of torture and execution. Diocletian, the Roman emperor from 284-305, issued four decrees in a little more than a year in his efforts to stamp out Christianity. The first edict ordered all Christian churches to be destroyed, all sacred books to be burned, all religious meetings to be stopped, and all Christians to be demoted from high positions. The second edict called for all religious leaders to be imprisoned. The third edict called for the imprisoned leaders either to offer sacrifice or to be executed. The fourth edict called for all Christians to offer sacrifice. During this time, there were mass executions of as many as one hundred Christians at one time. Show the students examples from a missionary magazine or a newspaper of similar persecution of Christians in the present time.

4. Many Christians impressed the soldiers and on-lookers with their bravery and loyalty to Christ in the midst of torture and under the threat of death. The faith of these Christians, the strength and courage they showed, seemed to be beyond human ability. Often the watching pagans became Christians in order to find the joy and the courage that the martyrs had. Have the students write a one-page, modern-day story in which a Christian witnesses by his or her actions to a person who has no faith in God.

5. The love and loyalty that the martyrs had for God was greater than any physical pain, any humiliation, any danger or threat. They would not submit even when the Emperor Nero had Christians covered with pitch and set on fire as human torches to light the way for his night drive through the park. They stood firm in faith even when he had some Christians sewn into animal skins and left in the woods so that he and his guests could go hunting for Christians as for wild animals. These and other persecuted Christians realized that Jesus had suffered not only from physical pain, but also from mockery and humiliation. Accompany the

students to the parish church to pray the Stations of the Cross. Let this prayer be a reminder that Jesus was the first to suffer in order to give courage to all His followers who suffer for Him.

See Supplement for July 1.

JULY 3: THOMAS

During the Eucharistic Prayer, the priest displays the Host for everyone to see. What do you say at this moment? You might say, "My Lord and my God." Do you know who is recorded in the Gospel as having said those faith-filled words the very first time? It was Thomas, one of the twelve apostles.

Thomas was most likely a Galilean fisherman, like Peter, James, and John. Jesus called him, and he followed generously. One day a messenger came to tell Jesus that His friend Lazarus was quite sick. Mary and Martha, the sisters of Lazarus, asked Jesus to come and cure their brother. The apostles knew this would be a dangerous trip for Jesus because He had many enemies living around Jerusalem. At this time Thomas said he would be very glad to go with Jesus, and even to die with Him.

But on Easter Sunday evening, when the apostles reported that the Risen Lord Jesus had appeared to them, Thomas refused to believe them. He insisted that he would not believe unless he could put his finger into the wound in Jesus' side. He was referring to the wound that resulted when a soldier pierced Jesus' side with a spear while He hung on the cross.

A week later, Jesus appeared again to the apostles. This time Thomas was there. Jesus called him over and told him to put his finger into the wound. Thomas was very ashamed of his unbelief. He fell to his knees and said, "My Lord and my God." Then Jesus said something that should give us great courage and trust. He told Thomas, "You believe because you can see me. Happy are those who have not seen and yet believe" (John 20:29).

We do not know for sure what happened to Thomas later on. Tradition says that he went to India and preached there. Perhaps he was martyred there, too. The Catholic people of India believe firmly that he is their special apostle and patron.

SUGGESTIONS

1. Tell the students that throughout the day they can turn to God and realize they are in His presence by using short prayers. Encourage them today to use the prayer of Thomas: "My Lord and my God."
2. Thomas realized that he was wrong. In front of the other apostles, he was willing to show that he was sorry. Discuss how the apostles might have felt when Thomas admitted he was wrong. Then have the students share how they feel when someone admits to a whole group that he or she is wrong. Finally have them write a prayer in their journals in which they ask for the grace to always admit when they are wrong.

3. Direct the class to assume a prayerful posture. Then invite the students to imagine that they are Thomas. Read aloud John 20:24-29 slowly. After the reading, pause for silent reflection. Then end with the Sign of the Cross.
4. According to the Gospel, Thomas was a twin. If there are any twins in the class, have them share the advantages of being a twin. Have a special prayer in class for all twins.
5. Faith is a free gift from God. Faith can be nourished and should be treasured by those who have received this gift. Have the students compose an original act of faith and print it on a card. Ask them to listen reflectively to a song about faith and then to sign their cards. Post these cards around the room or encourage the students to keep them in their journals.
6. Thomas is the patron of architects. Have the students study the architecture of their parish church. Then have them make sketches of the exterior of their church.

JULY 4: ELIZABETH OF PORTUGAL

Elizabeth was a Spanish princess when she married the King of Portugal in 1255. Very early in her life as queen, she began to help the poor. One story about her generosity is well known. She was on her way into the city carrying a bag of money from the royal treasury. Elizabeth intended giving the money to the poor people she would meet. Instead she met her husband, the king. He suspected that Elizabeth was taking money from the state funds, and he decided to scold her. So he asked his queen what she was carrying hidden under her cape. Elizabeth opened up the bag and the king saw a large number of beautiful roses. Of course he did not scold her.

We are not sure that the story is true, but we do have proof that Elizabeth was very generous to her people. She built a hospital, an orphanage, and a shelter for poor travelers. Besides these good deeds, she spent time and effort to make peace between the fighting members of her family. The king was a good ruler but not a very good husband and father. In fact, Elizabeth finally wore herself out trying to make peace between the king and their only son, who was warring against his father.

Statues and pictures of Elizabeth often show her holding an olive branch or a dove. Why are these appropriate symbols for her?

SUGGESTIONS

1. The sister of Elizabeth's grandmother was Elizabeth of Hungary. Have the students compare the lives of these two saints.
2. Elizabeth treated all people as equal. Have the students give examples of ways that people try to provide equal opportunities for the blind, the deaf,

and those who are mentally, emotionally, or physically disabled.

3. Elizabeth spent much time, energy, and prayer trying to reconcile her husband and her son. Share an experience of a time when you tried to be a reconciler. Invite the students to share their experiences also. Then discuss the risks involved in trying to reconcile two people, and the words and actions that might help. Finally, close by praying the Prayer of St. Francis or an original prayer for peace.

4. Elizabeth was well known for giving shelter to the homeless and feeding the hungry. Divide the students into pairs and have them quiz each other on the spiritual and corporal works of mercy. The list of these works can be found in the section of their text titled "Some Things Every Catholic Should Know."

5. As queen, Elizabeth respected and protected the rights of those who were powerless and poor. Through such actions, she promoted justice in the world. Have the students copy this prayer for justice from the Mass for the Progress of Peoples. Encourage them to pray it often.

> Father,
> you have given all peoples one common origin,
> and your will is to gather them as one family in yourself.
> Fill the hearts of all men with the fire of your love
> and the desire to ensure justice for all their brothers and sisters.
> By sharing the good things you give us
> may we secure justice and equality for every human being,
> an end to all division,
> and a human society built on love and peace.
>
> We ask this through our Lord Jesus Christ, your Son,
> who lives and reigns with you and the Holy Spirit,
> one God, for ever and ever.

JULY 5: ANTHONY ZACCARIA

Anthony Zaccaria is one of those saints who lived a short life full of service to others. He was born in Cremona, Italy, in 1502. He studied medicine and became a doctor. While he was busy healing bodies, he kept wishing he could be a priest in order to heal souls.

After a few years, he entered the seminary and was ordained a priest at the age of 26. Anthony took the great St. Paul for his model and patron. His days were filled with preaching in churches and on street corners. Because several men wanted to join him in his work, Anthony founded a religious order. He called his group Barnabites in honor of Barnabas, the companion of Paul.

At the very time that Luther was dividing the Church in Germany, Anthony and his followers were drawing half-hearted Catholics back to their faith. He encouraged Catholics to receive Holy Communion often, even every day. He had his priests conduct missions in the local parishes. He tried hard to stir up the faith of the Catholic people.

When Anthony was only 36 years old, he died, exhausted from his hard work of preaching, teaching, and traveling. He is usually pictured with a symbol of the Eucharist, a crucifix, or with St. Paul.

SUGGESTIONS

1. Anthony studied medicine before he became a priest. Have the students think of the many times that doctors have helped them since their birth. Encourage them to write a prayer for those doctors in their journals.

2. Doctors take the Hippocratic Oath, promising to preserve life. Every Christian should be dedicated to preserving life, which is created by God. Have the students find this oath (in the encyclopedia) and explain the name *Hippocratic*. Give them the following list and have them check the ways they help to protect life.

_____ make every human being feel important and welcome

_____ give money to the missions so that others may have a decent life

_____ compliment younger brothers and sisters honestly and often

_____ volunteer to help others who seem in need

Challenge the students to add other items to the list.

3. Anthony encouraged Catholics to receive Holy Communion often. Lead the students in a discussion on the importance of the Eucharist to help them appreciate this sacrament more. Have them examine the words of a eucharistic hymn and paraphrase a stanza in their journals. Hymns in praise of the Eucharist can be found in the monthly missalette, or the words could be written on an overhead projector. Suggestions for songs include "O Sacrament Most Holy," "Humbly Let Us Voice Our Homage," "Sing, My Tongue, the Savior's Glory," "Gift of Finest Wheat."

4. Anthony took St. Paul as a model for his life. Have the students make a chart comparing the two saints. Refer to the Acts of the Apostles, 13-28, for more information on St. Paul.

5. Anthony was keenly aware of the many half-hearted Catholics who were not experiencing the joy and peace of God's love. Have the students list

the ways in which Anthony tried to help these Catholics. Then have them think about the people in their own parish who may feel lonely or are uninvolved. Tell the students to brainstorm on ways they can reach out to such people. Help them decide on one thing they can do to welcome or encourage these people. Tell the students that their efforts to help others will build real community in their parishes.

JULY 6: MARIA GORETTI

Maria was only twelve years old when she was stabbed to death. She chose death rather than consent to sin.

In 1890 Maria was born into a poor family living near Anzio, Italy. When she was ten years old, the family moved to a farm near Nettuno, not far from Rome. Her family was so poor that they shared a home and the work on the farm with the Serenelli family. Just two years later, Maria's father died, leaving his wife with several small children.

Maria's mother had to take over the farm work in order to support her family. The managing of the home came to be Maria's job — cooking, cleaning, mending. So she was at home alone a great deal.

Nineteen-year-old Alessandro Serenelli was attracted to Maria. He saw her beauty and innocence and loving personality. One day he came in from the fields and tried to persuade Maria to commit a sexual sin with him. She resisted with great firmness. Alessandro dragged her inside the house. Because he was so terribly angry, he stabbed Maria fourteen times, even when she told him that what he wanted to do was a serious sin.

Maria lived until the next day. Before she died, she forgave Alessandro. He was arrested and sentenced to prison for thirty years. At first he was very angry and resentful. After six years of prison life, Alessandro said Maria appeared to him in a dream and gave him a bouquet of lilies. This impressed him so deeply that he spent the rest of his prison term trying to make up for his crime. He became a prayerful man.

When he was released from prison, he visited Maria's mother to ask for forgiveness. She gladly forgave him. Then Alessandro entered a monastery to do penance for his attack on Maria. In 1950 Maria was canonized, and her mother attended the ceremonies.

SUGGESTIONS

1. Maria was only twelve years old when she chose to die for her faith rather than have sexual relations outside of marriage. Have the students pray silently for all young people who are struggling with temptations against chastity or who feel trapped in sinful circumstances. Because the Blessed Virgin wants to help all Christians be chaste, close by having the class pray the Hail Mary.

2. Write the following list on the board:

   HELPS FOR CHASTITY
   - Good reading
   - Friendship with Jesus through the sacraments
   - Good choice of friends
   - Correct information (especially from parents)
   - Daily prayer
   - Respect for ourselves
   - Awareness that sex is a sacred gift and not a "toy" to be played with
   - Decent jokes
   - Right conscience

   Then discuss with the students the answer to this question: "How can each of these things help a person to be chaste?"

3. Explain to the students how forgiveness was the key to Alesandro's conversion. Review with them the importance of Jesus' death to make up for our sins. Discuss our belief that God will forgive every sin and help each person to make a fresh start. Then have the students read silently and think about Colossians 3:5-11.

4. Review the sixth commandment. Direct the students to write down one situation in which teens might be led to disobey this commandment and ways this temptation could be avoided or overcome. Have them write an answer a priest might give to the following problem: "Father, I can't get rid of impure thoughts. They bother me day and night. I just don't know how to change. What can I do?" Let volunteers read their answers on how to avoid temptations or overcome them.

5. Have the class compile a list of current television and radio shows, movies, and books that are wholesome entertainment and promote Christian values.

6. Discuss with the students modern society's general acceptance of premarital sex. Then clarify for them the Church's stand on premarital sex, contraception, and abortion, and the reasoning behind that stand. "Human Sexuality in Our Time — What the Church Teaches" (St. Paul Editions) is a good reference.

JULY 11: BENEDICT

Benedict. His name means "blessed." His most famous monastery, Monte Cassino, has been destroyed and rebuilt three times. His monks follow the motto "Ora et labora" which means "Pray and work."

This man, Benedict, was born in Nursia, Italy, about 480. His parents were rather rich, so they sent him to Rome to be educated. After a few years, when he

was about seventeen years old, he decided to leave Rome and become a hermit. He was disgusted with the wild student life all around him. With the help of another older monk, Benedict found a lonely cave on Mount Subiaco about fifty miles south of Rome. He lived there for three years. Gradually men recognized his holiness and wanted to live the way he did.

Sometime around 529, Benedict led a group of monks still further south, and he built Monte Cassino. This monastery became the best known of all Benedictine abbeys. At Monte Cassino Benedict wrote his famous Rule. This rule of life based on Scripture was written to help all the monks live a common life. The first duty of his monks was liturgical prayer. The Benedictine monasteries that spread over much of Europe became centers of learning, agriculture, hospitality, and medicine. Benedict's monks helped make good the damage caused by the barbarian invaders. It was Pope Gregory the Great who encouraged the Benedictines to move north past the Alps.

The date of Benedict's death is uncertain, but 547 seems to be correct. In pictures and church windows, Benedict is usually shown with a copy of his Rule. In 1964 Pope Paul VI named him the patron of all Europe.

SUGGESTIONS

1. Benedict wrote a rule of life that all the Benedictine monks followed. Other saints also wrote common rules for various communities. For example, St. Athanasius wrote a rule for St. Anthony of the Desert and his followers. Everyone who belonged to the same community followed the same rule of life, which was based on the Gospel. Have the students discuss why they need rules at home, at school, and among friends. Have them list rules they follow each day at home, at school, etc.

2. Hospitality is part of the Benedictine rule of life. Have the students design a bulletin board with the theme of *Hospitality*. Or have them invite guests, such as the school maintenance personnel or people in the neighborhood, to come to class for a short program. Let the class plan the program and supply refreshments.

3. Monks and nuns take the vows of poverty, chastity, and obedience. List the three vows on the board. Have the students listen to each of the following statements and then name the vow that would counteract the *attitude* expressed:

1) Cecilia insists upon doing things her own way, no matter what people tell her. She insists even when she suspects that they may be right. (Obedience.)

2) If you ask William to help you, he always says, "If you pay me for it, then I will help you." (Poverty.)

3) Lisa is always trying new makeup and clothes because she wants to date senior boys. She tries to act older and sophisticated in order to get their attention. But the boys who date her don't seem to respect her as a person. (Chastity.)

4) Sharon's father cannot depend on Sharon to do what he asks of her without a loud argument and slamming of doors. (Obedience.)

5) I just got a new console for my room so that I have a place for my stereo, my phone, my 150 record albums, my tape deck, my microcomputer, and my television set. I bet none of you have as much as I do. (Poverty.)

4. Benedict recognized the value of having a responsible leader in charge. He believed that God's will came through the person in authority, who made decisions according to the Gospels and the rule of life. Benedict encouraged his monks to obey without delay. Challenge the students to obey promptly when their parents or teachers ask them to do things that are right.

5. Plan a visit to a Benedictine monastery or show slides of a monastery in order to help the students understand the customs of the Benedictine order. Interested students may research and report to the class on famous monasteries like Monte Cassino, Cluny, Beuron, Stanhope, and Solemnes. Or they might find copies of illuminated manuscripts created by medieval monks.

6. Benedict had the monks memorize the psalms. He and his monks would meet seven times a day to pray certain psalms. Write one line from a psalm on the board each day and encourage the students to pray that psalm prayer during the day. After some time, they will have many short prayers that they can pray from memory. The following are some lines you might use:

Psalm 119:164
"Seven times daily I praise you."

Psalm 43:3
"Send out your light and your truth, let these be my guide."

Psalm 42:11
"Put your hope in God: I shall praise him yet, my savior, my God."

Psalm 42:1
"As a doe longs for running streams, so longs my soul for you, my God."

Psalm 91:14
"I rescue all who cling to me, I protect whoever knows my name."

Psalm 94:22
"My God is a rock where I take shelter."

JULY 13: HENRY

Civil leaders face many pressures because of their positions. They must consider the needs of a variety of different groups, find solutions to complicated problems, and often be solely responsible for decisions that affect the lives of many people. In the tenth century, civil leaders were not elected, and so they did not have to worry about pleasing their subjects in order to stay in office. Because of this custom, emperors and kings often took advantage of the luxury and honor of their office without responsibly working for the good of their people. They would choose to ignore or to squelch conflict rather than to deal justly with it. In the midst of these circumstances, Henry, the son of the Duke of Bavaria, gave the example of a Christlike leader.

Henry was born in 973. By the time he was 34 years old, he had become emperor of Germany. As a ruler, Henry concentrated on the good of his people. He built monasteries, helped the poor, fought against unjust seizure of power, and relieved all kinds of oppression. In 1014 he was crowned emperor of the Holy Roman Empire. That title made him ruler of Germany, Austria, Switzerland, Belgium, Holland, and northern Italy, as we know these countries today.

Henry was well known for his missionary spirit and for his protection of the pope in times of trouble. He died in 1024.

SUGGESTIONS

1. Ask the students to find out who the current leaders in their city, county, state, and country are. Then have them compose petitions to God the Father for these leaders, asking that they may have qualities like those of Jesus. During a class prayer time, ask each student to read his or her petition. For each petition, have the class respond, "Father, guide our leaders."

2. Henry was a Christian emperor who acted justly. Lead the students in a discussion on the importance of having Christian leaders in government. Discuss the danger of having leaders who do not value the God-given dignity and rights of each human person.

3. List on the board some of the basic rights that God has given to all people. You might wish to use this partial list from *Peace on Earth,* an encyclical letter written by Pope John XXIII in 1963. This list includes the right

   • to life and a worthy standard of living

   • to a good reputation

   • to be informed truthfully about public events

   • to a basic education

   • to honor God according to a person's conscience and to worship freely

   • to take part in public affairs and to contribute to the good of the country.

Explain to the students that government leaders have a responsibility to protect these basic human rights for every person. Then have the students list the corresponding duty that accompanies each right. For example, the right to a good reputation implies that each person must safeguard the reputation of all other people.

4. As a Christian leader, Henry realized that people looked to him for a good model, or example, to follow. Have the students write in their journals the names of two or three people who look to them for good example. Then have them write a short paragraph explaining how they can give a good example to these people.

5. Henry used his power to protect the pope. Have the students brainstorm ways that they can show support for the present pope.

Also see Supplement for July 14.

JULY 14: CAMILLUS OF LELLIS

Can a lawyer become a canonized saint? Why not? Thomas More did. Can a young, uneducated girl be canonized? Of course. Look at Maria Goretti. Well, then, how about someone who had been a soldier for many years? Yes, even a one-time soldier. Camillus, who was born in southern Italy in 1550, was the son of a professional soldier. He trained to be a military man like his father. As a young man, he joined the Venetian army to fight the Turks. By this time he had become a rough and reckless gambler. A serious wound in his leg forced him to go to St. James Hospital in Rome.

Here he saw the sad condition of the patients. He wanted to help them, but he was dismissed from the hospital because he began to gamble again. Camillus tried to join a monastery but he could not live the lifestyle. Finally he returned to St. James Hospital in Rome and settled down. Other young men in the hospital were inspired by his change of behavior. They joined him and together they formed a religious order called the Servants of the Sick.

In the meantime, Camillus had become a priest. He devoted the rest of his life to his priestly duties and to caring for the sick. His men became pioneers in setting up proper diets, in providing fresh air, and in separating patients with contagious diseases. During a war in Hungary, his followers formed the first recorded military field ambulance corps. Right up until his death in 1614, Camillus worked hard for sick people — especially the poor. Today he is the patron of Catholic nurses. Yes, anyone can become a saint if he or she really wants to.

SUGGESTIONS

1. For many years Camillus lived without a purpose in life. He pursued only pleasure. Have the stu-

dents find two articles in the newspaper: one an example of a person seeking *passing* happiness, the other an example of a person seeking *lasting* happiness. In a paragraph, have the students contrast the two situations.

2. Before he began to follow Christ, Camillus used gambling as a crutch to help him get through each day and to help him escape from the important things in life. Have the students list the crutches that some teens rely on to help them escape from life's problems. The following might be included on the list: withdrawal, over-conformity, sexual experimenting, frequent fighting, refusal to eat, drugs, and alcohol. Discuss with the students what these teens are missing in life and how they can be helped.

3. Camillus de Lellis is an example of a very poor person who reached out to help others who were poor. Direct the students to find and read the story of Matt Talbot, a reformed alcoholic. Have them compare the lives of the two men. Point out that God never gives up on loving and helping a person, no matter how hopeless his or her condition appears.

4. Camillus was very devoted to the sick and the dying. Review with the students the Sacrament of the Anointing of the Sick. Then direct them to number a paper from 1-8 and take a short quiz on this sacrament, answering true or false.

   QUIZ

   The Sacrament of the Anointing of the Sick . . .

   1) may be celebrated at home, in a hospital, or in a church. (T)
   2) brings peace and courage to a person who may be faced with continued suffering. (T)
   3) may be given to a sick person before surgery for a serious illness. (T)
   4) is another name for the Sacrament of Penance. (F)
   5) assists in restoring the physical health of a person, if this is God's will. (T)
   6) is given *only* to the dying. (F)
   7) uses olive oil for the anointing and as a sign of the rite. (T)
   8) is sometimes celebrated within a parish Mass. (T)

5. Camillus was well known for repeating these words adapted from Matthew's gospel: "I was sick and you visited me." He really sensed the presence of Christ in those who were sick and dying. Prepare the students for a visit to a home for the elderly. Help them imagine themselves in the position of the individuals in that home. Guide them to think of what they can say and do to make their visit uplifting. Help them to be understanding and

patient with the elderly by explaining some of the handicaps the people might have. After the visit, hold a follow-up discussion. Allow the students to share their feelings and insights. Ask them how much they have gained from the experience.

6. Have the students write a letter to someone they know who is in the military or who is hospitalized. Encourage them to share with the person some interesting, upbeat things that are happening in their own lives.

JULY 15: BONAVENTURE

Shortly after Bonaventure's death, it was written, "At the funeral there was much sorrow and tears; for the Lord had given him this grace, that all who saw him were filled with an immense love for him." What is the life story of this much-loved man?

Bonaventure was born about 1221 in Italy, not far from Naples. He was baptized John. The story is told that when he was about four years old, he was deathly sick. His mother begged Francis of Assisi to come and cure her child. Francis simply touched the little boy, and he was cured instantly. As an adult, Bonaventure entered the Franciscan order. He went to Paris, where he met the great Thomas Aquinas. They both studied at the famous University of Paris. After some years, Bonaventure became the Father General, the person in charge of the Franciscan order. He was appointed a cardinal shortly before his death in 1274.

Bonaventure wrote many books about theology. He wanted to teach everyone how to live closely with God.

SUGGESTIONS

1. Bonaventure kept a crucifix in his room and looked at it from time to time to remind himself to imitate Jesus, Who died for us, as completely as possible. Distribute pictures of Jesus crucified or small crucifixes to the students to keep on their desks or in their prayer corners at home. Tell them the religious object is a reminder that they are to imitate Jesus as completely as possible and to attract others to Him.

2. As head of the Franciscan order, Bonaventure guided the friars to a better understanding of the poverty in which they were called to live. Have the students give practical examples of teens who are living these aspects of the virtue of poverty:
   • spending money wisely
   • not bragging about what they own
   • depending on God for help
   • living inexpensively

3. Bonaventure traveled a great deal, visiting the various groups in his order so that he could better understand the needs and problems of the Franciscans in his care. Throughout his years in

authority, he relied on the gifts of the Holy Spirit that he received in Baptism and that were strengthened within him at Confirmation. Have the students memorize seven of these gifts: wisdom, understanding, counsel, fortitude or courage, knowledge, piety or reverence, fear of the Lord or awe.

4. Bonaventure spent much of his life contemplating various doctrines about God. He always wanted to learn more about the mysteries of his faith. Divide the class into groups and assign each group a topic related to the Catholic faith. These topics might include God the Father, Jesus, the Holy Spirit, Mary, the Church, parish life, the eucharistic liturgy, and one of the sacraments. Have the students in each group pool their knowledge and list all they know about their topic. Then have each group read the list to the whole class.

5. Bonaventure greatly loved the saints and wrote an excellent biography of St. Francis of Assisi, the founder of the Franciscans. Using a marker, draw a picture of a shelf of books at the top of a large sheet of poster paper. There should be one book for every person in the class, and there should be enough room left at the bottom of the paper for the students' summaries of the books.

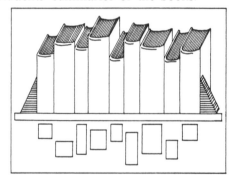

Distribute small sheets of lightly colored paper and have the students write a short synopsis of the life of a saint whose biography they have read. They should put the title and author of the book at the top of the paper. Then direct each student to write the *title* and *author* of the book he or she has read on the spine of a book in the picture. Add a title and author from your own reading. Arrange the synopses underneath in an attractive way, and ask the class to think of a clever caption for the chart. Post the completed project in the hall.

JULY 16: OUR LADY OF MOUNT CARMEL

On one side of the mountain top, the many priests of the god Baal stood next to the stone altar dedicated to their false god. They had been praying aloud all day, but no god had answered them. On the other side, the prophet Elijah stood alone next to a stone altar dedicated to the Lord God, Yahweh. That day Yahweh sent fire from heaven onto the altar, proving

that He, Yahweh, was the one true God. The Old Testament records this showdown on Mount Carmel in northern Palestine (1 Kings 18:16-39).

During the many centuries between that event and the year 1156, people who wanted a quiet place to pray and to live closely with God, began to come together on Mount Carmel. A large monastery was built there to honor the Mother of God. The members of the monastery were called Carmelites.

In 1251, according to the tradition of the Carmelites, the Blessed Virgin Mary appeared to St. Simon, the sixth General, or person in charge of the Carmelite Order, and gave him a scapular. The scapular was a long piece of cloth falling from the wearer's shoulders, in front and in back, down to the ankles. All the members of that Carmelite community wore a similar scapular. Today some religious men and women still wear the full scapular. Most of us are familiar with a scapular of two small pieces of cloth connected by narrow cord or braid. It is worn over the shoulders. Wearing a scapular medal or the shortened scapular has become a popular way of honoring the Blessed Mother. July 16 is a major feast for all Carmelite priests and sisters.

SUGGESTIONS

1. Show the students the picture of Our Lady of Mount Carmel. Have them recall the times they have previously seen a picture, statue, or stained glass window of Mary under this title.

2. People often privately honor Mary by giving her special titles. Some titles, such as Our Lady of Fatima, refer to a place. Others, such as Our Lady of the Snows, refer to a symbol. Have the students find as many titles of Mary as possible. Post a long piece of paper on which students can add new titles as they discover them. Finally, let the students make up their own title for Mary, based on their own experiences. Have them compose an original prayer to her.

3. Mountains are frequently referred to in both the Old and New Testaments as places to meet God, places to pray, places to seek refuge. Put this biblical matching exercise on the board, or make copies of it. Have the students work on it in pairs.

MOUNTAIN MATCHING

Match the Scripture reference with the name of a mountain or with an event that occurred on a mountain. Write the answers on the lines.

1) Matthew 21:1 _____
2) Matthew 4:8 _____
3) Mark 3:13 _____
4) Matthew 17:1 _____
5) Matthew 5:1 _____
6) Mark 6:46 _____
7) Luke 4:29 _____
8) Hebrews 12:22 _____

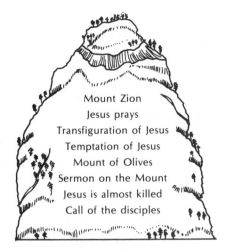

Mount Zion
Jesus prays
Transfiguration of Jesus
Temptation of Jesus
Mount of Olives
Sermon on the Mount
Jesus is almost killed
Call of the disciples

MOUNTAIN MATCHING exercise answers are:

1) Mount of Olives
2) Temptation of Jesus
3) Call of the disciples
4) Transfiguration of Jesus
5) Sermon on the Mount
6) Jesus prays
7) Jesus is almost killed
8) Mount Zion

4. Discover how much the students already know about the scapular. Then review with them other sacramentals (things or actions) that are reminders of Christ, Mary, and the saints. Some of these sacramentals would be the cross, medals, statues, the Sign of the Cross, the Stations of the Cross, and the Rosary. Guide them to see that these sacramentals are to help us remember that God is present and that He loves us.

5. Tell the story of Elijah, or have the students volunteer to read parts of it in 1 Kings 18:16-39. Then discuss with the class the courage, the faith, and the perseverance of Elijah. Finally, have the students select the single most important lesson that can be learned from this event.

JULY 21: LAWRENCE OF BRINDISI

Do you know anyone who can speak eight different languages? No? Then meet Lawrence of Brindisi.

He was born in Italy in 1559. After he was ordained a priest, he devoted his life to preaching the truths of our faith. He was most attentive to correcting the errors that so many Reformation preachers were spreading. Because he was able to speak in many languages, he became a popular and powerful preacher in several different countries.

Lawrence became known for his goodness, his simplicity, and his prudence as a teacher. He was especially devoted to the Blessed Virgin. Her feasts of the Immaculate Conception and the Assumption were two of his favorites. Besides being the superior

general of 9,000 Capuchin friars in Italy, France, Belgium, Spain, and Switzerland, Lawrence had a splendid reputation as a missionary and as a diplomat. In 1959, Pope John XXIII declared that Lawrence should be considered a Doctor of the Church.

SUGGESTIONS

1. Have the students find other saints whose devotion to Mary brought them closer to Jesus. Make a chart with the name of each saint and a small paragraph on the saint's devotion to Mary. You might wish to give a prayer card with a picture of Our Lady to any students who contribute to the chart.

2. One of Lawrence's gifts was the ability to communicate. He used his talent in languages to show God's love and truth to others. Have the students consider a modern means of communication: the telephone. Lead them in a discussion of ways that they can use the phone to help or hinder the spread of truth and love.

3. As a teacher, Lawrence showed qualities of simplicity, goodness, and prudence. Have the students list the positive qualities of one of their favorite teachers of the past. Then have them write a letter to this teacher, explaining how much they appreciated these positive qualities, and send the letter to him or her.

4. Have the students list the various roles of service that Lawrence fulfilled in spreading the Good News: priest, preacher, teacher, superior general, missionary, and diplomat. Then tell them to list as many roles of service in the Church today as they can. Finally, have them choose three roles that they may be fulfilling in ten years and have them write a sentence on each role, explaining their choice.

JULY 22: MARY MAGDALENE

Mary, the sister of Martha and Lazarus; Mary, the sinner who washed Jesus' feet with her tears; Mary, one of the women who cared for Jesus and his apostles on their journeys; Mary, present on Calvary; Mary, visiting the tomb very early on Easter morning . . . . Will the real Mary Magdalene please stand up?

There is some uncertainty about whether Mary Magdalene can be identified with all these Marys. Matthew, Mark, and John record that Mary of Magdala was present at the crucifixion of Jesus and that she was among the women who visited the tomb on Easter morning. Luke mentions only the Easter incident.

What we know for sure is that Mary Magdalene was near Jesus in his darkest hour, and again in His most glorious hour. For centuries Mary has been considered a model of complete generosity and of sincere sorrow for sin.

SUGGESTIONS

1. Mary of Magdala loved Jesus so much that she stood by Him while He hung on the cross. Ask the students to consider their own friendship with the Lord. Have them write in their journals ways that He shows His love for them and ways that they show their love for Him.

2. Mary was the first to proclaim the Good News of the Resurrection. Have the students listen to the account from John 20:11-18. Then have them write in their journals an imaginary letter in which Mary Magdalene recounts the events to her friend.

3. Mary Magdalene has been considered by many artists and devout Christians as a person who admitted her sins and was very sorry for them. Have the students study and memorize the prayer from the Penitential Rite of the Mass. Have them use the one that begins, "I confess to almighty God . . . ."

4. One of the Jewish prayer forms that Mary might have used is called the *berakah*, or thanksgiving prayer. This prayer contains both praise and petition. Have the students write original berakahs using the following pattern:

   First sentence: "Blessed be the Lord . . . ." (Add what God has done for you.)

   Second sentence: "May He . . . ." (Write your petition.)

   When the students are finished, light a prayer candle (check fire regulations) and have a short prayer service in which the students pray their berakahs. They might also print their prayers neatly on colored construction paper for display.

5. Have the students suggest how Mary Magdalene might have felt after the burial of Jesus. Then direct them to picture the scene of the garden and the tomb early on Easter Sunday morning, when it was still dark. Have them put themselves in Mary Magdalene's place as you read aloud John 20:1-18. Finally close with the prayer for the feast of Mary Magdalene from the Liturgy of the Hours.

   Father,
   your Son first entrusted to Mary Magdalene
   the joyful news of his resurrection.
   By her prayers and example
   may we proclaim Christ as our living Lord
   and one day see him in glory,
   for he lives and reigns with you and the
      Holy Spirit,
   one God, for ever and ever. Amen.

JULY 23: BRIDGET OF SWEDEN

A Christian mystic is a person who has received a special gift of prayer from God. Because this type of prayer is a free gift given to the persons whom God chooses, no one can control it or earn it. This mystical prayer, an experience of a special union with God in love, was given to Bridget of Sweden. She often had visions of Christ's passion. However, like other Christian mystics, Bridget was also very practical and down-to-earth in living out the gospel of Jesus.

Bridget was born in 1303 into the family of a wealthy landowner in Sweden. When she grew up, she became a very good wife and mother. One of her eight children, Catherine of Sweden, became a canonized saint. Once Bridget was invited to become the chief lady-in-waiting to the queen. She lived at the court for two years. While she was there, she tried to encourage the queen and king to live holy lives.

After her husband's death, she founded an order of nuns known as the Bridgetines, who made great contributions to the culture of Scandinavia. She showed a loving concern for the poor and the sick, and many people came to her for help.

Bridget made many pilgrimages around Italy and even to the Holy Land. She spent her last years in Rome. Like Catherine of Siena, she urged the pope to leave Avignon in France and return to Rome, the center of Christianity. Bridget died in Rome in 1373, ending a busy and holy life.

SUGGESTIONS

1. Bridget had many vocations. She was a wife, mother, founder, and advisor to the pope. Have interested students compare her with other Catholic women who have had a variety of vocations: Jane Frances de Chantal, Cornelia Connelly, and Elizabeth Ann Seton, for example.

2. Bridget did a great deal of penance in her life. Sometimes very small acts can be very difficult. Have the students consider the penance and charity of small things, such as not interrupting others in conversation and being punctual for class, meals, carpools, and curfews. Encourage the students to choose for a day a penance that would show their love and care for others.

3. Have interested students research and report to the class on the life of Bridget's daughter, Catherine of Sweden, and on the Bridgetines, also known as the Order of the Most Holy Savior.

4. Bridget often thought about the Passion of Christ. Have the students spend time looking at a crucifix and thinking about the sufferings that Jesus accepted for the sins of all of us. Then play a record or have a prayerful reading of a Scripture passage dealing with Christ's passion.

5. Tell the students that some other Christian mystics are Teresa of Avila, John of the Cross, Catherine of Genoa, Catherine of Siena, and Julianna of Norwich. Explain to them that these mystics did their normal life's work, but were always drawn to union with God. Eventually they became united with God in every aspect of their lives. Direct interested students to do more research on Christian mystics.

JULY 25: JAMES

We read in Matthew's Gospel (Mt 20:20-28) that the mother of James and John asked Jesus to give her sons a high position in His kingdom. Here is an adapted version of that conversation:

Mother: Good morning, Master. I would like to talk to you about my two sons. Here they are: fine, strong, young men.

Jesus: Yes, they are fine people. I am glad they are among my close followers.

Mother: They are very happy to be Your friends. Because I love them so much, I want to ask You for a favor. When You finally set up Your kingdom and have Your thrones all ready, will you let James sit on one side of You and John on the other? They will be a great help to You.

Jesus: (Looking at James and John) If you sit on my right and my left side in the kingdom, you will have to drink the same bitter cup of suffering I am going to drink. Can you do that?

James and John: Oh, yes, Master, of course. We will be strong enough to stand with You whatever happens.

Jesus: I want you to share in my sufferings, but only my Father will decide who will sit at my right and my left side. For now, just stay with me and be my friends.

Jesus called James to follow Him very early in His public life. Along with Peter and John, James was one of the favored three to witness the transfiguration of Jesus, the raising of Jairus' daughter, and the agony in the garden on Holy Thursday night.

We do not know very much about James' life. Tradition says he may have traveled to Spain. During the Middle Ages, there was a famous shrine to St. James at Compostella in Spain. Luke records in the Acts of the Apostles: "It was about this time that King Herod started persecuting certain members of the Church. He beheaded James the brother of John" (Acts 12:1-2).

James is a very popular saint in England. Over 400 churches are dedicated to him in that country.

SUGGESTIONS

1. James and John were known as *Boanerges*, which means "sons of thunder." They seem to have had strong tempers. Explain to the students the difference between constructive anger and destructive anger. Have them read Mark 3:1-6 for an example of Jesus' anger. Explain that His anger was *constructive* because He helped the man and was trying to teach the Pharisees the truth. Then direct the students look up these examples of *destructive* anger: Acts 19:23-41, Luke 9:51-56, Luke 15:25-32. Have the following sentences written on the board and ask the students to match one of the Scripture passages with each one:

1) People who feel sorry for themselves may get angry at imagined injustice. _____
2) People may act violently and less than human when they get angry. _____
3) People who see an injustice may want to correct it with revenge and punishment. _____

The answers are as follows:
1) Luke 15:25-32
2) Acts 19:23-41
3) Luke 9:51-56

2. At three special times in Jesus's life, He invited only Peter, James, and John to stay with Him, according to Scripture. Have the students look up each Scripture text: Matthew 17:1-8; Mark 14:32; Luke 8:40-56. Then ask them to imagine that they are James and have them write a diary entry for each event as he might have written it.

3. Lead the students in a prayer for modern missionaries.

PRAYER FOR MISSIONARIES
For love of You, Lord,
they walk among new family
on a distant path.
Bless their minds and thoughts,
bless the words they say,
so that in hearing their voices
Your Word will be known.
Bless the work they do
and the love they give,
so that Your own care will be seen
as they heal the sorrows and
mend the pain of Your poor ones.
Bless them with the gift of
seeing the Gospel come to new life
as their people learn the meaning
of the peace of Christ.
For love of You, Lord,
they walk among new family
on a distant path.
Help me to walk with them
each day
in prayer.
(Society for the Propagation of the Faith)

4. Put this acrostic on the board and give the students the following clues. Have them solve the puzzle as a class.

```
_ _ _ _ _ _ A _
        _ P _ _ _
      _ O _ _
    _ _ _ _ S
_ _ _ _   _ _ T _ _ _ _ _ _
    _ _ L _ _ _
      _ E _ _ _ _ _
```

- James' work before he became an apostle. (Fisherman.)
- Country that has a special shrine for James. (Spain.)
- James' brother. (John.)
- First apostle to die for Christ. (James.)
- Nickname for James and his brother. (Sons of Thunder.)
- Country with 400 churches dedicated to James. (England.)
- James' father. (Zebedee.)

5. For the liturgical celebration of the feast of St. James, the celebrant wears a red vestment. Review with the students various colors for the liturgical feasts and the symbolism for those colors. Put the following chart on the board and have them complete it. Answers are given in parentheses.

FEAST: Feast of apostles, martyrs, Pentecost, Good Friday

VESTMENT COLOR: _____ (Red)

MEANING: Fire, love, blood, victim for sin, sacrifice

FEAST: _____ (Advent, Lent)

VESTMENT COLOR: _____ (Violet)

MEANING: Repentance, expectation

FEAST: Feasts of Our Lord, Our Lady, virgins, confessors

VESTMENT COLOR: White

MEANING: _____ (Joy)

FEAST: Sundays in Ordinary Time

VESTMENT COLOR: _____ (Green)

MEANING: Hope

Note: On some solemn occasions, silver or gold vestments may be substituted for white.

JULY 26: JOACHIM AND ANN

Did you know that your grandparents have a pair of patron saints? Well, they do — St. Joachim and St. Ann. They were Mary's parents, and so they were the grandparents of Jesus.

We really do not know very much about these saints. Many details we would like to know are hidden deep in the mystery of time. Tradition says that they took their daughter to the Temple in Jerusalem when she was very young. They understood that Mary was a special child, so they dedicated her to God. The name "Ann" means "grace" and has many forms: Annette, Anita, Dina, Hannah, Nancy, Anna. The name "Joachim" means "the Lord will judge" and it, too, has different forms: Joaquin in Spanish and Joachimo in Italian.

SUGGESTIONS

1. Joachim and Ann were Mary's parents. Have the students make a list of the qualities of a good mother and another of a good father. Then have them compare their two lists. Next have them list the qualities of a good daughter or son. Finally, have them find good advice for parents and children in the Book of Proverbs. Possible references are Proverbs 1:8, 4:1, 10:1, 13:1, and 18:22.

2. Encourage the students to contact their grandparents through a letter, phone call, an invitation to a family meal, or a visit. Allow students to share with the class any positive results of their experiences.

3. Suggest that the students take baked goods, a little gift, or an offer of an hour's free help to a neighborhood couple who are expecting a baby.

4. To honor parents, have the students make collages of the gifts, talents, and positive Christian qualities of their parents. Direct them to give the finished pieces to their parents.

5. Put these scrambled names of famous father-mother pairs in the Bible on the board. Challenge the students to unscramble them and to list the names of the children in each family

VEE / MAAD

BARRMAH / HRSAA

BRAKEEH / ACSAI

CREAZAHIH / BLIAHETZE

Answers:

Adam and Eve, whose children were Cain, Abel, Seth.

Abraham and Sarah, whose child was Isaac.

Issac and Rebekah, whose children were Esau and Jacob.

Zechariah and Elizabeth, whose child was John the Baptist.

JULY 29: MARTHA

One of the most precious things in life is to have a home where you can go at any time and find people who accept, love, and understand you. Jesus found such a home in Bethany, at the house of a woman named Martha. She welcomed Him and served Him, and they developed a special bond of friendship.

Martha lived with her sister Mary. Like many other pairs of sisters, these two women were very different in personality. Martha was energetic and outspoken, while Mary was quiet and reflective. Jesus loved both of them and appreciated the gifts that each one had.

The Gospel of Luke records that once, when Jesus was visiting, Martha came to Him with a problem and with her own solution. She was frustrated by all the work she was doing. Her solution was to get her sister Mary to help. After all, Mary was just sitting at the feet of Jesus listening to His words. Martha wanted Jesus to tell Mary to help. But Jesus saw the situation differently. He showed Martha that because she was worrying so much, she did not have time to enjoy being with Him and listening to His words.

Another time, recorded in John's Gospel, both sisters sent a message to Jesus that their brother, Lazarus, was ill. They knew Jesus would come and cure him; they trusted in His loving care for them. When Jesus did come, Lazarus had already been dead for four days. As soon as she heard that Jesus was nearby, Martha, a woman of action, went out to meet Him, while Mary stayed in the house. In her grief over the loss of her brother, Martha told Jesus honestly what she had expected from Him. Jesus asked her to believe that He was the resurrection and that He had power to give eternal life to all who believe in Him. Without really understanding this mystery, Martha trusted Jesus totally and said, "I believe that you are the Christ, the Son of God, the one who was to come into this world" (John 11:27). That day Jesus raised her brother Lazarus from the dead to show that He has power over life and death and the power to give eternal life. The home Jesus found in Bethany was not only in the house but in the faithful heart of a woman named Martha.

SUGGESTIONS

1. Jesus was a guest at Martha and Mary's house in Bethany. Ask the students what they imagine would happen if Jesus came to visit in their homes. Then direct them to write an original, imagined story about a time when Jesus visited their homes.

2. Martha is the patroness of cooks. In honor of Martha, direct the students to carry out one of the following activities:
   - make cards, awards, or decorations for the cafeteria personnel
   - cook or bake something special for their own families
   - show special appreciation to the person who prepares the evening meals in their homes
   - prepare fruit sherbet during class, using the following recipe: Dissolve one cup sugar into two cups whipping cream. Let students take turns stirring. Add one half cup fruit, lemon, grape, or orange juice for flavor. Put in 8″ pan and freeze for three hours.

3. Martha lived in Bethany, which was a large town about two miles east of Jerusalem. Have the students look up the following Scripture texts and describe what happened at Bethany in each one.

   Matthew 26:6-7
   (Woman anoints Jesus at the home of Simon the leper.)

   Matthew 21:17
   (Jesus spent the night.)

   Mark 11:11
   (Jesus stayed there during the night.)

   John 12:1
   (Jesus raised Lazarus from the dead. The home of Lazarus.)

   Luke 24:50
   (Jesus ascends.)

4. In the Bible, Martha is a woman who helped God's plan of salvation by serving Jesus. Review with the students other women of the Bible who also had a role to play in salvation history. Some examples are Hannah, who showed perseverance in prayer (1 Samuel 1:1-20); Ruth, who showed loyalty and responsibility to duty (the Book of Ruth); Judith, who showed courage and faith (the Book of Judith).

5. Martha is well known for her service to others. As an act of loving service, have the students design tray decorations to send to a hospital or home for the elderly. A simple decoration can be made with scissors, glue, and scraps of paper. Direct the students to follow these directions:
   - Fold a piece of stiff white paper, 10″ x 4″, in half lengthwise so that the paper stands independently.
   - Designate one side to be the front.
   - Decide on a symbol of the season, such as a leaf, 3D flower, smiling sun, or little garden, and make the pieces of the symbol from scraps of construction paper.
   - Glue the symbol on one corner of the front of the paper.
   - Neatly print a line from a psalm or a cheery message across the front of the paper.

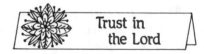
Trust in the Lord

JULY 30: PETER CHRYSOLOGUS

How does a bishop guide Christians to the truth when they are living a pagan life-style and are confused by false teachers? Peter Chrysologus found a way — the short homily.

Around 431, Peter, a deacon, became bishop of Ravenna, Italy. At this time, many Christians in his diocese were following false teachings and living according to unchristian values. Peter became well known as an outstanding preacher, whose brief homilies were filled with suggestions for living a moral life. He often based his homilies on the sections of the Bible that were used in the daily prayer of the Church, the "Liturgy of the Hours." He also preached to catechumens preparing for Baptism, explaining the Apostles' Creed and the Our Father.

Peter also found an opportunity to advise Eutyches, one of these false teachers. At the bishops' meeting in Constantinople in 448, Eutyches firmly denied that Jesus was both God and Man. Finally, unable to convince him of the truth, the bishops refused Eutyches the right to teach his false ideas. Eutyches then went to Peter for help. But Peter said, "In the interest of peace and the faith we cannot judge in matters of faith without the consent of the Roman bishop (the pope)." In this way Peter encouraged Eutyches to accept the authority of the Church.

Peter Chrysologus believed that knowledge is a great support for the Christian faith and a great way to improve the human mind. He encouraged education as a God-given opportunity and obligation. He urged Christians to learn as much as their capabilities and talents allowed. Around 450 Peter died in the same place where he had been born: Imola, Italy. Thirteen centuries later, Pope Benedict XIII declared him a Doctor of the Church because of his outstanding homilies.

SUGGESTIONS

1. Peter was greatly concerned with the immorality of society. Many people were content to live by the capital sins. Explain to the students that the capital, or chief, sins are the source of many other sins. Pride is the one sin that is found in every other sin. Have the students find definitions for the seven capital sins: pride, covetousness or greed, lust, anger, gluttony, envy, sloth or laziness.

2. In his short homilies, Peter tried to help Christians turn from sin to live as Christ lived. Have the students brainstorm ways of overcoming temptations to sin. You might wish to include the following ideas:

   • List all the benefits from overcoming the temptation and all the consequences of failing to overcome the temptation.

   • Pray for the strength to overcome temptation.

   • Practice acts of penance to strengthen yourself against temptation.

   • Get support from someone who wants you to overcome temptation.

   • Memorize a line from Scripture and repeat it when faced with temptation. Examples of passages are Romans 8:37, 12:9; 1 Corinthians 10:31; Galatians 5:25; Colossians 2:6, 3:16; 1 Peter 5:9.

3. The Church today has preserved 138 of Peter's homilies. Have the students look through magazines and cut out a picture which could be used as a starter for a Sunday homily on the readings. Then have them glue the picture on a piece of paper, choose a fitting Scripture text, and write a short homily under the picture.

4. Peter's homilies were based on Scripture. Have the students pair up and find examples of various types of biblical literature. Direct them to copy the following list and to find examples from the New Testament for each type of literature.

LIST

a) parable
b) prayer
c) letter
d) history
e) apocalyptic writing

POSSIBLE ANSWERS

a) Good Shepherd, vine and branches, Good Samaritan
b) Our Father, Zechariah's canticle in Luke 1:68-79, Mary's Magnificat in Luke 1:46-55
c) Any epistle
d) Acts of the Apostles
e) Revelation

5. Peter held all forms of learning in high esteem. Arrange for the students to tutor younger children in the school for several half-hour sessions. Discuss with them how this can help both the younger children and themselves.

JULY 31: IGNATIUS OF LOYOLA

Have you ever daydreamed about being a great hero? Perhaps you see yourself as a paramedic rescuing people from an icy lake. Or as the President making courageous decisions in the face of a panic-stricken nation. Perhaps you are a four-star general heroically maneuvering whole regiments to safety while under attack. These dangerous adventures appear very exciting and challenging in dreams. As a young man, Ignatius of Loyola learned that dangerous adventures could become painful experiences.

Born in 1491, Ignatius was the youngest son in a noble family of eleven children. While still a young man, he spent several years as a soldier, fighting in defense of Spain, his native country. At the age of thirty, he was seriously wounded. One leg was badly shattered and the other one was broken. The field surgeons set both legs and sent Ignatius home to the Loyola castle. But one leg was so badly set that it had to be broken again and reset. Even this operation was unsuccessful, so a third surgery was performed. Since this was in the days before anesthesia, Ignatius suffered unbelievable pain.

During his long recuperation, he began to read — not the novels he wanted, but what was available: a life of Jesus and a book about the saints. This action was the beginning of his conversion. Later, he spent several days in prayer at the Benedictine monastery in Montserrat. Then he journeyed on to Manresa, where he led a rugged, disciplined life for about a year. During this time he began to write his famous "Spiritual Exercises," a guide for those who want to live a truly Christian life.

Ignatius, now in his middle thirties, decided to fill in his neglected education. He returned to school with students less than half his age. After ten hard years, he was ready for the University of Paris. Here he met six young men who joined him in forming a new religious community. One of these men, Francis Xavier, later became the great Apostle of India. The members of the small community offered their service to the pope, for whatever he wanted them to do. By this time, the group of seven were ordained priests who had taken the three vows of poverty, chastity, and obedience. Ignatius called his community the Company of Jesus. Today they are better known as the Society of Jesus or the Jesuits.

Ignatius introduced several new regulations into his Society. The priests did not wear a special habit, as the Benedictines, Franciscans, and Dominicans did. Jesuits had shorter hours of community prayer. They were trained to work with people wherever people needed them. Their main work was teaching in schools, colleges, and universities. And they became great missionaries. They were a strong force in fighting false teachings throughout Europe.

When Ignatius died in 1556, more than 1,000 Jesuits were scattered across North and South America, Europe, China, and Japan. Georgetown University, the oldest Catholic institution of higher learning in the United States, was founded by the Jesuits in 1789. Other Jesuits besides Ignatius have become canonized saints; among them are Edmund Campion, Francis Xavier, Isaac Jogues, Robert Southwell, Peter Claver, and Robert Bellarmine.

SUGGESTIONS

1. Ignatius founded his Society to give the greatest possible service to the Church and to the pope. Have the students copy this prayer for the pope and pray it often:

   Father in heaven, protect our pope, _____ (name). Fill him with Your compassion so that he can live the gospel in loving service to all people. Lead him in the footsteps of Peter, who, filled with the Holy Spirit, first guided the Church. Amen.

2. Ignatius had a great zeal for promoting God's glory, for spreading God's kingdom, and for making this a better world. Divide the class into groups and plan a panel discussion on the topic "How have saints influenced the world?"

3. Many men from the Society of Jesus have been canonized. The Franciscan and Dominican orders also have canonized saints. Have each student choose a saint from one of these orders and draw a picture of that person. Direct the students to write a three-sentence summary of the life of the saint under the picture. Mount these on colored construction paper and post them. You might wish to title the display JESUIT HALL OF SAINTS, DOMINICAN HALL OF SAINTS, FRANCISCAN HALL OF SAINTS.

4. Ignatius valued being faithful to a duty, to what was right, to principles and beliefs. He stressed fidelity to God, to others, to self. Help the students realize that they have many opportunities to show fidelity. Put the following list on the board and allow them to add their own examples:

   I show fidelity when I

   • keep promises.
   • keep secrets.
   • avoid criticism of others behind their backs.
   • speak out about injustice.
   • do a job with care.
   • keep the commandments.

5. Ignatius strongly encouraged a daily examination of conscience. Have the students try this form of prayer by following these directions:

   • Find a quiet place (in church when possible) where you can be for five or ten minutes.
   • Calm the thoughts that are in your mind.
   • Ask the Holy Spirit for help.
   • Review your thoughts, words, and actions of the day so far.
   • Ask: Are my thoughts, words and actions like those of Christ? Am I the person Jesus expects me to be?
   • Choose one thing to improve on for the rest of the day.

AUGUST 1: ALPHONSUS LIGUORI

Do you know anyone who expects to be a fully registered lawyer by the time he or she is sixteen? Probably not. Alphonsus did achieve just that unusual goal. He was born in 1696 to the rich Liguori family of Naples, Italy. Because he was a very intelligent boy, and because the school system was very different at that time, he finished school and began to practice law when he was sixteen. After eleven years, he became so disturbed by the corruption in the courts of Naples that he gave up his career and began to study for the priesthood.

The poor, the ignorant, and the neglected people attracted him. Eventually other young men joined Alphonsus in his efforts to meet the spiritual needs of the poor. Finally he began a religious order of priests known as the Redemptorists. Their goal was to preach and to teach, especially in remote rural areas and in the slums of the cities. His order worked hard to fight Jansenism, a heresy that held the doctrine of predestination and advocated an "extremely rigorous code of morals and asceticism." It was responsible for keeping many Catholics from receiving Jesus in the Eucharist. Alphonsus, as a priest and later as a bishop, wrote many sermons, books, and articles to encourage devotion to Jesus in the Blessed Sacrament. He was also deeply devoted to the Blessed Virgin Mary.

Alphonsus was a friendly, kind man, full of quiet humor. The last years of his life brought him problems of weakening health, misunderstanding, and even a certain amount of failure. But through it all, he kept his awareness of the presence of Christ in his life. In this way he never lost his faith and hope. He died in 1787. In 1871 he was declared a Doctor of the Church.

SUGGESTIONS

1. Remembering Alphonsus' great devotion to Jesus in the Blessed Sacrament, encourage the students to go to a local church to spend a few minutes in the Lord's eucharistic presence.

2. As a lawyer, Alphonsus showed a keen sense of justice. He gave up being a lawyer only because he realized that his clients' causes were often unjust. Have the students share any experiences they have had of taking a stand for justice. Or have them describe incidents when people they knew stood up for justice. Finally, discuss how working for justice is acting as Jesus acted.

3. For his major writing on morality, a three-volume work, Alphonsus mentioned 800 authors in 70,000 references. Have each student find a quotation on the Christian life from a respected author. Direct the students to write their quotations and the authors on slips of paper. Collect the papers. Each day, choose a paper and write that quotation on the board as the thought for the day.

4. Alphonsus repeatedly spoke and wrote about the overwhelming love of God. Have the students memorize this short prayer, which Alphonsus used in his Way of the Cross.

> I love You, my beloved Jesus; I love You more than myself. I repent with my whole heart of having offended You. Never permit me to separate myself from You again. Grant that I may love You always, and then do with me what You will.

5. Bring to class old copies of *Liguorian*, a magazine published by the Redemptorists and named after St. Alphonsus. Depending on the number of magazines you have, distribute them to individuals or to groups of students who should examine the magazines with these questions in mind: What subjects are treated? How do the Redemptorists carry on the work of St. Alphonsus? Have individuals or groups report their findings to the class.

6. Alphonsus was a person of many talents. Besides writing poetry and books, he was a gifted musician and composed hymns. Have the students draw upon their own talents and put on a talent show for another class. Have the announcer dedicate the program to St. Alphonsus.

AUGUST 2: EUSEBIUS OF VERCELLI

Early in the fourth century, a very dangerous heretic named Arius became quite popular. He spread the false teaching that Jesus was not really divine. He taught that Jesus was a good man, but only a man. It has been called "the most devastating of the early heresies."

In 325 the bishops gathered for a meeting in Nicea and condemned Arius and his teaching. At this council, they formulated the Nicene Creed, which listed the basic beliefs of the Catholic faith. They drew on an early baptismal creed from Jerusalem.

Thirty years later, another council was held in Milan because the Arians were still causing a good deal of trouble. Eusebius, the bishop of Vercelli in northern Italy, attended this meeting. Before the bishops began any discussion, Eusebius insisted that each bishop sign a copy of the Nicene Creed. This act was to strengthen them in their belief in basic Catholic doctrine. At this council, Arius was condemned again as a false teacher.

The emperor, who favored Arius, was not pleased with Eusebius. So when Eusebius refused to condemn his fellow bishop Athanasius, who also fought Arianism, the emperor became angry. He sent Eusebius into exile in Palestine. The Arians in Palestine continued to harass Eusebius, but he held to his convictions. He was forced to endure exile in Egypt, too, When the emperor died, Eusebius returned to Italy and continued to fight Arianism for the rest of his life. He was deeply concerned that all priests everywhere should teach the Catholic faith as it had been handed on from the apostles.

SUGGESTIONS

1. Even during his exile, Eusebius remained loyal to the Church and the Gospel message. Have the students look up the following Scripture quotations on being faithful:

Proverbs 12:22	2 Timothy 3:14
Psalm 119:30	Revelation 1:5
Luke 16:10	Revelation 2:10

Then have the students write an original prayer asking for help to be faithful to Christ and His Church.

2. Eusebius was exiled for defending the truths of faith and upholding St. Athanasius. In exile, Eusebius must have been lonely and discouraged at times. But as soon as he was allowed to return to his own country, he resumed his efforts as defender of the faith. Ask the students to consider the last time they felt lonely or discouraged. Have them explain the situation and their reactions in their journals. Then have them look up Isaiah 41:10-13 and copy a phrase that will give them courage in the future.

3. Eusebius translated a commentary on the psalms. Have the students consider four types of psalms: *praise* psalms, which show wonder or excitement with creation; *thanksgiving* psalms, which show gratitude; *repentance* psalms, which show sorrow for displeasing God; *wisdom* psalms, which ask for guidance. Have the students work in pairs to find samples of each type of psalm. Then have each pair create a psalm mobile. Distribute index cards, and instruct the students to use one card for each type of psalm. They should put the type of psalm and a quotation on one side and a cut-out magazine picture that reflects the quotation on the other side. Punch holes in each card and attach the cards to a coat hanger with pieces of colored yarn.

4. Eusebius risked his life to defend the truth that Jesus is both true God and true Man. Have the students discuss the way that Jesus reflected these two natures in His public life. Then read the following situations taken from the Scriptures and ask the students to raise their hands if the example shows the power of God and to keep their hands lowered if the example shows the human side of Jesus:

- Jesus asks the woman for a drink of water. (Man.)

- Jesus touches the blind man's eyes, and he can see. (God.)

- Jesus falls asleep in the boat. (Man.)

- Jesus has dinner with a Pharisee. (Man.)

- Jesus walks on top of the water one night. (God.)

- Jesus tells someone that his sins are forgiven. (God.)

Then have students volunteer to give an example to the class.

5. Eusebius had a strong faith in all that Jesus taught. Have the students, in a spirit of faith, recite the Nicene Creed, which they can find in their textbooks or missalettes.

AUGUST 4: JOHN VIANNEY

"Can I help you, sir?" the fruit vendor at the city market in Ars asked the stranger. "Well, yes. I'm looking for the priest, John Vianney. People in my village are saying strange things about him, and I would like to know if the reports are true." "What kind of things have you heard?" inquired the vendor, smiling in a knowing way. "Oh, unusual stories," the gentleman answered. "Someone told me that the devil set fire to his bed a few weeks ago. And that he has seen the Blessed Virgin Mary and spoken to her. Are these stories true?"

"Why don't you go over there to his church and get in that long line waiting to go to confession to Father Vianney?"

"Confession? What will that tell me?"

"You had best try it out for yourself. Father Vianney will most likely tell you about some secret sins that you committed long ago. Talk to him, and then come back and let me know what you think about him. We call him a saint — and that he is."

In 1805, at the age of nineteen, John Vianney decided to enter a seminary to study for the priesthood. After several months, he had to leave because his previous schooling had not prepared him to attend lectures in Latin. He went to live with a friend who was a priest and who tutored him. This priest finally persuaded the bishop to ordain John, not for his learning but for his holiness.

After a few years, Father Vianney was assigned to Ars, a small village in rural France that contained about fifty families. The people there were very careless about practicing their faith, so they were not happy with this young new priest who was eager to draw them back to God and Christian living. Some of the parish members caused trouble by lying about him, by acting violently against him, by refusing to cooperate with him. They were hoping that he would give up and leave. But instead, Father Vianney increased his prayers, his fasting, and his penances. And God's love began to reach people's hearts.

Gradually people began to come to celebrate the Eucharist and the Sacrament of Reconciliation, and to really listen to his homilies. Within a few years, Father Vianney was spending ten hours a day in the confessional during the winter months, and almost fifteen hours every day during the summer. People from all over France, and even from other countries, came to consult him and to ask for help when they were in trouble. In fact, the French government built a special railroad line to Ars just to take care of all the pilgrims.

Father Vianney paid no attention to these signs of honor. He continued his hard yet simple way of prayer, fasting, and penance. He was strict with his parishioners, but a hundred times more strict with himself. Finally at the age of 73, he was worn out physically. People were calling him a saint long before he died. He was canonized in 1925 and is the patron saint of parish priests.

SUGGESTIONS

1. John lacked proper schooling and a natural ability for learning. Yet he became a priest and a saint. Guide the students to see that God's love for individuals is not based on a person's intelligence, talents, personality, grades, popularity, or money. Help them to appreciate the value that each person has in God's eyes. Direct the students to compose a prayer in their journals thanking God for His love.

2. Father Vianney is the patron of parish priests. Encourage the students to decide on prayers they could offer for the priests of the local parish. Have one student design the front of a card for these priests. Guide the class to compose an inside message that mentions the feast of John Vianney, includes a note of encouragement, and explains that prayers have been offered for the priests by the class. Finally, have every student sign the card and have a volunteer deliver the card to the priests.

3. John drew people to Christ by praying and sacrificing for them. In this way, he was a channel through which God's grace could work within the hearts of the people. Encourage the students to think of one person whom they want to draw to Christ. Have them write in their journals a resolution about prayer and sacrifice that they might offer daily for this person.

4. John heard confessions from midnight to the following evening on a regular basis. He stopped only to celebrate the Eucharist, to pray much, and to eat and sleep a bit. Every day he had people waiting in line. John seemed to have the gift of reaching people's hearts and telling them about the sins of their past lives. Have the students consider whether they would have chosen the Sacrament of Reconciliation with this saintly priest. Then review the steps for celebrating the Sacrament of Reconciliation.

5. John met several people in his life who also became well known. Because he used to care for beggars in his family's home, he once met St. Benedict Joseph Labre. He also met Pauline Jaricot, the founder of the Society for the Propagation of the Faith. Have the students research the lives of these people and share their findings with the class.

6. John gave away his furnishings, his belongings, and the clothes and food that the neighbors brought him. Once he received a black velvet cape as an award and sold it to buy food for the poor. Remind the students that in 1979, Mother Teresa of Calcutta won the Nobel Peace Prize and used the money to help the poor. Then have the class decide on a project to raise money for the poor.

AUGUST 5: DEDICATION OF ST. MARY MAJOR

When you hear the word "church," what do you think of? Do you think of the priests and people of your own parish? Do you think of a Sunday morning when families of the parish gather to celebrate the eucharistic liturgy? Do you picture a stately building with a round dome, pointed towers, and stained glass windows? The word "church" has a variety of meanings.

Today's feast focuses our attention on a church building, a basilica called St. Mary Major. Tradition says that in August, 352, the Blessed Virgin Mary appeared to a wealthy nobleman in Rome. She asked that a church be built on the spot where he would find snow. On that summer day, snow did mysteriously appear and a church was built on the spot and dedicated to Our Lady of the Snows.

Apart from the story, however, we know that a church was built on that spot in the fourth century and was rebuilt in 434. The church was also rededicated to Mary, the Mother of God. This title of Mary was protected by the ecumenical council of Ephesus. Today St. Mary Major is the largest church in the world dedicated to Our Lady. This church is called a patriarchal church, one where the pope officiates on certain occasions. There is a special altar in this church used by the Holy Father and by others with special permission. On a deeper level, this feast reminds us that Mary has been reverenced throughout the history of the Church as our Mother. "All generations will call me blessed" (Luke 1:48).

SUGGESTIONS

1. Take the class to a Marian shrine on the property or in the church. Sing a hymn to Mary and pray the Magnificat from Luke 1:46-55. This prayer has become a model prayer of praise for the Church. It might fittingly be used after Communion.

2. Have each student mention one good quality of their parish. Then have them give examples of

how they, as part of the Church, can help the parish in living out this quality.

3. Have the class list ways in which Christians show love for Mary. The list might include the following practices and/or others the students suggest: wearing a medal; participating in a May crowning; naming a child after Mary; dedicating a school, hospital, or church to Mary; praying the rosary; becoming a member of the Legion of Mary; remembering to celebrate her feast days. The students might also consult the diocesan directory to find names of religious communities and other organizations that have Mary for a patroness.

4. Have students research shrines of Our Lady, such as the ones in Knock, Ireland; Guadalupe; Lourdes; Fatima; and Czestochowa, Poland. Direct them to share the information and any pictures they find with the class. Encourage the students to look for shrines located in their own diocese or within easy access. They might even plan a pilgrimage to such a nearby shrine.

5. Make a large chart on the name of Mary. In the middle of the chart, have a student design the letters MARY. Then have the students search for the variations of that name in all languages. As they discover a name, have them print it somewhere on the chart. Possible starters are Miriam, Marisa, Maura (Ireland), and Mitzi (Austria).

AUGUST 6: TRANSFIGURATION

The synoptic Gospels contain a number of passages that show Jesus' divinity shining through His humanity. One of these is the passage on the Transfiguration.

Some time before He died on the cross, Jesus took Peter, James, and John up a high mountain — probably Mount Tabor. There, while the apostles watched, Jesus' face began to shine much more brightly than the sun. His garments became as white as snow.

Suddenly Moses and Elijah appeared, standing on each side of Jesus. The three of them talked together for a brief time about Jesus' coming passion and death. Then Peter, not really knowing what he was saying, exclaimed, "Lord . . . it is wonderful for us to be here; if you wish, I will make three tents here, one for you, one for Moses and one for Elijah" (Matthew 17:4).

While Peter was still speaking, a bright cloud gathered and covered the apostles with its shadow. Then the apostles heard a voice saying, "This is my Son, the Beloved; he enjoys my favor. Listen to him" (Matthew 17:5). Peter, James, and John fell to the ground because they were so frightened. The next moment, Jesus touched them and told them not to fear. When they looked up, there was no one in sight except Jesus, looking like His ordinary self.

As they walked down the mountain, Jesus told the favored three to keep the whole experience a secret. They were permitted to tell others only after He had risen from the dead.

SUGGESTIONS

1. Write the following letter on stationery and put it in an envelope. Open the letter in class, read it to the students, and ask them to guess who could have written a letter like this.

> Dearly Beloved,
> As I am here in prison, awaiting execution, I feel the urge to write to you, pleading with you to be faithful to Christ. I am aware that you have shown loyalty to Christ and His teachings, and I thank God for it; but, still, these few words may raise your spirits when you are tempted to give up. Realize that what we have taught you about the coming of Jesus in glory and power are not figments of our imagination, but actual truths, for we saw Jesus on the mount arrayed in glory and heard the voice from heaven announce, "This is my beloved Son." Let me repeat: Jesus will come again, this time in glory and majesty. Keep this truth in mind when the going is rough. It will be a lamp to light your way through the dark night until the morning star appears and the coming of dawn brings light to your heart.
>
> To Jesus be glory.
> (Adapted from 2 Peter 1:12-19)

After the students have guessed, tell them that this is adapted from Peter's second letter, written while he was in prison. Then guide them to see that Peter used the Transfiguration event to give courage to suffering Christians.

2. Have interested students make a shadow play of the Transfiguration event. They may experiment with lighting effects for the play.

3. In the Bible, a cloud may be an actual sign of rain or it may be a symbol to show that God is mysteriously present. Have the students divide into pairs and look up the following quotations. Then have them indicate on a piece of paper which quotations connect the cloud with weather and which refer to God's presence or glory.

1 Kings 18:44 (weather)
Exodus 13:21-22 (presence)
Isaiah 25:5 (weather)
Jude 12 (weather)
Luke 12:54 (weather)
Matthew 17:5 (presence)
Exodus 19:16-20 (presence)
1 Kings 8:10-13 (presence)
1 Corinthians 10:1 (presence)

4. Direct the students to search through songbooks and to copy sentences that refer to "glory." Then have the students choose a sentence from their list,

print it neatly on a bookmark, and decorate the bookmark. Encourage them to use the bookmark and to praise the God of glory whenever they see it.

5. Duplicate the following word search. Challenge the students to find ten words that refer to the Transfiguration account.

```
M J Z R E C C B
O O Q U I L H M
U H S G L O R Y
N N M F I U I S
T S O N G D S T
A J S W H I T E
I T E N T K E R
N R S X W P R Y
```

The answers are mountain, John, tent, Moses, glory, cloud, Son, white, Christ, mystery.

AUGUST 7: SIXTUS II AND HIS COMPANIONS

In 257, when Sixtus became pope, he did not know how long he would be able to serve the young Church. Being a Christian had suddenly become dangerous. For awhile, Emperor Valerius had been gentle and appreciative of Christians. His palace had been filled with Christian high officials. Then overnight, he turned against them, accusing Christians of being enemies of the government. In the midst of this new threat, Pope Sixtus struggled for one year to guide the Church through many difficulties, some dealing with false teachers, some dealing with questions about Baptism.

Because of the persecution, Christians began to gather for their eucharistic celebrations in the catacombs throughout Rome. Frequently they would change the particular location or the time so they would not be found by suspicious Roman guards. Then one day, during the eucharistic celebration in the catacombs, Valerius' soldiers appeared. In full view of the community, the soldiers beheaded Sixtus and four deacons who were assisting him. The men were beheaded simply because they were Christians.

Will we ever have to give up our lives rather than deny that we follow Jesus? We really do not know. We do know that we would be wise to pray often — every day — for strength to remain loyal to Jesus.

SUGGESTIONS

1. The catacombs were damp, dark tunnels used as underground cemeteries in Rome. At times Christians met there secretly to find strength and joy in their celebration of the eucharistic liturgy. In our own time, during World War II, priests like the Dutch prisoner Titus Bradsma smuggled the Eucharist to other prisoners in the barracks of concentration camps. Or priests held secret Masses in the concentration camps while a group of Catholic prisoners stood huddled around them in the corner of a crowded room. Guide the students to see that the Eucharist has been a source of joy and strength to Christians of every age, no matter what their surroundings. Have the students write a paragraph in their journals explaining why the Eucharist can be a source of strength even in the worst circumstances.

2. Have the students explain how Sixtus showed Christian leadership to the early Christian community. Then direct them to give examples of how modern popes have shown leadership to today's Christians. For example, John Paul II, in his many travels, witnesses to the universal love that Christians should have for all people. Challenge the students to do research in a local library to find examples of leadership in the lives of recent popes: John XXIII, Paul VI, John Paul I, and John Paul II.

3. To help the students experience the situation of the early Christians, guide them in the following prayerful, imaginative experience:

   • For the next few minutes, close your eyes and let your imagination do the work.

   • Imagine that you are an early Christian walking down a crowded street. People are rushing past you as you make your way behind a building. You are looking for the hidden entrance to one of the catacombs. Earlier in the day, Deacon Lawrence had slipped a note into your hand while you were standing at the open market. The note in code warned you that the meeting place had been changed. Some Roman guards must have discovered the regular meeting place. So now you are trying to find where Pope Sixtus and the others are gathering for the celebration of the Eucharist. Through the dark tunnel, you grope your way until your eyes adjust to the darkness. Your longing for Jesus increases as you stop and listen for voices. Meeting Him in the Eucharist has become the source of courage for which you keep risking your life. Suddenly your heart stops. Standing before you are Pope Sixtus and the eleven other Christians gathered for worship. All of them are familiar faces to you. BUT . . . they are surrounded by Roman soldiers. You want to turn and run as you realize that this discovery will mean dungeon, starvation, and death for you. [Pause.]

You might wish to allow some silent time for the students to complete the story in their own minds. Finally, to end the experience, read this closing prayer to the class:

Lord, You gave strength and courage to the early Christians. They faced death in order to be loyal to You. For them, You were more important than everything else, including life itself. Now we live as Your followers. Give us that same strength. Make us courageous in following You in the face of difficulties and ridicule. Be more important to us than anything else, even life itself. Amen.

4. Have the students compose a message that an early Christian might send to Pope Sixtus or that the pope might send to a Christian, giving the place and time of the next celebration of the Eucharist. Direct the students to write the messages in secret code, since Christians were being persecuted. Then tell them to trade papers and decode one another's messages.

5. Have the students read through the first letter of Peter in the New Testament. Ask them to write down any attitudes toward suffering that they find expressed there. Finally have them describe a situation in which they could use these attitudes.

AUGUST 7: CAJETAN

Does your parish have a credit union? The idea for this kind of organization goes back to a priest named Cajetan, who lived during the fifteenth and sixteenth centuries. He was born in 1480 in Vincenza, Italy. At the University of Padua, he was an outstanding student in both theology and law. Cajetan became a priest, and with his education, he could have had a successful career in the Curia as an advisor to the pope. Instead he chose to serve the poor and the sick.

Before long, other men wanted to help him in his work, so he began a religious order called Theatines. Cajetan trained his fellow priests in the study of the Bible, in the truths of the Catholic faith, and in restoring prayerful ways of worship in the parishes. Always his followers looked after the poor and the sick in the cities.

In 1527 an army attacked Rome. Cajetan was treated very cruelly because he did not have the riches that the soldiers were looking for. He escaped to Venice, where he recovered his health. It was there that he began a "monte de pieta" (a mountain of compassion). This name was given to an organization that loaned money to needy people in return for pawned objects. Cajetan developed this plan to help people against usurers, men who charged enormous interest for lending money. During the last few years of his life, Cajetan spent many hours each day in prayer. He died in 1547, worn out after a life of loving service to the poor.

SUGGESTIONS

1. When Cajetan saw a need among the people of God, he either tried to help or he organized a group to meet that need. He was always willing to adapt to new circumstances. Have the students find out how their parish helps the poor or other disadvantaged people. Let them suggest how they themselves can help such people.

2. One of the goals of the Theatines was to urge priests to have a routine of prayer and study in their lives. Discuss with the students the good that a prayerful priest can do for the Church. Then have the students consider how they can foster vocations. Some ways are to pray for vocations, to encourage those who are thinking of joining the priesthood, and to appreciate priests who are already serving the Church.

3. Cajetan chose to spend his life working among the people, but he could have also spent his life working in the Curia. Explain to the students that the Curia is the whole group of advisors who work with the pope as he leads the Catholic Church. Have the students refer to *The Official Catholic Directory* (available in most parishes), Part I, for "Roman Curia." The diocesan chancery, which can be called the diocesan curia, is made up of the bishop and all the people who help him run the diocese. In the local diocesan directory, the students can find the diocesan structure. Have interested students find more information on the work of the local diocesan chancery and report to the class. They might each report on the work of one of the charitable organizations such as the hunger centers, justice committees, and Catholic Charities.

4. Cajetan taught that the sick are best served by those who love Christ and pray to Him often. Ask the students to think about this recommendation and write a paragraph explaining why it is true. To encourage those who work with the sick, have the students make prayer cards for the nurses and for all who are employed on a selected floor of a nearby hospital. Assist the students in choosing the floor and in delivering the prayer cards.

5. Often Cajetan spoke to the members of his order about the importance of the spiritual and corporal works of mercy. Draw the following crossword puzzle on the board — without the answers — and give each student a copy of the clues. Let students raise their hands when they think they have an answer.

CLUES ACROSS

4) Rose collects good paperback books to send to people in prison. In her own way, she visits the _____.

6) Angela spends two hours trying to convince a classmate not to cheat on a final exam. She is counseling the _____.

7) Jose's great uncle has been in a home for the elderly for five years. Every Sunday Jose and his father go to see his uncle. In this way, Jose visits the _____.

8) In the evenings Clare is crocheting an afghan for her next-door neighbor, who is an invalid. In this way, Clare can _____ the naked.

CLUES DOWN

1) Richard's family has three refugee children living with him. His family shelters the _____.

2) Barbara's aunt has died, and Barbara misses her very much. Barbara can still help her aunt if she will _____ for the dead.

3) Lawrence sometimes brings an extra sandwich or piece of fruit for the elderly man who lives near the school. He wants to _____ the hungry.

5) Louis is falsely accused of lying. Now he has a week's detention. Even though he is innocent, he still is able to bear this wrong _____.

AUGUST 8: DOMINIC

TRUTH — Dominic's motto and his goal. TRUTH — woven into every day of Dominic's life. TRUTH — defended by Dominic with courageous enthusiasm. TRUTH — lived in love among his friars in the community that he founded. In all things, Dominic was greatly devoted to the truth that he found in the Christ of the Gospel.

Around the year 1170, Dominic was born in Spain as the youngest of four children. He was educated by his uncle, a priest. After further studies, Dominic became a priest and joined a religious community. He and the other monks created a community similar to the community of the early Christians. Soon he became prior, or head of the community.

He might have lived his whole life in that monastery if he had not accompanied his bishop to northern Europe in 1204. At that time, he met heretics who were teaching false ideas about the Catholic faith. These teachings had begun in the town of Albi in France, so the heresy was called Albigensianism. These Albigensians taught that people do not have a free will to do God's will. They taught that marriage was bad, but suicide and the killing of elderly or fatally-ill people could be good. They claimed to be the true Church and said that everyone else was wrong. Many good Christians were confused. They could not see the errors in the heretics' teachings, and they admired the fact that the heretics lived strict lives with little comfort.

Dominic clearly saw the problem. He saw that missionaries had been sent by the pope to preach against the heresies, but they slept in hotels, rode in carriages, and had good meals. The uneducated Christians were not impressed with that kind of life-style. So Dominic thought of a new way to fight this heresy. His bishop, three Cistercian monks, and Dominic went from city to city preaching the simple truth of Christ. They used the Bible as their reference book. They went on foot, depending on donations for food, and hospitality for a place to sleep. Dominic's plan began to change the attitude of some Christians.

In 1206 Dominic began an order of religious women who would serve the women who returned to the Catholic faith from Albigensianism. These Dominican sisters would help them to get a fresh start in life. These sisters also were a great help to Dominic himself. At one point, events took a turn for the worse. Dominic's bishop companion died, and the Cistercian monks, frustrated by arguments with heretics, went back to their own monastery. A cruel war broke out between the heretics and some Church members. Dominic realized that cruelty and violence could never draw people to Christ, Who is the Truth. His mission seemed to be failing. At this time, he established his base near the convent of the Dominican sisters, who spent their days praying that he would be able to touch the hearts of the heretics. These sisters encouraged Dominic to keep trying.

By 1215, a few men had joined Dominic in his work of preaching. He took them to Toulouse and there founded a religious order called the Order of Preachers. This small group was the beginning of what is now the world-wide Dominican order. Dominic learned a great deal from his preaching and travels: the importance of education, of praying with Scripture, and of living in Christian poverty. Dominic urged his members to study day and night, at home and on journeys. He knew if they were not well-educated, they could be trapped by the clever arguments of heretics. Furthermore, he encouraged his members to spend hours praying with Scripture and contemplating the Word of God. Then they would be ready to preach to the people what they had learned from God in prayer. Dominic also realized that in order to be true witnesses of the Gospel, Dominicans could not be wealthy. They had to live in poverty as Jesus had done. They had to travel from city to city, preaching as Jesus had preached.

Dominic was a trail blazer in that he formed a community different from most of the other orders. While other monks did manual labor and vowed to stay in the same monastery for life, the Dominican friars studied, prayed, traveled, and preached. In some ways they were like another new order: the Franciscans. But there was one important difference between the two groups: Dominic's order tried to reach the well-educated, those who were deceived by heresy because they thought they understood their faith, while Francis and his friars appealed to the poor and uneducated who wanted to love God and be joyful in Him.

Dominic knew how important is the truth of Christ and His Church. So even while he was establishing his order, he began a preaching mission through northern Italy. In 1221, while he was on this mission, he died — only six years after he had founded his community.

Dominic was a very loving person who was easy to live with. He was able to draw the members of his community together and to inspire them to love and forgive one another. He was canonized in 1234, only thirteen years after his death.

Dominic is outstanding for his love of truth, his clear thought, his organizing ability, and his sensitive, loving nature that reached out to all people. For Dominic, love for people was part of his love for God and for the Church.

SUGGESTIONS

1. Dominic was a powerful preacher, who had a way of convincing people of the truth. Direct the students to write a thirty-second PA announcement to persuade the students to follow Christ, to read the Bible, or to join wholeheartedly in participating in the liturgy. Have the most convincing announcements read over the PA.

2. Dominicans have always valued the Word of God. Dominic knew most of the Gospel of Matthew and the letters of Paul by memory. Have the students make flashcards with the name of a book of the Bible on one side and the abbreviation of the book on the reverse side. Let them make up games using these cards. Then challenge the students to memorize and recite the names of the books of the Bible in order, in a minute or less.

3. Rose Hawthorne, the daughter of the famous American novelist Nathaniel Hawthorne, was a wealthy woman in her own right. However, she used her wealth to begin a community of Dominican Sisters who care for incurably ill cancer patients. Have a volunteer read her life story and report to the class.

4. Dominic wanted his friars to be well educated and have a thorough knowledge of religion. To help the students assess their participation in religious classes, distribute a checklist that they can use in each religion class for a week. Have them use this scale for evaluation: VG = very good; G = good; NI = needs improvement.

RELIGION CLASS CHECKLIST

1) I had the necessary materials when class began: text, pencil, pen, paper.

2) I was paying attention when class began.

3) I participated by asking or answering questions.

4) I actively cooperated in the activities of the lesson.

5) I did the written work neatly and completely.

	M	T	W	Th	F
1					
2					
3					
4					
5					

At the end of the week, have the students write in their journals, describing the results of their week-long survey and suggesting some improvements for themselves.

5. Tell the students the following story:

Once when Dominic was traveling in Rome, he had a dream in which Mary was pointing to two men who would help to save the world from evil. Dominic recognized himself as one of the men, but he did not recognize the other person. The following day, a ragged beggar came up to him while he was praying in church. He recognized this beggar as the other person Mary had pointed out. The beggar was Francis of Assisi.

Some say that Dominic and Francis became friends and exchanged belts. This exchange explains why the Dominicans wear black belts and the Franciscans wear white belts. For many years the meeting of the two founders was remembered by both orders. On St. Dominic's feast day, Franciscans came to celebrate Mass with the Dominicans and then the two groups ate a meal together. On Francis' feast day, the Dominicans came to the Franciscan churches to celebrate together.

Ask the students to suggest reasons why two saints, such as Dominic and Francis, could save the world from evil.

AUGUST 10: LAWRENCE

"Where's the money?" demanded the Roman official harshly. Deacon Lawrence looked surprised. "What money?" he asked. "The Church's gold and silver," answered the official. "We know that you're in charge of the treasury, Lawrence. The government has a right to confiscate those funds. Hand them over." The official began to look annoyed. He had seen that Pope Sixtus II and four other deacons had been executed. But he didn't want to kill this deacon until he had the wealth in his hands. Lawrence responded, "Yes, I will show you the real treasures of the Church, but you have to give me time to prepare. Give me three days." Because he suspected that he, too, might be arrested, Lawrence had already sold the gold chalice and the other sacred items and had given the money to the poor.

But Lawrence was true to his promise. In three days the official returned. He saw before his eyes rows and rows of lepers, orphans, blind and lame people, and widows. Lawrence's comment was, "These are the treasure of the Church."

This incident that has come down from the early centuries shows how well Lawrence had put on the mind and heart of Christ. That special love he had for the weak, the helpless, and those whom others rejected, and the special dignity he saw in each person made him an excellent deacon. The deacons in the Church were to serve others, especially the poor. Lawrence valued the poor more than he did his own life.

The Roman official was so angry with Lawrence that he had a huge grill built and placed over burning coals. In this way, he hoped that Lawrence would die very slowly and painfully from the burning heat. But Lawrence was filled with good humor and joy while he died. The onlookers were amazed. But how could they understand that Lawrence was happy and excited about seeing the most important person in his life face to face — Jesus Christ?

SUGGESTIONS

1. St. Lawrence was a deacon in the early Church, not a priest. The word *deacon* comes from the Greek word "diakonia," which means service. Deacons of the early Church often helped widows, orphans, the poor and the elderly. Help the students grow in love for the elderly. Acquire a list of names of senior citizens from a parish minister to the elderly or home for the elderly. Have each student choose a name and write a letter of introduction as a Christian pen pal to this person. The students might include their pictures, original drawings, poems, or information about their present activities. Send these letters to the club or place of residence of these senior citizens. Be sure each letter has a return address.

2. The role of the deacon is to assist priests with some of their duties. Teach the students to distinguish between transitional deacons and permanent deacons. Transitional deacons are preparing for ordination to the priesthood. Permanent deacons are ordained only to the diaconate. Have the students ask the pastor of the parish about permanent deacons in the parish or young men from the parish who are transitional deacons in the seminary. Invite a deacon, transitional or permanent, to speak to the class about his role of service in the Church.

3. Lawrence is said to have laughed and joked while he was slowly dying. Have the students read 2 Corinthians 9:6-10, which describes a cheerful giver. Then have the students consider that though they may not be called to die as martyrs for Christ, they will certainly have to experience some difficulties in practicing their religion. If they show they honor their parents by obeying a curfew, for instance, they might have to suffer the teasing of their friends. Direct the students to write a prayer in their journals, asking for courage to be faithful to Jesus when a sacrifice is required of them.

4. Suggest that the students direct a service activity for the school. On a designated day, have the students give an opening announcement over the PA in which they challenge all the students in the school to do three acts of service to show their love for others. During the last class of the day, have the students distribute paper strips of various colors (1" x 5") to all classes. Each student in the school should receive one strip for every act of service he or she did. Direct the students to write one act of service that they really did on each strip of paper. Then have the classes glue the strips into interlocking loops and form a paper chain. Have classes attach the chains to other class chains. Decorate the halls with these service chains.

5. Lawrence's attitude toward the poor can be learned from his words and actions. Ask the students to write a paragraph in which they explain how their own words and actions reveal their attitude toward the poor. Then have them discuss how the school shows its attitude toward the poor. Finally, have the students pray silently for all those who are suffering, are without food and shelter, are neglected or ignored.

AUGUST 11: CLARE

Name the outstanding quality of true friendship. Is it loyalty, which keeps friends together through painful, discouraging times as well as through good times? Is it having the same goals, the same values? Is it the ability to help each other become the best person possible? Is it being comfortable together so that no one has to put on an act? Clare and Francis of Assisi had a strong, true friendship that reflected all these qualities. But they had something more: their mutual, deep love of Jesus, which made them want to live according to the Gospel.

Clare was born in 1194 into a wealthy family of Assisi, Italy. As a teenager, she became aware that Francis, the handsome, wealthy leader of the young in Assisi, had greatly changed. He used to spend a great deal of money having a good time and treating others to a good time. Now he had no money, no possessions, no family to call his own. He dressed in a brown robe, begged for food, and lived on the streets. Yet he seemed to enjoy life more than ever.

Clare was puzzled by his behavior. But gradually she saw that the real source of his joy and inner peace was his living in poverty like Jesus. In 1211, Clare left home to join Francis. He cut off her long hair, gave her a rough woolen habit to wear, and took her to stay for awhile with the Benedictine sisters. When he found a little house near San Damiano Church, he moved Clare and the other women who had joined her into this little place and guided her in beginning a new religious order.

This small community wanted to live according to the rule of Francis. They slept on the floor each night, went barefoot, kept silence much of the day, and spent hours in prayer. They ate only when food was donated because they had no money to buy their own food. Clare became abbess, the head of this little community. But she did not spend her time giving orders. She eagerly chose the hardest work to do herself; she helped the healthy as well as those who were ill. Her example inspired the others to trust in God.

In 1240 and again in 1241, the convent and the whole city were threatened by an invasion of the Saracens. Panic spread. Clare told her sisters not to be afraid but to trust in Jesus. She herself prayed to Jesus in the Blessed Sacrament to save His people. Both times the convent and the whole city were spared.

Clare died on August 11, 1253, after twenty-seven years of illness. The community that she began is still in existence today. The sisters are called the Poor Clares, and they continue to follow the spirit and the rule of St. Francis. These sisters continue to radiate the joy and peace that comes from living in Christian poverty like Jesus.

SUGGESTIONS

1. Clare acted as a peacemaker when the city of Assisi was threatened by the violence of a Saracen invasion. She prayed to Jesus in the Blessed Sacrament for help. Review with the students the procedure for Eucharistic Devotion, which is concluded with Benediction. If possible, let the students participate in a Eucharistic Devotion, or have them at least pray the Divine Praises, which may be used at the conclusion of Eucharistic Devotion.

2. Poor Clares have an inner joy that is difficult to describe. Have students research this order and report to the class. Or arrange for the class to visit a Poor Clare monastery to learn about the life and customs of these sisters.

3. Like her friend Francis, Clare felt wonder and awe at the beauty of nature and the reflection of God in nature. In honor of Clare, post colorful nature scenes around the room for the day. Whenever they look at a scene, the students should praise God for the beauty He has created.

4. Have the students make flower baskets for another class, neighbors, or shut-ins who belong to the parish. Give them these directions to follow:

   • Roll a piece of construction paper (8 ½″ x 11″) into a cone and fasten it with staples or glue.

   • Decorate the cone with paper designs, scraps of materials, and ribbon.

   • Attach yarn or ribbon to the top of the cone for a handle.

   • Print a Scripture quote on a small strip of stiff paper (3″ x 1 ½″) and tie the strip to the handle. Possible quotes are Psalm 96:11-12; Psalm 150:6; Isaiah 35:1; Luke 12:27.

   • Fill the cone with real or plastic flowers, or make flowers from tissue paper.

   Now the cones are ready to be hung on the doorknobs of those the students wish to surprise.

5. Clare realized the value of silence. Silence helps people to become aware of God's presence near them and in their hearts. Have the students listen to and reflect on the following questions:

   • Where is there silence in my life? When I take a test in school? In my bedroom at night? During Mass? While I'm waiting in line for something?

   • How do I feel when there is silence? Peaceful? Relaxed? Restless? It depends?

   Then discuss why some people love silence and others fill up every moment with music or other sounds.

6. Clare had a joyful and grateful heart. She enjoyed the simple things in life. Through the following exercise, help the students to reflect on the blessings in their lives: Have them fold a paper in four parts. Direct them to label each part with one of these headings: PERSONS, QUALITIES IN MYSELF, PLACES, THINGS. Then ask them to list under each heading the things (people) for which they are grateful. Finally, have each student choose one item from the list for a class litany of thanksgiving. For example, a student might say, "For my parents who care for me." As each student reads a prayer, have the class respond, "We thank You, Lord." Close with the doxology: "Glory to the Father . . . ."

AUGUST 13: PONTIAN AND HIPPOLYTUS

During the Roman persecution of the early Church, not all Christians were sentenced to death. Some were sentenced to forced labor in metal or salt mines. These convicted Christians marched to the mine shaft two by two, chained together with murderers, political prisoners, thieves, and slaves. Once confined below the ground, the convict spent his time in endless work. No one came out alive.

How did the Christians keep up their courage in those suffocating places? Their faith in Jesus Christ and the power of His love kept them going. Some of the walls in the mines had words or phrases scratched on them — words that expressed this faith to other suffering Christians. "You will live . . . you will live in Christ . . . You will live for ever . . . life . . . life . . . life."

In 235 Hippolytus and Pontian were among those sentenced to the mines. Hippolytus was the most important writer in the Church at that time. But he was also very critical and wanted the Church to be very strict with sinners. When Pope Callistus chose to be forgiving, as Jesus was, Hippolytus became very upset. He gathered followers around himself and became antipope. In 230 Pontian became pope, and Hippolytus still refused to change his position. He caused much unrest and confusion among Christian communities, and Pontian could not seem to change him.

In 235 under the persecution of Maximus, Pontian was sentenced to hard labor in the mines of Sardinia. He resigned as pope so that someone else could lead the Church. Then he went into the mines. That same year Hippolytus was also arrested and condemned to the mines in Sardinia. In that dark, damp prison, the forgiving love of Christ finally penetrated Hippolytus' heart and he was reconciled to Pontian. The two of them died in those mines, united in the love of God. They are martyrs for Christ and recognized as saints in the Church.

SUGGESTIONS

1. The early Christians like Pontian and Hippolytus gladly faced torture and death. Write the following coded message on the board. Have the students decode it to find out the secret of the joy of martyrs. HINT: Each letter of the message represents the letter that comes directly before it in the alphabet.

    XF IBWF WJDUPSZ UISPVHI KFTVT

    The answer is WE HAVE VICTORY THROUGH JESUS.

2. Pontian was a pope and martyr. Have interested students make a chart of the first thirty-two popes. Tell them to record the length of each pope's term and the manner of death of each one. (Cf., *Catholic Almanac; Butler's Lives of the Saints.*)

3. Celebrating birthdays is a popular custom. The Church usually celebrates the feast day of a saint on the day of his or her death. Have the students discuss the reasons for this custom.

4. The early Christians had to live among people who actually praised the capital sins and treated them as popular behavior. Have the students list the capital sins in a column on a sheet of paper: pride, covetousness (greed), lust, anger, gluttony, envy, sloth (laziness). Next to each sin, have them write one action a person could do to avoid that sin (e.g., pride: Praise another person's success instead of your own.).

5. Pontian and Hippolytus witnessed to Christ by their lives in the face of exile and cruel treatment. Help the students grow in this kind of courage. Divide the class into three groups and give each group one of the following Scripture references: Matthew 10:17-23; 2 Corinthians 4:7-18; 2 Corinthians 6:3-10. Have each group practice reading the assigned passage aloud, either by having each person take a line to read or by having two sides alternate. Use these in a short prayer service in honor of the early Christian martyrs. Begin with a song such as "Be Not Afraid" (Dufford) from the album *Earthen Vessels* (NALR). Then have each group give the scriptural selection. Finally, have spontaneous petitions to give the students an opportunity to ask for courage and strength for themselves and for other Christians.

See Supplement for August 14.

AUGUST 15: ASSUMPTION

Millions of people were tortured and killed during the Holocaust of World War II. This terrible tragedy led many people to wonder about human life. How valuable is a single human life? How valuable are the lives of the elderly, the unborn, the terminally ill? Are their lives worth as much as those of people who are healthy and active, working, and raising families?

God Who created human life gives it value. Jesus gave His life on the cross to redeem each individual human person. By doing this, Jesus stated, "Your life is worth My dying to save you." Through His own resurrection, Jesus showed us the glory of our resurrection and of our living in the Holy Spirit. Jesus promised that the body and soul of a person, separated at death, will be joined together again in glory at the Last Judgment. The person will be whole for all eternity. The feast of Mary's Assumption is a preview of what our lives will be. At the end of her earthly life, Mary was assumed, or taken up into heaven body and soul. She did not have to wait for the end of the world, as we do. God granted her this special privilege because of her sinlessness and her fulness of grace.

The Church has always believed in Mary's assumption into heaven. But on November 1, 1950, Pope Pius XII focused the attention of the whole world on the Assumption of Mary as a dogma and mystery of our faith. This mystery shows us that God wants every human person, body and soul, to be in glory forever, just as Mary is now. This dogma shows how important every single human life is. Pope Pius XII hoped that by thinking about Mary's assumption, people all over the world would develop a deeper respect for their own lives, their own bodies. He also hoped that people would grow in that same respect for the lives of others.

SUGGESTIONS

1. Bring to class various artists' interpretations of the Assumption. Ask the students to explain how the artist represented Mary and to imagine why he or she included certain details in the painting.

2. Give the students one minute to write down all the words they can think of that remind them of heaven. Have the person with the longest list read it to the class. Then discuss with the students why these words may have come to be associated with heaven. Finally read to the class 1 Corinthians 2:9.

3. Review the Glorious Mysteries of the Rosary. Divide the class into five groups and assign one mystery to each group. Direct the students to write a brief explanation and prayer for their mystery. Then have the class pray the Glorious Mysteries of the Rosary. Before each decade, have a volunteer from the appropriate group read the group's prayer meditation to the class. Remind the students to think about each mystery as they recite the prayers.

4. Mary now experiences the glory of God. Challenge the students to find Scripture passages that refer to God's glory. Write one reference on the board and have the students stand as soon as they locate the exact quotation in their Bibles. Then have one of the standing students read the quotation aloud while the others are seated and listening. Put the next reference on the board and repeat the procedure. These are some possible quotations:

Ephesians 1:17	Isaiah 6:3
Numbers 14:21	Mark 10:37
Psalm 29:1-2	1 Samuel 2:8
Habakuk 2:14	Romans 1:20
Psalm 19:1	Jeremiah 14:21
Luke 24:26	1 Timothy 3:16

5. In the United States, the Assumption is a holy day of obligation. All Catholics gather for the celebration of the Eucharist on the vigil or on the feast day itself. Discuss with the students what lessons the citizens of the United States can learn from this Marian feast.

6. Since the last part of the sixth century, the Eastern Catholic Churches have celebrated the feast of the Dormition of Mary, which eventually led to our feast of the Assumption. The Dormition is the "falling asleep of Mary" at the end of her earthy life. Tell the students that Mary's peaceful crossing over from earthly life to heavenly life is due to Jesus, Who died to free her and all of us from the power of death.

7. Divide the class into groups. Give each group a variety of songbooks and a specific time limit. Have them find and list the names of songs that deal with Jesus' resurrection or His victory over death. Then, as a class, sing one of these songs or a Marian song.

8. Have the students discuss the reasons why the following actions are wrong: neglect of proper food and sleep, violence, pornography, smoking.

AUGUST 16: STEPHEN OF HUNGARY

"Might makes right." "Take everything you can get." "The strongest person gets the best." "Don't try to cooperate — try to win!" The people who settled near the Danube River in the tenth century were used to following these principles. They were a violent and superstitious people. Often one of these tribes would invade a part of Western Europe, destroying property and stealing valuable objects. The tribes themselves were separate from one another and were often fighting among themselves or taking revenge for some offense.

The national leader of these people was Geza. When Geza's son, Vajk, was born, people expected the boy to take his father's place as leader of this area called Hungary. Then Geza and his son learned about Jesus Christ and Christianity. They were both baptized. Vajk received Stephen as his baptismal name. As a young adult, Stephen married a girl named Gisela, whose brother became the future emperor, Henry II. When Geza died, Stephen had to lead the country. He wanted all the Hungarian people to become Christians. First, he asked Pope Sylvester II if he could be a king instead of a national leader like his father. The pope agreed and sent a special crown, which still exists today. On Christmas Day, 1000, Stephen was crowned the first king of Hungary. Then, as king, he made unity a special goal and brought the various tribes into one nation.

Hoping to plant Christianity in the hearts of the Hungarian people, he made three other important decisions. He invited the Benedictine monks of Germany and Italy to come as missionaries to his people. He built churches and had them decorated with sculptures, colorful mosaics, and murals depicting truths of the Catholic faith. He encouraged the people to come to the churches and to value their local priests.

Stephen was very popular with the poor. He often went among them, giving donations. One time the crowd of beggars became so excited that they knocked the king to the ground. But Stephen laughed and assured them that he would continue to share his wealth with them. Stephen's love for the poor also kept his officials from getting too powerful and abusing the poor and the weak.

Stephen counted on his son Emeric to take his place as king when he died. He is believed to have written "Mirror of Princes" in order to explain to his son how to be a good Christian king. However, young Emeric was killed in a hunting accident, and Stephen faced many family quarrels over who should be the next king. Finally in 1038 he died and was buried at the Church of Our Lady of Buda in Hungary. Stephen was an outstanding leader, a dedicated Christian, and a strong defender of the Church. He is the patron saint of Hungary.

SUGGESTIONS

1. Read the following selection from *Mirror of Princes* to the class. Have the students imagine that they are Emeric and their father is giving them this advice:

Be humble in this life, that God may raise you up in the next. Be truly moderate and do not punish or condemn anyone immoderately. Be gentle so that you may never oppose justice. Be honorable so that you may never voluntarily bring disgrace on anyone. Be chaste so that you may avoid all the foulness of lust like the pangs of death. All these virtues I have noted above make up the royal crown, and without them no one is fit to rule here on earth or attain to the heavenly kingdom.

Read the section again and have the students write in their journals one idea from it that they think would be good advice for themselves.

2. Stephen is recognized as the real founder of the state of Hungary. So that the students can see how the Christian influence spread in that country, have them research Hungarian customs and traditions. Encourage them to share their findings with the class.

3. Stephen was a devoted Christian. Have the students make flashcards with a "duty of a Catholic Christian" on one side and a practical example of how that duty is lived on the reverse side. For example:

To join in the missionary spirit and apostolate of the Church.

Beth collects rosaries and postage stamps for the missions.

To do penance, including abstaining and fasting from food on the appointed days.

Every Friday, Greg skips all desserts.

Then have the students pair up and drill each other on the duties of a Catholic Christian. When they finish, have them switch partners and continue the drill.

4. Stephen realized that Christianity would help his people in all areas of their lives. Explain to the students that through the Second Vatican Council and through the letters of the popes and bishops, the Church helps all people to apply Christian principles to the problems in the world today. Have each student choose a world problem. Direct the students to write a short report in which they first state the issue and then explain the Church's view of the issue. Encourage them to discuss their research with their parents. Topics might include world hunger, prejudice, the wasting of natural resources, the arms race, abortion, and poverty.

5. Review with the students the names of their local and national leaders. Then discuss with them the Christian qualities that these leaders will need in order to do their job well. Lead the students in a litany in which they pray for these officials, asking God for a special quality that these leaders will need. The response to each petition might be "Bless our leaders, Lord."

AUGUST 18: JANE FRANCES DE CHANTAL

See December 12, her former feast day, on page 55.

AUGUST 19: JOHN EUDES

"You always say you're sorry, but you never change." "He has been a problem, he is a problem, and he will be a problem." "We might as well give up trying to help her. She's hopeless." John Eudes refused to accept comments like these. He believed that every person has value and dignity from God. He believed that God's merciful love is unlimited. His convictions were so strong that he helped many people whose situations might have seemed hopeless to others. He encouraged priests and many other Christians to respond in love to God. His image for divine love was the Sacred Heart of Jesus.

Born in Normandy, France in 1601, John was educated by Jesuits at Caen. This training helped prepare him to become a priest and to join a religious community, the Oratorians. Using his outstanding gifts as preacher and confessor, he traveled from parish to parish giving missions, which are like parish renewals. His travels convinced him that parish priests needed support in becoming men of prayer and action. He held frequent conferences for them in which he outlined their duties as shepherds of God's people. Later John started his own society of priests called the Congregation of Jesus and Mary. The members were dedicated to promoting good seminary training, which would form Christlike priests for the parishes.

The love that impelled Jesus to reach out to the crippled, the abandoned, and the rejected also impelled John to feel compassion for the women and young girls who were trying to escape from a life of prostitution. He wanted a place for them to live, a refuge from their former way of life. To serve the women in these refuges, he established a society of religious women called the Congregation of Our Lady of the Refuge. Through the years, this congregation has expanded, now serving the needs of delinquent girls around the world.

St. John Eudes has been called the Apostle of the Sacred Heart because he revived this devotion through his writings, his preaching, and his own life of loving service. He died in France in 1680.

SUGGESTIONS

1. Because John appreciated the great love of Jesus for everyone, he promoted devotion to the Sacred Heart of Jesus. Review with the students First Friday Devotions. Also make this short prayer part of the daily class prayer.

   Jesus, King and Center of all hearts, Rule supreme in our classroom and in every heart.

2. When John worked to bring prostitutes and other outcast women back to God, he was following the example of Jesus. In Jesus' time, the Jews believed that God scorned these women, but in His dealings with them Jesus showed how loved they were. Have the students read the following passages: John 4:5-26, 39-42; John 8:1-11; Luke 7:36-50; and then direct them to answer these questions in their journals.

   1) How did Jesus and the woman meet?

   2) How did Jesus treat the woman?

   3) How did the woman react to Jesus?

3. Early in his career, John gave missions encouraging people to turn from a life of sin and adopt a life of virtue, according to God's plan. Put the following scrambled words on the board. Then have the students list the seven capital sins on their papers, unscramble the virtues on the board, and match each virtue with its opposite sin.

   Virtues

YTSIROGEEN	TATISCHY
METREPECNA	NLPCSDIIIE
MILIUHYT	ELTSSENNEG
SINDFREIHP	

These are the answers:
pride — humility
covetousness (greed) — generosity
lust — chastity
envy — friendship
gluttony — temperance
anger — gentleness
sloth (laziness) — discipline

4. St. Maria Euphrasia Pelletier entered the Congregation of Our Lady of the Refuge in 1814 and eventually started a new branch called Sisters of Our Lady of Charity of the Good Shepherd. These sisters have helped many delinquent girls to get a fresh start in life by believing in their own God-given value. Mother Euphrasia, as she is called, also started a group of contemplative religious dedicated to reparation for sins. Former prostitutes who wanted to follow Christ in religious life were among those who could join this community. Formerly called the Sister Magdalens, the community is now called the Contemplatives of the Cross. Have interested students research these communities or the Congregation of Jesus and Mary and report their findings to the class.

5. The Apostleship of Prayer is a spiritual society dedicated to the Sacred Heart of Jesus. The association was begun by a Jesuit in France in 1844 and has spread throughout the world under the direction of the Jesuits. The members offer their daily prayers, works, sufferings, and joys to God to make up for their sins and the sins of all people. Have the students explain in their own words the ideas contained in the Morning Offering from the Apostleship of Prayer. Then have the students memorize the prayer by saying it regularly and thoughtfully.

MORNING OFFERING

O Jesus, through the Immaculate Heart of Mary, I offer You my prayers, works, joys, and sufferings of this day in union with the Holy Sacrifice of the Mass throughout the world. I offer them for all the intentions of Your Sacred Heart: the salvation of souls, reparation for sin, the reunion of all Christians. I offer them for the intentions of our bishops and of all Apostles of Prayer, and in particular for those recommended by our Holy Father this month.

AUGUST 20: BERNARD OF CLAIRVAUX

Parents are often surprised by their children. Bernard's wealthy parents were no exception. At the age of 22, Bernard decided to become a monk. The most likely choice for him was to enter the monastery at Cluny. The Benedictine monks there had a reputation for holiness, and the place was alive with young, enthusiastic men. Instead Bernard chose to enter a poor, crumbling monastery called Citeaux, which was only a few miles from his home. Those monks, most of whom were elderly, faithfully followed the Holy Rule of St. Benedict, as did the monks at Cluny. However the monks at Citeaux lived a stricter life of prayer, silence, and penance. Bernard was so eager about his choice that, by the time he left home, thirty-one other men decided to enter with him. Among these potential monks were four of his brothers, his uncle, and his cousin.

All these new people brought vitality to Citeaux. Within three years, the place was flourishing, and Bernard was sent to start a new monastery in a place that came to be named Clairvaux. As abbot, Bernard wanted to establish a life-style opposite to the worldly, powerful ways of the rich. In that first year he was very strict about meals (sometimes the only food was barley bread and boiled beech leaves), work, prayers, and sleep. Then he himself became sick, and through his illness, he learned to be more gentle and understanding about the human needs of the monks. After that, the monastery thrived.

During his busy years as abbot, Bernard often longed for solitude and time to live a simple, monk's life. However, almost daily he received visitors and letters from people asking for advice and help. He gave much time and effort to each request, whether it came from a king, a bishop, or a poor peasant. Because of his ability to settle disputes, Bernard was also called on to travel to various countries to give advice on important affairs of Church and of government. He was fearless in giving his opinion and also highly respected for his insight into very difficult problems.

One serious matter arose in 1130, when the newly elected Pope Innocent II faced the rising popularity of an antipope named Anacletus. The latter's claim to be pope threatened to split the Church in a schism. Bernard traveled to various countries asking government and Church leaders to support the true pope. Finally Anacletus lost his power and Innocent II returned as official bishop of Rome.

When Bernard was chosen as an official preacher for the Second Crusade, he inspired many soldiers and pilgrims to join the cause for Christ. However, the Crusade failed because of the cruelty and greed of some of those who joined the group, and Bernard was unjustly blamed for the failure.

In 1153 Bernard became very ill and died. His varied accomplishments have given him many titles. For his reform of monastic life at Citeaux and Clairvaux, he is known as the founder of the Cistercian Order. For all the good advice he gave and for his inspiring preaching, he has been called the "honey-tongued teacher." Because he was an influential figure in government and Church matters, he is known as "the man of the twelfth century." He has been named a Doctor of the Church for his many writings on the love of God, on Scripture, on the spiritual life, and on Mary.

SUGGESTIONS

1. After Bernard had left home, his father and his younger brother also decided to be monks. Have the students write a paragraph about a time when someone in their own family gave a good example, and other family members were inspired to do good acts. Write a paragraph to share with the class and allow volunteers to share theirs as well.

2. The monastery of Clairvaux came to be known as the "monastery of light." Bernard wanted the monks to shine as the light of Christ in a dark world. Have the students memorize the Beatitudes, which reflect the happiness of life according to God's values.

3. Direct interested students to research how these orders are related: Benedictines, Cistercians, Trappists. Have the students find out if there are any monasteries of these religious in the locality.

4. Bernard loved the Scripture and taught that we can reach God by studying Christ's life in the New Testament. Explain to the students that each gospel writer presents Jesus from a different point of view. Divide the class into four groups. Direct group one to find five examples from Matthew's gospel that show that Jesus is a teacher. Direct group two to find five examples from Mark's gospel that show Jesus' sufferings. Direct group three to find five examples from Luke's gospel that show Jesus as a loving savior reaching out to the poor, to women, to the Gentiles. Have group four count the number of times that the terms *Son, Son of the Father, Son of God,* or *only Son of God* are used in John's gospel in referring to Christ. As the evangelist explains in his first conclusion, "These are recorded so that you may believe that Jesus is the Christ, the Son of God and that believing this you may have life through his name" (John 20:31).

5. Bernard is often pictured with a beehive as an emblem, and he has been chosen by beekeepers as a patron. Some candlemakers have also chosen Bernard as patron. Discuss with the students why such associations are fitting for St. Bernard. The students could also consider the idea of choosing patrons for yearbooks, school plays, and other activities. Have a student look up the definition of *patron* and *patroness* in the dictionary. Then direct pairs of students to name five saints they know and decide on a group of people, a career, or an institution for which each saint might be chosen as patron.

AUGUST 21: PIUS X

"I was born poor, I lived poor, I will die poor." These words were part of the will that Pope Pius X left at his death on August 20, 1914.

He was born Giuseppe Melchiorre Sarto, the second of ten children. His father was a poor parish clerk in the village of Riese, Italy, and his mother worked as a seamstress. At eleven, Giuseppe received a place at the high school. Every day he walked the five miles to school and back. Then at the age of fifteen, he began attending the local seminary. When his father died, Giuseppe wanted to leave school, come home, and help with the family. He realized that his mother would face even greater poverty than she had when his father was alive. However, his mother would not let him give up studying for the priesthood.

In 1858 he was ordained, and he worked as a parish priest for the next seventeen years. He believed his call was to encourage the poor to lead strong Christian lives and to help them overcome financial problems. But the bishop had other ideas. Recognizing his gifts and talents, the bishop named Giuseppe spiritual director of the major seminary and chancellor of the diocese. Later, he became a bishop and then a cardinal.

In 1903, in a surprising turn of events, this little-known cardinal was elected by a ballot of fifty out of sixty-two votes to become Pope Pius X. He took his motto, "restore all things in Christ," from Paul's letter to the Ephesians. As pope he tried to fulfill his motto in many ways. He emphasized how important the Eucharist is in the life of all Christians and recommended frequent Mass and even daily Communion. He directed that children as young as seven years, who have reached the age of reason, should be allowed to receive Jesus in the Eucharist. He initiated important changes in Church music and public worship. To promote the study of Scripture, he began a biblical institute. He gave the first official impetus and pastoral direction to the modern liturgical renewal, which flowered in the Vatican II Council's "Constitution on the Sacred Liturgy" and in the subsequent reforms.

Pope Pius X believed that real order and peace among individuals, groups, and nations could be achieved only through social justice and charity. He sponsored and sheltered refugees with his own resources. He wrote an encyclical on June 7, 1912, encouraging the Latin American bishops to make efforts to improve the treatment of Indians working on plantations. Tirelessly he worked to stop the world from going to war. August 4, 1914, was the eleventh anniversary of his becoming pope. At this time, Europe entered World War I. Pius X was heartbroken, saying, "I would gladly give my life to save my poor children from this ghastly scourge." Just a few weeks after the war started, Pope Pius X died. All his life he had been poor. Now having used up his money to help the poor, he really did die poor. He commonly used the expression: "I am a poor man and Jesus Christ is all."

SUGGESTIONS

1. Pope Pius X was greatly concerned about world peace, as all his successors have been. Discuss with the students the popes' and bishops' stand on world peace. Have them suggest some ways in which they can help to promote world peace.

2. Pope Pius X is called the "Pope of the Eucharist." Tell the students to design posters encouraging the Christian faithful to receive Jesus in the Eucharist at each eucharistic liturgy they attend. Have the students also encourage reverence and prayerful preparation in their posters. They might wish to use lines from a eucharistic song or prayer and symbols of the Eucharist. Display these posters in the school hall or in church.

3. Pope Pius X was interested in public worship. Have the students make a flowchart to show how the liturgical seasons follow in the Church year. Tell them to include Advent, Christmas, Epiphany, Ordinary Time, Lent, Easter Triduum, Easter, Time after Easter, and Season of Ordinary Time after Pentecost.

4. Pope Pius X chose a line from Scripture as his motto for his papacy. Have the students think of a line from Scripture or look through the letters of the New Testament for a motto which they could adopt in their own lives. Direct them to print this motto in their journals and design the page.

5. The pope had a great love and appreciation for the psalms of the Old Testament. He wished that in the *Liturgy of the Hours*, all the psalms could be prayed aloud within a week. Choose a psalm and have the students practice it in choric speech. A presentation of Psalm 100 in choric speech is given here. Divide the class into sides and choose four speakers. You may wish to use the following arrangement:

PSALM 100

Side 1
   Acclaim Yahweh, all the earth,
Side 2
   serve Yahweh gladly,
All
   come into his presence with songs of joy!
All
   Know that he, Yahweh, is God,
Speaker 1
   he made us

Speaker 1, 2
and we belong to him,

Speaker 1, 2, 3, 4
we are his people,

All
the flock he pastures.

Girls
Walk through his porticos giving thanks,

All
enter his courts praising him,

Boys
give thanks to him, bless his name!

Side 1
Yes, Yahweh is good,

Side 2
his love is everlasting,

All
his faithfulness endures from age to age.

AUGUST 22: QUEENSHIP OF MARY

In 1954, Pope Pius XII focused the attention of the whole Church on Mary when he declared a feast day honoring her queenship. The idea of Mary's royalty is already expressed within the Feast of the Assumption on August 15. The title of queen is one of the oldest titles given to Mary in Christian tradition. When Elizabeth spoke of Mary as "the mother of my Lord" (Luke 1:43), she was using the words that mean "queen-mother" in the Old Testament, according to the gospel of Luke.

Jesus is the Lord and King of heaven and earth. So Mary, who was chosen by the Father, was filled with the Holy Spirit, and was made the mother of Christ, can be considered queen. Like a queen, she stood at the cross on Calvary, supporting her kingly Son's sacrifice with her love, faith, and obedience.

Mary's power as queen is manifested in the tenderness of a loving mother who cares for her children. St. Bernard (feast August 20), who had a great devotion to Mary, often wrote books and sermons inspiring his listeners to turn to her. Here is something he wrote:

> In dangers, in doubts, in difficulties, think of Mary, call upon Mary . . . with her for guide, you shall never go astray; while invoking her, you shall never lose heart; so long as she is in your mind, you are safe from deception; while she holds your hand, you cannot fall; under her protection you have nothing to fear . . . .

SUGGESTIONS

1. Direct each student to cut out a crown (6″ x 10″) from construction paper. On the crowns, have the students neatly print a title of Mary that begins "Mary, Queen of _____." The students may create their own titles or choose titles given in this excerpt from the Litany of Loreto:

   Queen of Angels
   Queen of Patriarchs
   Queen of Prophets
   Queen of Apostles
   Queen of Martyrs
   Queen of Confessors
   Queen of Virgins
   Queen of All Saints
   Queen Conceived without Original Sin
   Queen Assumed into Heaven
   Queen of the Most Holy Rosary
   Queen of Peace

2. Have the students listen to the following words of Mary recorded in Scripture. Then have them identify to whom she is speaking, in what place she is speaking, and what event is happening.

   "Let what you have said be done to me." *Luke 1:38*
   (Angel Gabriel; Nazareth; Annunciation)

   "My soul proclaims the greatness of the Lord." *Luke 1:46*
   (Elizabeth; Judah; visit)

   "See how worried your father and I have been, looking for you." *Luke 2:48*
   (Jesus; Jerusalem; finding in the Temple)

   "They have no wine." *John 2:3*
   (Jesus; Cana; wedding)

   "Do whatever he tells you." *John 2:5*
   (servants; Cana; wedding)

3. Encourage the students to do a special act of kindness today for a person who has Mary or a form of Mary for a name.

4. Tell the students the story of Knute Rockne, who was one of the greatest college football coaches and a convert to Catholicism. Rockne, who made the forward pass popular, was well known for giving Notre Dame University football teams the ideals of sportsmanship and fortitude. He was killed in a plane accident on March 31, 1931, while flying over Kansas. When the rescuers found his body, he had a rosary still clutched in his hand. Have interested students learn more about this man and his appreciation for Mary and for the Catholic faith.

5. Mary has been given the title of Queen of Peace. Have the students discuss the reasons why this title is so important at the present time. Then remind them that in various appearances, such as at Fatima, Our Lady has reminded Christians to pray and to make sacrifices for world peace. Direct each student to write an original petition related to world peace. Then lead the class in a litany for peace. Use this response: "Queen of Peace, lead us to peace."

AUGUST 23: ROSE OF LIMA

Some saints have traveled around the world. Rose of Lima became a saint without ever leaving her backyard.

Gaspar de Flores and his wife, Maria de Olivia, were very proud of their little daughter, born on April 20, 1586. On Pentecost of that year, she was baptized Isabel de Flores, named after an aunt who was also her godmother. One day a household maid, amazed at the great beauty of the tiny baby, exclaimed that she looked just like a rose. Isabel's mother agreed and declared firmly that this child would be called "Rose" from then on. At the age of fourteen, she was confirmed, taking Rose as her Confirmation name.

Through her childhood and youth, Rose did not have the opportunity to attend school. She stayed at home and worked in the garden, growing a variety of beautiful flowers. Rose delighted in the butterflies, birds, and flowers that surrounded her, because they reminded her of God's beauty. She also learned to embroider on silk and create designs, usually of flowers.

Rose took St. Catherine of Siena as the model for her life. Even as a child, she wanted to live only for Jesus. She looked for difficult things to do to show her love for Him. She also built a prayer hut for herself in the backyard so she could have a place to be alone and pray. Then her parents ran into financial difficulties, and Rose found herself facing a real conflict. She had planned to enter a convent, become a sister, and live a life of vowed chastity. Her parents wanted her to marry so that they could get financial help from her husband. Finally Rose found an answer to this problem. To help her parents, she stayed home and sold her needlework and the flowers that she raised in the garden. At the same time, she joined the Third Order of St. Dominic. She wore the white habit and black veil of the Dominican sisters. She spent many more hours a day in her prayer hut. Eventually she began to live in that hut. But her love for God also led her to love the poor. In her parents' home, she set up one room as a free medical clinic for poor children and elderly people who were ill. This free service became the beginning of social service in Peru.

In the last years of her life, Rose became very ill, and she died on August 24, 1617. She was widely known and loved by both rich and poor. Huge crowds gathered when they heard about her death. Finally, because of the public commotion, her body had to be buried privately in the cloistered part of St. Dominic's Church.

SUGGESTIONS

1. Rose saw God's beauty in nature and often put fresh roses around her veil to please her mother. If fresh flowers are available in local gardens, bring some to class and display them for the day in honor of St. Rose. Or bring a potted plant to keep in the classroom.

2. Rose was able to resolve the conflict between responsibility to her family and her call to live a life of prayer and solitude. Have the students think of a time in their lives when two responsibilities seemed to contradict each other. For example, they may have had to babysit for a neighbor and clean their rooms on the same Saturday morning. Or they may have had homework and baseball practice on the same evening. Have them discuss ways in which they can resolve these conflicts. Guide them to find creative ways to do what God wills.

3. In Rose's time there were hospitals and medical services. One hospital even bordered on her family's property. But Rose insisted that the people offer free medical help for the poor. Through such charity, Rose made the people of the city aware of the needs of the poor. Have the students bring in articles from magazines or newspapers that show how organizations such as Catholic Relief Services and Catholic Charities are drawing attention to the needs of the poor.

4. Once a theology professor came to question Rose about the truths of the Catholic faith. Rose was not afraid, even though she had never had formal religious instruction. She gave him clear and direct answers based on her many hours of prayer and on the sermons she heard when she participated in Mass. Have the students consider themselves in a similar situation. How would they face the questioner? Then direct them to write an imaginary dialogue in which the professor asks them five questions about their Catholic faith and they answer the questions clearly and directly. Allow volunteers to read their dialogues to the class.

5. Rose joined the Third Order of St. Dominic. Invite someone from a third order to speak to the class about the role of third orders in the Church.

AUGUST 24: BARTHOLOMEW

Bartholomew is mentioned by name only four times in the whole New Testament. In the gospels of Matthew and Luke, he is one of the twelve apostles called by Jesus. Mark's gospel states that Bartholomew is one of the twelve apostles appointed to be Jesus' companions, to preach, and to cast out devils. In the Acts of the Apostles, the people who are in the upper room in Jerusalem waiting for the Holy Spirit to come are listed. Bartholomew is in the list of apostles who are waiting there with several women, including Mary, Jesus's mother. Of the four evangelists, John alone does not mention Bartholomew by name. John does, however, list a person named

Nathanael as an apostle. Some scholars feel that Bartholomew and Nathanael are two names for the same person. If this is the case, then John's gospel gives us a detailed account of Nathanael's (also Bartholomew's) first meeting with Jesus.

According to this report, Philip was so excited about meeting Jesus that he asked his friend Nathanael to come to meet Him also. Nathanael, who was from Cana, was scornful when he heard that Jesus was from Nazareth. He thought that Nazareth was unimportant and that nothing good could be produced there. Philip did not argue. Arguments don't bring people to Christ. Meeting Christ and getting to know Him is the way that people learn to love and follow Him. So Philip told Nathanael to come and see for himself.

On seeing Nathanael, Jesus recognized a person who was not proud, prejudiced, or scheming. Jesus told him that he was a man without deceit in his heart. "How could Jesus make a snap decision about my personality?" Nathanael must have thought. But Jesus showed that He had a supernatural knowledge about people and things. When Nathanael realized that Jesus knew him in a very deep way, he began to praise Jesus as the real Messiah.

Even if Nathanael and Bartholomew are not the same person, we still know that Bartholomew was one of the twelve apostles. Whenever the twelve were assembled for some event, he was present also.

Shortly after Pentecost, Bartholomew became a missionary in a foreign land. Armenians honor him as the apostle of their country.

SUGGESTIONS

1. Divide the class into three groups. Give each group three of the following Scripture references from the Gospel of John: 2:1-10; 2:13-22; 4:46-54; 5:1-9; 6:5-15; 9:1-7; 12:1-8; 12:12-17; 20:24-29; 21:1-14. Allow the students five or ten minutes to plan a pantomime for all three of their stories. Then have each group present its pantomimes, one at a time, while the rest of the class tries to guess the story.

2. As an apostle, Bartholomew was sent to evangelize others, to bring them the Good News of Jesus. He is believed to have been a foreign missionary. Have the students learn this prayer for the poor of the missions.

> The poor of the Missions are not abandoned, Lord. They are just waiting. Waiting for us who know You to know them too: to see You in them, to love You in them, to call them brother and sister, to share our faith with them. The poor of the Missions are not abandoned, Lord. They are just waiting. Help me to do my part so that they need not wait too long.

Then have the students take up a mission collection.

3. Have students read aloud Acts 5:34-39. Discuss with the class how the Church has lasted through these past two thousand years and how it can be traced back to Jesus and the apostles. Finally, to deepen the students' awareness of their bond with the past, pray the Apostles' Creed with them.

4. Direct the students to create models of various scenes from the Acts of the Apostles. Have them make figures out of colored pipe cleaners. Then have them design scenery and props out of scraps of paper and material.

5. Have the students look up the occasions when Bartholomew is mentioned in the Scriptures: Matthew 10:3; Mark 3:18; Luke 6:14; Acts of the Apostles 1:13. Then distribute small slips of paper to each student. Direct the students to go through the New Testament and find clues about each of the apostles. Have them write one clue on each slip of paper in the following way: "I am the apostle who _____." Collect the slips and put them in a box or envelope. Then have students draw a slip, read the clue, and name the apostle who fits the clue, Finally, encourage the students to memorize the names of the twelve apostles.

AUGUST 25: LOUIS OF FRANCE

A husband, a father, a soldier, a king, a peacemaker, a saint — who fits all these roles? Louis IX, King of France.

When King Louis VIII and Blanche of Castille married, they expected one of their children to become the next king of France. Of the twelve children they had, it was Louis, born on April 25, 1214, who succeeded his father.

Louis became king of France in 1226, at the age of twelve. However, his mother made most of the important decisions for the kingdom until her death. In 1234 he married Marguerite of Provence and with her had ten children. In 1244, King Louis organized a Crusade to the Holy Land. Though the Crusade failed, many soldiers remembered Louis' example. They remembered how he chose to share all the dangers and hardships of an ordinary soldier when, as the king-commander of the troops, he could have given himself privileges and had an easier time of it. They recalled how each decision he made was based on the moral principle of justice. But Louis' efforts to achieve justice, mercy, and peace can best be seen in the way he ruled France from 1254 to 1270.

As king, Louis had a great love for God and for the individuals in his kingdom. He built a chapel in Paris and an abbey in Royaumont. He supported the Cistercians, the Franciscans, and the Dominicans, religious orders serving the French people. He also built hospitals and encouraged learning. He reformed some of the social structures that were promoting injustice. His reforms helped the legal system in France to provide fair laws and just trials.

Until he died, Louis tried to follow the advice that he gave to his son, the future king of France:

> Dear Son, let your heart be gentle, compassionate, and charitable toward the poor, the feeble, the unfortunate, toward everyone you think to be suffering in mind or in body . . . Maintain the good customs of your kingdom, suppress those which are bad. Do not covet your people's goods, and do not oppress them with duties or taxes.
>
> (St. Louis' "Testament")

SUGGESTIONS

1. Besides ruling France, Louis was the father of ten children. Have the students discuss the responsibilities fathers have toward their families. Then have the students write letters to their fathers, expressing appreciation for all that their fathers have given them.

2. In France Louis promoted peace. Ask the students to brainstorm for various definitions of peace. Then have a student print the words PEACE IS . . . at the top of a long piece of shelf paper. Have each student contribute one definition to the list. Post the list and encourage the students to continue to add ideas as they find them.

3. Louis had a great interest in serving the physical, intellectual, and social needs of the people of France. Have the students resolve to do a kind act for someone who cannot return the kindness.

4. Louis tried to help individual people, and he also worked to make the structures of society more just. Have the students discuss how each of the following unjust situations could be changed to a just situation:

   • a system where imported products are inexpensive because factory workers in the importing country are getting a very low wage.

   • a system where fruits and vegetables are less expensive because migrant workers live in subhuman conditions.

   • a system in which Native Americans have suffered by losing their land and having their treaties broken.

5. As king, Louis dealt with issues of war and peace on an international level. As a parent, Louis was concerned that his children live peacefully together. Have the students choose one of the following sentences as a topic sentence and write a paragraph on family peace. Then have volunteers read their compositions to the class.

   Brothers and sisters should get along better than people who are unrelated.

   Brothers and sisters have a harder time apologizing to each other than to other people.

AUGUST 25: JOSEPH OF CALASANZ

"Educating poor children is a terrible idea! Joseph, are you crazy?"

"No, I'm not, Franco. This is the time to reach them . . . while they are young. Their heavenly Father loves them greatly. Surely we can help them to reach eternal life."

"Oh, so you plan to give them only religious instruction? Is that it?"

"Franco, this is an opportunity to develop the whole person — body and soul. We can teach them all subjects."

"But our society will fall apart. Once the poor have an education, once they see how the government works, once they get better skills and new ideas . . . Can't you see the danger, Joseph?"

"What I see is that we can both protect them from the evil of which they are now victims and gradually attract them to doing good."

"You are being so unreasonable, Joseph. No one offers free education to anyone, much less to poor children."

"Franco, truth is a free gift from God. Everyone has a right to an education. Open your heart to the poor, Franco. God has opened His heart to them."

Born in Spain on September 11, 1556, Joseph grew up in a wealthy family. While he was working as a tutor in Rome, he began to minister to many people suffering from plague and floods. Some considered him an apostle to the poor. He was especially troubled about the children of the poor. These young ones were growing up in violent and rough surroundings with no hope for a good future or for Christian training. So Joseph opened free schools in Europe. Getting good teachers who would be loving and patient with the students became more difficult as the number of students increased. First Pope Clement VIII and then his successor, Pope Paul V, encouraged Joseph to form a religious order of men who could staff the schools. Joseph envisioned these religious men as coworkers with the Lord in the service of education. More and more schools were opened. At this time, Joseph was elected the head of the Clerks Regular of the Religious Schools (also called the Piarists), the order he had founded. Then began intensive attacks both from without and from within the order. When students from private schools switched to the free schools, their former teachers were angry at the loss of funds and the shrinking enrollments. Many rich people were threatened by the thought that poor people were learning new ideas. These powerful people tried to stop the free schools.

Even worse, first one member and then another of his own order began to campaign against him. Joseph soon found himself surrounded by prejudice and misunderstanding. Unfortunately these men so convinced the pope that something might be wrong within the order that, at the age of 86, Joseph was arrested and had to stand trial before the Holy Office. As a result of this trial, Joseph's work was stopped and the members of his order became part of the regular diocese. In spite of all this, Joseph continued to respect and protect his persecutors from the angry comments of others. He never lost hope that one day his religious order would be restored and poor children would be served through its members. On August 25, 1648, Joseph died in Rome, without ever seeing his hope fulfilled. Twenty years later, Pope Clement IX completely restored the order, which continues to our present day.

❋ ❋ ❋ ❋ ❋ ❋ ❋ ❋ ❋ ❋ ❋ ❋ ❋ ❋ ❋ ❋ ❋ ❋ ❋ ❋

SUGGESTIONS

1. Joseph founded an order of priests dedicated to the work of educating poor children. John Baptiste de la Salle founded an order with the same ministry. Have the students compare the lives of these two saints and the societies in which they lived.

2. Joseph highly valued dedicated teachers who had zeal for their work. Have the students work on a project to give recognition to the teachers in the school. Divide the class into three crews. Have the photo crew take pictures of each teacher. Have the news crew interview each teacher and write a short summary of his or her background. Finally, have the publicity crew make a display of the photos and summaries.

3. Joseph suffered greatly from the lies of those who ruined his reputation. Ask the students to define the words *detraction* and *slander* and explain the effects these actions have, both on the person who is guilty of them and on the person who is victim of them. Then have the students discuss the damage done by listening to gossip. After the discussion, let them reflect quietly on the following questions:

   • In the past, have I damaged people's reputations by careless or critical words? Whose reputation have I hurt?

   • What have I done to repair the damage or make up for it?

Have the students pray quietly for God's forgiveness. Direct them to ask Him to give special help and grace to those people whom they may have hurt. Finally encourage them to speak and act kindly toward these persons.

4. At times Joseph helped others by telling them their weaknesses and encouraging them to change their behavior. Direct the students to list the common reactions some people have when they are told about one of their faults. Then tell the students to list the benefits that can come from having someone point out (in a kind and tactful way) one of their weaknesses. In their journals, have them record an occasion when someone pointed out one of their weaknesses. Tell them to write down their reaction and the result.

5. Joseph dedicated his whole life to Catholic education. Have the students discuss the value of Catholic schools. Allow them to work in pairs to create short radio commercials for Catholic education. Have them present these commercials to other classes or over the public address system to the school as a whole.

6. Joseph was deeply concerned about the well-being of poor children. Have the students make scrapbooks, original storybooks, or toys, and donate them to a day-care center, children's hospital, or children's home.

AUGUST 27: MONICA

Through her life, Monica shows us how faithfully God answers prayers. She was born in Tagaste, Numidia, in Africa, around 322. As a child she lived with her family, but she and her sisters were raised by an elderly servant. This wise woman had also raised Monica's father when he was a little child.

As a young girl, Monica had a shocking experience. According to the custom of the time, her parents would ask her to bring up wine from the cellar for them. Once Monica took a little sip of the wine before she brought it up. After that, she gradually began to drink just a little more each day. She thought no one knew about her secret action. Then, one day, Monica quarreled with the servant who used to accompany her to the cellar. The angry servant accused Monica of drinking too much. Young Monica was stunned. She realized that the maid, while trying to win a quarrel, had really helped her to face this temptation. She decided at this time to stop drinking, and she did stop. Overcoming this weakness helped Monica become a caring wife and mother.

When she was old enough, Monica was married to a pagan official named Patricius. They had at least three children: Navigius, Perpetua, and Augustine, who became a saint. Patricius was a man with a terrible temper. Gradually Monica learned to be patient and wait for the right moment to discuss matters with him or to explain her actions. By her constant forgiveness and love, she hoped to draw her husband to Christ. Before he died, Patricius was baptized a Christian! Because she and her husband seemed to get along so well, other wives with marriage problems asked Monica for advice. In this way she often used her painful experiences to help others.

Because of ugly rumors spread by unhappy servants, Monica's mother-in-law turned against her during the early part of her marriage. Using the same patient forgiveness, Monica was able to win her cooperation.

Another source of worry for her was her son, Augustine. He seemed so unsettled, so pagan, so wild. He was not yet baptized and was living an immoral life. Monica tried to penetrate the barrier that seemed to exist between her and her teenage son. She once attempted a dangerous ocean voyage in order to advise him. She prayed and fasted persistently for him. She even tried to convince the local bishop to speak to her son. But the bishop told Monica, "Not yet, he is not ready and would not listen." But he did promise her, "Surely the son of so many tears will not perish."

Clinging to these comforting words, Monica never gave up, but continued to pray and sacrifice year after year. Slowly, Augustine did change. With the help of the Holy Spirit, He began to realize that God loved him. When he finally gained courage to be baptized, his mother was one of the first persons he told, for she was with him in Milan at the time. In the fall of 387, after his baptism, Augustine planned to return to Tagaste with his mother, but she died at Ostia where they were waiting to embark for Africa. Their last conversation together was a beautiful sharing of longing for heaven. Monica is an example for all mothers who want their families to enjoy eternal life in Christ.

SUGGESTIONS

1. Have the students make thank-you cards or paper corsages for the mothers who work in or for the school. Direct the students to present these gifts with a reference to the feast of St. Monica.

2. Have the students work in groups to design a filmstrip entitled "Famous Women in the Church." Encourage them to use the *Saints and Feast Days* book, their textbooks, or current books and magazines for research. Direct the students to compose and tape a commentary to accompany the filmstrip. Have them select at least seven women, including two or three from the twentieth century.

3. Monica was raised by an elderly servant, who was highly respected by Monica's parents. This aged woman made a great impact on Monica's life. Let the students plan a party for residents in a nearby home for the elderly. Allow them to decide on a theme, make decorations, and plan entertainment. They should think up activities that they and the senior citizens can do together.

4. As a wife and mother, Monica was probably concerned about family meals. Have the students write the Before and After Meal Prayers from memory. Then encourage them to pray these prayers or another prayer before and after each meal.

5. Have the students write letters of appreciation to their mothers on the Feast of St. Monica. Encourage them to contribute to class prayers by offering spontaneous prayers for their mothers and all mothers.

AUGUST 28: AUGUSTINE

Have you ever tried to write the story of your life — your autobiography? Many people have — entertainers, political leaders, sports figures, saints. In one of the most famous autobiographies, *Confessions*, Augustine of Hippo tells the story of his struggle to find God.

Born on November 13, 354, Augustine grew up in Tagaste, Numidia, in Africa. To his pagan father, Patricius, and his Christian mother, Monica, he appeared a very intelligent but restless child. He spent his teen years as a student, but he put all his energy into finding the meaning of real love and of life. He tried wild parties, premarital sex, the study of philosophy, and a popular religious heresy called Manichaeism, but none of these satisfied him.

After he finished school, he was first a speech teacher in Rome and then a professor in Milan. In Milan he often listened to the sermons of St. Ambrose, the local bishop. Through these homilies, Augustine first learned to read the Scriptures prayerfully. Excited by this new discovery, he enrolled as a catechumen in the Catholic Church. However, he feared that he was too weak to follow Christ faithfully. And he really could not yet trust in God's great power and love for him. So he wavered back and forth about being baptized.

Then he received another jolt from God. One day, while he was praying to be freed from the trap of his sins, Augustine heard a voice like that of a child chanting repeatedly, "Take up and read. Take up and read." Augustine opened the Bible and read the first chapter his eyes fell upon. "Let us live decently as people do in the daytime: no drunken orgies, no promiscuity or licentiousness, and no wrangling or jealousy. Let your armor be the Lord Jesus Christ; forget about satisfying your bodies with all their cravings" (Romans 13:13-14). At that moment Augustine realized the answer to real love and the meaning of life. At the beginning of Lent in 387, he gave his name as a candidate for Baptism. Then on the night of the Easter Vigil, he finally entered into the dying with Christ and rose to new life in Him.

As a newly baptized Christian, Augustine decided to return to his birthplace to begin a new way of life. With his mother Monica, who had been visiting him in Milan at the time, he made arrangements for the trip. While they were waiting at Ostia to embark for Africa, Monica died, satisfied that her greatest desires for her son had been fulfilled. The day before her death, Monica and Augustine experienced some wonderful hours of prayerful conversation together. After his mother's death, Augustine mourned deeply for her and thanked God for the graces she had won for him. Eventually, he reached Tagaste, his home, and gave away all he had. Then he lived a quiet prayerful life with a group of friends.

However, his life soon changed. While visiting in the city of Hippo in 391, Augustine stopped to listen to the local bishop, Valerius. He was preaching on the shortage of priests in the Church. Suddenly a few people in the crowd shouted, "Let Augustine be our priest!" Augustine would have preferred to return to his life of quiet prayer, but the excited crowd persisted. Valerius was very happy about the way God showed His will for Augustine and soon ordained him as a priest. In 396, when Valerius died, Augustine became the new bishop of Hippo. He greatly loved the land and the people. In fact, he was interested in everything the people did and in every aspect of their lives. He worked to administer the diocese, counteract the false religious teachings that were popular in Africa, protect the people from corrupt government officials and foreign invaders, and care for the sick, the poor, and those in prison. During this busy time, Augustine gained overwhelming insight into how much God really loved and cared for him. His many sermons, letters, and books reflect the ever-deepening love he felt for God in return. He summed up his long search for God in the famous words: "You have made us, O God, for yourself, and our hearts shall find no rest until they rest with you."

In the spring of 430, a group of Vandals invaded the African province, causing destruction and violence. Many people panicked because it seemed that the whole world was being destroyed. For the next three months, the elderly Augustine continued to inspire Christian hope in his people, as he had done for the past thirty-four years. Not a detail of his life-style changed. He continued to pray much, to help the poor, to write the truth, and to preach the Gospel. He reminded the people that they belonged to Christ and no Vandal could rob them of true life. On August 28, 430, Augustine died of a high fever. His influence in the Church continues to this day.

SUGGESTIONS

1. Augustine's whole life was the searching and finding of the God of love. In their journals, have the students answer the following questions about their own lives:
   - When you were a small child, what did you think about God? What was Jesus like for you?
   - How do you see God now? Has your image of Jesus changed? How?
   - What do you hope for your friendship with God in the future?

2. Augustine was greatly influenced by listening to the sermons of Ambrose. Have the students recall a homily they have heard that impressed them. Then tell them to listen carefully to the homily at the next Sunday liturgy and report on the ideas in the next class.

3. Direct the students to write short autobiographies. They may wish to interview their parents for information about their earliest days. Encourage them to add anecdotes and photographs.

4. Previous to Augustine's experience of opening the Bible and reading Romans 13:13-14, he had heard the story of the conversion of St. Anthony of Egypt. Anthony happened to be in church one day and heard the Gospel reading of the rich young man. When Anthony heard the words from Luke 18:22-23, he went and sold all he had and became a monk. Just like Augustine later, Anthony felt that the words of Scripture applied directly to his own life. Have the students spend five minutes reading a passage from the New Testament silently. Then have them write in their journals how the passage they read could apply to their own lives.

5. Augustine appreciated the arts and education. He spent many years as a student and as a teacher. Have the students participate in a Creative Arts Fair. Direct each student to choose a particular area in the arts: music, crafts, dance, literature, art, or some hobby. Then have them design a project in that area. Set aside one day in which all students bring in their displays and explain their projects.

6. Some of the most touching words Augustine wrote are these: "Late have I loved you, O Beauty ever ancient, ever new, late have I loved you! You were within me, but I was outside, and it was there that I searched for you. You were with me, but I was not with you." Have the students reflect on his words and tell what they mean to them.

AUGUST 29: MARTYRDOM OF JOHN THE BAPTIST

In the Gospel, we read: "Herod Antipas married his brother's wife." For John the Baptist, this event was of major importance. Herod Antipas' decision to take his brother's wife in adultery would eventually lead to

John's imprisonment and death. From various parts of the gospels, let us piece together John's story.

As a youth, John had gone into the desert to fast and pray in order to learn what God wanted him to do with his life. Then one day, following the inspiration of God, he began to walk along the Jordan River bank, preaching to anyone who would listen. Like the prophets of the Old Testament, his message was always the same — turn from your sins, repent, and live for God.

John saw clearly how people can fool themselves into choosing evil actions. Fearlessly he jolted people into facing their own behavior. Sometimes he even pointed out their sins. Always he gave them hope and the challenge to live according to God's law. He did not recommend that people live in the desert or eat wild locusts, as he had done. Rather he told people to be honest and loving, to avoid violence and to do their jobs well. As a sign of their sincere repentance for sin, the people would confess their sins in some manner, and then John would baptize them in the Jordan River.

John was not afraid of wealthy religious leaders or powerful political officials. When Herod Antipas chose adultery, John publicly told him of the evil of taking another man's wife. Herodias, the brother's wife, wanted to kill John because she was so angry with him. But Herod Antipas respected and admired John for his courageous honesty. Unfortunately, however, Herod Antipas was too weak to change his life. Instead he arrested John and chained him in prison so he could no longer influence people against the king.

John's time in prison might have dragged on indefinitely if it had not been for a huge banquet Herod gave on his birthday. As entertainment, Salome, Herodias' daughter, danced for the guests. Herod Antipas was so impressed that he promised to give the young girl whatever she wanted. Her mother persuaded her to ask for only one thing: the head of John the Baptist on a platter.

Herod Antipas was too embarrassed to admit before his guests that he had made a foolish promise. He could not change his mind. Because he was afraid of what others would think, he had John executed and the head brought in on a platter.

Why are good people stopped by those filled with hatred and jealousy? After living his whole life for others, why was John so senselessly killed? By His dying and rising, Jesus gives us the hope that evil will eventually be overcome by good. "Do not be afraid of the sufferings that are coming to you . . . . Even if you have to die, keep faithful, and I will give you the crown of life for your prize" (Revelation 2:10).

SUGGESTIONS

1. Have a student read aloud Luke 3:3-18. Then tell the students to write an imaginary dialogue in which John gives advice to a banker, doctor, busy housewife, factory worker, or a person in another career.

2. John's approach to his mission was that Jesus must increase in the people's estimation and he must decrease. Have some student volunteers look up and read aloud the Scripture passages that tell what John said about Jesus: Mark 1:7-8; John 1:29-34; John 3:28-30. Then have a volunteer read what Jesus said about John: Luke 7:24-30. Finally, have students compose a group summary of the readings and write it on the board.

3. After spending his whole life announcing the Messiah's coming, John spent his last months in prison. Have the students read Mark 6:17-29 and Matthew 11:2-6. Encourage them to imagine how difficult it must have been for John to be chained in prison. Then have them write in their journals a monologue of what John might have thought while he was alone in prison.

4. Duplicate the following acrostic and have the students work it to discover many of the qualities that John the Baptist showed in his life.

MAKE AN ACROSTIC

John the Baptizer had many wonderful characteristics. The scrambled words name some of these good qualities. If you unscramble them, they will fit in the blanks after the initial letters.

STUJ	J _ _ _
BINTEDOE	O _ D _ _ _ _
LEHBUM	H _ _ B _ _
LEBON	N _ _ L _
RUTULHFT	T _ _ _ _ _ F U _
THOSNE	H _ _ _ _ _ T
RESNAET	E A _ _ _ S _
AVERB	B _ _ _ _
TENDAR	A R D _ _ _
UDENTRP	P _ _ D _ _ _ _
TEMATEPRE	T _ _ _ P _ R _ _
NITEPRID	I _ T _ R _ _ _ D
LEASOUZ	Z _ _ _ _ _ _
QUITEABLE	E Q U _ _ _ _ _
TEVERNER	R E _ _ _ _ _ N _

179

The answers are Just, Obedient, Humble, Noble, Truthful, Honest, Earnest, Brave, Ardent, Prudent, Temperate, Intrepid, Zealous, Equitable, and Reverent.

5. Sing with the students a song that refers to John's message of filling in valleys and bringing down mountains. Possible songs are "Exult, You Just Ones," (O'Connor) and "Let the Valleys Be Raised" (Schutte) from *Gentle Night* (NALR) or "Every Valley" (Dufford) from *Neither Silver Nor Gold* (NALR).

BIBLIOGRAPHY FOR SAINTS AND FEAST DAYS

Cunningham, Lawrence. *The Meaning of Saints*. San Francisco: Harper & Row, 1980.

Daughters of St. Paul. *Saints for Young People for Every Day of the Year*. Boston: St. Paul Editions, 1984.

Delaney, John J. *Dictionary of Saints*. Garden City, New York: Doubleday & Company, Inc., 1980.

—— , ed. *Saints for All Seasons*. Garden City, New York: Image Books (A Division of Doubleday & Company, Inc.), 1978.

Dollen, Charles, ed. *Prayer Book of the Saints*. Huntington, Indiana: Our Sunday Visitor, 1984.

Dooley, Kate. *The Saints Book*. Ramsey, New Jersey: Paulist Press, 1981.

Foley, Leonard, O.F.M., ed. *Saint of the Day*. Revised ed. Cincinnati, Ohio: St. Anthony Messenger Press, 1990.

Fox, Fr. Robert J. *Saints and Heroes Speak*. Huntington, Indiana: Our Sunday Visitor, 1977.

Kalberer, Augustine. *Lives of the Saints: Daily Readings*. Chicago: Franciscan Herald Press, 1976.

Langdon, Larry. *Children Celebrate: 39 Plays for Feasts*. Cincinnati, Ohio: St. Anthony Messenger Press, 1993.

Liptak, David Q. *Saints for Our Time*. Waldwick, New Jersey: Arena Lettres, 1976.

—— . *More Saints for Our Time*. Waldwick, New Jersey: Arena Lettres, 1983.

Lodi, Enzo. *Saints of the Roman Calendar*. New York: Alba House, 1992.

McBride, Alfred. *Saints Are People*. Dubuque, Iowa: Wm. C. Brown, 1981.

McGinley, Phyllis. *Saint-Watching*. New York: Doubleday, 1974.

Moran Patrick, R. *Day by Day with the Saints*. Huntington, Indiana: Our Sunday Visitor, 1985.

Nevins, Albert J. *A Saint for Your Name (Boys)* and *A Saint for Your Name (Girls)*. Huntington, Indiana: Our Sunday Visitor, 1980.

Walsh, Michael, ed. *Butler's Lives of the Saints*. Concise edition. New York: HarperCollins, 1991.

Woodward, Kenneth L. *Making Saints: How the Catholic Church Determines Who Becomes a Saint, Who Doesn't, and Why*. New York: Simon & Schuster, 1990.

Saints Kit by Mary Kathleen Glavich, S.N.D., and other Sisters of Notre Dame is available from Loyola University Press (Toll Free: 800-621-1008). It contains 201 illustrated lives of the saints and suggested student activities on cards. The material is adapted for students from *Saints and Feast Days*.

Supplement

SEPTEMBER 20: ST. ANDREW KIM TAEGON, ST. PAUL CHONG HASANG, AND THEIR COMPANIONS

One hundred thirteen Korean martyrs were canonized together in 1984. Among them were Andrew, a priest; Paul, a forty-five-year-old seminarian; Columba Kim, a twenty-six-year-old single woman; and a thirteen-year-old boy. Some ten thousand Catholics were martyred for their faith before religious freedom came to Korea in 1883. Today Korea has more than a million and a half Catholics.

During a Japanese invasion in 1592 some Koreans were baptized. Soon after, Korea cut itself off from the rest of the world. Around 1777 Catholic books came into the country, and a home Church began. When a Chinese priest secretly arrived about twelve years later, he found four thousand Catholics who had never seen a priest. Korea's first Christian community was made up entirely of laypersons. Between 1839 and 1867 there were fierce persecutions. One hundred three members of this community were martyred along with three bishops and seven priests from the Paris Foreign Mission Society.

Andrew Kim Taegon was the first native Korean priest. He was the son of converts. His father, a farmer, was martyred. Andrew was baptized when he was fifteen. He then attended the seminary in Macao, China, 1,300 miles away from home. After six years Andrew returned to Korea and assumed the job of bringing missionaries into the country secretly. He was arrested, tortured, and beheaded.

In a letter written to fellow Christians, Andrew states, "We have received baptism, entrance into the Church, and the honor of being called Christians. Yet what good will this do us if we are Christians in name only and not in fact?"

SUGGESTIONS

1. Report on the beginnings of the Church in Korea.
2. List ways you can strengthen your Christian faith.
3. Write a composition explaining how laypeople contribute to your parish community.
4. Compose a homily about being a Christian in fact.

SEPTEMBER 28: ST. LAWRENCE RUIZ AND HIS COMPANIONS

Lawrence Ruiz is the first Filipino canonized saint. He and fifteen others were martyred in or near Nagasaki, Japan. Besides Lawrence, there were two other laymen, two consecrated women, two brothers, and nine priests. The group included nine Japanese, four Spaniards, an Italian, and a Frenchman.

Lawrence had a Chinese father and a Filipino mother. The family lived in the Chinese section of Manila in the Philippines in the early seventeenth century. Lawrence learned Spanish from the Dominicans whom he served as altar boy and sacristan. He became a professional calligrapher, printing documents in beautiful penmanship. As a member of the Confraternity of the Holy Rosary, he prayed the fifteen mysteries of the rosary each week.

In 1636, when Lawrence was a young father with two sons and a daughter, he was implicated in a murder. To avoid arrest, he joined a missionary group of three Dominican priests, another priest, and a layman who was a leper. Only on the ship did Lawrence learn the group was headed for Japan, where Catholics were being persecuted.

In Japan the six men were arrested. After being imprisoned for a year, they were sent to Nagasaki to be tried. Before the Japanese judges, Lawrence declared, "I am a Christian. I shall die for God, and for God I would give many thousands of lives. So do with me what you please." As the Catholics were tortured, they encouraged one another to be killed rather than give up the faith. At one point Lawrence asked whether by giving up the faith he would be freed. When he received no direct answer, his faith grew stronger. All six men were put to a cruel death in 1637. In 1987 they were canonized with ten others who spread the faith in Japan, the Philippines, and Taiwan.

SUGGESTIONS

1. Discuss why some people give up the faith today.
2. Write a report about the Catholic faith in Japan.
3. Find out how you can help missionaries. Write to Holy Childhood Association, 1720 Massachusetts Avenue NW, Washington, DC 20036.
4. Make a poster about your faith.

OCTOBER 6: BLESSED MARIE-ROSE DUROCHER

Marie-Rose Durocher was born in 1811 in a village near Montreal, Canada, the tenth of eleven children. She had a good education. Her brother became a priest. Marie-Rose thought about becoming a Sister, but her health was not good enough. When Marie-Rose was eighteen and her mother died, she began to work in her brother's parish. For thirteen years she was housekeeper, hostess, and parish worker. Her goodness earned her the title "the saint of Beloeil."

Both Marie-Rose's spiritual director and Bishop Bourget of Montreal encouraged her to found a teaching community. Marie-Rose was against the idea. Finally, with two friends, she began a boarding school for thirteen girls. In 1843, with the help of other

Sisters, the Oblates of Mary Immaculate, she founded the Sisters of the Holy Names of Jesus and Mary.

The six years Marie-Rose lived as a Sister were filled with poverty, difficulties, and sickness. She practiced penance and was quite strict with her community. A great love for the crucified Jesus gave her strength.

Marie-Rose's order was devoted to religious education for the poorest children. It began a mission in Oregon in 1959 and is now an international congregation.

Marie-Rose died in 1849 and was beatified in 1982.

SUGGESTIONS

1. Write a composition about ways to learn more about the Catholic faith.

2. Learn how organizations like the Catholic Church Extension Society and the Knights of Columbus help spread the faith. Choose one and write a report on it.

3. Meet with a group of classmates and share the story of how you have learned about your faith.

4. Try to assist with religious education in your parish. For instance, you might be a helper in the Sunday preschool program.

NOVEMBER 18: ST. ROSE PHILIPPINE DUCHESNE

Rose Philippine Duchesne was born in France in 1769 and named for St. Rose of Lima, the first saint of the New World. A Jesuit missionary sometimes visited her home and told stories about the Native Americans. This might have sparked Rose's interest in them.

Rose attended a school taught by the Visitation Sisters. When she was seventeen and her family was looking for a husband for her, Rose told them she wanted to become a Visitation Sister. Her family objected, but Rose joined the community. When the French Revolution forced religious communities to leave their convents, Rose returned home. She continued to live as a religious. She cared for the sick, visited prisoners, and taught.

At that time St. Madeleine Sophie Barat was starting the Society of the Sacred Heart, a new community of Sisters. At the age of thirty-three, Rose joined them. She expressed a wish to go to America as a missionary, but it wasn't until she was forty-nine years old that her dream came true. She and four other Sisters were sent at the request of the bishop of St. Louis. They spent eleven weeks crossing the ocean and seven weeks on the Mississippi to reach St. Louis.

Rose was dismayed to discover that there was no work with the Native Americans in St. Louis. In fact, the Sisters were unexpected. The bishop sent them to a log cabin on the frontier, where they opened the first free school for girls west of the Mississippi. Altogether Rose founded six convents from New Orleans to St. Louis. With courage and trust in God, she and the Sisters educated poor children.

Finally, when Mother Duchesne was seventy-one years old, she was allowed to resign as American superior. Father Pierre De Smet was asking the Sisters to open a school for Native Americans in Kansas. Mother Duchesne asked to go. Although she could not speak the language or teach, she could pray. In Kansas she spent four hours in the morning and four hours in the evening praying in the chapel every day. The Native Americans called her "Woman Who Always Prays." There is a story that one day a Native American child placed kernels of corn on the skirt of Mother Duchesne's habit. He came back hours later and found them unmoved.

When her health failed, Mother Duchesne returned to Missouri. There she lived a simple life of prayer and penance until her death on November 18, 1852. She was canonized in 1988.

SUGGESTIONS

1. Find out more about the Catholic firsts in the United States: the first bishop, the first church, the first saint, the first Catholic school.

2. On a map locate Kansas and the cities of St. Louis, New Orleans, and St. Charles.

3. Compose a prayer for Native Americans or find one of their prayers and pray it.

4. Make a report on Kateri Tekakwitha or the North American Martyrs.

NOVEMBER 23: BLESSED MIGUEL AGUSTÍN PRO

On November 23, 1927, Father Miguel Pro, a lively, fun-loving young Jesuit, faced the firing squad with a small cross in one hand and a rosary in the other. He had refused a blindfold and had asked only for time to pray. Not long before, he had offered his life to God for the faith of the Mexican people. Now God was accepting his sacrifice.

Miguel Pro was born January 13, 1891, in Guadalupe, Mexico, one of eleven children of a mining engineer. After his two older sisters became Sisters, he joined the Jesuits in 1911. A year before that, a severe persecution had begun in Mexico. While Miguel was in the novitiate, soldiers broke into the building and set fire to the library. The novices were sent out to escape to study in other countries. Miguel, dressed as a peasant, fled to California. After studying there for a while, he was sent to Spain, Nicaragua, and Belgium, where he was ordained in 1925. Study was hard for Miguel, especially since he suffered from a stomach illness that was eventually remedied by surgery. His fellow Jesuits referred to him as "the brother who is convinced that God wants him to be a saint."

Father Pro returned to Mexico City in 1926, and within a month the government banned public worship. Secretly priests ministered to the faithful, celebrating the Eucharist in their homes, preaching, baptizing, and hearing confessions. Father Pro usually lived with his parents. He rode through Mexico City on his bicycle, distributing Communion at stations and providing clothing for the poor. Disguised as a mechanic, an office worker, or even a beggar, he courageously served the Catholic Mexicans.

Father Pro's quick thinking and pranks helped him in many narrow escapes. Once, when the police were following him, he turned a corner and saw a Catholic woman he knew. He winked at her and took her arm. When the police turned the corner, they saw not a priest but only a loving couple walking down the street.

On November 13 an assassination attempt was made on a Mexican general. A bomb was thrown from a car that had once belonged to Father Pro's brother. Police arrested Father Pro and his two younger brothers. These brothers were members of the National League for the Defense of Religious Rights, but they had had nothing to do with the failed assassination attempt.

When the man behind the plot heard that Father Pro had been arrested, he confessed. But the authorities wanted to teach the Catholics a lesson. With no witnesses and no trial, Father Pro and his two brothers were condemned to death. Reporters, photographers, and others were invited to a special execution. Father Pro's sense of humor could not save him this time.

One of the officers who had captured Father Pro led him out of jail to be executed. With tears in his eyes he begged Father to forgive him. Miguel put his arm around him and said, "You have not only my forgiveness but my thanks." He also softly told the members of the firing squad, "May God forgive you all."

Father Pro heard the guns being cocked. With arms spread as if on a cross, he shouted, "Long live Christ the King!" before a bullet silenced him. The real criminal and one of Miguel's brothers were also shot, but his other brother was pardoned at the last moment.

Although the government forbade a public funeral, thousands of people came to Father Pro's wake. They knew that he had died for them. Miguel Pro was beatified on September 25, 1988.

SUGGESTIONS

1. Write a composition about what the Eucharist means to you.

2. Compose a prayer to Father Pro or write a poem about him.

3. Find out about recent martyrs in El Salvador: the six Jesuits with their housekeeper and her daughter; Jean Donovan and Sisters Ita Ford, Maura Clarke, and Dorothy Kazel; and Archbishop Oscar Romero. Write a report.

4. Prepare a report on the Jesuits: their founder, their mission, their life, and their work today.

NOVEMBER 24: ST. ANDREW DUNG-LAC AND HIS COMPANIONS

Vietnam's history has long been marked by the cross. It includes several severe persecutions of Catholics. Pope John Paul II canonized together the 117 Vietnamese martyrs, who had been beatified in four groups from 1900 to 1951. St. Andrew, a parish priest, is one of them.

Of the 117 who died between the years 1820 and 1862, ninety-six were Vietnamese, eleven were Spanish, and ten were French. The group included eight bishops, fifty priests, and fifty-nine lay Catholics.

The Portuguese brought the faith to Vietnam. In 1615 Jesuits opened the first permanent mission in Da Nang to minister to Japanese Catholics who had been driven from Japan. The king of one of the three kingdoms of Vietnam banned all foreign missionaries. Priests went into hiding in Catholic homes.

Later in the nineteenth century three more persecutions occurred—one caused by the emperor's thinking that Christians were in favor of his son, who was rebelling against him. Foreign missionaries too were martyred. The last to be martyred were seventeen laypersons, one only nine years old. That year, 1862, a treaty with France gave religious freedom to Catholics. Persecutions continued, however.

In this century Catholics in North Vietnam fled to the South in great numbers. The Church now in Vietnam is strong and committed to the faith. Vietnamese Catholics and Catholics worldwide have been inspired by the Vietnamese martyrs, who were canonized in 1988.

SUGGESTIONS

1. Find out about Vietnamese Catholics in the United States: their locations and their religious communities of priests, brothers, and sisters.

2. Write an essay about what the faith means to you.

3. Faith is shown not only by dying for it but by living for it. Make a list of difficult things you do as a result of your faith.

4. Copy the words of a hymn about faith. Comment on what they say to you.

5. Find out about the distribution of Catholics in the world today.

DECEMBER 9: BLESSED JUAN DIEGO

Juan Diego, an Aztec Indian who lived near Mexico City, was born in 1474. His Indian name was Cuauhlatohuac, which means "the eagle who speaks." Juan Diego and his wife, María Lucía, were converts to the faith. They walked fourteen miles to Mass and religious instructions every Saturday and Sunday. When Juan was fifty-seven years old and a widower, he had an experience that changed his life.

On December 9, 1531, as Juan was walking to Mass, a beautiful lady dressed as an Aztec maiden and surrounded by light appeared. She told him she was the Immaculate Virgin Mary, the Mother of the true God. She expressed her desire to have a shrine built there at Tepeyac Hill so that she could show her love for the people. She said, "Ask for my help. Here I will listen to people's prayers and I will help them." Mary then asked Juan to tell the bishop of her desire.

When Juan went to the bishop, the bishop didn't believe him. Juan returned to the lady and suggested she send someone who could talk better to the bishop. Mary told Juan that he was the one she had chosen for this work and that she would bless him for helping her. Juan visited the bishop again. This time the bishop told him to ask "his Lady" for a sign that she was truly the Mother of God. When Juan asked Mary for a sign, she told him to return the next day for it.

In the meantime, however, Juan's Uncle Bernardino became very ill, and Juan had to stay home to care for him. By Tuesday his uncle was dying, so Juan went for a priest. On the way he met the Holy Virgin. Embarrassed, he apologized for not meeting her the day before. Mary replied, "Now listen to me. Do not let anything bother you, and do not be afraid of any illness, pain, or accident. Am I not here, your Mother? Are you not under my shadow and protection? What more could you want? Don't worry about your uncle. He is well already."

Mary then told Juan to go to the top of the hill and gather the flowers he would find growing there. Juan knew that nothing grew on that rocky hill, let alone in the middle of winter! However, he did as the Virgin had told him and climbed the hill. At the top he found gorgeous roses! He picked them and brought them to Mary, who arranged them in his tilma, or cloak, which María Lucía had made. Mary told Juan to take them to the bishop.

When the bishop saw Juan, he asked what he had in his tilma. Juan opened it, letting the fragrant roses fall in a shower to the floor. You can imagine the bishop's surprise at seeing roses in winter! Yet, he saw an even greater miracle: there on Juan's tilma a life-size image began to appear, beautifully painted! Juan gasped! It was his "Lady"!

The bishop cried out, "The Immaculate!" Then he knelt and with tears asked the Blessed Mother's pardon for not believing Juan.

On that same day, Mary appeared to Juan's uncle and cured him. Uncle Bernardino went to the bishop and told how he had been cured. He also gave the bishop a message from the Virgin, saying that she would "crush the serpent's head." The bishop did not understand the Indian's language. He heard the Indian word for "crush the serpent," which sounded like "Guadalupe," the name of Mary's shrine in Spain. Thinking that the Virgin wanted the new shrine to have the same name, the bishop called her Our Lady of Guadalupe.

The picture of Our Lady of Guadalupe has meaningful symbols. Its main message is that Mary loves us and wants to help us. The cloak itself is made from the rough fibers of a cactus plant. This type of material cannot be painted on, nor will the material last more than twenty years. Yet after 450 years the picture on the cloak remains fresh and beautiful! It can be seen above the main altar in the Basilica of Our Lady of Guadalupe in Mexico. The Church celebrates the feast of Our Lady of Guadalupe on December 12.

Juan Diego spent the rest of his life, seventeen years, traveling throughout central Mexico, telling the story of his experience and bringing others to the faith. He remained poor, simple, and humble and had a great devotion to the Eucharist. People called him "the pilgrim" because he always walked alone and seemed to be praying. It is said that through his efforts eight million Aztec Indians were converted to Catholicism.

Juan Diego died on May 30, 1548, and was beatified in 1990.

SUGGESTIONS

1. God and Mary, the Mother of God, show concern for the poor. Plan a way to raise money for the poor. Send the money you collect to an organization such as Catholic Relief Services, 1011 First Avenue, New York, NY 10022.

2. Write a report about the Basilica of Our Lady of Guadalupe.

3. List five other titles of Mary and give a brief description of the meaning of each.

4. Make a habit of praying three Hail Marys each night before going to bed.

5. Write a poem or prayer to Mary.

6. Tell at least one other person the story of Our Lady of Guadalupe.

JANUARY 6: BLESSED ANDRÉ BESSETTE

The most unexpected people can be saints. André Bessette was sickly all his life. He failed at any job he tried. He could barely read or write. Yet he became famous and well loved for his holiness.

André, the eighth of twelve children, was born in 1845 in Montreal and baptized Alfred. His parents, who were French-Canadians, died early. André was adopted when he was twelve years old and became a farmhand. Later he tried being a shoemaker, a baker, and a blacksmith, but he was unsuccessful.

Then André joined the Congregation of the Holy Cross, but at the end of a year he was told to leave because of his bad health. Luckily, a wise bishop convinced the community to allow André to remain. Brother André became the doorkeeper at the College of Notre Dame for forty years.

André had a statue of St. Joseph on the windowsill in his room. André spent many hours praying during the night. Soon it was discovered that André had healing powers. He would visit the sick, pray with them, rub them with oil, and they would be cured. Before long, throngs of people were coming to him for healing and spiritual direction. André would say, "It is St. Joseph who cures. I am just his little dog." André ministered to people eight to ten hours a day. In the meantime four secretaries were kept busy handling the eighty thousand letters André received each year.

The Holy Cross community had tried for many years to buy land nearby. André buried a medal of St. Joseph on the property, and suddenly the owners sold the land. Then André raised money to build first a small chapel there and then a church. For years he cut students' hair for five cents and saved the money. At the church he received visitors. Cured people left behind their crutches and canes. It took fifty years to build St. Joseph's Oratory, which is probably the world's main shrine to St. Joseph.

André, the weak failure, let God use him to accomplish great things and became known as "the Miracle Man of Montreal." He died on January 6, 1937, and was beatified in 1982.

SUGGESTIONS

1. Find out more about St. Joseph's Oratory in Montreal.
2. Attend an anointing of the sick at your parish.
3. Visit or send a homemade get-well card to someone who is ill.
4. Write a report on the gift of healing in the Church today.
5. Compose a poem or essay about St. Joseph.

MARCH 3: BLESSED KATHARINE DREXEL

In 1889 newspaper headlines read, "Gives Up Seven Million." The article told about Katharine Drexel, an heiress from Philadelphia, who had decided to join the Sisters of Mercy.

Katharine was born November 26, 1858. Her father was an international banker, and the family had a private railroad car. Katharine's mother was a Baptist Quaker who died when Katharine was five months old. Her father married a devout Catholic woman. The Drexels were good Catholics who even had a chapel in their house. Mr. Drexel prayed for a half hour each evening, and Mrs. Drexel opened her home to the poor three days a week. Like any wealthy girl, Katharine had received an excellent education, traveled, and made her debut into society.

When Katharine's stepmother became ill with cancer, Katharine nursed her for three years until she died. This experience made her think about values in life and about becoming a nun. Then, after visiting the western part of the United States, she became concerned about the Native Americans.

One day Katharine had a chance to meet Pope Leo XIII. She asked him to send more missionaries to Wyoming to help her friend Bishop James O'Connor. The pope asked, "Why don't you become a missionary?"

After pondering the pope's suggestion, Katharine visited the chief of the Sioux and began helping at the missions. She joined the Sisters of Mercy in Pittsburgh to make a two-year novitiate. Then in 1891 she made her vows as the first Sister of the Blessed Sacrament. Her order was dedicated to sharing the Gospel and the life of the Eucharist among Native Americans and black peoples. The old Drexel summer home in Pennsylvania was the Sisters' first convent.

After three-and-a-half years of training, Mother Drexel and other Sisters opened a boarding school in Santa Fe, New Mexico. She spent her life and her $12-million inheritance on her work. In the end, she had established fifty missions for Native Americans in sixteen states, a system of Catholic schools for African-Americans, forty mission centers, and twenty-three rural schools. She had also made the Church and the country more aware of the needs of the poor and had spoken out against racial and other injustices.

Mother Drexel's greatest educational achievement was founding Xavier University in New Orleans, the first university for African-Americans in the United States.

A heart attack at the age of seventy-seven forced Katharine to retire. She spent the rest of her days praying in a small room overlooking the sanctuary until she died at ninety-six on March 3, 1955. She was beatified in 1988.

SUGGESTIONS

1. Make a report on the life of Pierre Toussaint, Martin de Porres, Thea Bowman, Archbishop James P. Lyke, or another famous black Catholic.

2. Find out about the Josephite Fathers and prepare a report on them.

3. Discuss with a group how the Native-American and African-American cultures contribute to the richness of the Catholic Church.

4. Pray for an end to prejudice and racism.

5. Contribute some of your own money to an organization that promotes the welfare of Native Americans or black peoples.

MAY 10: BLESSED DAMIEN

The Gospels record several occasions when Jesus reached out to lepers with kindness and healing. Centuries later, Father Damien became another Christ, devoting his life to these poor people, the outcasts of society.

Joseph de Veuster was born in Belgium on January 3, 1840, the son of well-to-do peasants. While at college he decided God was calling him to be a priest. He joined the Congregation of the Sacred Hearts of Jesus and Mary, the same community his older brother had joined, and he took the name Damien. When illness prevented his brother from sailing to the missions in Hawaii, Damien offered to go in his place. He arrived in Hawaii and was ordained in Honolulu.

For nine years Damien served the people in different villages. He was interested in a settlement for people with leprosy, Hansen's Disease, on the island of Molokai. The colony was very poor, and there was not a single doctor or priest on the island. Father Damien offered to go to Molokai and work with the lepers.

In 1873 all the lepers who could still walk came to meet the boat to see the priest who wanted to work with them. They were sure he wouldn't stay very long when he saw what life there was like. Lepers often have unpleasant sores, and some even lose parts of their body because of the disease. Those lepers who were not very ill sometimes lived a wild life because there were no laws and no police on the island.

Father Damien got busy right away, cleaning up the huts, nursing the very sick people, and trying new medicines. Those able to help were put to work building decent houses. Father Damien not only preached and offered Mass but also built roads, water systems, orphanages, and churches and acted as sheriff, counselor, and undertaker. He even organized a choir and a band! He made the people feel they were important, so they began to take better care of themselves and their property. Through his efforts, many people turned away from their immoral habits. Damien also begged for money to help his eight hundred lepers.

For ten years Father Damien was the only priest on the island. He had permission to stay there permanently.

At Mass on Sundays Father Damien always began his homily with "My dear lepers." One day he said, "My fellow lepers." At first it was very quiet. Then people began to sob. They knew that their beloved Father Damien had gotten the disease. Even when ill, he carried on his work until a month before his death. He also suffered from attacks on his reputation and from the misunderstanding of other priests.

Joseph Dutton, a layman from Vermont who was called Brother Joseph, joined Father Damien in his work and stayed for forty-four years. A group of Franciscan Sisters from New York under the leadership of Mother Marianne Cope also came to help.

After working with the lepers for sixteen years, Father Damien died on April 15, 1889, at the age of forty-nine. He is called the Martyr of Molokai.

SUGGESTIONS

1. Discuss with your classmates how some groups of people are regarded as lepers today. Consider what is being done to help them.

2. Propose ways your class can help suffering people, such as volunteering at a soup kitchen or nursing home or raising money for Food for the Poor, Covenant House, or research in the fight against AIDS, cancer, or multiple sclerosis.

3. Help your class adopt a person who is ill. You and your classmates might write and send cards to the person and pray for him or her each day.

4. Find out about a person today who dedicates time, money, or his or her life to helping a suffering group of people. Write a report on the person.

5. Find and read stories in the Gospels of Jesus' encounters with lepers.

6. Research and write a report on Brother Joseph Dutton or Mother Marianne Cope.

JULY 1: BLESSED JUNÍPERO SERRA

A number of large cities in California—such as San Francisco, Santa Barbara, and San Diego—began with the efforts of one man: a five-foot-two-inch Franciscan named Junípero Serra. This Father of California is proof that in weakness God's power is shown.

José Miguel Serra was born the son of a farmer in Spain on November 24, 1713. When he first applied to the Franciscans, they turned him down because of his frail appearance. He joined this order later, however, when he was seventeen. He took the name Junípero, after Juniper, the beloved companion of St. Francis. As a priest, he taught philosophy, earned a doctorate in theology, and taught theology at a university. He was a popular preacher. Then he requested to be a missionary. He wrote, "All my life I have wanted to be a missioner. I have wanted to carry the Gospel teachings to those who have never heard of God and the kingdom he has prepared for them."

In 1749 Father Serra wrote a final letter to his parents, whom he would never see again. Then he sailed for Mexico with other Franciscans, including Father Palou, a former student, who became his confessor and biographer. The ninety-eight-day journey was an ordeal. There was not enough fresh food and water, and the thirst was almost unbearable. Near Mexico a storm drove the ship off course and almost wrecked it. Father Serra wrote home that he was the only religious who did not get seasick.

After landing in Mexico, Father Serra and another friar walked the three hundred miles to Mexico City. On the way, Father Serra was bitten on the left leg by a poisonous insect. For the rest of his life this leg caused him pain and made him lame. The travelers stopped at the shrine of Our Lady of Guadalupe. There Father Serra dedicated his work among the Indians to her.

After a training period in Mexico City, Father Serra went to work with the Pame Indians for eight years. Then he worked as a traveling missioner in many cities.

In 1767 the viceroy of Mexico forced all Jesuits to leave the country, and Junípero was made president of their fourteen missions in Lower California. Then, when the Spaniards took over Upper California in 1769, Junípero went with them. At the age of fifty-six and with his leg and foot swollen, he traveled the nine hundred miles on muleback to San Diego, where he founded the territory's first mission of the nineteen he planned. Altogether Junípero established nine of the twenty-one Franciscan missions along the Pacific Coast: San Diego, San Carlos Borromeo, San Antonio de Padua, San Gabriel, San Luis Obispo, San Francisco, San Juan Capistrano, Santa Clara, and San Buenaventura. He baptized about six thousand Native Americans.

The missions were communities of Native Americans in which everything was held in common. The Indians were taught to grow crops and raise livestock. They learned to read and write, to sing, and to paint. Most exciting for Father Serra, they learned about the faith and asked to become Catholics.

Father Serra made his favorite mission, San Carlos in Carmel, his headquarters. There he had a room with only one window, a wooden pallet for a bed, a chair, and a small table.

Junípero loved the Indians as a father. He walked thousands of miles visiting his missions. Often he came into conflict with authorities because of their mistreatment of the Indians. He made the long trip back to Mexico City, arriving close to death, in order to meet with the military commander and to establish rules that protected the Indians and the missions. Once, when an Indian uprising at San Diego left a Franciscan and several others dead, Father Serra pleaded that the Indians held for the killings be released.

When Junípero was dying, he insisted on walking to chapel for Holy Communion. Father Palou and some Indian converts were with him when he died on August 28, 1784. Indians stayed with the body through the night. Father Palou recorded that at the funeral the weeping of the congregation drowned out the singing. Father Serra is buried at the Carmel mission.

Father Serra's statue stands in the Hall of Fame at the Capitol in Washington, D.C. When this tribute to the founders of the United States was planned, Father Serra was nominated by the state of California. In 1935 the Serra Club was founded to foster vocations and promote Catholicism in the United States. A United States airmail stamp issued in 1988 bears the picture of Junípero Serra. Even a mountain in California is named for him: Junípero Serra Peak. Father Junípero Serra was beatified in 1988.

SUGGESTIONS

1. Discuss or write a paper explaining how Catholics your age witness to the faith.

2. Find out about the missions Junípero Serra founded.

3. Explore ways you can support the missions to the Native Americans today.

4. Read about Blessed Kateri Tekakwitha.

5. Give some thought to your vocation in life. Do you have a desire to be a missionary? Why?

JULY 14: BLESSED KATERI TEKAKWITHA

Kateri Tekakwitha is called "Lily of the Mohawks." Her name Tekakwitha means "putting things in order." She put her life in order in a short time.

Kateri was a Mohawk Indian born in 1656 in what is now Auriesville, New York, ten years after Isaac Jogues and his companions were martyred there. Her mother was a Christian Algonquin Indian, and her father was a pagan Mohawk chief. Her parents and a brother died of smallpox when she was only four. The disease left Kateri's eyes weak and her face scarred.

Anastasia, a friend of Kateri's mother, took care of her and told her stories about the Christian God. When Anastasia left to go to Canada, where there were Christians, Kateri's uncle, a Mohawk chief, took Kateri as his daughter.

When Kateri's uncle and aunts wanted her to marry, she refused. She felt that the Great Spirit was the only one she could love. This angered her uncle.

Kateri learned more about God from a missionary and asked to be baptized. She was baptized on Easter Sunday. It was hard for Kateri to live as a Christian. Her people expected her to work in the fields on Sunday, the Lord's Day. Sometimes they didn't feed her. Children made fun of her and threw stones at her. Kateri endured this for two years.

Finally a priest advised Kateri to go to Canada, where she would be with other Christians. One day, when her uncle was not home, she left for Canada with a Christian named Hot Ashes. When Kateri's uncle discovered she was missing, he followed her but did not catch her.

Kateri brought with her a note for a Canadian priest from the missionary priest that said, "I send you a treasure, Katherine Tekakwitha. Guard her well." Kateri lived an outstanding Christian life. She went to Mass daily, made frequent visits to the Blessed Sacrament, and prayed the rosary often. She cared for the sick and the old and taught the children. She did much penance.

Kateri suffered from bad headaches. She was not strong and could eat very little. On April 17, 1680, when she died at the age of twenty-four, the scars on her face disappeared and she was beautiful. Her last words were, "Jesus, I love you." Kateri Tekakwitha was beatified in 1980.

SUGGESTIONS

1. Spend extra time with the Blessed Sacrament.
2. Write a report about missionaries who worked with Native Americans.
3. Find out about Catholic Native Americans today. Write a report on one of their parishes or on ways they adapt liturgy to their culture.
4. Draw a picture of a scene from Kateri's life.
5. Think of a difficult thing you can do today as a silent way to say to Christ, "I love you." Write it down and do it.

AUGUST 14: ST. MAXIMILIAN MARY KOLBE

Maximilian Kolbe was born in Poland on January 8, 1894, and was named Raymond. His parents entered a monastery, and Maximilian joined the Franciscans at age thirteen. He studied in Rome and was ordained. Maximilian had a great devotion to Mary Immaculate. He worked to spread devotion to her, even traveling to Japan and India to do so. His pockets were always full of Miraculous Medals to distribute. He published good Catholic literature, including a monthly magazine called *The Knight of the Immaculate*. Through this magazine, which had a million subscribers, Father Kolbe taught the Gospel under Mary's protection to all nations. He founded spiritual centers named City of Mary Immaculate. In Japan he established the City at Nagasaki. After the atomic bomb was dropped on Nagasaki, the City was unharmed.

During the Second World War, Father Maximilian Kolbe gave shelter to thousands of Polish people, both Christians and Jews. He risked his life to help these suffering people. On February 17, 1941, he was arrested and sent to prison in Warsaw. There he was given a convict's uniform and the number 16670. He was sent to the Nazi concentration camp at Auschwitz, where he endured very hard work and beatings that almost killed him. Even then he secretly heard confessions and spoke to the other prisoners about God's love. When food was brought in, he stepped aside for the other prisoners. Sometimes there was nothing left for him.

One day a prisoner escaped from the camp. As a result, the officers said ten men must die by starvation in an underground pit. They chose ten men to die. One man cried out, "My wife, my children! I shall never see them again!" Father Kolbe stepped forward and offered to take the man's place.

In the pit, Father Kolbe led the nine men in prayer and song to Mary, God's Mother. He lifted their spirits. After two weeks, when Father Kolbe was the only one still alive, an executioner killed him with an injection. His body was burned with the other prisoners'. No doubt Maximilian Kolbe was pleased that his death occurred on August 14, 1941, the vigil of Mary's Assumption, so that now each year this vigil is his feast day. He was canonized in 1982.

Maximilian's mother told the story that when he was ten he had a vision of Mary holding out two crowns to him. Mary asked which he wanted, the white crown of purity or the red crown of martyrdom. Maximilian answered, "Both."

SUGGESTIONS

1. List ways that devotion to Mary is shown today.
2. Write a report on the Miraculous Medal.
3. Discuss with a classmate where Father Kolbe found the power to give his life for another.
4. Make a habit of praying three Hail Marys a day.